THE COMPLETE NORTHERN IRELAND FC 1882-2020

Dirk Karsdorp

British Library Cataloguing in Publication Data
A catalogue record for this book is available from the British Library

ISBN 978-1-86223-444-4

Copyright © 2020, SOCCER BOOKS LIMITED. (01472 696226)
72 St. Peter's Avenue, Cleethorpes, N.E. Lincolnshire, DN35 8HU, England

All rights are reserved. No part of this publication may be reproduced, stored in a retrieval system or transmitted, in any form or by any means, electronic, mechanical, photocopying, recording, or otherwise, without the prior written permission of Soccer Books Limited.

Printed in the UK by Severn

FOREWORD

When Ireland played their first ever game against England at Bloomfield Park, Belfast on 18th February 1882, the country was still part of the United Kingdom. This remained the case until the partition of Ireland in 1921 when many of the Southern Counties broke away from the United Kingdom to form the Irish Free State (later the Republic of Ireland). The Irish Football Association, previously the governing body of football for the whole of Ireland, subsequently took responsibility for football in the newly-formed province of Northern Ireland alone and all the games played by Ireland prior to the partition are considered to 'belong' to Northern Ireland. Interestingly enough, it wasn't until 1948 that the Irish F.A. ceased to select players born in the South of Ireland.

This book contains statistics for all of the officially-recognised full international games played by Ireland up to 1921 and for Northern Ireland from this date to the end of 2020. Other titles in this series are also available covering the matches played by England, Scotland, Wales and the Republic of Ireland. and we have also published new books containing complete statistics for the international matches of Belgium, Italy and the Netherlands.

Although we have endeavoured to include statistics which are as complete as possible, inevitably there are omissions with one or two small pieces of information missing for some games. Most notably, the times at which goals were scored were not recorded for a few of the earliest games and also for a number of games between Northern Ireland and Wales (although the goalscorers themselves are known). In such cases, the following symbol has been used to indicate that the time of the goal is not known: "#".

Additionally, for many of the games between Northern Ireland and Wales, the names of the referees have not been recorded by statisticians of either country and this is indicated in the text itself.

1. 18.02.1882
IRELAND v ENGLAND 0-13 (0-5)

Bloomfield Park, Belfast

Referee: Robert Kennedy (Ireland)   Attendance: 2,500

IRELAND: James Hamilton, John McAlery (Cap), David Rattray, Donald Martin, John Hastings, James Buckle, William McWha, John Robert Davison, John Sinclair, Alex Dill, Samuel Johnston.

ENGLAND: John Frederick P. Rawlinson, Alfred Thomas Carrick Dobson, Doctor Haydock Greenwood, Frederick William Hargreaves, Robert Stuart King, Edward Charles Bambridge (Cap), Horace Hutton Barnet, Arthur Brown, James Brown, Oliver Howard Vaughton, Henry Alfred Cursham.

Goals: Oliver Howard Vaughton (#, #, #, #, #), Arthur Brown (#, #, #, #), James Brown (#, #), Henry Alfred Cursham (#), Edward Charles Bambridge (#)

2. 25.02.1882
WALES v IRELAND 7-1 (4-1)

The Racecourse, Wrexham

Referee: Robert Lythgoe (England)   Attendance: 2,000

WALES: Harry Adams, John Richard Morgan (Cap), John Powell, Frederick William Hughes, William Williams, William Pierce Owen, Edward Gough Shaw, Charles Frederick Ketley, John Henry Price, John Roberts, John Vaughan.

IRELAND: James Hamilton, William Crone, John McAlery (Cap), Donald Martin, John Hastings, John Robert Davison, William McWha, John Condy, John Sinclair, Alex Dill, Samuel Johnston.

Goals: John Richard Morgan (10), John Price (#, #, #, #), William Pierce Owen (#, #) / Samuel Johnston (20)

3. 24.02.1883
ENGLAND v IRELAND 7-0 (4-0)

Liverpool Cricket Ground, Liverpool

Referee: John McDowall (Scotland)   Attendance: 2,500

ENGLAND: Harry Albemarle Swepstone, Percy John de Paravincini, Henry Thomas Moore, John Hudson (Cap), Stuart Macrae, Oliver Whateley, Francis William Pawson, Harry Chester Goodhart, Arthur Tempest Blakiston Dunn, William Nevill Cobbold, Henry Alfred Cursham.

IRELAND: James Rankin, James Watson, David Rattray, Thomas Molyneux, Donald Martin (Cap), William Morrow, Renwick Potts, William McWha, John Robert Davison, John Reid, Ned Spiller.

Goals: Oliver Whateley (15, 47), William Cobbold (17, 19), Arthur Tempest Blakiston Dunn (43, 80), Francis Pawson (88)

4. 17.03.1883
IRELAND v WALES 1-1 (0-0)

Ulster Cricket Ground, Ballynafeigh, Belfast

Referee: John McDowell (Scotland)   Attendance: 1,000

IRELAND: James Rankin, James Watson, David Rattray, Thomas Molyneux, John Hastings, William Morrow, Renwick Potts, William McWha, John Robert Davison (Cap), Ned Spiller, Alex Dill.

WALES: Harry Adams, Frederick William Hughes, John Powell (Cap), John Price Davies, William Williams, John Jones I, Robert Davies, Walter Hugh Roberts, John Henry Price, John Arthur Eyton-Jones, John Vaughan.

Goals: William Morrow (67) / Walter Hugh Roberts (50)

5. 26.01.1884   British Championship
IRELAND v SCOTLAND 0-5 (0-2)

Ulster Cricket Ground, Ballynafeigh, Belfast

Referee: Thomas Hindle (England)   Attendance: 2,000

IRELAND: Robert John Hunter, Matt Wilson, William Crone, John Hastings, Thomas Molyneux, Alex Dill, Edward Arthur Spiller, John Gibb, William Morrow, John Robert Davison (Cap), Arthur Gaussen.

SCOTLAND: John Inglis, John Forbes, Walter Arnott (Cap), John Graham, William Fulton, Robert Brown, Samuel Thomson, James Gossland, John Wilson Goudie, William Harrower, J. McAulay.

Goals: William Harrower (12, 86), James Gossland (35, 80), John Wilson Goudie (60),

6. 09.02.1884   British Championship
WALES v IRELAND 6-0 (1-0)

The Racecourse, Wrexham

Referee: Robert Sloan (England)   Attendance: 2,000

WALES: Elias Owen, Charles Conde, Walter Davies, William Tanat Foulkes, Peter Griffiths, Henry Valentine Edwards, William Pierce Owen (Cap), Robert Davies, Edward Gough Shaw, John Arthur Eyton-Jones, Robert Albert Jones.

IRELAND: Robert John Hunter, Matt Wilson, William Crone, Thomas Molyneux, Henry Lockhart, Robert Redmond, John Robert Davison (Cap), John Gibb, John Reid, Ned Spiller, Alex Dill.

Goals: Edward Shaw (20, 68), William Pierce Owen (55, 70), Robert Albert Jones (59), John Arthur Eyton-Jones (82)

7.   23.02.1884   British Championship
IRELAND v ENGLAND 1-8 (0-4)
Ulster Cricket Ground, Ballynafeigh, Belfast
Referee: Thomas Lawrie (Scotland)   Attendance: 3,000
IRELAND: Robert John Hunter, Matt Wilson, William Crone, John Hastings, Thomas Molyneux, Alex Dill, Ned Spiller, William McWha, Samuel Johnston, John Robert Davison (Cap), Arthur Gaussen.
ENGLAND: William Crispin Rose, Alfred Thomas Carrick Dobson, Joseph Beverley, Norman Coles Bailey (Cap), Stuart Macrae, Edward Johnson, George Holden, Arthur Leopold Bambridge, Arthur Tempest Blakiston Dunn, Edward Charles Bambridge, Henry Alfred Cursham.
Goals: William McWha (88) / Edward Johnson (#, 15), Edward Bambridge (#, #), Henry Alfred Cursham (#, #, #), Arthur Leopold Bambridge (76)

8.   28.02.1885   British Championship
ENGLAND v IRELAND 4-0 (1-0)
Whalley Range, Manchester
Referee: James McKillop (Scotland)   Attendance: 6,000
ENGLAND: William John Herbert Arthur, Percy Melmoth Walters, Arthur Melmoth Walters, Norman Coles Bailey (Cap), James Henry Forrest, Joseph Morris Lofthouse, Benjamin Ward Spilsbury, James Brown, Francis William Pawson, William Nevill Cobbold, Edward Charles Bambridge.
IRELAND: Anthony Henderson, George Hewison, Frederick William Moorehead, Thomas Molyneux, William John Houston, William Eames, William McWha, John Robert Davison (Cap), John Gibb, George McGee, Alex Dill.
Goals: Edward Charles Bambridge (43), James Brown (#), Benjamin Ward Spilsbury (75), Joseph Morris Lofthouse (77)

9.   14.03.1885   British Championship
SCOTLAND v IRELAND 8-2 (4-0)
First Hampden Park, Glasgow
Referee: William Pierce Dix (England)   Attendance: 6,000
SCOTLAND: William Chalmers, Hugh McHardy, James Niven, Robert Robinson Kelso, John Campbell McLeod McPherson (Cap), Alexander Barbour, John Marshall, William Turner, Alexander Higgins, Robert Calderwood, Walter Lamont.
IRELAND: Anthony Henderson, George Hewison, William Johnston, Robert Muir, William John Houston, William Eames (Cap), Thomas McLean, Joseph Sherrard, John Gibb, George McGee, Alex Dill.
Goals: Walter Lamont (10), William Turner (12), Robert Calderwood (15), John Marshall (35), Alexander Higgins (51, 60, 70), Alexander Barbour (53) / John Gibb (81, 89)

10.   11.04.1885   British Championship
IRELAND v WALES 2-8 (2-0)
Ulster Cricket Ground, Ballynafeigh, Belfast
Referee: John McDowell (Scotland)   Attendance: 1,500
IRELAND: Anthony Henderson, William Johnston, William Eames (Cap), Thomas Molyneux, Robert Muir, William McWha, William James Hamilton, William Drummond Hamilton, John Gibb, George McGee, Alex Dill.
WALES: Robert Herbert Mills-Roberts, Frederick Robert Jones, Alfred Owen Davies, Thomas Burke, John Owen Vaughan, Humphrey Jones (Cap), Robert Davies, William Owen, Job Wilding, Herbert Sisson, John Roach
Goals: Thomas Molyneux (23), Alex Dill (40) / William Owen (50), Thomas Burke (52), Herbert Sisson (55, 59, 60), John Roach (64, 89), Humphrey Jones (69)

11.   27.02.1886   British Championship
WALES v IRELAND 5-0 (1-0)
The Racecourse, Wrexham
Referee: Richard Gregson (England)   Attendance: 700
WALES: Albert Malcolm Hersee, Robert Roberts, Seth Powell, John Owen Vaughan, William Stafford Bell, Humphrey Jones (Cap), William Roberts, Job Wilding, Richard Hersee, Herbert Sisson, Thomas Bryan.
IRELAND: Shaw Gillespie, Edward R. Whitfield, James Watson (Cap), Thomas Molyneux, William Crone, Alexander McArthur, John McClatchey, James Williams, Richard Henry Smyth, John Lemon, Edward Roper.
Goals: William Roberts (#), Job Wilding (#), Richard Hersee (#), Thomas Bryan (#), Herbert Sisson (#)

12.   13.03.1886   British Championship
IRELAND v ENGLAND 1-6 (1-2)
Ulster Cricket Ground, Ballynafeigh, Belfast
Referee: James McKillop (Scotland)   Attendance: 4,500
IRELAND: Shaw Gillespie, James Watson, Oliver Devine, Thomas Molyneux, William Crone, John Hastings (Cap), William Turner, John Condy, Samuel Johnston, John McClatchey, James Williams.
ENGLAND: William Crispin Rose, Percy Melmoth Walters (Cap), Richard Baugh, George Shutt, Ralph Tyndall Squire, Charles Frederick Dobson, John Edward Leighton, Frederick Dewhurst, Tinsley Lindley, Benjamin Ward Spilsbury, Thelwell Mather Pike.
Goals: James Williams (15) / Benjamin Ward Spilsbury (#, #, #, #), Frederick Dewhurst (#), Tinsley Lindley (#)

13.　20.03.1886　British Championship
IRELAND v SCOTLAND　2-7　(2-5)
Ulster Cricket Ground, Ballynafeigh, Belfast

Referee: Wolstenholme (Ireland)　Attendance: 3,000

IRELAND: Shaw Gillespie, Oliver Devine, James Watson, William Crone, Thomas Molyneux, John Hastings (Cap), John McClatchey, Samuel Johnston, John Gibb, John Condy, William Turner.

SCOTLAND: James Connor, Andrew Thomson, William McLeod, John Cameron, Leitch Keir, Robert Fleming, John Alexander Lambie (Cap), Charles Winton Heggie, William Turner, James McCrory Gourlay, Michael Dunbar.

Goals: John Condy (19), Samuel Johnston (44) / Charles Winton Heggie (15, 18, 25, 60), John Lambie (35), Michael Dunbar (40), James McCrory Gourlay (75)

14.　05.02.1887　British Championship
ENGLAND v IRELAND　7-0　(4-0)
Bramall Lane, Sheffield

Referee: Alexander Hunter (Wales)　Attendance: 6,000

ENGLAND: William John Herbert Arthur, Robert Henry Howarth, Charles Mason, George Haworth, Edward Brayshaw, James Henry Forrest, James Sayer, Frederick Dewhurst, Tinsley Lindley, William Nevill Cobbold, Edward Charles Bambridge (Cap).

IRELAND: Shaw Gillespie, Frederick Browne, William Fox, Archibald Rosbotham, William Leslie, William Crone, Jim Allen, John Gibb (Cap), Olphert Stanfield, James Small, Nathaniel Brown.

Goals: Frederick Dewhurst (2, 87), William Cobbold (25, 49), Tinsley Lindley (27, 43, 49)

15.　19.02.1887　British Championship
SCOTLAND v IRELAND　4-1　(2-1)
First Hampden Park, Glasgow

Referee: Alexander Hunter (Wales)　Attendance: 1,000

SCOTLAND: John Edward Doig, Andrew Whitelaw, Robert Smellie, John Weir, Thomas McMillan, James Hutton, Thomas James Jenkinson, John Alexander Lambie (Cap), William Wilson Watt, James Lowe, William Johnstone.

IRELAND: Shaw Gillespie, William Fox, James Watson, Robert Moore, Archibald Rosbotham, Robert Baxter, John Reid, Olphert Stanfield, Frederick Browne, John Peden, John Gibb (Cap).

Goals: William Wilson Watt (5), Thomas Jenkinson (43), William Johnstone (55), James Lowe (75) / Frederick Browne (41)

16.　12.03.1887　British Championship
IRELAND v WALES　4-1　(2-0)
Oldpark Avenue, Belfast

Referee: James McKillop (Scotland)　Attendance: 4,000

IRELAND: Shaw Gillespie (Cap), Frederick Browne, James Watson, Joseph Sherrard, Archibald Rosbotham, Oliver Devine, Robert Moore, Robert Baxter, John Gibb, Olphert Stanfield, John Peden.

WALES: Robert Roberts, Alfred William Townsend, Samuel Jones, Henry Valentine Edwards (Cap), Alexander Hunter, Ernest Percival Whitley Hughes, Henry Wilmshurt Sabine, William Roberts, John Doughty, George Griffiths, William Haighton Turner.

Goals: Olphert Stanfield (20), Frederick Browne (44), John Peden (65), Joseph Sherrard (70) / Henry Wilmshurt Sabine (55)

17.　03.03.1888　British Championship
WALES v IRELAND　11-0　(5-0)
The Racecourse, Wrexham

Referee: Thomas Hindle (England)　Attendance: 2,000

WALES: Robert Herbert Mills-Roberts, Dr. Alfred Owen Davies (Cap), John Powell, Reuben Humphreys, Joseph Davies, David Jones, William Ernest Pryce-Jones, Job Wilding, John Doughty, Edmund Gwynne Howell, Roger Doughty.

IRELAND: John Clugston, George Forbes, William Crone, Joseph Sherrard, Archibald Rosbotham, Oliver Devine, Arthur Gaussen, Olphert Stanfield (Cap), John Barry, James Wilton, John Peden.

Goals: John Doughty (#, #, #), Roger Doughty (#, #), Edmund Gwynne Howell (#, #), Job Wilding (#, #, #, #)

18.　24.03.1888　British Championship
IRELAND v SCOTLAND　2-10　(2-7)
Solitude, Belfast

Referee: Robert Parlane (Scotland)　Attendance: 5,000

IRELAND: Ralph Lawther, Robert Wilson, Frederick Browne, James Forsythe, Archibald Rosbotham, Thomas Molyneux, William Dalton, Olphert Stanfield (Cap), John Barry, John Lemon, William Turner.

SCOTLAND: John McLeod, Duncan Stewart (Cap), Archibald McCall, Allan Stewart, George Dewar, Andrew Jackson, Neil McCallum, John Robertson Gow, William Alexander Dickson, Thomas Breckenridge, Ralph Allan Aitken.

Goals: John Lemon (18), William Dalton (24) / George Dewar (5), William Alexander Dickson (8, 33, 40, 45), Thomas Breckenridge (15), Ralph Allan Aitken (25), Neil McCallum (53), Robert Wilson (65 own goal), Allan Stewart (88)

19. 07.04.1888 British Championship
IRELAND v ENGLAND 1-5 (1-3)
Ulster Cricket Ground, Ballynafeigh, Belfast
Referee: James McKillop (Scotland)   Attendance: 7,000
IRELAND: Ralph Lawther, Madesto Silo, Frederick Browne, James Forsythe, Archibald Rosbotham, William Crone, Arthur Gaussen, Olphert Stanfield (Cap), John McVicker, James Wilton, John Peden.
ENGLAND: Robert John Roberts, Alfred James Aldridge, Percy Melmoth Walters, Robert Holmes, Henry Allen, Charles Shelton, William Isaiah Bassett, Frederick Dewhurst, Tinsley Lindley (Cap), Albert Allen, Dennis Hodgetts.
Goals: William Crone (32) / Frederick Dewhurst (10), Albert Allen (14, 39, 60), Tinsley Lindley (#)

20. 02.03.1889 British Championship
ENGLAND v IRELAND 6-1 (3-1)
Anfield Road, Liverpool
Referee: Alfred Owen Davies (Wales)   Attendance: 6,000
ENGLAND: William Rowley, Thomas Clare, Alfred James Aldridge, Charles Wreford-Brown, David Weir, Alfred Shelton, Joseph Morris Lofthouse, Frank Ernest Burton, James Brant Brodie (Cap), Henry Butler Daft, John Yates.
IRELAND: John Clugston, Manliffe Fraser Goodbody, James Watson, Alexander Crawford, Archibald Rosbotham, Samuel Cooke, Arthur Gaussen, Olphert Stanfield (Cap), John Barry, James Wilton, John Peden.
Goals: David Weir (#), John Yates (#, #, 35), James Brant Brodie (#), Joseph Morris Lofthouse (#) / James Wilton (10)

21. 09.03.1889 British Championship
SCOTLAND v IRELAND 7-0 (4-0)
Ibrox Park, Glasgow
Referee: William Stacey (England)   Attendance: 6,000
SCOTLAND: John Edward Doig, James Adams, Thomas Michael McKeown, Thomas Robertson (Cap), David Calderhead, John Buchanan, Francis Watt, Thomas McInnes, William Groves, Robert Boyd, David George Black.
IRELAND: John Clugston, John McVicker, Robert Crone, John Thompson, James Christian, William Crone, Samuel Torrans, Olphert Stanfield, John Gibb (Cap), James Wilton, John Peden.
Goals: Francis Watt (7, 10), David George Black (25), William Groves (32, 50, 65), Thomas McInnes (80)

22. 27.04.1889 British Championship
IRELAND v WALES 1-3 (1-2)
Ulster Cricket Ground, Ballynafeigh, Belfast
Referee: Thomas Park (Scotland)   Attendance: 1,500
IRELAND: John Clugston, Allan Elleman, James Watson, Alexander Crawford, Lionel Vaughan Bennett, John Reid, Arthur Gaussen, Olphert Stanfield (Cap), James Percy, John Lemon, John Gillespie.
WALES: Samuel Gladstone Gillam, William Jones, David Jones, Ernest Percival Whitley Hughes, Thomas Patrick McCarthy, Patrick Leary, Joseph Davies, William Owen (Cap), George Alfred Owen, Richard Henry Jarrett, William Lewis
Goals: Olphert Stanfield (10) / Richard Jarrett (20, 44, 60)

23. 08.02.1890 British Championship
WALES v IRELAND 5-2 (2-2)
Old Racecourse, Shrewsbury
Referee: James McKillop (Scotland)   Attendance: 3,000
WALES: Samuel Gladstone Gillam, Robert Lee Roberts, William Jones, Peter Griffiths, Abel Hayes, Humphrey Jones (Cap), David Morral Lewis, William Ernest Pryce-Jones, William Owen, Albert Richard Wilcock, John Charles Henry Bowdler.
IRELAND: William Gailbraith, Robert Crone, Robert Stewart, William Crone, John Reynolds, John Reid, William Dalton, George Gaffikin, Samuel Johnston, Samuel Torrans, John Peden.
Goals: William Owen (6), Albert Wilcock (27), David Morral Lewis (#), William Ernest Pryce-Jones (56, 90) / William Dalton (11, 44)

24. 15.03.1890 British Championship
IRELAND v ENGLAND 1-9 (0-3)
Ulster Cricket Ground, Ballynafeigh, Belfast
Referee: James McKillop (Scotland)   Attendance: 6,000
IRELAND: John Clugston, Robert Stewart, Robert Crone, James Williamson, Samuel Spencer, Samuel Cooke, Allan Elleman (Cap), Olphert Stanfield, James Wilton, Robert McIlvenny, John Reynolds.
ENGLAND: Robert John Roberts, Richard Baugh, Charles Mason, John Barton, Charles Perry, James Henry Forrest (Cap), Joseph Morris Lofthouse, James Kenneth Davenport, Fred Geary, Nathaniel Walton, William John Townley.
Goals: John Reynolds (70) / Fred Geary (15, 60, 80), William John Townley (16, 84), Joseph Morris Lofthouse (40), James Davenport (46, 75), John Barton (88)

25.   29.03.1890   British Championship
IRELAND v SCOTLAND 1-4 (1-1)
Ulster Cricket Ground, Ballynafeigh, Belfast
Referee: William Stacey (England)   Attendance: 5,000
IRELAND: John Clugston, Robert Stewart (Cap), Robert Crone, John Reid, Samuel Spencer, Samuel Cooke, William Dalton, George Gaffikin, Olphert Stanfield, Samuel Torrans, John Peden.
SCOTLAND: John McLeod (Cap), Richard Hunter, James Rae, John Russell, Isaac Begbie, David Mitchell, Thomas Wylie, Gilbert Rankin, John McPherson, John Bell, David Baird.
Goals: John Peden (25) / Gilbert Rankin (13, 85), John "Kitey" McPherson (60), Thomas Wylie (86)

26.   07.02.1891   British Championship
IRELAND v WALES 7-2 (4-2)
Ulsterville, Belfast
Referee: Robert Harrison (Scotland)   Attendance: 6,000
IRELAND: John Clugston, Manliffe Fraser Goodbody, Robert Morrison, Alexander Crawford (Cap), John Reynolds, Richard Moore, William Dalton, George Gaffikin, Olphert Stanfield, Samuel Torrans, John Peden.
WALES: Richard Turner, Robert Roberts, Robert Arthur Lloyd, Peter Griffiths, John Mates, Arthur Lea, Joseph Davies, William Owen (Cap), Albert Thomas Davies, Benjamin Lewis, John Charles Henry Bowdler.
Goals: William Dalton (19), Olphert Stanfield (22, 34, 42, 80), George Gaffikin (60), Samuel Torrans (63) / Robert Roberts (10), Albert Thomas Davies (37)

27.   07.03.1891   British Championship
ENGLAND v IRELAND 6-1 (3-0)
Molineux, Wolverhampton
Referee: Richard Thomas Gough (Wales)   Att: 15,231
ENGLAND: William Crispin Rose, Joseph Thomas Marsden, Alfred Underwood, Albert Edward James Matthias Bayliss, Charles Perry, James Brant Brodie, William Isaiah Bassett, George Huth Cotterill, Tinsley Lindley (Cap), Arthur George Henfrey, Henry Butler Daft.
IRELAND: John Clugston, George Forbes, Robert Morrison, Alexander Crawford (Cap), John Reynolds, Richard Moore, Thomas Whiteside, Olphert Stanfield, William McCabe, Robert McIlvenny, John Peden.
Goals: George Cotterill (15), Arthur George Henfrey (17), Henry Butler Daft (35), Tinsley Lindley (60, 83), William Isaiah Bassett (63) / Thomas Whiteside (61)

28.   28.03.1891   British Championship
SCOTLAND v IRELAND 2-1 (1-0)
Celtic Park, Glasgow
Referee: William Stacey (England)   Attendance: 8,000
SCOTLAND: George Gillespie (Cap), Donald Currie Sillars, William Paul, Thomas Hamilton, James Cleland, James Campbell, James Low, William Bowie, Robert Clements, Thomas Smith Waddell, James Fraser.
IRELAND: Joseph Loyal, William Gordon, George Forbes, Alexander Crawford (Cap), John Reynolds, Richard Moore, William Dalton, George Gaffikin, Olphert Stanfield, David Brisby, Samuel Torrans.
Goals: James Low (6), Thomas Smith Waddell (60) / Alexander Crawford (70)

29.   27.02.1892   British Championship
WALES v IRELAND 1-1 (1-0)
Penrhyn Park, Bangor
Referee: James Campbell (Scotland)   Attendance: 4,000
WALES: James Trainer (Cap), Smart Arridge, David Jones, William Hughes, Caesar August Llewelyn Jenkyns, Robert Roberts, Robert Davies I, Archibald Middleship Bastock, William Lewis, John Charles Henry Bowdler, Benjamin Lewis.
IRELAND: John Clugston, William Gordon, Robert Stewart, Nathaniel McKeown, Samuel Spencer (Cap), William Cunningham, William Dalton, George Gaffikin, Olphert Stanfield, Samuel Torrans, John Peden.
Goals: Benjamin Lewis (15) / Olphert Stanfield (87)

30.   05.03.1892   British Championship
IRELAND v ENGLAND 0-2 (0-1)
Solitude, Belfast
Referee: Robert Harrison (Scotland)   Attendance: 7,000
IRELAND: John Clugston, William Gordon (Cap), Robert Stewart, Nathaniel McKeown, Samuel Spencer, William Cunningham, William Dalton, George Gaffikin, Olphert Stanfield, Samuel Torrans, John Peden.
ENGLAND: William Rowley, Alfred Underwood, Thomas Clare, John Davies Cox, John Holt, Michael Whitham, William Charles Athersmith, John Hargreaves Pearson, John Henry George Devey, Henry Butler Daft (Cap), Dennis Hodgetts.
Goals: Henry Butler Daft (44, 47)

31.　19.03.1892　British Championship
IRELAND v SCOTLAND 2-3 (1-2)
Solitude, Belfast

Referee: John Taylor (Wales)　Attendance: 10,500

IRELAND: John Clugston, William Gordon (Cap), Robert Stewart, Nathaniel McKeown, Samuel Spencer, William Cunningham, William Dalton, George Gaffikin, James Williamson, Olphert Stanfield, Samuel Torrans.

SCOTLAND: Andrew Baird, George Alexander Bowman, John Drummond, Robert Marshall, Thomas Robertson (Cap), Peter Dowds, William Gulliland, David Murray McPherson, James Ellis, William Allan Lambie, Alexander Lowson Keillor.

Goals: James Williamson (38), George Gaffikin (78) / Alexander Lowson Keillor (25), William Allan Lambie (28), James Ellis (60)

32.　25.02.1893　British Championship
ENGLAND v IRELAND 6-1 (4-1)
Perry Barr, Birmingham

Referee: Thomas Park (Scotland)　Attendance: 10,000

ENGLAND: Charles Christopher Charsley, Alban Hugh Harrison, Frederick Raymond Pelly, Albert Smith, William Norman Winckworth, Norman Charles Cooper, Robert Topham, Gilbert Oswald Smith, George Huth Cotterill (Cap), Walter Evelyn Gilliat, Rupert Renorden Sandilands.

IRELAND: John Clugston, William Gordon, Robert Stewart, Alexander Crawford, Samuel Spencer, William Cunningham, James Small (Cap), George Gaffikin, Olphert Stanfield, Samuel Torrans, John Peden.

Goals: Walter Gilliat (10, 18, 30), Gilbert O. Smith (43), William Winckworth (60), Rupert Renorden Sandilands (75) / George Gaffikin (12)

33.　25.03.1893　British Championship
SCOTLAND v IRELAND 6-1 (4-1)
Celtic Park, Glasgow

Referee: John Taylor (Wales)　Attendance: 12,000

SCOTLAND: John Lindsay, James Adams, Robert Smellie, William Maley, James Kelly (Cap), David Mitchell, William Sellar, Thomas Smith Waddell, James Hamilton, Alexander McMahon, John Campbell.

IRELAND: John Clugston, William Gordon, Robert Torrans, Nathaniel McKeown, Samuel Johnston, Samuel Torrans, James Small (Cap), George Gaffikin, James Williamson, James Wilton, John Peden.

Goals: Alexander McMahon (5), James Hamilton (15), Samuel Torrans (20 own goal), William Sellar (27, 80), James Kelly (50) / George Gaffikin (44)

34.　08.04.1893　British Championship
IRELAND v WALES 4-3 (2-1)
Solitude, Belfast

Referee: James Campbell (Scotland)　Attendance: 3,000

IRELAND: John Clugston, William Gordon, Robert Stewart, Alexander Crawford, Nathaniel McKeown, Samuel Johnston, James Small (Cap), George Gaffikin, Olphert Stanfield, James Wilton, John Peden.

WALES: Samuel Jones, Alfred William Townsend, Oliver David Shepston Taylor, Arthur Lea (Cap), John Evans, Edward Morris, James Vaughan, William Owen, John Butler, George Alfred Owen, Edwin James.

Goals: John Peden (5, 50, 58), James Wilton (82) / William Owen (8), George Alfred Owen (34, 80)

35.　24.02.1894　British Championship
WALES v IRELAND 4-1 (1-0)
St Helen's Rugby Ground, Swansea

Referee: James Campbell (Scotland)　Attendance: 7,000

WALES: James Trainer (Cap), Smart Arridge, Oliver David Shepston Taylor, Robert Samuel Jones, Thomas Chapman, Abel Hayes, John Evans, Benjamin Lewis, William Lewis, John Charles Rea, Edwin James.

IRELAND: Thomas Gordon, Robert Stewart, Samuel Torrans (Cap), Nathaniel McKeown, John Burnett, Robert Milne, William Dalton, George Gaffikin, Olphert Stanfield, William Kennedy Gibson, James Barron.

Goals: William Lewis (55, 82), Edwin James (65, 75) / Olphert Stanfield (20)

36.　03.03.1894　British Championship
IRELAND v ENGLAND 2-2 (1-0)
Solitude, Belfast

Referee: Thomas Park (Scotland)　Attendance: 8,000

IRELAND: Thomas Scott, Robert Stewart, Samuel Torrans (Cap), Samuel Johnston, John Burnett, Robert Milne, William Dalton, George Gaffikin, Olphert Stanfield, William Kennedy Gibson, James Barron.

ENGLAND: Joseph Reader, Robert Henry Howarth, Robert Holmes (Cap), John Reynolds, John Holt, James William Crabtree, Harry Chippendale, James Whitehead, John Henry George Devey, Dennis Hodgetts, Frederick Spiksley.

Goals: Olphert Stanfield (70), William Kennedy Gibson (87) / John Henry George Devey (40), Frederick Spiksley (55)

37. 31.03.1894   British Championship
IRELAND v SCOTLAND 1-2 (0-2)
Solitude, Belfast

Referee: Edward Phennah (Wales)   Attendance: 6,000

IRELAND: Thomas Scott, Robert Stewart, Samuel Torrans, Nathaniel McKeown, John Burnett, Robert Milne, William Dalton, George Gaffikin, Olphert Stanfield (Cap), William Kennedy Gibson, James Barron.

SCOTLAND: Francis Barrett, David Crawford, John Drummond, Robert Marshall (Cap), William Longair, David Stewart, John Daniel Taylor, James Blessington, David Alexander, Robert Scott, Alexander Lowson Keillor.

Goals: Olphert Stanfield (65) / Samuel Torrans (25 own goal), John Daniel Taylor (28)

38. 09.03.1895   British Championship
ENGLAND v IRELAND 9-0 (5-0)
County Cricket Club, Derby

Referee: James Robertson (Scotland)   Attendance: 8,000

ENGLAND: John William Sutcliffe, James William Crabtree, Robert Holmes (Cap), Rabbi Howell, Thomas Henry Crawshaw, James Albert Turner, William Isaiah Bassett, Stephen Bloomer, John Goodall, Francis Becton, Joseph Alfred Schofield.

IRELAND: Thomas Gordon, Hugh Gordon, Samuel Torrans, Hymie McKie, Robert Milne (Cap), John Burnett, Thomas Morrison, George Gaffikin, Olphert Stanfield, William Sherrard, Thomas Jordan.

Goals: Samuel Torrans (3 own goal), Steve Bloomer (4, 58), Francis Becton (15, 60), William Isaiah Bassett (30), Rabbi Howell (36), John Goodall (65, 87)

39. 16.03.1895   British Championship
IRELAND v WALES 2-2 (1-0)
Solitude, Belfast

Referee: William Jope (England)   Attendance: 6,000

IRELAND: Thomas Scott, Hugh Gordon, Lewis Irwin Scott, Hymie McKie, Robert Milne, John Burnett, Thomas Morrison, William Sherrard, Thomas Jordan (Cap), George Warrington Gaukrodger, George Gaffikin.

WALES: James Trainer (Cap), Smart Arridge, James Alfred Edwards, George Williams, Thomas Chapman, John Leonard Jones, William Henry Meredith, Joseph Davies, Harry Trainer, William Parry, William Lewis.

Goals: George Gaukrodger (32), Thomas Jordan (42) / Harry Trainer (10, 85)

40. 30.03.1895   British Championship
SCOTLAND v IRELAND 3-1 (1-1)
Celtic Park, Glasgow

Referee: Thomas Mitchell (England)   Attendance: 15,000

SCOTLAND: Daniel McArthur, John Drummond (Cap), Daniel Doyle, James Simpson, David Kennedy Russell, Neil Gibson, John Daniel Taylor, Thomas Smith Waddell, John "Kitey" McPherson, John Walker, William Allan Lambie.

IRELAND: Thomas Scott, Joseph Ponsonby, Lewis Irwin Scott, Hymie McKie, Thomas E. Alexander, Thomas McClatchey, Thomas Morrison, William Sherrard, Olphert Stanfield (Cap), William Kennedy Gibson, James Barron.

Goals: John Walker (20, 75), William Allan Lambie (40) / William Sherrard (35)

41. 29.02.1896   British Championship
WALES v IRELAND 6-1 (4-0)
The Racecourse, Wrexham

Referee: James Cooper (England)   Attendance: 3,000

WALES: Samuel Jones I, Charles Frederick Parry (Cap), John Samuel Matthias, Joseph Rogers, Price Foulkes White, John Leonard Jones, William Henry Meredith, David Henry Pugh, Arthur Grenville Morris, John Charles Rea, William Lewis.

IRELAND: Thomas Scott, Joseph Ponsonby, Samuel Torrans, Sam McCoy, Robert Milne, John Campbell, Edward Turner, Giddy Baird, Olphert Stanfield (Cap), James McCashin, John Peden.

Goals: William Lewis (9, 20), William Meredith (22, 84), Arthur Grenville Morris (34), David Henry Pugh (60) / Edward Turner (70)

42. 07.03.1896   British Championship
IRELAND v ENGLAND 0-2 (0-1)
Solitude, Belfast

Referee: James Robertson (Scotland)   Attendance: 12,000

IRELAND: Thomas Scott, Joseph Ponsonby, Samuel Torrans, James Fitzpatrick (Cap), Robert Milne, Hugh Gordon, Giddy Baird, James Kelly, Olphert Stanfield, Edward Turner, John Peden.

ENGLAND: George Berkeley Raikes, Lewis Vaughn Lodge, William John Oakley, James William Crabtree, Thomas Henry Crawshaw, George Kinsey, William Isaiah Bassett, Stephen Bloomer, Gilbert Oswald Smith (Cap), Edgar Wallace Chadwick, Frederick Spiksley.

Goals: Gilbert Oswald Smith (40), Stephen Bloomer (75)

43. 28.03.1896 British Championship
IRELAND v SCOTLAND 3-3 (3-2)
Solitude, Belfast
Referee: James Cooper (England)   Attendance: 8,000
IRELAND: Thomas Scott, Joseph Ponsonby, Samuel Torrans, Hugh Gordon (Cap), Robert Milne, James Fitzpatrick, Giddy Baird, Denis Morrogh, Olphert Stanfield, James Barron, John Peden.
SCOTLAND: Kenneth Anderson, Peter Meechan, John Drummond, Neil Gibson, James Kelly (Cap), George Hogg, Patrick Murray, James Blessington, Robert Smyth McColl, John Cameron, William Allan Lambie.
Goals: James Barron (20, 32), Robert Milne (43 pen) / Robert Smyth McColl (7, 25), Patrick Murray (85)

44. 20.02.1897 British Championship
ENGLAND v IRELAND 6-0 (3-0)
Trent Bridge Cricket Ground, Nottingham
Referee: Thomas Robertson (Scotland)   Attendance: 13,490
ENGLAND: John William Robinson, William John Oakley, William Williams, Bernard Middleditch, Thomas Henry Crawshaw, Ernest Needham, William Charles Athersmith, Stephen Bloomer, Gilbert Oswald Smith (Cap), George Frederick Wheldon, Thomas Henry Bradshaw.
IRELAND: Thomas Scott, Joseph Ponsonby, Samuel Torrans, John Pyper, Robert Milne, George McMaster, James Campbell, George Hall, Olphert Stanfield, John Darling, James Barron (Cap).
Goals: Stephen Bloomer (19, 85), George Wheldon (30, 33, 55), William Charles Athersmith (75)

45. 06.03.1897 British Championship
IRELAND v WALES 4-3 (1-3)
Solitude, Belfast
Referee: Thomas Robertson (Scotland)   Attendance: 10,000
IRELAND: Thomas Scott, William Kennedy Gibson, Samuel Torrans, John Pyper, Joseph Ponsonby (Cap), George McMaster, James Campbell, Olphert Stanfield, James Pyper, John Peden, James Barron.
WALES: James Trainer (Cap), James Alfred Edwards, Charles Frederick Parry, Sydney Darvell, Caesar August Llewelyn Jenkyns, John Leonard Jones, William Henry Meredith, David Henry Pugh, Morgan Maddox Morgan-Owen, William Nock, John Charles Rea.
Goals: James Barron (7), Olphert Stanfield (62), John Pyper (66), John Peden (68) / William Meredith (19, 36), Caesar August Llewelyn Jenkyns (27)

46. 27.03.1897 British Championship
SCOTLAND v IRELAND 5-1 (4-0)
Ibrox Park, Glasgow
Referee: James Cooper (England)   Attendance: 15,000
SCOTLAND: Matthew Dickie, Duncan McLean, John Drummond (Cap), Neil Gibson, William Urquhart Baird, David Stewart, Thomas Pollock Low, John "Kitey" McPherson, Robert Smyth McColl, Alexander King, William Allan Lambie.
IRELAND: James Thompson, Joseph Ponsonby (Cap), Samuel Torrans, John Pyper, Robert Milne, George McMaster, James Campbell, Olphert Stanfield, James Pyper, John Darling, John Peden.
Goals: John "Kitey" McPherson (5, 70), Neil Gibson (15), Robert Smyth McColl (25), Alexander King (40) / James Pyper (62)

47. 19.02.1898 British Championship
WALES v IRELAND 0-1 (0-0)
The Oval, Llandudno
Referee: Thomas Robertson (Scotland)   Attendance: 6,000
WALES: John Morris, Charles Frederick Parry (Cap), Smart Arridge, George Williams, John Henry Edwards, John Leonard Jones, William Henry Meredith, Thomas John Thomas, William Lewis, Albert Lockley, John Charles Rea.
IRELAND: Thomas Scott, William Kennedy Gibson (Cap), Michael Cochrane, William Anderson, Robert Milne, John Lytle, James Campbell, John Thompson Mercer, James Pyper, James McCashin, John Peden.
Goal: John Peden (85)

48. 05.03.1898 British Championship
IRELAND v ENGLAND 2-3 (1-2)
Solitude, Belfast
Referee: Thomas Robertson (Scotland)   Attendance: 12,000
IRELAND: Thomas Scott, William Kennedy Gibson, Samuel Torrans, William Anderson, Robert Milne, Michael Cochrane, James Campbell (Cap), John Thompson Mercer, James Pyper, John Peden, Joseph McAllen.
ENGLAND: John William Robinson, William John Oakley, William Williams, Frank Forman, Thomas Morren, James Albert Turner, William Charles Athersmith, Charles Henry Richards, Gilbert Oswald Smith (Cap), Benjamin Walter Garfield, George Frederick Wheldon.
Goals: James Pyper (18), Joseph McAllen (70) / Gilbert Oswald Smith (37), William Charles Athersmith (42), Thomas Morren (47)

49. 26.03.1898   British Championship
IRELAND v SCOTLAND 0-3 (0-2)

Solitude, Belfast

Referee: John Lewis (England)   Attendance: 5,000

IRELAND: Thomas Scott, William Kennedy Gibson, Samuel Torrans, William Anderson, Robert Milne, Michael Cochrane (Cap), James Campbell, John Thompson Mercer, James Pyper, James McCashin, John Peden.

SCOTLAND: Kenneth Anderson, Robert Robinson Kelso (Cap), Daniel Doyle, William Thomson, David Kennedy Russell, Alexander King, William Graham Stewart, John Campbell, Robert Smyth McColl, John Walker, Thomas Robertson.

Goals: Thomas Robertson (30), Robert Smyth McColl (42), William Graham Stewart (70)

50. 18.02.1899   British Championship
ENGLAND v IRELAND 13-2 (5-0)

Roker Park, Sunderland

Referee: Allen Hamilton (Scotland)   Attendance: 13,000

ENGLAND: John Hillman, Philip Bach, William Williams, Frank Forman, James William Crabtree, Ernest Needham, William Charles Athersmith, Stephen Bloomer, Gilbert Oswald Smith (Cap), James Settle, Frederick Ralph Forman.

IRELAND: James Lewis, John Pyper, Samuel Torrans, Joseph Ponsonby, Robert Milne, Michael Cochrane, James Campbell, John Thompson Mercer, John Waring, John Wattie, Joseph McAllen (Cap).

Goals: Frank Forman (15), Frederick Ralph Forman (15, 52), William Athersmith (25), Gilbert O. Smith (27, 55, 60, 75), Stephen Bloomer (37, 89), James Settle (53, 55, 80) / Joseph McAllen (65 pen), James Campbell (88)

51. 04.03.1899   British Championship
IRELAND v WALES 1-0 (0-0)

Grosvenor Park, Belfast

Referee: Charles Sutcliffe (England)   Attendance: 10,000

IRELAND: James Lewis, John Pyper, Samuel Torrans, Archibald Goodall, Robert Milne, John Taggart, Thomas Morrison, James Meldon, John Daniel Hanna, Joseph McAllen (Cap), John Peden.

WALES: James Trainer, Charles Edward Thomas, Horace Elford Blew, George Richards, John Leonard Jones (Cap), Edward Hughes, Frederick Charles Kelly, Robert Atherton, Edwin James, David Charles Davies, William James Jackson.

Goal: James Meldon (60)

52. 25.03.1899   British Championship
SCOTLAND v IRELAND 9-1 (5-0)

Celtic Park, Glasgow

Referee: Charles Sutcliffe (England)   Attendance: 11,000

SCOTLAND: Matthew Dickie, Nicol Smith, David Storrier (Cap), Neil Gibson, Alexander John Christie, Alexander King, John Campbell, Robert Cumming Hamilton, Robert Smyth McColl, Davidson Berry, John Bell.

IRELAND: James Lewis (Cap), Samuel Swan, Thomas Foreman, William Anderson, Archibald Goodall, John McShane, George Sheehan, James Meldon, James Pyper, James McCashin, Joseph McAllen.

Goals: Robert Smyth McColl (2, 35, 46), Alexander Christie (8), Robert Cumming Hamilton (15, 60), John Bell (40), John Campbell (70, 85) / Archibald Goodall (54)

53. 24.02.1900   British Championship
WALES v IRELAND 2-0 (0-0)

The Oval, Llandudno

Referee: Charles Sutcliffe (England)   Attendance: 6,000

WALES: Leigh Richmond Roose, David Jones (Cap), Charles Richard Morris, Samuel James Brookes, Robert Morris, William Clare Harrison, William Henry Meredith, William Thomas Butler, Richard Jones, Thomas David Parry, David Charles Davies.

IRELAND: Thomas Scott, John Pyper, Michael Cochrane, John McShane, Archibald Goodall, Hugh Maginnis, George Sheehan (Cap), Thomas Morrison, John Henry Kirwan, Alfred Kearns, Joseph McAllen.

Goals: Thomas Parry (73), William Henry Meredith (87 pen)

54. 03.03.1900   British Championship
IRELAND v SCOTLAND 0-3 (0-2)

Solitude, Belfast

Referee: Charles Sutcliffe (England)   Attendance: 6,000

IRELAND: James Lewis, John Pyper, Michael Cochrane, John McShane (Cap), John Barry, Hugh Maginnis, James Campbell, John Darling, Patrick McAuley, Joseph McAllen, Alfred Kearns.

SCOTLAND: Henry George Rennie, Nicol Smith, Robert Glen, Neil Gibson, Henry James Hall Marshall (Cap), William Orr, William Graham Stewart, Robert Walker, John Campbell, Patrick Callaghan, Alexander Smith.

Goals: John Campbell (8, 83), Alexander Smith (23)

55. 17.03.1900   British Championship
IRELAND v ENGLAND 0-2 (0-2)
Lansdowne Road, Dublin

Referee: John Marshall (Scotland)   Attendance: 8,000

IRELAND: Matthew Michael Reilly, John Pyper, Michael Cochrane, John McShane, Archibald Goodall, Hugh Maginnis, George Sheehan, James Campbell, James Pyper, Joseph McAllen, Alfred Kearns.

ENGLAND: John William Robinson, William John Oakley, James William Crabtree, William Harold Johnson, John Holt, Ernest Needham, Arthur John Turner, Daniel Cunliffe, Gilbert Oswald Smith (Cap), Charles Sagar, Alfred Ernest Priest.

Goals: William Harold Johnson (12), Charles Sagar (16)

56. 23.02.1901   British Championship
SCOTLAND v IRELAND 11-0 (5-0)
Celtic Park, Glasgow

Referee: Richard Thomas Gough (Wales)   Att: 15,000

SCOTLAND: George Chappell McWattie, Nicol Smith, Bernard Battles, David Kennedy Russell, George Anderson, John Tait Robertson, John Campbell, John Campbell, Robert Cumming Hamilton (Cap), Alexander McMahon, Alexander Smith.

IRELAND: Samuel McAlpine, William Kennedy Gibson (Cap), Samuel Torrans, Patrick Farrell, James Connor, Michael Cochrane, James Scott, James Smith, James Campbell, Harry O'Reilly, Robert Clarke.

Goals: Alexander McMahon (6, 15, 40, 50), David Kennedy Russell (25), John Campbell (30, 65), Robert Cumming Hamilton (55, 60, 70, 80)

57. 09.03.1901   British Championship
ENGLAND v IRELAND 3-0 (1-0)
The Dell, Southampton

Referee: Thomas Robertson (Scotland)   Attendance: 8,000

ENGLAND: John William Robinson, Charles Burgess Fry, William John Oakley (Cap), William Jones, Thomas Henry Crawshaw, Ernest Needham, Arthur John Turner, Reginald Erskine Foster, George Albert Hedley, Herbert Ernest Banks, John Cox.

IRELAND: James Nolan-Whelan, William Kennedy Gibson, Peter Boyle, James Connor, Archibald Goodall (Cap), Joseph Burnison, Thomas Black, Robert Rea, John Mansfield, Isaac Doherty, Robert Clarke.

Goals: Thomas Crawshaw (9), George Albert Hedley (81), Reginald Erskine Foster (83)

58. 23.03.1901   British Championship
IRELAND v WALES 0-1 (0-1)
Solitude, Belfast

Referee: Charles Sutcliffe (England)   Attendance: 7,000

IRELAND: James Nolan-Whelan, William Kennedy Gibson (Cap), Samuel Torrans, Patrick Farrell, Robert Milne, Joseph Burnison, James Campbell, James Smith, H. McKelvie, Harry O'Reilly, Joseph McAllen.

WALES: Leigh Richmond Roose, Samuel Meredith, Charles Richard Morris, Maurice Pryce Parry, Robert Morris (Cap), William Clare Harrison, William Henry Meredith, John Owen Jones, Arthur William Green, Thomas David Parry, Ephrahim Williams.

Goal: John Owen Jones (55)

59. 22.02.1902   British Championship
WALES v IRELAND 0-3 (0-1)
Arms Park, Cardiff

Referee: Arthur Kingscott (England)   Attendance: 7,000

WALES: Robert Owen Evans, Horace Elford Blew, Hugh Jones, Maurice Pryce Parry, Edward Hughes, John Leonard Jones (Cap), Frederick Charles Kelly, Thomas Jenkins, Roger Evans, Ephrahim Williams, Richard Morris.

IRELAND: James Nolan-Whelan, William Kennedy Gibson (Cap), William McCracken, John Darling, Robert Milne, Harold Nicholl, John Thompson Mercer, James Maxwell, Andrew Gara, Alfred Kearns, John Henry Kirwan.

Goals: Andrew Gara (40, 60, 75)

60. 01.03.1902   British Championship
IRELAND v SCOTLAND 1-5 (0-1)
Grosvenor Park, Belfast

Referee: Frederick Bye (England)   Attendance: 15,000

IRELAND: James Nolan-Whelan, William Kennedy Gibson, John Pyper, John Darling, Archibald Goodall, Robert Milne (Cap), James Campbell, Thomas Morrison, Andrew Gara, Alfred Kearns, Joseph McAllen.

SCOTLAND: Henry George Rennie, Nicol Smith, John Drummond, George Brown Key, Albert Thoroughgood Buick (Cap), John Tait Robertson, William McCartney, Robert Walker, Robert Cumming Hamilton, John Campbell, Alexander Smith.

Goals: Robert Milne (89) / Robert Cumming Hamilton (43, 70, 74), Robert Walker (49), Albert Thoroughgood Buick (76)

61. 22.03.1902   British Championship
IRELAND v ENGLAND 0-1 (0-0)

North-East Gound, Balmoral, Belfast

Referee: Thomas Robertson (Scotland)   Attendance: 12,000

IRELAND: Matthew Michael Reilly, William McCracken, Peter Boyle, John Darling, Robert Milne (Cap), Harold Nicholl, John Thompson Mercer, Thomas Morrison, Andrew Gara, Alfred Kearns, John Henry Kirwan.

ENGLAND: William George, Robert Crompton, James Iremonger, Albert Wilkes, William Bannister, Frank Forman (Cap), William Hogg, Stephen Bloomer, John Calvey, James Settle, Frederick Blackburn.

Goal: James Settle (86)

62. 14.02.1903   British Championship
ENGLAND v IRELAND 4-0 (1-0)

Molineux, Wolverhampton

Referee: William Nunnerley (Wales)   Attendance: 24,240

ENGLAND: Thomas Baddeley, Howard Spencer (Cap), George Molyneux, William Harold Johnson, Thomas Holford, Harry Hadley, Harry Davis, John Sharp, Vivian John Woodward, James Settle, Arthur Lockett.

IRELAND: William Scott, William McCracken, George McMillan, John Darling, Robert Milne, Archibald Goodall (Cap), James Campbell, James Maxwell, James Sheridan, Harold Alexander Sloan, John Henry Kirwan.

Goals: Vivian John Woodward (19, 52), John Sharp (63), Harry Davis (87)

63. 21.03.1903   British Championship
SCOTLAND v IRELAND 0-2 (0-1)

Celtic Park, Glasgow

Referee: Thomas Kirkham (England)   Attendance: 17,000

SCOTLAND: Henry George Rennie, Archibald Colin Gray, John Drummond (Cap), John Cross, Peter Robertson, William Orr, David Lindsay, Robert Walker, William Porteous, Finlay Ballantyne Speedie, Alexander Smith.

IRELAND: William Scott, Alexander McCartney, Peter Boyle, John Darling, Robert Milne (Cap), Hugh Maginnis, John Thompson Mercer, James Sheridan, Maurice Joseph Connor, Thomas Shanks, John Henry Kirwan.

Goals: Maurice Joseph Connor (9), John Henry Kirwan (83)

64. 28.03.1903   British Championship
IRELAND v WALES 2-0 (0-0)

Solitude, Belfast

Referee: Frederick Thomas Kirkham (England)   Att: 14,000

IRELAND: William Scott, Alexander McCartney, Peter Boyle (Cap), John Darling, Archibald Goodall, Hugh Maginnis, John Thompson Mercer, James Maxwell, Maurice Joseph Connor, James Sheridan, John Henry Kirwan.

WALES: Robert Owen Evans, Samuel Meredith, Charles Richard Morris (Cap), George Richards, Robert Morris, Thomas Davies, William Henry Meredith, William Wynn, William Davies, Richard Morris, Robert Atherton.

Goals: Archibald Goodall (76), James Sheridan (88)

65. 12.03.1904   British Championship
IRELAND v ENGLAND 1-3 (0-2)

Solitude, Belfast

Referee: Thomas Robertson (Scotland)   Attendance: 15,000

IRELAND: William Scott, William McCracken, Peter Boyle, Robert Milne, Archibald Goodall (Cap), Hugh Maginnis, John Thompson Mercer, James Sheridan, Maurice Joseph Connor, John Henry Kirwan, Henry Redmond Buckle.

ENGLAND: Thomas Baddeley, Robert Crompton (Cap), Herbert Burgess, Herod Ruddlesdin, Thomas Henry Crawshaw, Alexander Leake, William Frederick Brawn, Alfred Common, Vivian John Woodward, Joseph William Bache, George Henry Davis.

Goals: John Henry Kirwan (49) /
Joseph William Bache (12), Alfred Common (16, 65)

66. 21.03.1904   British Championship
WALES v IRELAND 0-1 (0-0)

The Cricket Ground, Bangor

Referee: Frederick Thomas Kirkham (England)   Att: 10,000

WALES: David Davies, Horace Elford Blew, Charles Richard Morris, Maurice Pryce Parry, Edward Hughes, John Leonard Jones (Cap), Alfred Ernest Watkins, Walter Martin Watkins, Arthur William Green, Richard Morris, Robert Atherton.

IRELAND: William Scott, William McCracken, Alexander McCartney, James English McConnell, Robert Milne, Hugh Maginnis, John Thompson Mercer, Thomas Shanks, Archibald Goodall (Cap), Hugh Kirkwood, John Henry Kirwan.

Goal: William McCracken (77 pen)

67. 26.03.1904   British Championship
IRELAND v SCOTLAND 1-1 (0-1)
Dalymount Park, Dublin
Referee: Thomas Kirkham (England)   Attendance: 1,000
IRELAND: William Scott, William McCracken, Alexander McCartney, James English McConnell, Robert Milne (Cap), Hugh Maginnis, James Campbell, James Sheridan, Harry O'Reilly, Harold Alexander Sloan, John Henry Kirwan.
SCOTLAND: Henry George Rennie, Thomas Alexander Skinner Jackson, John Cameron, George Hunter Henderson, Charles Bellany Thomson, John Tait Robertson (Cap), John Walker, Robert Walker, Robert Cumming Hamilton, Hugh Wilson, Alexander Smith.
Goals: James Sheridan (70) / Robert Hamilton (22)

68. 25.02.1905   British Championship
ENGLAND v IRELAND 1-1 (0-0)
Ayresome Park, Middlesbrough
Referee: Thomas Robertson (Scotland)   Attendance: 21,700
ENGLAND: Reginald Garnet Williamson, William Balmer, John Carr, Samuel Wolstenholme, Charles Roberts, Alexander Leake, Richard Bond, Stephen Bloomer, Vivian John Woodward, Stanley Schute Harris (Cap), Frank Booth.
IRELAND: William Scott, William McCracken, Alexander McCartney, John Darling, James Connor, Harold Nicholl, Harold Alexander Sloan, James Sheridan, Neill Murphy, Thomas Shanks, John Henry Kirwan (Cap).
Goals: Stephen Bloomer (55) /
Reginald Garnet Williamson (48 own goal)

69. 18.03.1905   British Championship
SCOTLAND v IRELAND 4-0 (2-0)
Celtic Park, Glasgow
Referee: Thomas Kirkham (England)   Attendance: 35,000
SCOTLAND: William Hay Howden, Donald McLeod, William McIntosh, Neil Gibson (Cap), Charles Bellany Thomson, James Hay, James McMenemy, Robert Walker, James Quinn, Peter Somers, George Wilson.
IRELAND: William Scott, Alexander McCartney, William McCracken, John Darling, James Connor, James English McConnell, John Thompson Mercer, James Maxwell, Neill Murphy, Charles O'Hagan, John Henry Kirwan (Cap).
Goals: Charles Bellany Thomson (14 pen, 61 pen), Robert Walker (35), James Quinn (50)

70. 08.04.1905   British Championship
IRELAND v WALES 2-2 (2-2)
Solitude, Belfast
Referee: Frederick Thomas Kirkham (England)   Att: 15,000
IRELAND: Robert Reynolds, William McCracken, George McMillan, John Darling, James Connor, Samuel Johnston, Andrew Hunter, James Maxwell, Neill Murphy, Charles O'Hagan, John Henry Kirwan (Cap).
WALES: John Tracey Morgan, Horace Elford Blew, Charles Richard Morris, George Richards, Edward Hughes (Cap), John Hughes, William Henry Matthews, Walter Martin Watkins, William Davies, William Jones, Robert Atherton.
Goals: Neill Murphy (25), Charles O'Hagan (45) /
Walter Martin Watkins (20), Robert Atherton (#)

71. 17.02.1906   British Championship
IRELAND v ENGLAND 0-5 (0-2)
Solitude, Belfast
Referee: Thomas Robertson (Scotland)   Attendance: 16,000
IRELAND: James Sherry, John Darling, Hugh McIlroy, John Wright, Robert Milne, James English McConnell, Andrew Hunter, Thomas Stephen Mulholland, Valentine Harris, Charles O'Hagan, John Henry Kirwan (Cap).
ENGLAND: James Ashcroft, Robert Crompton, Herbert Smith, Benjamin Warren, Colin Campbell McKechnie Veitch, Albert Edward Houlker, Richard Bond, Samuel Hulme Day, Arthur Samuel Brown, Stanley Schute Harris (Cap), Albert Arthur Gosnell.
Goals: Richard Bond (26, 89), Arthur Samuel Brown (32), Stanley Schute Harris (56), Samuel Hulme Day (70)

72. 17.03.1906   British Championship
IRELAND v SCOTLAND 0-1 (0-0)
Dalymount Park, Dublin
Referee: Frederick Bye (England)   Attendance: 8,000
IRELAND: Frederick McKee, George Willis, John Darling, John Wright, Robert Milne, Joseph Ledwige, Andrew Hunter, Thomas Stephen Mulholland, Thomas Waddell, Charles O'Hagan, John Henry Kirwan (Cap).
SCOTLAND: Henry George Rennie, Donald McLeod, David Alexander Hill, James S. Young, Charles Bellany Thomson (Cap), John May, Gladstone Hamilton, Robert Walker, James Quinn, Thomas Tindal Fitchie, Alexander Smith.
Goal: Thomas Tindal Fitchie (52)

73. 02.04.1906   British Championship
WALES v IRELAND 4-4 (3-2)
The Racecourse, Wrexham

Referee: Frederick Thomas Kirkham (England)   Att: 5,000

WALES: Leigh Richmond Roose, James Roberts, Horace Elford Blew (Cap), Edwin Hughes, Morgan Maddox Morgan-Owen, Edward Hughes, William Jones, Hugh Morgan-Owen, Arthur William Green, Richard Jones II, Robert Ernest Evans.

IRELAND: Frederick McKee, George Willis, John Darling, John Wright, Robert Milne, Joseph Ledwige, Andrew Hunter, James Maxwell, Charles O'Hagan, Harold Alexander Sloan, John Henry Kirwan (Cap).

Goals: Arthur Green (#, #, #), Hugh Morgan-Owen (#) / James Maxwell (72), Harold Alexander Sloan (10, 25, 74)

74. 16.02.1907   British Championship
ENGLAND v IRELAND 1-0 (0-0)
Goodison Park, Liverpool

Referee: Thomas Robertson (Scotland)   Attendance: 25,325

ENGLAND: Samuel Hardy, Robert Crompton (Cap), John Carr, Benjamin Warren, William John Wedlock, Robert Murray Hawkes, John Rutherford, John George Coleman, George Richard Hilsdon, Joseph William Bache, Harold Payne Hardman.

IRELAND: William Scott, William McCracken, Alexander McCartney, John Wright, James Connor, James English McConnell, John Blair, Valentine Harris, Harold Alexander Sloan (Cap), Charles O'Hagan, Samuel Young.

Goal: Harold Payne Hardman (53)

75. 23.02.1907   British Championship
IRELAND v WALES 2-3 (1-1)
Solitude, Belfast

Referee: Frederick Thomas Kirkham (England)   Att: 12,000

IRELAND: James Sherry, John Seymour, Alexander McCartney, John Wright (Cap), Charles Crothers, George McClure, John Blair, Valentine Harris, Harold Alexander Sloan, Charles O'Hagan, John Henry Kirwan.

WALES: Leigh Richmond Roose, James Roberts, Lloyd Davies, George Latham, George Owen Williams, Llewelyn Davies, William Henry Meredith (Cap), William Jones, Arthur Howell Hughes, Richard Morris, Gordon Peace Jones.

Goals: Charles O'Hagan (10), Harold Alexander Sloan (80) / Richard Morris (12), William Henry Meredith (#), William Jones (#)

76. 16.03.1907   British Championship
SCOTLAND v IRELAND 3-0 (1-0)
Celtic Park, Glasgow

Referee: John Lewis (England)   Attendance: 26,000

SCOTLAND: William Muir, Thomas Alexander Skinner Jackson, William Barbour Agnew, William Key, Charles Bellany Thomson (Cap), Alexander McNair, Alexander Bennett, Robert Walker, Frank O'Rourke, Peter Somers, John Fraser.

IRELAND: William Scott, George Willis, Alexander McCartney, John Wright (Cap), James Connor, George McClure, John Blair, James Maxwell, Edward McGuire, Charles O'Hagan, Samuel Young.

Goals: Frank O'Rourke (40), Robert Walker (48), Charles Bellany Thomson (82 pen)

77. 15.02.1908   British Championship
IRELAND v ENGLAND 1-3 (1-1)
Solitude, Belfast

Referee: Thomas Robertson (Scotland)   Attendance: 22,600

IRELAND: William Scott (Cap), Alexander Craig, Alexander McCartney, Valentine Harris, James Connor, George McClure, John Blair, Denis Hannon, Harold Victor Aitken Mercer, Samuel Burnison, Samuel Young.

ENGLAND: Harry Mart Maskery, Robert Crompton, Jesse Pennington, Benjamin Warren, William John Wedlock, Evelyn Henry Lintott, John Rutherford, Vivian John Woodward (Cap), George Richard Hilsdon, James Edward Windridge, George Wall.

Goals: Denis Hannon (13) / George Richard Hilsdon (7, 85), Vivian John Woodward (88)

78. 14.03.1908   British Championship
IRELAND v SCOTLAND 0-5 (0-2)
Dalymount Park, Dublin

Referee: James Ibbotson (England)   Attendance: 9,000

IRELAND: William Scott (Cap), Alexander Craig, Alexander McCartney, Valentine Harris, James Connor, James English McConnell, John Blair, Denis Hannon, William Andrews, Charles O'Hagan, Samuel Young.

SCOTLAND: Henry George Rennie, James Mitchell, William Barbour Agnew, John May, Charles Bellany Thomson (Cap), James Hill Galt, Robert Bryson Templeton, Robert Walker, James Quinn, Robert Smyth McColl, William Lennie.

Goals: James Quinn (3, 55, 70, 75), James Hill Galt (23)

79. 11.04.1908   British Championship
WALES v IRELAND   0-1 (0-1)
Athletic Ground, Aberdare

Referee: James Ibbotson (England)   Attendance: 6,000

WALES: Robert Owen Evans, Horace Elford Blew, Jeffrey Woodward Jones, Ernest Peake, Maurice Pryce Parry, Ioan Haydn Price, William Henry Meredith, Richard Morris, Walter Martin Watkins (Cap), Albert Victor Hodgkinson, Thomas Daniel Jones.

IRELAND: William Scott, Alexander Craig (Cap), Alexander McCartney, John Darling, James English McConnell, Valentine Harris, Andrew Hunter, William Hamilton, Harold Alexander Sloan, Charles O'Hagan, Henry Redmond Buckle.

Goal: Harold Alexander Sloan (28)

80. 13.02.1909   British Championship
ENGLAND v IRELAND   4-0 (0-0)
Park Avenue, Bradford

Referee: James Stark (Scotland)   Attendance: 28,000

ENGLAND: Samuel Hardy, Robert Crompton, Joseph Richard Cottle, Benjamin Warren, William John Wedlock, Evelyn Henry Lintott, Arthur Berry, Vivian John Woodward (Cap), George Richard Hilsdon, James Edward Windridge, George Arthur Bridgett.

IRELAND: William Scott, James Balfe, Alexander McCartney, Valentine Harris (Cap), John Darling, George McClure, Andrew Hunter, William Lacey, William Greer, Charles O'Hagan, Samuel Young.

Goals: George Richard Hilsdon (50, 87 pen), Vivian John Woodward (60, 80)

81. 15.03.1909   British Championship
SCOTLAND v IRELAND   5-0 (2-0)
Ibrox Park, Glasgow

Referee: James Mason (England)   Attendance: 23,000

SCOTLAND: James Brownlie, James Main, James Watson, William Walker, James Stark (Cap), James Hay, Alexander Bennett, James McMenemy, Alexander Thomson, Alexander MacFarlane, Harold McDonald Paul.

IRELAND: William Scott, Alexander Craig, Alexander McCartney, Valentine Harris (Cap), James English McConnell, Harold Alexander Sloan, Andrew Hunter, William Lacey, William Greer, Charles Webb, John Henry Kirwan.

Goals: James McMenemy (15, 77), Alex MacFarlane (20), Alexander Thomson (48), Harold McDonald Paul (84)

82. 20.03.1909   British Championship
IRELAND v WALES   2-3 (1-1)
Grosvenor Park, Belfast

Referee: James Stark (Scotland)   Attendance: 8,000

IRELAND: William Scott, John Seymour, Alexander McCartney, Valentine Harris (Cap), James Connor, James English McConnell, Andrew Hunter, William Lacey, William Greer, Charles Webb, Jack Slemin.

WALES: Leigh Richmond Roose, Charles Richard Morris (Cap), Jeffrey Woodward Jones, George Latham, Ernest Peake, Lloyd Davies, William Henry Meredith, George Arthur Wynn, William Davies, William Jones, Ioan Haydn Price.

Goals: William Lacey (30), Andrew Hunter (75) / William Jones (#), George Arthur Wynn (#), William Henry Meredith (#)

83. 12.02.1910   British Championship
IRELAND v ENGLAND   1-1 (1-0)
Solitude, Belfast

Referee: Alexander Jackson (Scotland)   Attendance: 8,000

IRELAND: William Scott (Cap), Samuel Burnison, Patrick McCann, Valentine Harris, James English McConnell, John Darling, William Thomas James Renneville, William Lacey, James Murray, John Murphy, Frank Thompson.

ENGLAND: Samuel Hardy, Herbert Morley, Arthur Cowell, Andrew Ducat, William John Wedlock, William Bradshaw, Richard Bond, Harold John Fleming, Vivian John Woodward (Cap), Joseph William Bache, Albert Edward Hall.

Goals: Frank Thompson (43) / Harold John Fleming (51)

84. 19.03.1910   British Championship
IRELAND v SCOTLAND   1-0 (0-0)
Windsor Park, Belfast

Referee: John Thomas Howcroft (England)   Att: 18,000

IRELAND: William Scott (Cap), Samuel Burnison, P. McCann, Valentine Harris (110), James English McConnell, John Darling, William Thomas James Renneville, William Lacey, James Murray, John Murphy, Frank Thompson.

SCOTLAND: James Brownlie, George Law, James Mitchell, William Walker, William Loney, James Hay (Cap), George William Llyod Sinclair, John Kay McTavish, James Quinn, Alexander Higgins, Robert Bryson Templeton.

Goal: Frank Thompson (54)

85. 11.04.1910   British Championship
WALES v IRELAND 4-1 (3-0)

The Racecourse, Wrexham

Referee: James Mason (England)   Attendance: 8,000

WALES: Leigh Richmond Roose, Lloyd Davies, Charles Richard Morris (Cap), Edwin Hughes, Ernest Peake, Llewelyn Davies, William Henry Meredith, John "Love" Jones, Evan Jones, Arthur Grenville Morris, Robert Ernest Evans.

IRELAND: John O'Hehir, James Balfe, Patrick McCann, Valentine Harris, James English McConnell (Cap), John Darling, William Thomas James Renneville, William Lacey, James Murray, John Murphy, Frank Thompson. Trainer: William Crone

Goals: Robert Evans (#, #), Arthur Grenville Morris (#, #) / John Darling (47 pen)

86. 28.01.1911   British Championship
IRELAND v WALES 1-2 (0-0)

Windsor Park, Belfast

Referee: Thomas Rowbotham (England)   Att: 15,000

IRELAND: William Scott (Cap), Samuel Burnison, P.J. Thunder, Valentine Harris, James Connor, Henry Vernon Hampton, William Thomas James Renneville, William Lacey, William Halligan, James Lowry Macauley, Frank Thompson.

WALES: Robert Owen Evans, Thomas John Hewitt, Charles Richard Morris (Cap), Edwin Hughes, Ernest Peake, Llewelyn Davies, William Henry Meredith, George Arthur Wynn, William Davies, Arthur Grenville Morris, Edward Thomas Vizard.

Goals: William Halligan (#) / William Davies (50), Arthur Grenville Morris (75)

87. 11.02.1911   British Championship
ENGLAND v IRELAND 2-1 (1-0)

Baseball Ground, Derby

Referee: David Phillips (Scotland)   Attendance: 20,000

ENGLAND: Reginald Garnet Williamson, Robert Crompton (Cap), Jesse Pennington, Benjamin Warren, William John Wedlock, Albert Sturgess, John Simpson, Harold John Fleming, Albert Shepherd, George Woodger, Robert Ernest Evans.

IRELAND: William Scott (Cap), Samuel Burnison, Patrick McCann, Valentine Harris, James Connor, Henry Vernon Hampton, William Lacey, Denis Hannon, John McDonnell, James Lowry Macauley, Frank Thompson.

Goals: Albert Shepherd (18), Robert Ernest Evans (87) / James Lowry Macauley (88)

88. 18.03.1911   British Championship
SCOTLAND v IRELAND 2-0 (1-0)

Celtic Park, Glasgow

Referee: Herbert Bamlett (England)   Attendance: 32,000

SCOTLAND: James Brownlie, Donald Cameron Colman, John Walker, Andrew Aitken (Cap), Charles Bellany Thomson, James Hay, Angus Douglas, James McMenemy, William Reid, Alexander Higgins, Alexander Smith.

IRELAND: William Scott (Cap), Samuel Burnison, Patrick McCann, Valentine Harris, James Connor, Henry Vernon Hampton, William Lacey, Denis Hannon, John McDonnell, Charles Webb, Thomas Walker.

Goals: William Reid (23), James McMenemy (53)

89. 10.02.1912   British Championship
IRELAND v ENGLAND 1-6 (1-3)

Dalymount Park, Dublin

Referee: Alexander Jackson (Scotland)   Attendance: 15,000

IRELAND: William Scott (Cap), Samuel Burnison, Patrick McCann, Valentine Harris, Patrick O'Connell, Henry Vernon Hampton, William Lacey, Michael Hamill, William Halligan, James Lowry Macauley, Frank Thompson.

ENGLAND: Samuel Hardy, Robert Crompton (Cap), Jesse Pennington, James Thomas Brittleton, William John Wedlock, William Bradshaw, John Simpson, Harold John Fleming, Bertram Clewley Freeman, George Henry Holley, John Mordue.

Goals: Michael Hamill (35) / Harold John Fleming (12, 44, 60), George Henry Holley (17), Bertram Clewley Freeman (50), John Simpson (85)

90. 16.03.1912   British Championship
IRELAND v SCOTLAND 1-4 (1-2)

Windsor Park, Belfast

Referee: Herbert Bamlett (England)   Attendance: 12,000

IRELAND: John Hanna, George Willis, Alexander Craig, John Darling, Patrick O'Connell, Joseph Moran, John Houston, James McKnight, James Lowry Macauley, Joseph Enright, Samuel Young.

SCOTLAND: James Brownlie, Alexander McNair (Cap), John Walker, James Eadie Gordon, Wilfrid Lawson Low, Alexander Bell, George William Llyod Sinclair, Robert Walker, William Reid, Walter Campbell Allison Aitkenhead, Robert Bryson Templeton.

Goals: James McKnight (42 pen) / Walter Aitkenhead (8, 23), William Reid (60), Robert Walker (70)

91. 13.04.1912   British Championship
WALES v IRELAND 2-3 (1-0)
Ninian Park, Cardiff
Referee: Herbert Bamlett (England)   Attendance: 10,000
WALES: Robert Owen Evans, Llewelyn Davies, Moses Richard Russell, Edwin Hughes, Leonard Francis Newton, Joseph Thomas Jones, William Henry Meredith (Cap), James William Williams, William Davies, David Walter Davies, John Hugh Evans.
IRELAND: John Hanna, Alexander Craig, William George McConnell, Henry Vernon Hampton, B. Brennan, David Rollo, John Houston, Denis Hannon, John McDonnell, John McCandless, Frank Thompson.
Goals: William Davies (30), David Walter Davies (53) / John McCandless (#), B. Brennan (#), John McCandless (#)

92. 18.01.1913   British Championship
IRELAND v WALES 0-1 (0-1)
Grosvenor Park, Belfast
Referee: John Hargreaves Pearson (England)   Att: 8,000
IRELAND: William Scott (Cap), Samuel Burnison, Patrick McCann, David Rollo, Leo Donnelly, Henry Vernon Hampton, John Houston, William Lacey, John McDonnell, John McCandless, Frank Thompson.
WALES: William Ellis Bailiff, Thomas John Hewitt, Llewelyn Davies (Cap), George Latham, Ernest Peake, Joseph Thomas Jones, William Henry Meredith, David Walter Davies, Walter Otto Davis, James Roberts, John Hugh Evans.
Goal: James Roberts (15)

93. 15.02.1913   British Championship
IRELAND v ENGLAND 2-1 (1-1)
Windsor Park, Belfast
Referee: Alexander Jackson (Scotland)   Attendance: 20,000
IRELAND: William Scott, William George McConnell, Peter Warren, Henry Vernon Hampton, Valentine Harris (Cap), William Andrews, John Houston, Denis Hannon, William Gillespie, James Lowry Macauley, Frank Thompson.
ENGLAND: Reginald Garnet Williamson, Robert Crompton (Cap), Robert William Benson, Francis Cuggy, Thomas Wilkinson Boyle, George Utley, John Mordue, Charles Murray Buchan, George Washington Elliott, Joseph Smith, George Wall.
Goals: William Gillespie (43, 60) / Charles Buchan (35)

94. 15.03.1913   British Championship
IRELAND v SCOTLAND 1-2 (1-2)
Dalymount Park, Dublin
Referee: Arthur Adams (England)   Attendance: 12,000
IRELAND: William Scott, William George McConnell, Peter Warren, William Andrews, Valentine Harris (Cap), Henry Vernon Hampton, John Houston, James McKnight, William Gillespie, James Lowry Macauley, Frank Thompson.
SCOTLAND: James Brownlie, Donald Cameron Colman (Cap), John Walker, Robert Mercer, Thomas Logan, Peter Nellies, Alexander Bennett, James Eadie Gordon, William Reid, James Anderson Croal, George Robertson.
Goals: James McKnight (42) / William Reid (16), Alexander Bennett (32)

95. 19.01.1914   British Championship
WALES v IRELAND 1-2 (1-2)
The Racecourse, Wrexham
Referee: Isaac Baker (England)   Attendance: 5,000
WALES: Edward John Peers, Llewelyn Davies, Lloyd Davies (Cap), Edwin Hughes, Ernest Peake, Joseph Thomas Jones, William Henry Meredith, Evan Jones, Walter Otto Davis, William Jones, Edward Thomas Vizard.
IRELAND: Frederick McKee, William George McConnell, Alexander Craig, Valentine Harris (Cap), Patrick O'Connell, David Rollo, H. Seymour, Samuel Young, William Gillespie, William Lacey, Louis Bookman.
Goals: Evan Jones (60 pen) / Samuel Young (#), William Gillespie (#)

96. 14.02.1914   British Championship
ENGLAND v IRELAND 0-3 (0-2)
Ayresome Park, Middlesbrough
Referee: Alexander Jackson (Scotland)   Attendance: 25,000
ENGLAND: Samuel Hardy, Robert Crompton (Cap), Jesse Pennington, Francis Cuggy, Franklin Charles Buckley, William Watson, Charles William Wallace, Daniel Shea, George Washington Elliott, Edwin Gladstone Latheron, Henry Martin.
IRELAND: Frederick McKee, William George McConnell, Alexander Craig, Henry Vernon Hampton, Patrick O'Connell (Cap), Michael Hamill, David Rollo, Samuel Young, William Gillespie, William Lacey, Frank Thompson.
Goals: William Lacey (6, 80), William Gillespie (36)

97. 14.03.1914   British Championship
IRELAND v SCOTLAND 1-1 (0-0)
Windsor Park, Belfast

Referee: Herbert Bamlett (England)   Attendance: 31,000

IRELAND: Frederick McKee, William George McConnell, Alexander Craig, Valentine Harris, Patrick O'Connell (Cap), Michael Hamill, John Houston, Robert Nixon, Samuel Young, William Lacey, Frank Thompson.

SCOTLAND: James Brownlie, Joseph Dodds, Alexander McNair (Cap), James Eadie Gordon, Charles Bellany Thomson, James Hay, Alexander Pollock Donaldson, James McMenemy, William Reid, Andrew Wilson, Joseph Donnachie.

Goals: Samuel Young (89) / Joseph Donnachie (70)

98. 25.10.1919   British Championship
IRELAND v ENGLAND 1-1 (0-1)
Windsor Park, Belfast

Referee: Thomas Dougray (Scotland)   Attendance: 30,000

IRELAND: William O'Hagan, William McCandless, William McCracken, William Emerson, Michael Hamill, William Lacey (Cap), James Ferris, Alfred Snape, Joseph Gowdy, Patrick Gallagher, David Lyner.

ENGLAND: Samuel Hardy, Joseph Smith, Arthur Egerton Knight (Cap), John James Bagshaw, Sidney Bowser, William Watson, Robert Joseph Turnbull, Jack Carr, John Gilbert Cock, Joseph Smith, Joseph Charles Hodkinson.

Goals: James Ferris (70) / John Gilbert Cock (1)

99. 14.02.1920   British Championship
IRELAND v WALES 2-2 (1-0)
The Oval, Belfast

Referee: Isaac Baker (England)   Attendance: 30,000

IRELAND: William O'Hagan, Robert Manderson, David Rollo, William McCandless, Michael Hamill, William Emerson (Cap), David Lyner, William Lacey, William Gillespie, James Ferris, John McCandless.

WALES: William Ellis Bailiff, Harold Millership, Moses Richard Russell (Cap), Thomas James Matthias, Joseph Thomas Jones, Frederick Charles Keenor, William Henry Meredith, William Jones, Stanley Charles Davies, Ivor Jones, John Hugh Evans.

Goals: William McCandless (#), William Emerson (#) / Stanley Charles Davies (#, #)

100. 13.03.1920   British Championship
SCOTLAND v IRELAND 3-0 (2-0)
Celtic Park, Glasgow

Referee: James Mason (England)   Attendance: 39,750

SCOTLAND: Kenneth Campbell, Alexander McNair (Cap), James Blair, James Bowie, Wilfrid Lawson Low, James Eadie Gordon, Alexander Pollock Donaldson, James McMenemy, Andrew Nesbit Wilson, Andrew Cunningham, Alan Lauder Morton.

IRELAND: Elisha Scott, Robert Manderson, David Rollo, Michael Hamill, William Lacey, William Emerson (Cap), Patrick Robinson, Patrick Gallagher, Edward A. Brookes, William Gillespie, John McCandless.

Goals: Andrew Nesbit Wilson (8), Alan Lauder Morton (42), Andrew Cunningham (55)

101. 23.10.1920   British Championship
ENGLAND v IRELAND 2-0 (1-0)
Roker Park, Sunderland

Referee: Alexander Jackson (Scotland)   Attendance: 22,000

ENGLAND: John William Mew, Richard Downs, Frederick Edwin Bullock, Andrew Ducat, Joseph McCall (Cap), Arthur Grimsdell, Samuel Chedgzoy, Robert Kelly, William Henry Walker, Frederick Morris, Alfred Edward Quantrill.

IRELAND: Elisha Scott, David Rollo, William McCandless, Robert McCracken, William Lacey, William Emerson, Patrick J. Kelly, James Ferris, John Francis Doran, William Gillespie, John McCandless.

Goals: Robert Kelly (8), William Henry Walker (47)

102. 26.02.1921   British Championship
NORTHERN IRELAND v SCOTLAND 0-2 (0-1)
Windsor Park, Belfast

Referee: Arthur Ward (England)   Attendance: 35,000

NORTHERN IRELAND: Elisha Scott, James Mulligan, David Rollo, William Lacey, Ernest Edwin Smith, Michael Terence O'Brien, Samuel McGregor, James Ferris, Daniel McKinney, Michael Hamill, Louis Bookman.

SCOTLAND: Kenneth Campbell, John Marshall, William McStay, Joseph Harris, John Alexander Graham, James McMullan, Alexander McNab, Thomas Miller, Andrew Nesbit Wilson (Cap), Joseph Cassidy, Alexander Troup.

Goals: Andrew Nesbit Wilson (11 pen), Joseph Cassidy (89)

103. 09.04.1921   British Championship
WALES v NORTHERN IRELAND 2-1
Vetch Field, Swansea

Referee: John Thomas Howcroft (England)   Att: 12,000

WALES: Edward John Peers, Moses Richard Russell, Harold Millership, Frederick Charles Keenor, Robert William Matthews, Thomas James Matthias, William James Hole, Ivor Jones, Stanley Charles Davies, Richard William Richards, Edward Thomas Vizard.

NORTHERN IRELAND: Elisha Scott, David Rollo, William McCandless, William Lacey, Michael Scraggs, John Harris, Patrick Robinson, John Brown, Robert James Chambers, Allan Mathieson, Louis Bookman.

Goals: William James Hole (#), Stanley Charles Davies (#) / Robert James Chambers (#)

104. 22.10.1921   British Championship
NORTHERN IRELAND v ENGLAND 1-1 (1-1)
Windsor Park, Belfast

Referee: Alexander Jackson (Scotland)   Attendance: 30,000

NORTHERN IRELAND: Elisha Scott, William McCracken, David Rollo, Robert McCracken, Michael Scraggs, William Emerson, William Lacey, William Gillespie, John Francis Doran, Allan Mathieson, Louis Bookman.

ENGLAND: Jeremiah Dawson, Thomas Clay, Thomas Lucas, Frank Moss, George Wilson (Cap), Percival Henry Barton, Samuel Chedgzoy, William John Kirton, Ernest Simms, William Henry Walker, George Harrison.

Goals: William Gillespie (30) / William Kirton (35)

105. 04.03.1922   British Championship
SCOTLAND v NORTHERN IRELAND 2-1 (0-1)
Celtic Park, Glasgow

Referee: Arthur Ward (England)   Attendance: 36,000

SCOTLAND: Kenneth Campbell, John Marshall, Donald McKinlay, James Hogg, William Cringan, Thomas Allan Muirhead, Alexander Pollock Donaldson, James D. Kinloch, Andrew Nesbit Wilson, Andrew Cunningham (Cap), Alexander Troup.

NORTHERN IRELAND: Francis Collins, William McCracken, William McCandless, Robert McCracken, Michael Terence O'Brien, William Emerson, William Lacey, Patrick Gallagher, Robert William Irvine, William Gillespie, David Lyner.

Goals: Andrew Nesbit Wilson (60, 83) / William Gillespie (42)

106. 01.04.1922   British Championship
NORTHERN IRELAND v WALES 1-1
Windsor Park, Belfast

Referee: Arthur Ward (England)   Attendance: 20,000

NORTHERN IRELAND: Joseph Alexander Cuthbert Mehaffy, William McCracken, John Joseph Curran, Robert McCracken, Michael Terence O'Brien, William Emerson, David Lyner, William Crooks, John Francis Doran, William Gillespie, Joseph Toner.

WALES: Edward John Peers, Moses Richard Russell, James Henry Evans, Herbert Price Evans, Joseph Thomas Jones, Thomas James Matthias, Stanley Charles Davies, Frederick Charles Keenor, Leonard Stephen Davies, Ivor Jones, John Hugh Evans.

Goals: William Gillespie (#) / Leonard Stephen Davies (#)

107. 21.10.1922   British Championship
ENGLAND v NORTHERN IRELAND 2-0 (0-0)
The Hawthorns, West Bromwich

Referee: Alexander Jackson (Scotland)   Attendance: 20,173

ENGLAND: Edward Hallows Taylor, Joseph Smith, Jack Harry Harrow, Frank Moss, George Wilson, Arthur Grimsdell (Cap), David William Mercer, James Marshall Seed, Frank Raymond Osborne, Henry Chambers, Owen Williams.

NORTHERN IRELAND: Alfred Harland, David Rollo, John Joseph Curran, William Emerson, Ernest Edwin Smith, Francis Gerald Morgan, David Lyner, Robert William Irvine, Patrick Nelis, William Gillespie, James Burns.

Goals: Henry Chambers (66, 85)

108. 03.03.1923   British Championship
NORTHERN IRELAND v SCOTLAND 0-1 (0-0)
Windsor Park, Belfast

Referee: Arthur Ward (England)   Attendance: 30,000

NORTHERN IRELAND: Thomas Farquarharson, William McCracken, John Joseph Curran, Samuel Johnstone Irving, George Moorehead, William Emerson, Hamilton McKenzie, Patrick Gallagher, George Hull Reid, William Gillespie, William Moore.

SCOTLAND: William Harper, John Hutton, James Blair (Cap), David Morton Steele, David Morris, Neil McBain, Alexander Archibald, John White, Andrew Nesbit Wilson, Joseph Cassidy, Alan Lauder Morton.

Goal: Andrew Nesbit Wilson (69)

109. 14.04.1923   British Championship
WALES v NORTHERN IRELAND   0-3
The Racecourse, Wrexham

Referee: George Nunnerley (England)   Attendance: 12,222

WALES: George Alfred Godding, Moses Richard Russell, Edward Parry, Robert Frederick John, Frederick Charles Keenor, William Jennings, William James Hole, Ivor Jones, Leonard Stephen Davies, Edward Thomas Vizard, John Hugh Evans.

NORTHERN IRELAND: Thomas Farquharson, John Alexander Mackie, Andrew Kennedy, Samuel Johnstone Irving, Ernest Edwin Smith, William Emerson, David Lyner, Patrick Gallagher, Robert William Irvine, William Gillespie, Joseph Toner.

Goals: Robert William Irvine (#, #), William Gillespie (#)

110. 20.10.1923   British Championship
NORTHERN IRELAND v ENGLAND   2-1 (1-1)
Windsor Park, Belfast

Referee: Alexander Jackson (Scotland)   Attendance: 23,000

NORTHERN IRELAND: Thomas Farquharson, Andrew McCluggage, John Joseph Curran, Samuel Johnstone Irving, Ernest Edwin Smith, William Emerson, John Brown, Thomas Croft, Robert William Irvine, William Gillespie, Joseph Toner.

ENGLAND: Edward Hallows Taylor, Alfred George Bower, Samuel John Wadsworth, Harry Harold Pantling, George Wilson (Cap), Thomas Meehan, Kenneth Edward Hegan, Robert Kelly, Joseph Bradford, Henry Chambers, Frederick Edward Tunstall.

Goals: William Gillespie (16), Thomas Croft (70) / Joseph Bradford (11)

111. 01.03.1924   British Championship
SCOTLAND v NORTHERN IRELAND   2-0 (0-0)
Celtic Park, Glasgow

Referee: George Noel Watson (England)   Att: 30,000

SCOTLAND: William Harper, John Hutton (Cap), James Hamilton, Peter Kerr, David Morris, James McMullan, James Greig Reid, Andrew Cunningham, Hugh Kilpatrick Gallacher, Thomas Cairns, Alan Lauder Morton.

NORTHERN IRELAND: Thomas Farquharson, David Rollo, William McCandless, Samuel Johnstone Irving, Michael Terence O'Brien, Francis Gerald Morgan, Daniel McKinney, Patrick Gallagher, Robert William Irvine, William Gillespie, John McGrillen.

Goals: Andrew Cunningham (85), David Morris (89)

112. 15.03.1924   British Championship
NORTHERN IRELAND v WALES   0-1
Windsor Park, Belfast

Referee: Arthur Kingscott (England)   Attendance: 40,000

NORTHERN IRELAND: Thomas Farquharson, David Rollo, William McCandless, Joseph Gowdy, Michael Terence O'Brien, Samuel Johnstone Irving, John Brown, Patrick Gallagher, Patrick McIlvenny, William Gillespie, Joseph Toner.

WALES: Albert Gray, Moses Richard Russell, John Jenkins, Herbert Price Evans, Frederick Charles Keenor, William Jennings, William Davies, John Barry Nicholls, Leonard Stephen Davies, Richard William Richards, Edward Thomas Vizard.

Goal: Moses Richard Russell (# penalty)

113. 22.10.1924   British Championship
ENGLAND v NORTHERN IRELAND   3-1 (1-0)
Goodison Park, Liverpool

Referee: Peter Craigmyle (Scotland)   Attendance: 25,000

ENGLAND: James Frederick Mitchell, Warneford Cresswell, Samuel John Wadsworth (Cap), Frederick William Kean, Henry Healless, Percival Henry Barton, Samuel Chedgzoy, Robert Kelly, Henry Bedford, William Henry Walker, Frederick Edward Tunstall.

NORTHERN IRELAND: Thomas Farquharson, Robert Manderson, Andrew Kennedy, James Chatton, Michael Terence O'Brien, Samuel Johnstone Irving, William Lacey, Patrick Gallagher, Robert William Irvine, William Gillespie, Joseph Toner.

Goals: Robert Kelly (15), Henry Bedford (60), William Henry Walker (79) / William Gillespie (77)

114. 28.02.1925   British Championship
NORTHERN IRELAND v SCOTLAND   0-3 (0-3)
Windsor Park, Belfast

Referee: George Noel Watson (England)   Att: 41,000

NORTHERN IRELAND: Thomas Farquharson, Robert Manderson, William McCandless, James Chatton, Michael Terence O'Brien, Samuel Johnstone Irving, Donald Martin, Patrick Gallagher, Edward Carrol, William Gillespie, Joseph Toner.

SCOTLAND: William Harper, James Nelson, William McStay, David Ditchburn Meiklejohn, David Morris (Cap), Robert Hunter Brown Bennie, Alexander Skinner Jackson, James Dunn, Hugh Kilpatrick Gallacher, Thomas Cairns, Alan Lauder Morton.

Goals: David Ditchburn Meiklejohn (4), Hugh Gallacher (25), James Dunn (35)

115. 18.04.1925   British Championship
WALES v NORTHERN IRELAND 0-0
The Racecourse, Wrexham

Referee: Ernest Pinkston (England)   Attendance: 10,000

WALES: Albert Gray, Edward Parry, John Jenkins, John Reginald Blacknall Moulsdale, Frederick Charles Keenor, Robert Frederick John, William Davies, Stanley Charles Davies, James Jones, Leonard Stephen Davies, Jesse Thomas Williams.

NORTHERN IRELAND: Elisha Scott, David Rollo, William Henry McConnell, John Garrett, Michael Terence O'Brien, Samuel Johnstone Irving, Tom Cowan, Patrick Gallagher, Andrew Sloan, Hugh Leonard Meek, Henry Wilson.

116. 24.10.1925   British Championship
NORTHERN IRELAND v ENGLAND 0-0
Windsor Park, Belfast

Referee: William Nunnerley (Wales)   Attendance: 35,000

NORTHERN IRELAND: Elisha Scott, David Rollo, William Henry McConnell, Joseph Gowdy, James Chatton, Thomas Sloan, Andrew Bothwell, Robert William Irvine, Hugh Davey, James Hopkins, David McMullan.

ENGLAND: Benjamin Howard Baker, Thomas Smart, Francis Carr Hudspeth, Frederick William Kean, George Henry Armitage, Thomas George Bromilow, Sidney William Austin, Sydney Charles Puddefoot, Claude Thesiger Ashton (Cap), William Henry Walker, Arthur Reginald Dorrell.

117. 13.02.1926   British Championship
NORTHERN IRELAND v WALES 3-0
Windsor Park, Belfast

Referee: Peter Craigmyle (Scotland)   Attendance: 25,000

NORTHERN IRELAND: Elisha Scott, Walter Brown, William Henry McConnell, Samuel Johnstone Irving, Michael Terence O'Brien, Thomas Sloan, Andrew Bothwell, Alexander Steele, Samuel Curran, William Gillespie, David McMullan.

WALES: Arthur Ivor Brown, Edward Parry, Thomas Jones, John Newnes, Robert William Matthews, David Evans, William Davies, Leonard Stephen Davies, John Fowler, Stanley Charles Davies, Ivor Jones.

Goals: William Gillespie (#), Samuel Curran (#, #)

118. 27.02.1926   British Championship
SCOTLAND v NORTHERN IRELAND 4-0 (2-0)
Ibrox Park, Glasgow

Referee: George Noel Watson (England)   Att: 30,000

SCOTLAND: William Harper, John Hutton, William McStay (Cap), Peter Wilson, John McDougall, Robert Hunter Brown Bennie, Alexander Skinner Jackson, Andrew Cunningham, Hugh Kilpatrick Gallacher, Thomas Bruce McInally, Adam McLean.

NORTHERN IRELAND: Elisha Scott, Robert Manderson, Thomas Watson, Samuel Johnstone Irving, Joseph Gowdy, Thomas Sloan, Andrew Bothwell, Alexander Steele, Samuel Curran, William Gillespie, John Mahood.

Goals: Hugh Kilpatrick Gallacher (13, 60, 66), Andrew Cunningham (40)

119. 20.10.1926   British Championship
ENGLAND v NORTHERN IRELAND 3-3 (1-2)
Anfield Road, Liverpool

Referee: Evan Charles Sambrook (Wales)   Att: 20,000

ENGLAND: Albert McInroy, Warneford Cresswell, Samuel John Wadsworth (Cap), Willis Edwards, John Henry Hill, George Henry Green, Joseph Walter Spence, George Brown, Norman Bullock, William Henry Walker, James William Ruffel.

NORTHERN IRELAND: Elisha Scott, David Rollo, William Henry McConnell, Joseph Gowdy, Francis Gerald Morgan, Samuel Johnstone Irving, Andrew Bothwell, Robert William Irvine, Hugh Davey, William Gillespie, Joseph Toner.

Goals: George Brown (8), Joseph Walter Spence (47), Norman Bullock (80) /
William Gillespie (5), Hugh Davey (44), Robert Irvine (51)

120. 26.02.1927   British Championship
NORTHERN IRELAND v SCOTLAND 0-2 (0-1)
Windsor Park, Belfast

Referee: George Noel Watson (England)   Att: 40,000

NORTHERN IRELAND: Elisha Scott, Andrew McCluggage, William Henry McConnell, Joseph Gowdy, Thomas Sloan, David McMullan, John McGrillen, Patrick Gallagher, Hugh Davey, Samuel Johnstone Irving, Joseph Toner.

SCOTLAND: John Diamond Harkness, John Hutton, William McStay (Cap), Thomas Allan Muirhead, James Davidson Gibson, Thomas Craig, Alexander Skinner Jackson, James Dunn, Hugh Kilpatrick Gallacher, James Howieson, Alan Lauder Morton.

Goals: Alan Lauder Morton (44, 88)

121. 09.04.1927   British Championship
WALES v NORTHERN IRELAND 2-2 (2-0)
Ninian Park, Cardiff
Referee: Ernest Pinkston (England)   Attendance: 10,000
WALES: Sidney John Vivian Leonard Evans, Thomas Jones, William Jennings, Frederick Charles Keenor, Thomas Percival Griffiths, David Evans, David Rees Williams, Wilfred Leslie Lewis, Leonard Stephen Davies, Charles Jones, David Sidney Nicholas.
NORTHERN IRELAND: Elisha Scott, Andrew McCluggage, William Henry McConnell, Samuel Johnstone Irving, Thomas Sloan, Michael Terence O'Brien, Andrew Bothwell, Robert William Irvine, Harold Johnston, William Gillespie, Harold McCaw.
Goals: David Rees Williams (#, #) / Harold Johnston (#, #)

122. 22.10.1927   British Championship
NORTHERN IRELAND v ENGLAND 2-0 (1-0)
Windsor Park, Belfast
Referee: Thomas Dougray (Scotland)   Attendance: 30,000
NORTHERN IRELAND: Elisha Scott, Andrew McCluggage, William Henry McConnell, Samuel Johnstone Irving, Francis Gerald Morgan, Thomas Sloan, Robert James Chambers, Robert William Irvine, Hugh Davey, William Gillespie, John Mahood.
ENGLAND: Arthur Edward Hufton, Thomas Cooper, Herbert Jones, Henry Nuttall, John Henry Hill (Cap), Harry Storer, Joseph Harold Anthony Hulme, Stanley George James Earle, William Ralph Dean, John Ball, Louis Antonia Page.
Goals: Herbert Jones (36 own goal), John Mahood (72)

123. 04.02.1928   British Championship
NORTHERN IRELAND v WALES 1-2
Windsor Park, Belfast
Referee: H. Hopkinson (England)   Attendance: 27,563
NORTHERN IRELAND: Elisha Scott, Andrew McCluggage, William Henry McConnell, Samuel Johnstone Irving, Francis Gerald Morgan, Thomas Sloan, Robert James Chambers, James Dunne, Hugh Davey, Patrick McConnell, John Mahood.
WALES: Daniel Lewis, Benjamin David Williams, Thomas John Evans, Samuel Bennion, Frederick Charles Keenor, Robert Frederick John, William James Hole, William Davies, Wilfred Leslie Lewis, Leonard Stephen Davies, Rev. Hywel Davies.
Goals: Robert James Chambers (#) /
William Davies (#), Wilfred Leslie Lewis (#)

124. 25.02.1928   British Championship
SCOTLAND v NORTHERN IRELAND 0-1 (0-1)
Firhill Park, Glasgow
Referee: Arthur Ward (England)   Attendance: 55,000
SCOTLAND: Allan McClory, John Hutton, William McStay, Thomas Allan Muirhead (Cap), David Ditchburn Meiklejohn, Thomas Craig, Henry McGill Ritchie, James Dunn, James Edward McGrory, George Stevenson, Alan Lauder Morton.
NORTHERN IRELAND: Elisha Scott, Andrew McCluggage, Robert Hamilton, Samuel Johnstone Irving, George Moorehead, Francis Gerald Morgan, Robert James Chambers, Robert William Irvine, Samuel Curran, James Ferris, John Mahood.
Goal: Robert James Chambers (10)

125. 22.10.1928   British Championship
ENGLAND v NORTHERN IRELAND 2-1 (1-1)
Goodison Park, Liverpool
Referee: Evan Sambrook (Wales)   Attendance: 34,000
ENGLAND: John Hacking, Thomas Cooper, Ernest Blenkinsop, Willis Edwards (Cap), John William Barrett, Austin Fenwick Campbell, Joseph Harold Anthony Hulme, Ernest William Hine, William Ralph Dean, Joseph Bradford, James William Ruffel.
NORTHERN IRELAND: Elisha Scott, Andrew McCluggage, Robert Hamilton, Samuel Johnstone Irving, Thomas Sloan, Francis Gerald Morgan, Robert James Chambers, Robert William Irvine, Joseph Bambrick, William Gillespie John Mahood.
Goals: Joseph Hulme (26), William Ralph Dean (77) /
Joseph Bambrick (34)

126. 02.02.1929   British Championship
WALES v NORTHERN IRELAND 2-2
The Racecourse, Wrexham
Referee: James Victor Pennington (England)   Att: 12,000
WALES: Albert Gray, Ernest James Morley, Arthur Albert Lumberg, Samuel Bennion, Frederick Charles Keenor, Stanley James Bowsher, William Davies, Eugene O'Callaghan, Albert William Mays, Leonard Stephen Davies, Frederick Windsor Warren.
NORTHERN IRELAND: Elisha Scott, Andrew McCluggage, William McCandless, Joseph Miller, James H. Elwood, Alexander Steele, Robert James Chambers, Richard William Morris Rowley, Joseph Bambrick, Lawrence Cumming, John Mahood.
Goals: Albert Mays (#), Frederick Windsor Warren (#) /
John Mahood (#), Andrew McCluggage (# penalty)

127. 23.02.1929   British Championship
NORTHERN IRELAND v SCOTLAND 3-7 (2-4)
Windsor Park, Belfast
Referee: Albert Edward Fogg (England)   Att: 35,000
NORTHERN IRELAND: Elisha Scott, Andrew McCluggage, Hugh Flack, Joseph Miller, George Moorehead, Alexander Steele, Robert James Chambers, Richard William Morris Rowley, Joseph Bambrick, Lawrence Cumming, John Mahood.
SCOTLAND: John Diamond Harkness, Douglas Herbert Gray, Daniel Blair, Thomas Allan Muirhead, David Ditchburn Meiklejohn, James McMullan (Cap), Alexander Skinner Jackson, William Stewart Chalmers, Hugh Kilpatrick Gallacher, Alexander Wilson James, Alan Lauder Morton.
Goals: Richard Rowley (#), Joseph Bambrick (#, #) / Hugh Kilpatrick Gallacher (3, 9, 14, 51, 76), Alexander Skinner Jackson (36, 82)

128. 19.10.1929   British Championship
NORTHERN IRELAND v ENGLAND 0-3 (0-2)
Windsor Park, Belfast
Referee: Thomas Small (Scotland)   Attendance: 40,000
NORTHERN IRELAND: Elisha Scott, Samuel Russell, Robert Hamilton, Joseph Miller, James H. Elwood, William McCleery, Harold Anthony Duggan, Richard William Morris Rowley, Joseph Bambrick, Lawrence Cumming, Peter J. Kavanagh.
ENGLAND: John Henry Brown, Warneford Cresswell, Ernest Blenkinsop, Willis Edwards (Cap), Ernest Arthur Hart, Albert Frank Barrett, Hugh Adcock, Ernest William Hine, George Henry Camsell, Joseph Bradford, Eric Frederick George Brook.
Goals: Ernest Hine (37 pen), George Henry Camsell (42, 80)

129. 01.02.1930   British Championship
NORTHERN IRELAND v WALES 7-0 (2-0)
Celtic Park, Belfast
Referee: Thomas Crewe (England)   Attendance: 25,000
NORTHERN IRELAND: Alfred Gardiner, Andrew McCluggage, Robert Fulton, William McCleery, John Jones, Thomas Sloan, Robert James Chambers, Richard William Morris Rowley, Joseph Bambrick, James McCambridge, John Mahood.
WALES: Richard Prytherch Finnegan, Arthur Ronald Hugh, Thomas Jones, Edward Lawrence, Frederick Charles Keenor, John Pugsley, William Davies, Bertie Williams, Tudor James Martin, Stanley Charles Davies, Frederick Cook.
Goals: Joseph Bambrick (6 goals), Andrew McCluggage (#)

130. 22.02.1930   British Championship
SCOTLAND v NORTHERN IRELAND 3-1 (1-1)
Celtic Park, Glasgow
Referee: Arthur Joseph (England)   Attendance: 30,000
SCOTLAND: Robert Colin Middleton, Douglas Herbert Gray, William Wiseman, James Davidson Gibson, David Ditchburn Meiklejohn (Cap), Thomas Craig, Alexander Skinner Jackson, George Stevenson, Hugh Kilpatrick Gallacher, Alexander Wilson James, Alan Lauder Morton.
NORTHERN IRELAND: Alfred Gardiner, Samuel Russell, Robert Hamilton, Robert McDonald, John Jones, Thomas Sloan, Robert James Chambers, Robert William Irvine, Joseph Bambrick, James McCambridge, Harold McCaw.
Goals: Hugh Gallacher (32, 61), George Stevenson (70) / Harold McCaw (40)

131. 20.10.1930   British Championship
ENGLAND v NORTHERN IRELAND 5-1 (0-0)
Bramall Lane, Sheffield
Referee: James Thomson (Scotland)   Attendance: 35,000
ENGLAND: Henry Edward Hibbs, Frederick Roy Goodall (Cap), Ernest Blenkinsop, Alfred Henry Strange, Thoms Leach, Austin Fenwick Campbell, Samuel Dickinson Crooks, Gordon Hodgson, James Hampson, Harry Burgess, William Eric Houghton.
NORTHERN IRELAND: Elisha Scott, Andrew McCluggage, Robert Fulton, John Jones, William Reid, William McCleery, Harold Anthony Duggan, Robert William Irvine, James Dunne, William Gillespie, Harold McCaw.
Goals: Harry Burgess (14, 42), James Hampson (31), Samuel Dickinson Crooks (38), William Eric Houghton (44) / James Dunne (80)

132. 21.02.1931   British Championship
NORTHERN IRELAND v SCOTLAND 0-0
Windsor Park, Belfast
Referee: H. E. Hull (England)   Attendance: 20,000
NORTHERN IRELAND: Alfred Gardiner, John McNinch, Robert Fulton, William McCleery, John Jones, Thomas Sloan, Hugh Blair, Edward Falloon, Frederick C. Roberts, John Geary, Harold McCaw.
SCOTLAND: John Thomson, James Sermagour Crapnell, Joseph Nibloe, Peter Wilson, George Walker, Frank Robert Hill, John Livingstone Murdoch, Peter Scarff, Benjamin Collard Yorston, Robert Low McPhail, Alan Lauder Morton (Cap).

133. 22.04.1931   British Championship
WALES v NORTHERN IRELAND   3-2
The Racecourse, Wrexham

Referee: William Percy Harper (England)   Att: 11,000

WALES: William Ronald John, Benjamin David Williams, Wynne Crompton, Frederick Charles Keenor, Thomas Percival Griffiths, David Thomas Richards, Cuthbert Phillips, David Astley, Thomas Bamford, Wilfred Bernard James, Frederick Windsor Warren.

NORTHERN IRELAND: John Diffin, Andrew McCluggage, Robert Fulton, Samuel Johnstone Irving, John Jones, William McCleery, Harold Anthony Duggan, Richard William Morris Rowley, James Dunne, James McCambridge, Harold McCaw.

Goals: Cuthbert Phillips (#), Thomas Percival Griffiths (#), Frederick Windsor Warren (#) / James Dunne (#), Richard William Morris Rowley (#)

134. 19.09.1931   British Championship
SCOTLAND v NORTHERN IRELAND   3-1 (2-1)
Ibrox Park, Glasgow

Referee: Isaac Caswell (England)   Attendance: 40,000

SCOTLAND: Robert Hepburn, Daniel Blair, Robert McAulay, Alexander Massie, David Ditchburn Meiklejohn (Cap), George Clark Phillips Brown, James Crawford, George Stevenson, James Edward McGrory, Robert Low McPhail, James Connor.

NORTHERN IRELAND: Alfred Gardiner, John McNinch, Robert Hamilton, William McCleery, John Jones, William Alexander Gowdy, Hugh Blair, Richard William Morris Rowley, James Dunne, John Geary, Robert James Chambers.

Goals: George Stevenson (5), James Edward McGrory (34), Robert Low McPhail (72) / James Dunne (20)

135. 17.10.1931   British Championship
NORTHERN IRELAND v ENGLAND   2-6 (1-3)
Windsor Park, Belfast

Referee: Hugh Watson (Scotland)   Attendance: 40,000

NORTHERN IRELAND: Alfred Gardiner, Samuel Russell, Robert Fulton, Robert McDonald, John Jones, William Mitchell, Robert James Chambers, Patrick McConnell, James Dunne, James McCambridge, James Kelly.

ENGLAND: Henry Edward Hibbs, Frederick Roy Goodall (Cap), Ernest Blenkinsop, Alfred Henry Strange, Thomas Graham, Austin Fenwick Campbell, Samuel Dickinson Crooks, John William Smith, Thomas Waring, Ernest William Hine, William Eric Houghton.

Goals: James Dunne (40), James Kelly (89) / John William Smith (10), Thomas Waring (12, 57), Ernest William Hine (22), William Eric Houghton (60, 82)

136. 05.12.1931   British Championship
NORTHERN IRELAND v WALES   4-0
Windsor Park, Belfast

Referee: Peter Snape (England)   Attendance: 10,000

NORTHERN IRELAND: Elisha Scott, John McNinch, Robert Fulton, William McCleery, Maurice Pyper, William Mitchell, Robert James Chambers, Robert William Irvine, Joseph Bambrick, William Millar, James Kelly.

WALES: Albert Gray, Sidney Wilfred Lawrence, Hugh Edward Foulkes, Samuel Bennion, Thomas Percival Griffiths, Emrys Ellis, Thomas John Jones, Wilfred Bernard James, Thomas Bamford, Walter William Robbins, John Edward Parris.

Goals: James Kelly (#, #), William Millar (#), Joseph Bambrick (#)

137. 17.09.1932   British Championship
NORTHERN IRELAND v SCOTLAND   0-4 (0-2)
Windsor Park, Belfast

Referee: William Harper (England)   Attendance: 40,000

NORTHERN IRELAND: Elisha Scott, William Cook, Robert Fulton, Edward Falloon, John Jones, William Alexander Gowdy, Edward Mitchell, Thomas Priestley, William Millar, Samuel English, James Kelly.

SCOTLAND: Alexander McLaren, Douglas Herbert Gray, James Sermagour Crapnell (Cap), Alexander Massie, John Ainslie Johnstone, William Telfer, James Crawford, George Stevenson, James Edward McGrory, Robert Low McPhail, James Munro King.

Goals: James Munro King (3), Robert Low McPhail (35, 67), James Edward McGrory (75)

138. 17.10.1932   British Championship
ENGLAND v NORTHERN IRELAND   1-0 (1-0)
Bloomfield Road, Blackpool

Referee: Hugh Watson (Scotland)   Attendance: 23,000

ENGLAND: Henry Edward Hibbs, Frederick Roy Goodall, Ernest Blenkinsop (Cap), Alfred Henry Strange, James Peter O'Dowd, Samuel Weaver, Samuel Dickinson Crooks, Robert Barclay, William Ralph Dean, Thomas Clark Fisher Johnson, Arthur Cunliffe.

NORTHERN IRELAND: Elisha Scott, William Cook, Robert Fulton, William Mitchell, John Jones, William McCleery, Harold Anthony Duggan, Patrick Moore, James Dunne, James Doherty, James Kelly.

Goal: Robert Barclay (30)

139. 07.12.1932   British Championship
WALES v NORTHERN IRELAND 4-1
The Racecourse, Wrexham

Referee: George Hewitt (England)   Attendance: 8,500

WALES: William Ronald John, Benjamin David Williams, Robert Frederick John, James Patrick Murphy, Thomas Percival Griffiths, David Thomas Richards, William Edward Richards, Eugene O'Callaghan, David Astley, Walter William Robbins, William Evans.

NORTHERN IRELAND: Elisha Scott, William Cook, Thomas Willighan, William Mitchell, John Jones, William McCleery, William Houston, Samuel English, James Dunne, James Doherty, James Kelly.

Goals: David Astley (#, #), Walter William Robbins (#, #) / Samuel English (#)

140. 16.09.1933   British Championship
SCOTLAND v NORTHERN IRELAND 1-2 (0-2)
Celtic Park, Glasgow

Referee: Edward Wood (England)   Attendance: 27,135

SCOTLAND: John Diamond Harkness, Andrew Anderson, Peter McGonagle (Cap), Alexander Massie, Alexander Low, William Telfer, James Murray Boyd, Alexander Venters, James Edward McGrory, Robert Low McPhail, James Munro King.

NORTHERN IRELAND: Elisha Scott, Thomas Willighan, Robert Fulton, John McMahon, John Jones, William Mitchell, Hugh Blair, Alexander Ernest Stevenson, David Kirker Martin, John Coulter, John Mahood.

Goals: Robert Low McPhail (60) / David Martin (8, 13)

141. 14.10.1933   British Championship
NORTHERN IRELAND v ENGLAND 0-3 (0-1)
Windsor Park, Belfast

Referee: Hugh Watson (Scotland)   Attendance: 40,000

NORTHERN IRELAND: Elisha Scott, Sydney Edward Reid, Robert Fulton, Walter McMillen, John Jones, Samuel Jones, Harold Anthony Duggan, Alexander Ernest Stevenson, David Kirker Martin, John Coulter, Thomas Priestley.

ENGLAND: Henry Edward Hibbs, Frederick Roy Goodall (Cap), Edris Albert Hapgood, Alfred Henry Strange, James Phillips Allen, Wilfred Copping, Samuel Dickinson Crooks, Albert Thomas Grosvenor, John William Anslow Bowers, Clifford Sydney Bastin, Eric Frederick George Brook.

Goals: Eric Frederick George Brook (30), Albert Grosvenor (51), John William Anslow Bowers (52)

142. 04.11.1933   British Championship
NORTHERN IRELAND v WALES 1-1
Windsor Park, Belfast

Referee: Mungo Charles Hutton (Scotland)   Att: 20,000

NORTHERN IRELAND: Elisha Scott, Sydney Edward Reid, Robert Fulton, William Mitchell, John Jones, Samuel Jones, E.J.Mitchell, Alexander Ernest Stevenson, David Kirker Martin, John Coulter, James Kelly.

WALES: Sidney John Vivian Leonard Evans, Sidney Wilfred Lawrence, David Owen Jones, Alfred Day, Harry Hanford, David Thomas Richards, Cuthbert Phillips, Eugene O'Callaghan, Ernest Matthew Glover, Thomas James Mills, Ernest Robert Curtis.

Goals: Samuel Jones (#) / Ernest Matthew Glover (#)

143. 20.10.1934   British Championship
NORTHERN IRELAND v SCOTLAND 2-1 (0-1)
Windsor Park, Belfast

Referee: Henry Norman Mee (England)   Att: 39,752

NORTHERN IRELAND: Elisha Scott, John Alexander Mackie, Robert Fulton, Walter McMillen, John Jones, William Mitchell, Harold Anthony Duggan, William Alexander Gowdy, David Kirker Martin, Alexander Ernest Stevenson, John Coulter.

SCOTLAND: James Dawson, Andrew Anderson, Peter McGonagle, Alexander Massie (Cap), James McMillan Simpson, Andrew Clark Herd, William Lawrence Cook, George Stevenson, James Smith, Patrick Gallacher, James Connor.

Goals: David Kirker Martin (76), John Coulter (89) / Patrick Gallacher (43)

144. 06.02.1935   British Championship
ENGLAND v NORTHERN IRELAND 2-1 (2-1)
Goodison Park, Liverpool

Referee: Willie Webb (Scotland)   Attendance: 32,000

ENGLAND: Henry Edward Hibbs, Charles George Male, Edris Albert Hapgood (Cap), Clifford Samuel Britton, John William Barker, Wilfred Copping, Samuel Dickinson Crooks, John Gilbert Bestall, Edward Joseph Drake, Clifford Sydney Bastin, Eric Frederick George Brook.

NORTHERN IRELAND: Thomas Breen, William Cook, Robert Fulton, William Alexander Gowdy, John Jones, William Mitchell, John Brown I, Peter Dermot Doherty, David Kirker Martin, Alexander Ernest Stevenson, John Coulter.

Goals: Clifford Sydney Bastin (18, 70) / Alexander Ernest Stevenson (50)

145. 27.03.1935   British Championship
WALES v NORTHERN IRELAND 3-1
The Racecourse, Wrexham

Referee: Peco Bauwens (Germany)   Attendance: 16,000

WALES: John Iorweth Hughes, Benjamin David Williams, Robert Frederick John, James Patrick Murphy, Thomas Percival Griffiths, David Thomas Richards, Idris Morgan Hopkins, Leslie Jenkin Jones, Charles Wilson Jones, Brynmor Jones, Cuthbert Phillips.

NORTHERN IRELAND: Thomas Breen, John Alexander Mackie, Robert Fulton, Keiller McCullough, John Jones, William Alexander Gowdy, Harold Anthony Duggan, John Brown I, Joseph Bambrick, Peter Dermont Doherty, John Coulter.

Goals: Charles Wilson Jones (#), Cuthbert Phillips (#), Idris Morgan Hopkins (#) / Joseph Bambrick (#)

146. 19.10.1935   British Championship
NORTHERN IRELAND v ENGLAND 1-3 (1-0)
Windsor Park, Belfast

Referee: Willie Webb (Scotland)   Attendance: 28,000

NORTHERN IRELAND: Elisha Scott, Sydney Edward Reid, Cecil Allan, William Mitchell, John Jones, Robert James Browne, John Brown I, Keiller McCullough, Joseph Bambrick, Peter Dermont Doherty, James Kelly.

ENGLAND: Edward Sagar, Charles George Male, Edris Albert Hapgood (Cap), Septimus Charles Smith, John William Barker, John Bray, Ralph Birkett, Edwin Raymond Bowden, Samuel Frederick Tilson, Raymond William Westwood, Eric Frederick George Brook.

Goals: John Brown (16) / Ralph Birkett (63), Samuel Tilson (66), Eric Frederick George Brook (85)

147. 13.11.1935   British Championship
SCOTLAND v NORTHERN IRELAND 2-1 (0-0)
Tynecastle Park, Edinburgh

Referee: Henry Nattrass (England)   Attendance: 30,000

SCOTLAND: John Jackson, Andrew Anderson, George Wilfred Cummings, Alexander Massie, James McMillan Simpson (Cap), Alexander Cockburn Hastings, James Delaney, Thomas Walker, Matthew Armstrong, William Mills, Douglas Duncan.

NORTHERN IRELAND: Elisha Scott, William Cook, Robert Fulton, Keiller McCullough, John Jones, William Mitchell, Harold Anthony Duggan, Alexander Ernest Stevenson, Joseph Bambrick, Peter Dermont Doherty, James Kelly.

Goals: Thomas Walker (58), Douglas Duncan (89) / James Kelly (49)

148. 11.03.1936   British Championship
NORTHERN IRELAND v WALES 3-2 (1-2)
Celtic Park, Belfast

Referee: Henry Nattrass (England)   Attendance: 20,000

NORTHERN IRELAND: Elisha Scott, William Cook, Robert Fulton, William Alexander Gowdy, John Jones, Robert James Browne, Noel Kernaghan, James Gibb, David Kirker Martin, Alexander Ernest Stevenson, James Kelly.

WALES: William Ronald John, Thomas Percival Griffiths, David Owen Jones, James Patrick Murphy, Harry Hanford, David Thomas Richards, Idris Morgan Hopkins, Cuthbert Phillips, David Astley, Brynmor Jones, William Evans.

Goals: James Gibb (#), Alexander Ernest Stevenson (#), Noel Kernaghan (#) / David Astley (#), Cuthbert Phillips (#)

149. 31.10.1936   British Championship
NORTHERN IRELAND v SCOTLAND 1-3 (1-1)
Windsor Park, Belfast

Referee: Thomas Thompson (England)   Attendance: 45,000

NORTHERN IRELAND: Thomas Breen, William Cook, Robert Fulton, Walter McMillen, John Jones, William Mitchell, Noel Kernaghan, Keiller McCullough, David Kirker Martin, John Coulter, James Kelly.

SCOTLAND: James Dawson, Andrew Anderson, Robert Francis Dudgeon Ancell, Alexander Massie, James McMillan Simpson (Cap), George Clark Phillips Brown, Alexander Dewar Munro, Thomas Walker, David McCulloch, Charles Edward Napier, Douglas Duncan.

Goals: Noel Kernaghan (25) / Charles Edward Napier (27), Alexander Dewar Munro (42), David McCulloch (63)

150. 18.11.1936   British Championship
ENGLAND v NORTHERN IRELAND 3-1 (1-1)
Victoria Ground, Stoke

Referee: Willie Webb (Scotland)   Attendance: 47,882

ENGLAND: George Henry Holdcroft, Charles George Male (Cap), Arthur Edward Catlin, Clifford Samuel Britton, Charles William Gee, Errington Ridley Liddell Keen, Frederic Worrall, Horatio Stratton Carter, Frederick Charles Steele, Clifford Sydney Bastin, Joseph Arthur Johnson.

NORTHERN IRELAND: Thomas Breen, William Cook, Robert Fulton, Keiller McCullough, John Jones, William Mitchell, John Brown I, Alexander Ernest Stevenson, Thomas Lawrence Davis, Peter Dermont Doherty, James Kelly.

Goals: Horatio Stratton Carter (30), Clifford Bastin (77), Frederic Worrall (85)

29

151. 17.03.1937   British Championship
WALES v NORTHERN IRELAND 4-1
The Racecourse, Wrexham

Referee: Arthur James Jewell (England)   Attendance: 19,000

WALES: Albert Gray, Herbert Gwyn Turner, David Owen Jones, James Patrick Murphy, Thomas Percival Griffiths, David Thomas Richards, Idris Morgan Hopkins, Brynmor Jones, Ernest Matthew Glover, Leslie Jenkin Jones, Frederick Windsor Warren.

NORTHERN IRELAND: Thomas Breen, William Cook, Robert Fulton, Thomas Henry Brolly, John Jones, William Mitchell, John Brown I, Peter Dermont Doherty, S.J. Banks, Alexander Ernest Stevenson, John Coulter.

Goals: Ernest Glover (#, #), Frederick Windsor Warren (#), Brynmor Jones (#) / Alexander Ernest Stevenson (#)

152. 23.10.1937   British Championship
NORTHERN IRELAND v ENGLAND 1-5 (0-2)
Windsor Park, Belfast

Referee: Willie Webb (Scotland)   Attendance: 36,000

NORTHERN IRELAND: Thomas Breen, William Edward Hayes, William Cook, William Mitchell, John Jones, Robert James Browne, Noel Kernaghan, Alexander Ernest Stevenson, David Kirker Martin, Peter Dermont Doherty, Owen Madden.

ENGLAND: Victor Robert Woodley, Bert Sproston, Samuel Barkas (Cap), William John Crayston, Stanley Cullis, Wilfred Copping, Albert Geldard, George William Hall, George Robert Mills, Leonard Arthur Goulden, Eric Frederick George Brook.

Goals: Alexander Ernest Stevenson (88) / George Robert Mills (10, 15, 55), George William Hall (62), Eric Frederick George Brook (87)

153. 10.11.1937   British Championship
SCOTLAND v NORTHERN IRELAND 1-1 (0-1)
Pittodrie Park, Aberdeen

Referee: Arthur James Jewell (England)   Attendance: 21,878

SCOTLAND: James Dawson, Andrew Anderson, George Wilfred Cummings, Duncan McKenzie, James McMillan Simpson (Cap), Alexander Cockburn Hastings, James Delaney, Thomas Walker, James Smith, Robert Low McPhail, Robert Reid.

NORTHERN IRELAND: Thomas Breen, William Edward Hayes, William Cook, Matthew Doherty, Walter McMillen, William Mitchell, John Brown I, James McAlinden, David Kirker Martin, Peter Dermont Doherty, John Coulter.

Goals: James Smith (49) / Peter Dermont Doherty (14)

154. 16.03.1938   British Championship
NORTHERN IRELAND v WALES 1-0
Windsor Park, Belfast

Referee: Herbert Reginald Mortimer (England)   Att: 15,000

NORTHERN IRELAND: James Franus Twoomey, William Cook, Robert Fulton, Thomas Henry Brolly, Walter McMillen, Robert James Browne, John Brown I, Paddy Farrell, Joseph Bambrick, Alexander Ernest Stevenson, John Coulter.

WALES: Albert Gray, Herbert Gwyn Turner, William Marshall Hughes, George Henry Green, Thomas George Jones, David Thomas Richards, Idris Morgan Hopkins, Leslie Jenkin Jones, Edwin Perry, Brynmor Jones, Frederick Windsor Warren.

Goal: Joseph Bambrick (#)

155. 08.10.1938   British Championship
NORTHERN IRELAND v SCOTLAND 0-2 (0-1)
Windsor Park, Belfast

Referee: Herbert Mortimer (England)   Attendance: 40,000

NORTHERN IRELAND: Thomas Breen, William Edward Hayes, William Cook, Walter McMillen, Matthew Augustine O'Mahoney, Robert James Browne, John Brown, James McAlinden, David Kirker Martin, Alexander Ernest Stevenson, John Coulter.

SCOTLAND: James Dawson, James Carabine (Cap), Andrew Beattie, William Shankly, James Dykes, George Denholm Paterson, James Delaney, Thomas Walker, John Crum, John Divers, Torance Gillick.

Goals: James Delaney (33), Thomas Walker (48)

156. 16.11.1938   British Championship
ENGLAND v NORTHERN IRELAND 7-0 (4-0)
Old Trafford, Manchester

Referee: Peter Craigmyle (Scotland)   Attendance: 40,386

ENGLAND: Victor Robert Woodley, William Walker Morris, Edris Albert Hapgood (Cap), Charles Kenneth Willingham, Stanley Cullis, Joseph Mercer, Stanley Matthews, George William Hall, Thomas Lawton, Joseph Eric Stephenson, James Christopher Reginald Smith.

NORTHERN IRELAND: James Franus Twoomey, William Edward Hayes, William Cook, Thomas Henry Brolly, Walter McMillen, Robert James Browne, David Cochrane, Alexander Ernest Stevenson, Henry Baird, Peter Dermont Doherty, John Brown.

Goals: Thomas Lawton (8), George Hall (36, 38, 40, 55, 65), Stanley Matthews (86)

157. 15.03.1939   British Championship
WALES v NORTHERN IRELAND 3-1
The Racecourse, Wrexham

Referee: Arthur Barton (England)   Attendance: 22,997

WALES: George Poland, Herbert Gwyn Turner, William Marshall Hughes, George Henry Green, Thomas George Jones, Donald John Dearson, Idris Morgan Hopkins, Leslie Mervyn Boulter, Ernest Matthew Glover, Brynmor Jones, Reginald Horace Cumner.

NORTHERN IRELAND: Thomas Breen, William Cook, Malcolm Partridge Butler, Thomas Henry Brolly, Johnny Leatham, Ned Weir, David Cochrane, Alexander Ernest Stevenson, Dudley Milligan, Peter Dermot Doherty, John Brown I.

Goals: Leslie Mervyn Boulter (#), Ernest Matthew Glover (#), Reginald Horace Cumner (#) / Dudley Milligan (#)

158. 28.09.1946   British Championship
NORTHERN IRELAND v ENGLAND 2-7 (0-3)
Windsor Park, Belfast

Referee: Willie Webb (Scotland)   Attendance: 57,111

NORTHERN IRELAND: Alex Russell, William Charles Gorman, Thomas Aherne, John James Carey, John Joseph Vernon, James Douglas, David Cochrane, James McAlinden, Edward James McMorran, Peter Dermont Doherty, Norman Lockhart.

ENGLAND: Frank Victor Swift, Lawrence Scott, George Francis Moutry Hardwick (Cap), William Ambrose Wright, Cornelius "Neil" Franklin, Henry Cockburn, Thomas Finney, Horatio Stratton Carter, Thomas Lawton, Wilfred Mannion, Robert Langton.   Manager: Walter Winterbottom

Goals: Norman Lockhart (75, 89) / Horatio Carter (1), Wilfred Mannion (7, 28, 61), Thomas Finney (60), Thomas Lawton (82), Robert Langton (83)

159. 27.11.1946   British Championship
SCOTLAND v NORTHERN IRELAND 0-0
Hampden Park, Glasgow

Referee: George Reader (England)   Attendance: 98,776

SCOTLAND: Robert Brown, George Lewis Young, David Shaw (Cap), William Bowie Campbell, Francis Brennan, Hugh Long, Gordon Smith, George Hamilton, William Thornton, James Duncanson, William Beveridge Liddell.

NORTHERN IRELAND: Edward Hinton, William Charles Gorman, James McBurney Feeney, Cornelius Joseph Martin, John Joseph Vernon, Peter Desmond Farrell, David Cochrane, John James Carey, David John Walsh, Alexander Ernest Stevenson, Thomas Joseph Eglington.

160. 16.04.1947   British Championship
NORTHERN IRELAND v WALES 2-1 (1-1)
Windsor Park, Belfast

Referee: Not recorded   Attendance: 41,000

NORTHERN IRELAND: Edward Hinton, William Charles Gorman, John James Carey, Josiah Walter Sloan, John Joseph Vernon, Peter Desmond Farrell, David Cochrane, Alexander Ernest Stevenson, David John Walsh, Peter Dermont Doherty, Thomas Joseph Eglington.

WALES: William Warren Shortt, Alfred Thomas Sherwood, William Marshall Hughes, Douglas Frederick Witcomb, John Vaughan Humphreys, William Arthur Ronald Burgess, William Maldwyn Griffiths, William Morris, Trevor Ford, Brynmor Jones, George Edwards.

Goals: Alexander Stevenson (#), Peter Dermont Doherty (#) / Trevor Ford (#)

161. 04.10.1947   British Championship
NORTHERN IRELAND v SCOTLAND 2-0 (1-0)
Windsor Park, Belfast

Referee: Thomas Smith (England)   Attendance: 52,000

NORTHERN IRELAND: Edward Hinton, Cornelius Joseph Martin, Thomas Aherne, William Walsh, John Joseph Vernon, Peter Desmond Farrell, David Cochrane, Samuel Smyth, David John Walsh, Alexander Ernest Stevenson, Thomas Joseph Eglington.

SCOTLAND: William Miller, George Lewis Young, John Shaw (Cap), Archibald Renwick MacAuley, William Alexander Woodburn, Alexander Rooney Forbes, James Delaney, James Watson, William Thornton, William Steel, William Beveridge Liddell.

Goals: Samuel Smyth (35, 54)

162. 05.11.1947   British Championship
ENGLAND v NORTHERN IRELAND 2-2 (0-0)
Goodison Park, Liverpool

Referee: Peter Fitzpatrick (Scotland)   Attendance: 67,980

ENGLAND: Frank Victor Swift, Lawrence Scott, George Francis Moutry Hardwick (Cap), Philip Henry Taylor, Cornelius "Neil" Franklin, William Ambrose Wright, Stanley Matthews, Stanley Harding Mortensen, Wilfred Mannion, Thomas Lawton, Thomas Finney.
Manager: Walter Winterbottom

NORTHERN IRELAND: Edward Hinton, Cornelius Joseph Martin, John James Carey, William Walsh, John Joseph Vernon, Peter Desmond Farrell, David Cochrane, Samuel Smyth, David John Walsh, Peter Dermont Doherty, Thomas Joseph Eglington.

Goals: Wilfred Mannion (82), Thomas Lawton (88) / David John Walsh (54), Peter Dermont Doherty (89)

163. 10.03.1948   British Championship
WALES v NORTHERN IRELAND 2-0 (1-0)
The Racecourse, Wrexham
Referee: Not recorded   Attendance: 33,160
WALES: Cyril Sidlow, Alfred Thomas Sherwood, Walley Barnes, Ivor Verdun Powell, Thomas George Jones, William George Baker, David Sidney Thomas, Aubrey Powell, Trevor Ford, George Lowrie, George Edwards.
NORTHERN IRELAND: Edward Hinton, Cornelius Joseph Martin, William Charles Gorman, William Walsh, John Joseph Vernon, Peter Desmond Farrell, David Cochrane, Samuel Smyth, David John Walsh, Peter Dermont Doherty, Thomas Joseph Eglington.
Goals: George Lowrie (#), George Edwards (#)

164. 09.10.1948   British Championship
NORTHERN IRELAND v ENGLAND 2-6 (0-1)
Windsor Park, Belfast
Referee: Willie Webb (Scotland)   Attendance: 53,629
NORTHERN IRELAND: William Smyth, John James Carey, Cornelius Joseph Martin, William Walsh, John Joseph Vernon, Peter Desmond Farrell, John Francis O'Driscoll, James McAlinden, David John Walsh, Charles Tully, Thomas Joseph Eglington.
ENGLAND: Frank Victor Swift, Lawrence Scott, John Robert Howe, William Ambrose Wright (Cap), Cornelius "Neil" Franklin, Henry Cockburn, Stanley Matthews, Stanley Harding Mortensen, John Edward Milburn, Stanley Clare Pearson, Thomas Finney.   Manager: Walter Winterbottom
Goals: David John Walsh (50, 89) / Stanley Matthews (27), John Edward Milburn (52), Stanley Mortensen (55, 60, 80), Stanley Clare Pearson (83)

165. 17.11.1948   British Championship
SCOTLAND v NORTHERN IRELAND 3-2 (1-2)
Hampden Park, Glasgow
Referee: W.H.E. Evans (England)   Attendance: 93,182
SCOTLAND: Robert Brown, John Govan, David Shaw, Robert Evans, George Lewis Young (Cap), William Yates Redpath, William Waddell, James Mason, William Houliston, William Steel, John Carmichael Kelly.
NORTHERN IRELAND: William Smyth, John James Carey, Thomas Roderick Keane, James Joseph McCabe, John Joseph Vernon, William Walsh, David Cochrane, Samuel Smyth, David John Walsh, Peter Dermont Doherty, John Francis O'Driscoll.
Goals: William Houliston (27), James Mason (72), William Houliston (89) / David John Walsh (1, 4)

166. 09.03.1949   British Championship
NORTHERN IRELAND v WALES 0-2 (/0-1)
Windsor Park, Belfast
Referee: Not recorded   Attendance: 22,880
NORTHERN IRELAND: Cecil Moore, John James Carey, Thomas Aherne, James Joseph McCabe, John Joseph Vernon, Peter Desmond Farrell, David Cochrane, Samuel Smyth, David John Walsh, Robert Anderson Brennan, John Francis O'Driscoll.
WALES: William Arthur Hughes, Walley Barnes, Alfred Thomas Sherwood, Roy Paul, Thomas George Jones, William Arthur Ronald Burgess, Harold Williams, William Rees, Trevor Ford, William Henry Lucas, George Edwards.
Goals: George Edwards (#), Trevor Ford (#)

167. 01.10.1949   British Championship,
4th World Cup Qualifiers
NORTHERN IRELAND v SCOTLAND 2-8 (0-5)
Windsor Park, Belfast
Referee: R.A. Mortimer (England)   Attendance: 50,000
NORTHERN IRELAND: Patrick Kelly, Gerard Columba Bowler, Alfred McMichael, Robert Denis Blanchflower, John Joseph Vernon, Raymond Osborn Ferris, David Cochrane, Samuel Smyth, Robert Anderson Brennan, Edward Crossan, John McKenna.
SCOTLAND: James Clews Cowan, George Lewis Young (Cap), Samuel Richmond Cox, Robert Evans, William Alexander Woodburn, George Graham Aitken, William Waddell, James Mason, Henry Miller Morris, William Steel, Lawrence Reilly.
Goals: Samuel Smyth (50, 59) /
Henry Miller Morris (2, 70, 89), William Waddell (5, 42 pen), William Steel (25), Lawrence Reilly (26), James Mason (80)

168. 16.11.1949   British Championship,
4th World Cup Qualifiers
ENGLAND v NORTHERN IRELAND 9-2 (4-0)
Maine Road, Manchester
Referee: Mervyn Griffiths (Wales)   Attendance: 69,762
ENGLAND: Bernard Reginald Streten, Bertram Mozley, John Aston, William Watson, Cornelius "Neil" Franklin, William Ambrose Wright (Cap), Thomas Finney, Stanley Harding Mortensen, John Frederick Rowley, Stanley Clare Pearson, Jack Froggatt.   Manager: Walter Winterbottom
NORTHERN IRELAND: Hugh Redmond Kelly, James McBurney Feeney, Alfred McMichael, Gerard Columba Bowler, John Joseph Vernon, James Joseph McCabe, David Cochrane, Samuel Smyth, Robert Anderson Brennan, Charles Tully, John McKenna.
Goals: John Rowley (6, 47, 56, 58), Jack Froggatt (25), Stanley Clare Pearson (33, 68), Stanley Mortensen (39, 50) / Samuel Smyth (55), Robert Anderson Brennan (75)

169. 08.03.1950   British Championship, 4th World Cup Qualifiers
WALES v NORTHERN IRELAND   0-0
The Racecourse, Wrexham

Referee: Reginald Leafe (England)   Attendance: 30,000

WALES: William Warren Shortt, Walley Barnes, Alfred Thomas Sherwood, Roy Paul, William John Charles, William Arthur Ronald Burgess, Harold Williams, William Rees, Trevor Ford, Francis Henry Scrine, Royston James Clarke.

NORTHERN IRELAND: Hugh Redmond Kelly, Gerard Columba Bowler, Thomas Aherne, Robert Denis Blanchflower, Cornelius Joseph Martin, Reginald Alphonso Ryan, John McKenna, Samuel Smyth, David John Walsh, Robert Anderson Brennan, Norman Lockhart.

170. 07.10.1950   British Championship
NORTHERN IRELAND v ENGLAND   1-4 (0-1)
Windsor Park, Belfast

Referee: George Mitchell   Attendance: 50,000

NORTHERN IRELAND: Hugh Redmond Kelly, Charles Gallogly, Alfred McMichael, Robert Denis Blanchflower, John Joseph Vernon, Wilbur Cush, John Peter Campbell, Edward Crossan, Edward James McMorran, Robert Anderson Brennan, John McKenna.

ENGLAND: Bert Frederick Williams, Alfred Ernest Ramsey, John Aston, William Ambrose Wright (Cap), Allenby Chilton, James William Dickinson, Stanley Matthews, Wilfred Mannion, John Lee, Edward Francis Baily, Robert Langton. Manager: Walter Winterbottom

Goals: Edward James McMorran (70) / Edward Francis Baily (43, 86), John Lee (64), William Ambrose Wright (85)

171. 01.11.1950   British Championship
SCOTLAND v NORTHERN IRELAND   6-1 (2-1)
Hampden Park, Glasgow

Referee: Benjamin Mervyn Griffiths (Wales)   Att: 83,142

SCOTLAND: James Clews Cowan, George Lewis Young (Cap), William McNaught, John Miller McColl, William Alexander Woodburn, Alexander Rooney Forbes, Robert Young Collins, James Mason, John McPhail, William Steel, William Beveridge Liddell.

NORTHERN IRELAND: Hugh Redmond Kelly, Charles Gallogly, Alfred McMichael, Robert Denis Blanchflower, John Joseph Vernon, Wilbur Cush, John Peter Campbell, J. Kevin McGarry, Edward James McMorran, Peter Dermont Doherty, John McKenna.

Goals: John McPhail (8, 13), William Steel (53, 57, 66, 79) / J. Kevin McGarry (43)

172. 07.03.1951   British Championship
NORTHERN IRELAND v WALES   1-2 (0-1)
Windsor Park, Belfast

Referee: Not recorded   Attendance: 12,000

NORTHERN IRELAND: Edward Hinton, William George Leonard Graham, William Edward Cunningham, James Joseph McCabe, John Joseph Vernon, William Dickson, William Hughes, Edward James McMorran, William Simpson, J. Kevin McGarry, Norman Lockhart.

WALES: Iorwerth Hughes, Walley Barnes, Alfred Thomas Sherwood, Roy Paul, William Raymond Daniel, William Arthur Ronald Burgess, William Maldwyn Griffiths, Noel Kinsey, Trevor Ford, Ivor John Allchurch, Royston James Clarke.

Goals: William Simpson (#) / Royston James Clarke (#, #)

173. 12.05.1951
NORTHERN IRELAND v FRANCE   2-2 (1-2)
Windsor Park, Belfast

Referee: Arthur Edward Ellis (England)   Att: 24,000

NORTHERN IRELAND: Edward Hinton, William George Leonard Graham, Alfred McMichael, Robert Denis Blanchflower, John Joseph Vernon, Raymond Osborn Ferris, William Bingham, J. Kevin McGarry, William Simpson, William Dickson, John McKenna.

FRANCE: Julien Darui, Guy Huguet, Robert Jonquet, Roger Marche (Cap), Antoine Cuissard, René Gallice, Antoine Bonifaci, Edouard Kargu, André Strappe, Jean Baratte, Edmond Haan.

Goals: Raymond Ferris (9 pen), William Simpson (62) / Jean Baratte (16), Antoine Bonifaci (28)

174. 06.10.1951   British Championship
NORTHERN IRELAND v SCOTLAND   0-3 (0-2)
Windsor Park, Belfast

Referee: W.H.E. Evans (England)   Attendance: 56,946

NORTHERN IRELAND: William Uprichard, William George Leonard Graham, Alfred McMichael, William Dickson, John Joseph Vernon, Raymond Osborn Ferris, William Bingham, James McIlroy, Edward James McMorran, Robert Peacock, Charles Tully.

SCOTLAND: James Clews Cowan, George Lewis Young (Cap), Samuel Richmond Cox, Robert Evans, William Alexander Woodburn, William Yates Redpath, William Waddell, Robert Johnstone, Lawrence Reilly, Thomas Bingham Orr, William Beveridge Liddell.

Goals: Thomas Bingham Orr (32), Robert Johnstone (44, 62)

175. 14.11.1951   British Championship
ENGLAND v NORTHERN IRELAND 2-0 (1-0)

Villa Park, Birmingham

Referee: Mervyn Griffiths (Wales)   Attendance: 57,889

ENGLAND: Gilbert Harold Merrick, Alfred Ernest Ramsey, Lionel Smith, William Ambrose Wright (Cap), Malcolm Williamson Barrass, James William Dickinson, Thomas Finney, John Sewell, Nathaniel Lofthouse, Leonard Horace Phillips, Leslie Dennis Medley.   Manager: Walter Winterbottom

NORTHERN IRELAND: William Uprichard, William George Leonard Graham, Alfred McMichael, William Dickson, John Joseph Vernon, Francis Joseph McCourt, William Bingham, Samuel Smyth, Edward James McMorran, James McIlroy, John McKenna.

Goals: Nathaniel Lofthouse (40, 83)

176. 19.03.1952   British Championship
WALES v NORTHERN IRELAND 3-0 (1-0)

Vetch Field, Swansea

Referee: Not recorded   Attendance: 30,000

WALES: William Warren Shortt, Walley Barnes, Alfred Thomas Sherwood, Roy Paul, William Raymond Daniel, William Arthur Ronald Burgess, William Isaiah Foulkes, William Morris, Trevor Ford, Ivor John Allchurch, Royston James Clarke.

NORTHERN IRELAND: William Uprichard, William George Leonard Graham, Alfred McMichael, Robert Denis Blanchflower, William Dickson, Francis Joseph McCourt, William Bingham, Samuel Donal D'Arcy, Edward James McMorran, James McIlroy, Norman Lockhart.

Goals: Walley Barnes (# penalty), Ivor John Allchurch (#), Royston James Clarke (#)

177. 04.10.1952   British Championship
NORTHERN IRELAND v ENGLAND 2-2 (1-1)

Windsor Park, Belfast

Referee: Douglas Gerrard (Scotland)   Attendance: 58,000

NORTHERN IRELAND: William Uprichard, William Edward Cunningham, Alfred McMichael, Robert Denis Blanchflower, William Dickson, Francis Joseph McCourt, William Bingham, Samuel Donal D'Arcy, Edward James McMorran, James McIlroy, Charles Tully.

ENGLAND: Gilbert Harold Merrick, Alfred Ernest Ramsey, William Eckersley, William Ambrose Wright (Cap), Jack Froggatt, James William Dickinson, Thomas Finney, John Sewell, Nathaniel Lofthouse, Edward Francis Baily, William Henry Elliott.   Manager: Walter Winterbottom

Goals: Charles Tully (15, 46) / Nathaniel Lofthouse (2), William Henry Elliott (87)

178. 05.11.1952   British Championship
SCOTLAND v NORTHERN IRELAND 1-1 (0-0)

Hampden Park, Glasgow

Referee: Robert Smith (Wales)   Attendance: 65,057

SCOTLAND: George Neil Farm, George Lewis Young (Cap), Samuel Richmond Cox, James Scoular, Francis Brennan, George Graham Aitken, Thomas Wright, James Tullis Logie, Lawrence Reilly, William Steel, William Beveridge Liddell.

NORTHERN IRELAND: William Uprichard, William George Leonard Graham, Alfred McMichael, Robert Denis Blanchflower, William Dickson, Francis Joseph McCourt, William Bingham, Samuel Donal D'Arcy, Edward James McMorran, James McIlroy, Charles Tully.

Goals: Lawrence Reilly (90) / Samuel Donal D'Arcy (80)

179. 11.11.1952
FRANCE v NORTHERN IRELAND 3-1 (2-1)

Stade Yves du Manoir, Colombes, Paris

Referee: Klaas Schipper (Holland)   Attendance: 52,399

FRANCE: Jean Ruminski, Lazare Gianessi, Robert Jonquet, Roger Marche (Cap), Antoine Bonifaci (26 Jean Baratte), Armand Penverne, Joseph Ujlaki, André Strappe, Raymond Kopa, Thadée Cisowski, Stanislas Curyl.

NORTHERN IRELAND: William Uprichard, William George Leonard Graham, Alfred McMichael, Robert Denis Blanchflower, William Dickson, Francis Joseph McCourt, William Bingham, Samuel Donal D'Arcy Edward James McMorran, Robert Peacock, Charles Tully.

Goals: Joseph Ujlaki (30), Raymond Kopa (36, 89) / Charles Tully (42)

180. 15.04.1953   British Championship
NORTHERN IRELAND v WALES 2-3 (1-3)

Windsor Park, Belfast

Referee: Not recorded   Attendance: 33,000

NORTHERN IRELAND: William Uprichard, James Joseph McCabe, Alfred McMichael, Robert Denis Blanchflower, William Dickson, Francis Joseph McCourt, William Bingham, James McIlroy, Edward James McMorran, Samuel Donal D'Arcy, Charles Tully.

WALES: William Warren Shortt, Derrick Sullivan, Alfred Thomas Sherwood, Roy Paul, William Raymond Daniel, William Arthur Ronald Burgess, Terence Cameron Medwin, William John Charles, Trevor Ford, Ivor John Allchurch, James Henry Griffiths.

Goals: Edward James McMorran (#, #) / William John Charles (#, #), Trevor Ford (#)

181. 03.10.1953   British Championship, 5th World Cup Qualifiers
NORTHERN IRELAND v SCOTLAND 1-3 (0-0)

Windsor Park, Belfast

Referee: Arthur Edward Ellis (England)   Att: 58,248

NORTHERN IRELAND: William Smyth, William Edward Cunningham, Alfred McMichael, Robert Denis Blanchflower, James Joseph McCabe, Wilbur Cush, William Bingham, James McIlroy, William Simpson, Charles Tully, Norman Lockhart.

SCOTLAND: George Neil Farm, George Lewis Young (Cap), Samuel Richmond Cox, Robert Evans, Francis Brennan, Douglas Cowie, William Waddell, Charles Fleming, John McPhail, James Watson, John Gillespie Henderson.

Goals: Norman Lockhart (72 pen) /
Charles Fleming (47, 69), John Gillespie Henderson (89)

182. 11.11.1953   British Championship, 5th World Cup Qualifiers
ENGLAND v NORTHERN IRELAND 3-1 (1-0)

Goodison Park, Liverpool

Referee: Robert Smith (Wales)   Attendance: 70,000

ENGLAND: Gilbert Harold Merrick, Stanley Rickaby, William Eckersley, William Ambrose Wright (Cap), Harry Johnstonon, James William Dickinson, Stanley Matthews, Albert Quixall, Nathaniel Lofthouse, Harold William Hassall, James Mullen.   Manager: Walter Winterbottom

NORTHERN IRELAND: William Smyth, William George Leonard Graham, Alfred McMichael, Robert Denis Blanchflower, William Dickson, Wilbur Cush, William Bingham, James McIlroy, William Simpson, Edward James McMorran, Norman Lockhart.

Goals: Harold Hassall (1, 57), Nathaniel Lofthouse (74) /
Edward James McMorran (54)

183. 31.03.1954   British Championship, 5th World Cup Qualifiers
WALES v NORTHERN IRELAND 1-2 (0-1)

The Racecourse, Wrexham

Referee: Charles Faultless (Scotland)   Attendance: 32,817

WALES: Alfred John Kelsey, Derrick Sullivan, Alfred Thomas Sherwood, Roy Paul, William Raymond Daniel, William Arthur Ronald Burgess, William Isaiah Foulkes, Noel Kinsey, William John Charles, Ivor John Allchurch, Royston James Clarke.

NORTHERN IRELAND: Harry Gregg, William George Leonard Graham, Alfred McMichael, Robert Denis Blanchflower, William Dickson, Robert Peacock, William Bingham, John Blanchflower, William John McAdams, James McIlroy, Peter James McParland.

Goals: William John Charles (80) / Peter McParland (1, 52)

184. 02.10.1954   British Championship
NORTHERN IRELAND v ENGLAND 0-2 (0-0)

Windsor Park, Belfast

Referee: Charles Edward Faultless (Scotland)   Att: 59,000

NORTHERN IRELAND: William Uprichard, Frank J.Montgomery, Alfred McMichael, Robert Denis Blanchflower, William Dickson, Robert Peacock, William Bingham, John Blanchflower, William Simpson, James McIlroy, Peter James McParland.

ENGLAND: Raymond Ernest Wood, William Anthony Foulkes, Roger William Byrne, John Edward Wheeler, William Ambrose Wright (Cap), Raymond John Barlow, Stanley Matthews, Donald George Revie, Nathaniel Lofthouse, John Norman Haynes, Brian Pilkington.
Manager: Walter Winterbottom

Goals: John Norman Haynes (75), Donald George Revie (77)

185. 03.11.1954   British Championship
SCOTLAND v NORTHERN IRELAND 2-2 (1-2)

Hampden Park, Glasgow

Referee: Alfred Bond (England)   Attendance: 46,200

SCOTLAND: William Alexander Fraser, George Lewis Young (Cap), William McNaught, Robert Evans, James Anderson Davidson, Douglas Cowie, William Waddell, Robert Johnstone, Patrick McCabe Buckley, William Fernie, Thomas Ring.

NORTHERN IRELAND: William Uprichard, William George Leonard Graham, William Edward Cunningham, Robert Denis Blanchflower, William Terence McCavana, Robert Peacock, William Bingham, John Blanchflower, William John McAdams, James McIlroy, Peter James McParland.

Goals: James Davidson (22), Robert Johnstone (74) /
William Bingham (24), William John McAdams (44)

186. 20.04.1955   British Championship
NORTHERN IRELAND v WALES 2-3 (2-2)

Windsor Park, Belfast

Referee: Not recorded   Attendance: 30,000

NORTHERN IRELAND: William Uprichard, William George Leonard Graham, Alfred McMichael, Robert Denis Blanchflower, Ernie McCleary, Thomas Casey, William Bingham, Edward Crossan, James Walker, James McIlroy, Norman Lockhart.

WALES: Alfred John Kelsey, Stuart Grenville Williams, Alfred Thomas Sherwood, Melvyn Charles, William Raymond Daniel, Derrick Sullivan, Derek Robert Tapscott, Trevor Ford, William John Charles, Ivor John Allchurch, Leonard Allchurch.
Trainer: Walley Barnes

Goals: Edward Crossan (#), James Walker (#) /
William John Charles (#, #, #)

187. 08.10.1955   British Championship
NORTHERN IRELAND v SCOTLAND 2-1 (2-0)
Windsor Park, Belfast

Referee: John Kelly (England)   Attendance: 48,000

NORTHERN IRELAND: William Uprichard, William George Leonard Graham, William Edward Cunningham, Robert Denis Blanchflower, William Terence McCavana, Robert Peacock, William Bingham, John Blanchflower, Francis Coyle, James McIlroy, Peter James McParland.

SCOTLAND: Thomas Younger, Alexander Hershaw Parker, Joseph McDonald, Robert Evans, George Lewis Young (Cap), Archibald Glen, Gordon Smith, Robert Young Collins, Lawrence Reilly, Robert Johnstone, William Beveridge Liddell.

Goals: John Blanchflower (7), William Bingham (16) / Lawrence Reilly (62)

188. 02.11.1955   British Championship
ENGLAND v NORTHERN IRELAND 3-0 (0-0)
Wembley, London

Referee: Mervyn Griffiths (Wales)   Attendance: 60,000

ENGLAND: Ronald Leslie Baynham, Jeffrey James Hall, Roger William Byrne, Ronald Clayton, William Ambrose Wright (Cap), James William Dickinson, Thomas Finney, John Norman Haynes, Bedford Alfred George Jezzard, Dennis James Wilshaw, William Perry.   Manager: Walter Winterbottom

NORTHERN IRELAND: William Uprichard, William Edward Cunningham, William George Leonard Graham, Robert Denis Blanchflower, William Terence McCavana, Robert Peacock, William Bingham, James McIlroy, Francis Coyle, Charles Tully, Peter James McParland.

Goals: Dennis James Wilshaw (50, 52), Thomas Finney (88)

189. 11.04.1956   British Championship
WALES v NORTHERN IRELAND 1-1 (1-0)
Ninian Park, Cardiff

Referee: Not recorded   Attendance: 37,510

WALES: Alfred John Kelsey, Alfred Thomas Sherwood, Melvyn Hopkins, Alan Charles Harrington, William John Charles, Roy Paul, Clifford William Jones, Derek Robert Tapscott, Trevor Ford, Ivor John Allchurch, Royston James Clarke.   Trainer: James Patrick Murphy

NORTHERN IRELAND: William Uprichard, William Edward Cunningham, Alfred McMichael, Robert Denis Blanchflower, John Blanchflower, Thomas Casey, William Bingham, James McIlroy, James Jones I, Edward James McMorran, Norman Lockhart.

Goals: Royston James Clarke (#) / James Jones (#)

190. 06.10.1956   British Championship
NORTHERN IRELAND v ENGLAND 1-1 (1-1)
Windsor Park, Belfast

Referee: Hugh Phillips (Scotland)   Attendance: 58,420

NORTHERN IRELAND: Harry Gregg, William Edward Cunningham, Alfred McMichael, Robert Denis Blanchflower, John Blanchflower, Thomas Casey, William Bingham, James McIlroy, James Jones I, William John McAdams, Peter James McParland.

ENGLAND: Reginald Derrick Matthews, Jeffrey James Hall, Roger William Byrne, Ronald Clayton, William Ambrose Wright (Cap), Duncan Edwards, Stanley Matthews, Donald George Revie, Thomas Taylor, Dennis James Wilshaw, Colin Grainger.   Manager: Walter Winterbottom

Goals: James McIlroy (10) / Stanley Matthews (3)

191. 07.11.1956   British Championship
SCOTLAND v NORTHERN IRELAND 1-0 (1-0)
Hampden Park, Glasgow

Referee: Reginald Leafe (England)   Attendance: 62,035

SCOTLAND: Thomas Younger, Alexander Hershaw Parker, John Davidson Hewie, John Miller McColl, George Lewis Young (Cap), Douglas Cowie, Alexander Silcock Scott, John Knight Mudie, Lawrence Reilly, James Wardhaug, William Fernie.

NORTHERN IRELAND: Harry Gregg, William Edward Cunningham, Alfred McMichael, Robert Denis Blanchflower, John Blanchflower, Thomas Casey, William Bingham, James McIlroy, Robert James Shields, Thomas A. Dickson, Peter James McParland.

Goal: Alexander Silcock Scott (25)

192. 16.01.1957   6th World Cup Qualifiers
PORTUGAL v NORTHERN IRELAND 1-1 (1-1)
José Alvalade, Lisboa

Referee: Marcel Lequesne (France)   Attendance: 30,000

PORTUGAL: CARLOS António do Carmo Costa GOMES, VIRGÍLIO Marques Mendes, ÂNGELO Gaspar Martins, José Maria Carvalho Pedroto, Manuel PASSOS Fernandes (Cap), António Henrique MONTEIRO da COSTA, HERNÂNI Ferreira da Silva, Manuel Vasques, JOSÉ Carvalho Santos Pinto ÁGUAS, Mário Esteves Coluna, Fernando Júlio Perdigão.   Trainer: Tavares da Silva

NORTHERN IRELAND: Harry Gregg, William Edward Cunningham, Alfred McMichael, Robert Denis Blanchflower, John Blanchflower, Thomas Casey, William Bingham, James McIlroy, Francis Coyle, Wilbur Cush, Peter James McParland.

Goals: Manuel Vasques (33) / William Bingham (7)

193. 10.04.1957   British Championship
NORTHERN IRELAND v WALES 0-0
Windsor Park, Belfast
Referee: Not recorded   Attendance: 30,000
NORTHERN IRELAND: Harry Gregg, William Edward Cunningham, Alfred McMichael, Robert Denis Blanchflower, Wilbur Cush, Robert Peacock, William Bingham, James McIlroy, James Jones, Thomas Casey, Peter James McParland.
WALES: Alfred John Kelsey, Leonard Trevor Edwards, Melvyn Hopkins, Melvyn Charles, William Raymond Daniel, David Lloyd Bowen, Terence Cameron Medwin, Derek Robert Tapscott, William John Charles, Thomas Royston Vernon, Clifford William Jones.   Trainer: James Patrick Murphy

194. 25.04.1957   6th World Cup Qualifiers
ITALY v NORTHERN IRELAND 1-0 (1-0)
Olimpico, Roma
Referee: Maurice Guigue (France)   Attendance: 70,000
ITALY: Roberto Lovati, Ardico Magnini (Cap), Sergio Cervato, Giuseppe Chiappella, Alberto Orzan, Armando Segato, Ermes Muccinelli, Carlo Galli, Edwing Firmani, Guido Gratton, Amleto Frignani.
Technical commission trainer: Alfredo Foni
NORTHERN IRELAND: Harry Gregg, William Edward Cunningham, Alfred McMichael, Robert Denis Blanchflower (Cap), Wilbur Cush, Thomas Casey, William Bingham, William Simpson, Edward James McMorran, James McIlroy, Robert Peacock.
Goal: Sergio Cervato (3)

195. 01.05.1957   6th World Cup Qualifiers
NORTHERN IRELAND v PORTUGAL 3-0 (1-0)
Windsor Park, Belfast
Referee: Hugh Philips (Scotland)   Attendance: 35,000
NORTHERN IRELAND: Harry Gregg, William Edward Cunningham, Alfred McMichael, Robert Denis Blanchflower, Wilbur Cush, Thomas Casey, William Bingham, William Simpson, Edward James McMorran, James McIlroy, Robert Peacock.
PORTUGAL: CARLOS António do Carmo Costa GOMES, VIRGÍLIO Marques Mendes, Francisco Torrão Pires, José Maria Carvalho Pedroto (Cap), EMÍDIO da Silva GRAÇA, Fernando da Silva Cabrita, HERNÂNI Ferreira da Silva, Manuel Vasques, JOSÉ Carvalho Santos Pinto ÁGUAS, SALVADOR Félix Martins, Domiciano Barrocal Gomes Cavém.   Trainer: Tavares da Silva
Goals: Thomas Casey (22), William Simpson (60), James McIlroy (70 pen)

196. 05.10.1957   British Championship
NORTHERN IRELAND v SCOTLAND 1-1 (0-0)
Windsor Park, Belfast
Referee: Leo Callaghan (Wales)   Attendance: 50,000
NORTHERN IRELAND: William Uprichard, William Edward Cunningham, Alfred McMichael, Robert Denis Blanchflower, John Blanchflower, Robert Peacock, William Bingham, William Simpson, William John McAdams, James McIlroy, Peter James McParland.
SCOTLAND: Thomas Younger, Alexander Hershaw Parker, Eric Caldow, John Miller McColl, Robert Evans, Thomas Henderson Docherty (Cap), Graham Leggat, Robert Young Collins, John Knight Mudie, Samuel Baird, Thomas Ring.
Goals: William Simpson (47) / Graham Leggat (58)

197. 06.11.1957   British Championship
ENGLAND v NORTHERN IRELAND 2-3 (0-1)
Wembley, London
Referee: Mervyn Griffiths (Wales)   Attendance: 40,000
ENGLAND: Edward Hopkinson, Donald Howe, Roger William Byrne, Ronald Clayton, William Ambrose Wright (Cap), Duncan Edwards, Bryan Douglas, Derek Tennyson Kevan, Thomas Taylor, John Norman Haynes, Alan A'Court.
Manager: Walter Winterbottom
NORTHERN IRELAND: Harry Gregg, Richard Matthewson Keith, Alfred McMichael, Robert Denis Blanchflower, John Blanchflower, Robert Peacock, William Bingham, Samuel McCrory, William Simpson, James McIlroy, Peter James McParland.
Goals: Alan A'Court (60), Duncan Edwards (80) / James McIlroy (30 pen), Samuel McCrory (60), William Simpson (73)

198. 04.12.1957   6th World Cup Qualifiers
NORTHERN IRELAND v ITALY 2-2 (1-1)
Windsor Park, Belfast
Referee: Thomas Mitchell (Northern Ireland)   Att: 53,000
NORTHERN IRELAND: Harry Gregg, Richard Matthewson Keith, Alfred McMichael, Robert Denis Blanchflower (Cap), John Blanchflower, Robert Peacock, William Bingham, James McIlroy, William John McAdams, Wilbur Cush, Peter James McParland.
ITALY: Ottavio Bugatti, Giuseppe Corradi, Sergio Cervato (Cap), Giuseppe Chiappella, Rino Ferrario, Armando Segato, Alcide Ghiggia, Juan Alberto Schiaffino, Gastone Bean, Guido Gratton, Miguel Montuori.
Technical commission trainer: Alfredo Foni
Sent off: Giuseppe Chiappella (83)
Goals: Wilbur Cush (27, 60) / Alcide Ghiggia (24), Miguel Montuori (50)

199. 15.01.1958   6th World Cup Play-Offs
NORTHERN IRELAND v ITALY 2-1 (2-0)

Windsor Park, Belfast

Referee: István Zsolt (Hungary)   Attendance: 43,000

NORTHERN IRELAND: William Uprichard, William Edward Cunningham, Alfred McMichael, Robert Denis Blanchflower (Cap), John Blanchflower, Robert Peacock, William Bingham, Wilbur Cush, William Simpson, James McIlroy, Peter James McParland.

ITALY: Ottavio Bugatti, Guido Vincenzi, Giuseppe Corradi, Giovanni Invernizzi, Rino Ferrario, Armando Segato (Cap), Alcide Ghiggia, Juan Alberto Schiaffino, Gino Pivatelli, Miguel Montuori, Dino Da Costa.
Technical commission trainer: Alfredo Foni

Sent off: Alcide Ghiggia (68)

Goals: James McIlroy (13), Wilbur Cush (28) / Dino Da Costa (56)

200. 16.04.1958   British Championship
WALES v NORTHERN IRELAND 1-1 (0-0)

Ninian Park, Cardiff

Referee: Not recorded   Attendance: 25,677

WALES: Alfred John Kelsey, Stuart Grenville Williams, Melvyn Hopkins, Alan Charles Harrington, Derrick Sullivan, David Lloyd Bowen, Leonard Allchurch, Ronald Hewitt, Terence Cameron Medwin, Ivor John Allchurch, Clifford William Jones. Trainer: James Patrick Murphy

NORTHERN IRELAND: Harry Gregg, William Edward Cunningham, Alfred McMichael, Robert Denis Blanchflower, Richard Matthewson Keith, Robert Peacock, William Bingham, Wilbur Cush, William Simpson, James McIlroy, Peter James McParland.

Goals: Richard Matthewson Keith (# own goal) / William Simpson (#)

201. 08.06.1958   6th World Cup, 1st Round
NORTHERN IRELAND v CZECHOSLOVAKIA 1-0 (1-0)

Orjans Vall, Halmstad

Referee: Friedrich Seipelt (Austria)   Attendance: 10,647

NORTHERN IRELAND: Harry Gregg, Richard Matthewson Keith, Alfred McMichael, Robert Denis Blanchflower (Cap), William Edward Cunningham, Robert Peacock, William Bingham, Wilbur Cush, Alexander Derek Dougan, James McIlroy, Peter James McParland.

CZECHOSLOVAKIA: Břetislav Dolejši, Gustáv Mráz, Jiří Čadek, Ladislav Novák (Cap), Svatopluk Pluskal, Josef Masopust, Václav Hovorka, Milan Dvořák, Jaroslav Borovička, Jan Hertl, Tadeáš Kraus. Trainer: Karel Kolský

Goal: Wilbur Cush (20)

202. 11.06.1958   6th World Cup, 1st Round
ARGENTINA v NORTHERN IRELAND 3-1 (1-1)

Orjans Vall, Halmstad

Referee: Sten Ahlner (Sweden)   Attendance: 14,174

ARGENTINA: Amadeo Raúl Carrizo, Pedro Rodolfo Dellacha (Cap), Federico Vairo, Juan Francisco Lombardo, Néstor Raúl Rossi, José Varacka, Oreste Osmar Corbatta, Ludovico Héctor Avio, Norberto Menéndez, Ángel Amadeo Labruna, Norberto Constante Boggio. Trainer: Guillermo Stábile

NORTHERN IRELAND: Harry Gregg, Richard Matthewson Keith, Alfred McMichael, Robert Denis Blanchflower (Cap), William Edward Cunningham, Robert Peacock, William Bingham, Wilbur Cush, Francis Coyle, James McIlroy, Peter James McParland.

Goals: Oreste Corbatta (38 pen), Norberto Menéndez (55), Ludovico Héctor Avio (60) / Peter James McParland (4)

203. 15.06.1958   6th World Cup, 1st Round
NORTHERN IRELAND v WEST GERMANY 2-2 (1-1)

Malmö Stadion, Malmö

Referee: Joaquim Fernandes de Campos (Portugal)
Attendance: 21,990

NORTHERN IRELAND: Harry Gregg, Richard Matthewson Keith, Alfred McMichael, Robert Denis Blanchflower (Cap), William Edward Cunningham, Robert Peacock, William Bingham, Wilbur Cush, Thomas Casey, James McIlroy, Peter James McParland.

WEST GERMANY: Fritz Herkenrath, Georg Stollenwerk, Erich Juskowiak, Horst Eckel, Herbert Erhardt, Horst Szymaniak, Helmut Rahn, Fritz Walter, Uwe Seeler, Hans Schäfer (Cap), Bernhard Klodt. Trainer: Josef Herberger

Goals: Peter James McParland (19, 60) / Helmut Rahn (21), Uwe Seeler (79)

204. 17.06.1958   6th World Cup, 1st Round
NORTHERN IRELAND v CZECHOSLOVAKIA 2-1 (1-1, 1-1) (AET)

Malmö Stadion, Malmö

Referee: Maurice Guigue (France)   Attendance: 6,196

NORTHERN IRELAND: William Uprichard, Richard Matthewson Keith, Alfred McMichael, Robert Denis Blanchflower (Cap), William Edward Cunningham, Robert Peacock, William Bingham, Wilbur Cush, John Scott, James McIlroy, Peter James McParland.

CZECHOSLOVAKIA: Břetislav Dolejši, Gustáv Mráz, Ján Popluhár, Ladislav Novák (Cap), Titus Buberník, Josef Masopust, Milan Dvořák, Pavol Molnár, Jiří Feureisl, Jaroslav Borovička, Zdeněk Zikán. Trainer: Karel Kolský

Sent off: Titus Buberník (102)

Goals: Peter James McParland (44, 99) / Zdeněk Zikán (20)

205. 19.06.1958   6th World Cup, Quarter-Final
FRANCE v NORTHERN IRELAND 4-0 (1-0)
Idrottsparken, Norrköping
Referee: Juan Gardeazábal Garay (Spain)   Att: 11,800
FRANCE: Claude Abbes, Raymond Kaelbel, Robert Jonquet (Cap), André Lerond, Armand Penverne, Jean-Jacques Marcel, Maryan Wisnieski, Just Fontaine, Raymond Kopa, Roger Piantoni, Jean Vincent.   Trainer: Albert Batteux
NORTHERN IRELAND: Harry Gregg, Richard Matthewson Keith, Alfred McMichael, Robert Denis Blanchflower (Cap), William Edward Cunningham, Wilbur Cush, William Bingham, Thomas Casey, John Scott, James McIlroy, Peter James McParland.
Goals: Maryan Wisnieski (44), Just Fontaine (56, 64), Roger Piantoni (68)

206. 04.10.1958   British Championship
NORTHERN IRELAND v ENGLAND 3-3 (1-1)
Windsor Park, Belfast
Referee: Robert Holley Davidson (Scotland)   Att: 58,000
NORTHERN IRELAND: Harry Gregg, Richard Matthewson Keith, William George Leonard Graham, Robert Denis Blanchflower, William Edward Cunningham, Robert Peacock, William Bingham, Wilbur Cush, Thomas Casey, James McIlroy, Peter James McParland.
ENGLAND: Colin Agnew McDonald, Donald Howe, Thomas Banks, Ronald Clayton, William Ambrose Wright (Cap), Wilfred McGuinness, Peter Brabrook, Peter Frank Broadbent, Robert Charlton, John Norman Haynes, Thomas Finney. Manager: Walter Winterbottom
Goals: Wilbur Cush (33), Robert Peacock (57), T. Casey (70) / Robert Charlton (38, 75), Thomas Finney (61)

207. 15.10.1958
SPAIN v NORTHERN IRELAND 6-2 (2-0)
Santiago Bernabeu, Madrid
Referee: Joaquin Fernandez Campos (Portugal)
Attendance: 120,000
SPAIN: Juan Alonso, Juan Carlos Díaz Quincoces, José Emilio Santamaría, Rafael Lesmes, Juan Santisteban, José María Zárraga (Cap), Justo Tejada, Ladislao Kubala, Alfredo Di Stéfano, Luis Suárez, Francisco Gento.
Trainer: Manuel Meana Vallina
NORTHERN IRELAND: William Uprichard, Richard Matthewson Keith, Alfred McMichael, Robert Denis Blanchflower, John T. Forde, Thomas Casey, William Bingham, Wilbur Cush, Peter James McParland, James McIlroy, Charles Tully.
Goals: Justo Tejada (3, 47, 77, 84), Ladislao Kubala (11 pen), Luis Suárez (57) / Wilbur Cush (49), James McIlroy (76)

208. 05.11.1958   British Championship
SCOTLAND v NORTHERN IRELAND 2-2 (0-0)
Hampden Park, Glasgow
Referee: John Harold Clough (England)   Att: 72,732
SCOTLAND: William Dallas Fyfe Brown, John Grant, Eric Caldow, David Craig MacKay (Cap), William Toner, Thomas Henderson Docherty, Graham Leggat, Robert Young Collins, David George Herd, Denis Law, John Gillespie Henderson. Manager: Matthew Busby
NORTHERN IRELAND: William Uprichard, Richard Matthewson Keith, Alfred McMichael, Robert Denis Blanchflower, William Edward Cunningham, Robert Peacock, William Bingham, Wilbur Cush, William Simpson, James McIlroy, Peter James McParland.
Goals: David George Herd (51), Robert Young Collins (54) / Eric Caldow (72 own goal), James McIlroy (76)

209. 22.04.1959   British Championship
NORTHERN IRELAND v WALES 4-1 (3-0)
Windsor Park, Belfast
Referee: Not recorded   Attendance: 45,000
NORTHERN IRELAND: Harry Gregg, Richard Matthewson Keith, Alfred McMichael, Robert Denis Blanchflower, William Edward Cunningham, Robert Peacock, William Bingham, James McIlroy, Wilbur Cush, Matthew James Hill, Peter James McParland.
WALES: Raymond Victor Rouse, Stuart Grenville Williams, Melvyn Hopkins, Victor Herbert Crowe, Derrick Sullivan, David Lloyd Bowen, Terence Cameron Medwin, Derek Robert Tapscott, Antonio Camilio Rowley, Ivor John Allchurch, Clifford William Jones.   Trainer: James Patrick Murphy
Goals: Peter James McParland (#), Robert Peacock (#), James McIlroy (#), Wilbur Cush (#) / Derek Robert Tapscott (#)

210. 03.10.1959   British Championship
NORTHERN IRELAND v SCOTLAND 0-4 (0-3)
Windsor Park, Belfast
Referee: Reginald Leafe (England)   Attendance: 59,000
NORTHERN IRELAND: Harry Gregg, Richard Matthewson Keith, Alfred McMichael, Robert Denis Blanchflower, William Edward Cunningham, Robert Peacock, William Bingham, Wilbur Cush, Alexander Derek Dougan, James McIlroy, Peter James McParland.
SCOTLAND: William Dallas Fyfe Brown, Eric Caldow, John Davidson Hewie, David Craig MacKay, Robert Evans (Cap), Robert Johnston McCann, Graham Leggat, John Anderson White, Ian St. John, Denis Law, George Mulhall. Manager: Andrew Beattie
Goals: Graham Leggat (25), John Davidson Hewie (34 pen), John Anderson White (41), George Mulhall (54)

211. 18.11.1959   British Championship
ENGLAND v NORTHERN IRELAND 2-1 (1-0)
Wembley, London
Referee: Leo Callaghan (Wales)   Attendance: 60,000
ENGLAND: Ronald Derrick Springettt, Donald Howe, Anthony Allen, Ronald Clayton (Cap), Kenneth Brown, Ronald Flowers, John Michael Connelly, John Norman Haynes, Joseph Henry Baker, Raymond Alan Parry, Edwin Holliday. Manager: Walter Winterbottom
NORTHERN IRELAND: Harry Gregg, Richard Matthewson Keith, Alfred McMichael, Robert Denis Blanchflower, William Edward Cunningham, Robert Peacock, William Bingham, John Andrew Crossan, Wilbur Cush, James McIlroy, Peter James McParland.   Manager: Peter Doherty
Goals: Joseph Henry Baker (16), Raymond Alan Parry (89) / William Bingham (88)

212. 06.04.1960   British Championship
WALES v NORTHERN IRELAND 3-2 (1-0)
The Racecourse, Wrexham
Referee: Not recorded   Attendance: 16,979
WALES: Alfred John Kelsey, Stuart Grenville Williams, Graham Evan Williams, Victor Herbert Crowe, Melvyn Tudor George Nurse, Colin Walter Baker, Terence Cameron Medwin, Philip Abraham Woosnam, Graham Moore, Thomas Royston Vernon, Clifford William Jones.
Trainer: James Patrick Murphy
NORTHERN IRELAND: Harry Gregg, Alexander Russell Elder, Alfred McMichael, Robert Denis Blanchflower, William Edward Cunningham, Wilbur Cush, William Bingham, James McIlroy, William Ian Lawther, Matthew James Hill, Peter James McParland.
Goals: Terence Cameron Medwin (#), Philip Abraham Woosnam (# penalty) / Robert Denis Blanchflower (# penalty), William Bingham (#)

213. 08.10.1960   British Championship
NORTHERN IRELAND v ENGLAND 2-5 (1-2)
Windsor Park, Belfast
Referee: Hugh Phillips (Scotland)   Attendance: 60,000
NORTHERN IRELAND: Harry Gregg, Richard Matthewson Keith, Alexander Russell Elder, Robert Denis Blanchflower, John T. Forde, Robert Peacock, William Bingham, James McIlroy, William John McAdams, Alexander Derek Dougan, Peter James McParland.
ENGLAND: Ronald Derrick Springettt, James Christopher Armfield, Michael McNeil, Robert William Robson, Peter Swan, Ronald Flowers, Bryan Douglas, James Peter Greaves, Robert Alfred Smith, John Norman Haynes (Cap), Robert Charlton.   Manager: Walter Winterbottom
Goals: William John McAdams (36, 53) / Robert Alfred Smith (15), James Peter Greaves (44, 63), Robert Charlton (50), Bryan Douglas (88)

214. 26.10.1960   7th World Cup Qualifiers
NORTHERN IRELAND v WEST GERMANY 3-4 (1-1)
Windsor Park, Belfast
Referee: Leopold Horn (Holland)   Attendance: 40,000
NORTHERN IRELAND: John McClelland, Richard Matthewson Keith, Alexander Russell Elder, Robert Denis Blanchflower (Cap), John T. Forde, Robert Peacock, William Bingham, James McIlroy, William John McAdams, Matthew James Hill, Peter James McParland.
WEST GERMANY: Hans Tilkowski, Herbert Erhardt (Cap), Karl-Heinz Schnellinger, Willi Giesemann, Leo Wilden, Horst Szymaniak, Richard Kreß, Albert Brülls, Uwe Seeler, Günther Herrmann, Gert Dörfel.   Trainer: Josef Herberger
Goals: William John McAdams (25, 51, 89) / Albert Brülls (6), Uwe Seeler (53), Gert Dörfel (54, 80)

215. 09.11.1960   British Championship
SCOTLAND v NORTHERN IRELAND 5-2 (2-0)
Hampden Park, Glasgow
Referee: Kevin Howley (England)   Attendance: 34,564
SCOTLAND: Lawrence Grant Leslie, Duncan Mackay, Eric Caldow (Cap), David Craig MacKay, John Boyd Plenderleith, James Curran Baxter, George Herd, Denis Law, Alexander Young, Ralph Laidlaw Brand, David Wilson.
NORTHERN IRELAND: Harry Gregg, Richard Matthewson Keith, Alexander Russell Elder, Robert Denis Blanchflower, John T. Forde, Robert Peacock, William Bingham, Walter Bruce, William John McAdams, James Joseph Nicholson, Peter James McParland.
Goals: Denis Law (8), Eric Caldow (43 pen), Alexander Young (78), Ralph Laidlaw Brand (81, 90) / Robert Blanchflower (48 pen), Peter James McParland (84)

216. 12.04.1961   British Championship
NORTHERN IRELAND v WALES 1-5 (0-3)
Windsor Park, Belfast
Referee: Not recorded   Attendance: 30,000
NORTHERN IRELAND: John McClelland, Richard Matthewson Keith, Alexander Russell Elder, Robert Denis Blanchflower, William Edward Cunningham, James Joseph Nicholson, Thomas C. Stewart, Alexander Derek Dougan, William John McAdams, James McIlroy, Peter James McParland.
WALES: Alfred John Kelsey, Stuart Grenville Williams, Melvyn Hopkins, Melvyn Charles, Melvyn Tudor George Nurse, Victor Herbert Crowe, Clifford William Jones, Philip Abraham Woosnam, Kenneth Leek, Ivor John Allchurch, George Graham Williams.   Trainer: James Patrick Murphy
Goals: Alexander Derek Dougan (#) / Melvyn Charles (#), Kenneth Leek (#), Ivor John Allchurch (#), Clifford William Jones (#, #)

217. 25.04.1961
ITALY v NORTHERN IRELAND 3-2 (1-0)

Comunale, Bologna

Referee: Jacques Devillers (France)   Attendance: 17,500

ITALY: Giorgio Ghezzi, Giacomo Losi, Mario Trebbi, Cesare Maldini, Sandro Salvadore, Giovanni Trapattoni, Bruno Mora, Romano Fogli, Bruno Nicolè (Cap) (75 Sergio Brighenti II), Omar Enrique Sivori, Gino Stacchini.
Trainer: Giovanni Ferrari

NORTHERN IRELAND: John McClelland, Richard Matthewson Keith, William James McCullough, Martin Harvey, William John Terence Neill, Robert Peacock (Cap), William Bingham, Alexander Derek Dougan, William Ian Lawther, William John McAdams, Peter James McParland.
Manager: Peter Doherty

Goals: Gino Stacchini (30, 58), Omar Enrique Sivori (78) / Alexander Derek Dougan (71), William John McAdams (72)

218. 03.05.1961   7th World Cup Qualifiers
GREECE v NORTHERN IRELAND 2-1 (1-0)

Panathinaikos, Athína

Referee: Eli Priessner (Israel)   Attendance: 15,000

GREECE: Konstantinos Valianos, Giágos Simantiris, Aristeídis Kamaras, Panagiótis Papoulidis, Konstantinos Polyhroniou (Cap), Neotákis Loukanidis, Andréas Stamatiadis, Andréas Papaemmanouil, Apóstolos Vasileiadis, Giórgos Sideris, Antonios Poseidon.   Trainer: Tryfonas Tzanetis

NORTHERN IRELAND: John McClelland, Richard Matthewson Keith, Alexander Russell Elder, Wilbur Cush, William John Terence Neill, Robert Peacock, William Bingham, James McIlroy, William John McAdams, Alexander Derek Dougan, Peter James McParland.

Goals: Andréas Papaemmanouil (10, 75) / James McIlroy (85)

219. 10.05.1961   7th World Cup Qualifiers
WEST GERMANY v NORTHERN IRELAND 2-1 (1-0)

Olympia, West-Berlin

Referee: Curt Lindberg (Sweden)   Attendance: 94,600

WEST GERMANY: Hans Tilkowski, Herbert Erhardt (Cap), Karl-Heinz Schnellinger, Jürgen Werner, Leo Wilden, Horst Szymaniak, Richard Kress, Günther Herrmann, Uwe Seeler, Klaus Stürmer, Albert Brülls.   Trainer: Josef Herberger

NORTHERN IRELAND: John McClelland, Richard Matthewson Keith, Alexander Russell Elder, Robert Denis Blanchflower (Cap), William John Terence Neill, Robert Peacock, William Bingham, Wilbur Cush, William John McAdams, James McIlroy, Peter James McParland.

Goals: Richard Kress (29), Albert Brülls (58) / James McIlroy (85)

220. 07.10.1961   British Championship
NORTHERN IRELAND v SCOTLAND 1-6 (1-3)

Windsor Park, Belfast

Referee: James Finney (England)   Attendance: 41,000

NORTHERN IRELAND: Harry Gregg, Edward James Magill, Alexander Russell Elder, Robert Denis Blanchflower, William John Terence Neill, Robert Peacock, Samuel Wilson, James McIlroy, William Ian Lawther, Matthew James Hill, James Christopher McLaughlin.

SCOTLAND: William Dallas Fyfe Brown, Duncan Mackay, Eric Caldow (Cap), Patrick Timothy Crerand, William McNeill, James Curran Baxter, Alexander Silcock Scott, John Anderson White, Ian St. John, Ralph Laidlaw Brand, David Wilson.
Manager: John Miller McColl

Goals: James Christopher McLaughlin (17) / David Wilson (14), Alexander Silcock Scott (34, 53, 79), Ralph Laidlaw Brand (38, 69)

221. 17.10.1961   7th World Cup Qualifiers
NORTHERN IRELAND v GREECE 2-0 (1-0)

Windsor Park, Belfast

Referee: Pietro Bonetto (Italy)   Attendance: 38,000

NORTHERN IRELAND: Harry Gregg, Edward James Magill, Alexander Russell Elder, Robert Denis Blanchflower (Cap), William John Terence Neill, James Joseph Nicholson, William Bingham, James McIlroy, William John McAdams, Wilbur Cush, James Christopher McLaughlin.

GREECE: Konstantinos Valianos, Aristeídis Kamaras, Dimítris Stefanakos, Athanásios Vasiliou, Konstantinos Polyhroniou (Cap), Panagiótis Papoulidis, Vasílis Mastrakoulis, Andréas Papaemmanouil, Dimítris Domazos, Giórgos Sideris, Antonios Poseidon.
Trainer: Antónis Migiakis

Sent off: Giórgos Sideris (60)

Goals: James Christopher McLaughlin (28, 57)

222. 22.11.1961   British Championship
ENGLAND v NORTHERN IRELAND 1-1 (1-0)

Wembley, London

Referee: Leo Callaghan (Wales)   Attendance: 30,000

ENGLAND: Ronald Derrick Springett, James Christopher Armfield, Ramon Wilson, Robert William Robson, Peter Swan, Ronald Flowers, Bryan Douglas, John Joseph Byrne, Raymond Crawford, John Norman Haynes (Cap), Robert Charlton.
Manager: Walter Winterbottom

NORTHERN IRELAND: Victor Hunter, Edward James Magill, Alexander Russell Elder, Robert Denis Blanchflower, William John Terence Neill, James Joseph Nicholson, William Bingham, Hugh Henry Barr, William John McAdams, James McIlroy, James Christopher McLaughlin.

Goals: Robert Charlton (20) / James McIlroy (81)

223. 11.04.1962   British Championship
WALES v NORTHERN IRELAND 4-0 (2-0)
Ninian Park, Cardiff

Referee: Not recorded   Attendance: 13,250

WALES: Alfred John Kelsey, Stuart Grenville Williams, Melvyn Hopkins, Peter Malcolm Lucas, Harold Michael England, William Terence Hennessey, Leonard Allchurch, Philip Abraham Woosnam, Melvyn Charles, Thomas Royston Vernon, Clifford William Jones.
Trainer: James Patrick Murphy

NORTHERN IRELAND: William Ronald Briggs, Richard Matthewson Keith, William Edward Cunningham, Robert Denis Blanchflower, William John Terence Neill, James Joseph Nicholson, William Humphries, William Cecil Johnston, James O'Neill, James Christopher McLaughlin, Robert Munn Braithwaite.

Goals: Melvyn Charles (#, #, #, #)

224. 09.05.1962
HOLLAND v NORTHERN IRELAND 4-0 (0-0)
Feijenoord, Rotterdam

Referee: Werner Treichel (West Germany)   Att: 30,000

HOLLAND: Peter van de Merwe, Roel Wiersma (Cap), Jan Renders, Fons van Wissen, Tonny Pronk, Bennie Muller, Sjaak Swart, Henk Groot, Tonny van der Linden, Co Prins, Piet van der Kuil.   Trainer: Elek Schwartz

NORTHERN IRELAND: Robert James Irvine, Richard Matthewson Keith, William Edward Cunningham, Martin Harvey, Robert Denis Blanchflower, James Joseph Nicholson, William Humphries, William Ian Lawther, William John McAdams, James McIlroy, Peter James McParland.

Goals: Sjaak Swart (48), Piet van der Kuil (51), Tonny van der Linden (70, 73)

225. 10.10.1962   2nd European Champs, 1st Round
POLAND v NORTHERN IRELAND 0-2 (0-1)
Śląski, Chorzów

Referee: Bertil Wilhelm Lööw (Sweden)   Att: 50,000

POLAND: Edward Szymkowiak, Henryk Szczepański (Cap), Władysław Kawula, Stanisław Oślizło, Ryszard Budka, Bernard Blaut, Lucjan Brychczy, Eugeniusz Faber, Jan Liberda, Norbert Gajda, Roman Lentner.   Manager: Czesław Krug.
Trainer: Ryszard Koncewicz

NORTHERN IRELAND: Robert James Irvine, Edward James Magill, Alexander Russell Elder, Robert Denis Blanchflower (Cap), Samuel Hatton, James Joseph Nicholson, William Humphries, Hugh Henry Barr, Alexander Derek Dougan, James McIlroy, William Bingham.   Manager: Robert Peacock

Goals: Derek Dougan (17), William Humphries (54)

226. 20.10.1962   British Championship
NORTHERN IRELAND v ENGLAND 1-3 (0-1)
Windsor Park, Belfast

Referee: James Barclay (Scotland)   Attendance: 53,750

NORTHERN IRELAND: Robert James Irvine, Edward James Magill, Alexander Russell Elder, Robert Denis Blanchflower, William John Terence Neill, James Joseph Nicholson, William Humphries, Hugh Henry Barr, Samuel Thomas McMillan, James McIlroy, William Bingham.

ENGLAND: Ronald Derrick Springettt, James Christopher Armfield (Cap), Ramon Wilson, Robert Frederick Moore, Brian Leslie Labone, Ronald Flowers, Michael Stephen Hellawell, Frederick Hill, Alan Peacock, James Peter Greaves, Michael O'Grady.   Manager: Walter Winterbottom

Goals: Hugh Henry Barr (62) /
James Peter Greaves (43), Michael O'Grady (75, 85)

227. 07.11.1962   British Championship
SCOTLAND v NORTHERN IRELAND 5-1 (1-1)
Hampden Park, Glasgow

Referee: James Finney (England)   Attendance: 58,734

SCOTLAND: William Dallas Fyfe Brown, Alexander William Hamilton, Eric Caldow (Cap), Patrick Timothy Crerand, John Francombe Ure, James Curran Baxter, William Henderson, John Anderson White, Ian St. John, Denis Law, George Mulhall.   Manager: John Miller McColl

NORTHERN IRELAND: Robert James Irvine, Edward James Magill, Alexander Russell Elder, Robert Denis Blanchflower, Samuel Hatton, James Joseph Nicholson, William Humphries, Samuel Thomas McMillan, Alexander Derek Dougan, James McIlroy, William Bingham.   Manager: Robert Peacock

Goals: Denis Law (40, 64, 77), William Henderson (79), Denis Law (87) / William Bingham (8)

228. 28.11.1962   2nd European Champs, 1st Round
NORTHERN IRELAND v POLAND 2-0 (1-0)
Windsor Park, Belfast

Referee: Othmar Huber (Switzerland)   Attendance: 28,900

NORTHERN IRELAND: Robert James Irvine, Edward James Magill, Alexander Russell Elder, Robert Denis Blanchflower (Cap), William John Terence Neill, James Joseph Nicholson, William Bingham, John Andrew Crossan, Alexander Derek Dougan, James McIlroy, Robert Munn Braithwaite.
Manager: Robert Peacock

POLAND: Edward Szymkowiak, Henryk Szczepański (Cap), Stanisław Oślizło, Włodzimierz Śpiewak, Antoni Nieroba, Ryszard Grzegorczyk, Józef Gałeczka, Lucjan Brychczy, Erwin Wilczek, Roman Lentner, Eugeniusz Faber.
Manager: Czesław Krug.   Trainer: Ryszard Koncewicz

Goals: John Andrew Crossan (9), William Bingham (64)

229. 03.04.1963   British Championship
NORTHERN IRELAND v WALES 1-4 (1-2)
Windsor Park, Belfast

Referee: Not recorded   Attendance: 25,000

NORTHERN IRELAND: Robert James Irvine, Edward James Magill, Alexander Russell Elder, Martin Harvey, Albert Campbell, William John Terence Neill, William Humphries, John Andrew Crossan, William John Irvine, James McIlroy, James Christopher McLaughlin.

WALES: David Michael Hollins, Melvyn Hopkins, Graham Evan Williams, Alwyn Derek Burton, Harold Michael England, Barrington Gerard Hole, Barrie Spencer Jones, Philip Abraham Woosnam, Graham Moore, Ivor John Allchurch, Clifford William Jones.   Trainer: James Patrick Murphy

Goals: Martin Harvey (#) /
Clifford William Jones (#, #, #), Philip Abraham Woosnam (#)

230. 30.05.1963   2nd European Champs, 2nd Round
SPAIN v NORTHERN IRELAND 1-1 (0-0)
San Mames, Bilbao

Referee: Cesare Jonni (Italy)   Attendance: 27,960

SPAIN: José Vicente Traín, Feliciano Ruiz Muñoz Rivilla, Luis María Echeberría, Severino Reija, Francisco García "Paquito", Enrique Pérez "Pachín", AMANCIO Amaro, Félix Ruiz, Delio Morollón, ADELARDO Rodríguez, Enrique Collar (Cap).   Trainer: José Villalonga

NORTHERN IRELAND: Robert James Irvine, Edward James Magill, Alexander Russell Elder, Martin Harvey, William John Terence Neill, William James McCullough, William Bingham, John Andrew Crossan, William John Irvine, William Humphries, Robert Munn Braithwaite.

Goals: AMANCIO Amaro (60) / William John Irvine (76)

231. 12.10.1963   British Championship
NORTHERN IRELAND v SCOTLAND 2-1 (1-0)
Windsor Park, Belfast

Referee: John Keith Taylor (England)   Attendance: 39,000

NORTHERN IRELAND: Harry Gregg, Edward James Magill, John Parke, Martin Harvey, William John Terence Neill, William James McCullough, William Bingham, William Humphries, Samuel Wilson, John Andrew Crossan, Matthew James Hill.   Manager: Robert Peacock

SCOTLAND: William Dallas Fyfe Brown, Alexander William Hamilton, David Provan, Patrick Timothy Crerand, John Francombe Ure, David Craig MacKay (Cap), William Henderson, John Anderson White, Ian St. John, David Wedderburn Gibson, George Mulhall.
Manager: John Miller McColl

Goals: William Bingham (25), Samuel Wilson (63) /
Ian St. John (49)

232. 30.10.1963   2nd European Champs, 2nd Round
NORTHERN IRELAND v SPAIN 0-1 (0-0)
Windsor Park, Belfast

Referee: Andries van Leeuwen (Holland)   Att: 45,809

NORTHERN IRELAND: Victor Hunter, Edward James Magill, John Parke, Martin Harvey, William John Terence Neill, William James McCullough, William Bingham, William Humphries, Samuel Wilson, John Andrew Crossan, Matthew James Hill.

SPAIN: José Casas "Pepín", Feliciano Ruiz Muñoz Rivilla, Fernando Olivella, Severino Reija, Ignacio Zoco, Félix Ruiz, Jesús María Pereda, Luis Del Sol, Domingo Zaldúa, Luis Suárez, Francisco Gento (Cap).   Trainer: José Villalonga

Goal: Francisco Gento (65)

233. 20.11.1963   British Championship
ENGLAND v NORTHERN IRELAND 8-3 (4-1)
Wembley, London

Referee: Leo Callaghan (Wales)   Attendance: 55,000

ENGLAND: Gordon Banks, James Christopher Armfield (Cap), Robert Anthony Thomson, Gordon Milne, Maurice Norman, Robert Frederick Moore, Terence Lionel Paine, James Peter Greaves, Robert Alfred Smith, George Edward Eastham, Robert Charlton.   Manager: Alfred Ramsey

NORTHERN IRELAND: Harry Gregg, Edward James Magill, John Parke, Martin Harvey, William John Terence Neill, William James McCullough, William Bingham, William Humphries, Samuel Wilson, John Andrew Crossan, Matthew James Hill.   Manager: Robert Peacock

Goals: Terence Lionel Paine (2, 37, 64), James Peter Greaves (21, 24, 60, 70), Robert Alfred Smith (48) /
John Andrew Crossan (44), Samuel Wilson (74, 85)

234. 15.04.1964   British Championship
WALES v NORTHERN IRELAND 2-3 (1-3)
Vetch Field, Swansea

Referee: Not recorded   Attendance: 10,343

WALES: Gareth Sprake, Royston Sidney Evans, Graham Evan Williams, Michael George Johnson, Harold Michael England, Barrington Gerard Hole, Barrie Spencer Jones, Graham Moore, Ronald Tudor Davies, Brian Cameron Godfrey, Clifford William Jones.   Trainer: David Bowen

NORTHERN IRELAND: Patrick Anthony Jennings, Edward James Magill, Alexander Russell Elder, Martin Harvey, William John Terence Neill, William James McCullough, George Best, John Andrew Crossan, Samuel Wilson, James Christopher McLaughlin, Robert Munn Braithwaite.

Goals: Brian Godfrey (#), Ronald Tudor Davies (#) /
James Christopher McLaughlin (#), Samuel Wilson (#), Martin Harvey (#)

235. 29.04.1964
NORTHERN IRELAND v URUGUAY 3-0 (1-0)
Windsor Park, Belfast

Referee: Ken Nawley (England)   Attendance: 23,000

NORTHERN IRELAND: Patrick Anthony Jennings, Edward James Magill, Alexander Russell Elder, Martin Harvey, William John Terence Neill, William James McCullough, George Best, John Andrew Crossan, Samuel Wilson, James Christopher McLaughlin, Robert Munn Braithwaite.

URUGUAY: Walter Taibo, William Ruben Martínez, Nelson Díaz, Héctor Carlos Cincunegui, Darcy Pereira, Elbio Ricardo Pavoni, Nelson Flores (Alberto Ferrero), Julio César Cortés, Mario Castro (Néstor Soria), Abayubá Ibañez, Juan Pintos. Trainer: Rafael Milans

Goals: John Andrew Crossan (2 penalties), Samuel Wilson (#)

236. 03.10.1964   British Championship
NORTHERN IRELAND v ENGLAND 3-4 (0-4)
Windsor Park, Belfast

Referee: William Brittle (Scotland)   Attendance: 58,000

NORTHERN IRELAND: Patrick Anthony Jennings, Edward James Magill, Alexander Russell Elder, Martin Harvey, William John Terence Neill, William James McCullough, George Best, John Andrew Crossan, Samuel Wilson, James Christopher McLaughlin, Robert Munn Braithwaite.

ENGLAND: Gordon Banks, George Reginald Cohen, Robert Anthony Thomson, Gordon Milne, Maurice Norman, Robert Frederick Moore (Cap), Terence Lionel Paine, James Peter Greaves, Frederick Pickering, Robert Charlton, Peter Thompson.   Manager: Alfred Ramsey

Goals: Samuel Wilson (52), James McLaughlin (55, 75) / Frederick Pickering (7), James Peter Greaves (15, 24, 27)

237. 14.10.1964   8th World Cup Qualifiers
NORTHERN IRELAND v SWITZERLAND 1-0 (0-0)
Windsor Park, Belfast

Referee: Hubert Burguet (Belgium)   Attendance: 28,598

NORTHERN IRELAND: Patrick Anthony Jennings, Edward James Magill, Alexander Russell Elder, Martin Harvey, William John Terence Neill, William James McCullough, George Best, John Andrew Crossan, Samuel Wilson, James Christopher McLaughlin, Robert Munn Braithwaite.

SWITZERLAND: Karl Elsener, André Grobéty, Ely Tacchella, Heinz Schneiter, Xavier Stierli, Richard Dürr, Jakob Kuhn, Kurt Armbruster, Philippe Pottier, Kurt Grünig, Jean-Claude Schindelholz.   Trainer: Alfredo Foni

Goal: John Andrew Crossan (46 pen)

238. 14.11.1964   8th World Cup Qualifiers
SWITZERLAND v NORTHERN IRELAND 2-1 (2-1)
Olympique de la Pontaise, Lausanne

Referee: Paul Schiller (Austria)   Attendance: 22,162

SWITZERLAND: Karl Elsener, André Grobéty, Ely Tacchella, Heinz Schneiter, Xavier Stierli, Richard Dürr, Jakob Kuhn, Georges Vuilleumier, Robert Hosp, René-Pierre Quentin, Jean-Claude Schindelholz.   Trainer: Alfredo Foni

NORTHERN IRELAND: Patrick Anthony Jennings, Edward James Magill, Alexander Russell Elder, Martin Harvey, Albert Campbell, John Parke, George Best, John Andrew Crossan, William John Irvine, James Christopher McLaughlin, Robert Munn Braithwaite.

Goals: René-Pierre Quentin (29), Jakob Kuhn (37) / George Best (12)

239. 25.11.1964   British Championship
SCOTLAND v NORTHERN IRELAND 3-2 (3-2)
Hampden Park, Glasgow

Referee: Geoffrey Powell (Wales)   Attendance: 48,752

SCOTLAND: Robert Campbell Forsyth, Alexander William Hamilton, James Kennedy, John Greig, John McGrory, Francis McLintock, William Semple Brown Wallace, Denis Law, Alan John Gilzean, James Curran Baxter (Cap), David Wilson. Manager: John Miller McColl

NORTHERN IRELAND: Patrick Anthony Jennings, Edward James Magill, Alexander Russell Elder, Martin Harvey, William John Terence Neill, John Parke, George Best, William Humphries, William John Irvine, John Andrew Crossan, Robert Munn Braithwaite.   Manager: Robert Peacock

Goals: David Wilson (10), Alan John Gilzean (17), David Wilson (31) / George Best (9), William John Irvine (19)

240. 17.03.1965   8th World Cup Qualifiers
NORTHERN IRELAND v HOLLAND 2-1 (1-1)
Windsor Park, Belfast

Referee: Tage Sørensen (Denmark)   Attendance: 35,000

NORTHERN IRELAND: William Ronald Briggs, John Parke, Alexander Russell Elder, Martin Harvey, William John Terence Neill, James Joseph Nicholson, William Humphries, John Andrew Crossan, William John Irvine, David Clements, George Best.

HOLLAND: Eddy Pieters Graafland, Frits Flinkevleugel, Rinus Israël, Daan Schrijvers (Cap), Cor Veldhoen, Bennie Muller, Piet Fransen, Gerard Bergholtz, Hennie van Nee, Henk Groot, Coen Moulijn.   Trainer: Denis Neville

Goals: John Crossan (11), William John Terence Neill (62) / Hennie van Nee (6)

241. 31.03.1965   British Championship
NORTHERN IRELAND v WALES 0-5 (0-2)
Windsor Park, Belfast

Referee: Not recorded   Attendance: 15,000

NORTHERN IRELAND: Robert James Irvine, John Parke, Alexander Russell Elder, Martin Harvey, William John Terence Neill, James Joseph Nicholson, William Humphries, John Andrew Crossan, William John Irvine, James Christopher McLaughlin, David Clements.

WALES: David Michael Hollins, Peter Joseph Rodrigues, Graham Evan Williams, Cyril Lea, Harold Michael England, Barrington Gerard Hole, Clifford William Jones, Ivor John Allchurch, Ronald Wyn Davies, Thomas Royston Vernon, Ronald Raymond Rees.   Trainer: David Bowen

Goals: Thomas Royston Vernon (#, #), Clifford Jones (#), Graham Evan Williams (#), Ivor John Allchurch (#)

242. 07.04.1965   8th World Cup Qualifiers
HOLLAND v NORTHERN IRELAND 0-0
Feijenoord, Rotterdam

Referee: William Clements (England)   Attendance: 61,954

HOLLAND: Eddy Pieters Graafland, Frits Flinkevleugel, Daan Schrijvers (Cap), Rinus Israël, Cor Veldhoen, Guus Haak, Theo Laseroms, Pierre Kerkhoffs, Co Prins, Henk Groot, Coen Moulijn.   Trainer: Denis Neville

NORTHERN IRELAND: Patrick Anthony Jennings, Edward James Magill, Alexander Russell Elder, Martin Harvey, William John Terence Neill, John Parke, George Best, John Andrew Crossan, William John Irvine, James Joseph Nicholson, Robert Munn Braithwaite.

243. 07.05.1965   8th World Cup Qualifiers
NORTHERN IRELAND v ALBANIA 4-1 (2-0)
Windsor Park, Belfast

Referee: Norman Mootz (Luxembourg)   Attendance: 16,017

NORTHERN IRELAND: Patrick Anthony Jennings, Edward James Magill, Alexander Russell Elder, Martin Harvey, William John Terence Neill, John Parke, William Humphries, John Andrew Crossan, William John Irvine, James Joseph Nicholson, George Best.

ALBANIA: Mikel Janku, Fathbardh Deliallisi, Skënder Halili, Fatmir Frashëri, Ali Mema, Lin Shllaku, Panajot Pano, Ramazan Rragami, Fiqiri Thoma Duro, Pavllo Bukoviku, Robert Jashari.   Trainer: Zyber Konçi

Goals: John Crossan (16, 31, 61 pen), George Best (85) / Robert Jashari (49)

244. 02.10.1965   British Championship
NORTHERN IRELAND v SCOTLAND 3-2 (1-1)
Windsor Park, Belfast

Referee: John Keith Taylor (England)   Attendance: 50,000

NORTHERN IRELAND: Patrick Anthony Jennings, Edward James Magill, Alexander Russell Elder, Martin Harvey, William John Terence Neill, James Joseph Nicholson, James McIlroy, John Andrew Crossan, William John Irvine, Alexander Derek Dougan, George Best.   Manager: Robert Peacock

SCOTLAND: William Dallas Fyfe Brown, Alexander William Hamilton, Edward Graham McCreadie, David Craig MacKay, William McNeill (Cap), John Greig, William Henderson, Denis Law, Alan John Gilzean, James Curran Baxter, John Hughes.   Manager: John Stein

Goals: Alexander Dougan (42), John Andrew Crossan (59), William John Irvine (89) / Alan John Gilzean (17, 81)

245. 10.11.1965   British Championship
ENGLAND v NORTHERN IRELAND 2-1 (1-1)
Wembley, London

Referee: Leo Callaghan (Wales)   Attendance: 70,000

ENGLAND: Gordon Banks, George Reginald Cohen, Ramon Wilson, Norbert Peter Stiles, John "Jack" Charlton, Robert Frederick Moore (Cap), Peter Thompson, Joseph Henry Baker, Alan Peacock, Robert Charlton, John Michael Connelly.   Manager: Alfred Ramsey

NORTHERN IRELAND: Patrick Anthony Jennings, Edward James Magill, Alexander Russell Elder, Martin Harvey, William John Terence Neill, James Joseph Nicholson, James McIlroy, John Andrew Crossan, William John Irvine, Alexander Derek Dougan, George Best.   Manager: Robert Peacock

Goals: Joseph Henry Baker (19), Alan Peacock (89) / William John Irvine (20)

246. 24.11.1965   8th World Cup Qualifiers
ALBANIA v NORTHERN IRELAND 1-1 (0-0)
Qemal Stafa, Tiranë

Referee: Petre Sotir (România)   Attendance: 16,381

ALBANIA: Mikel Janku, Fatmir Frashëri, Skënder Halili, Gëzim Kasmi, Ali Mema, Lin Shllaku, Foto Andoni, Ramazan Rragami, Medin Zhega, Mexhit Haxhiu, Bashkim Rudi.   Trainer: Loro Boriçi

NORTHERN IRELAND: Patrick Anthony Jennings, Edward James Magill, Alexander Russell Elder, Martin Harvey, William John Terence Neill, James Joseph Nicholson, James McIlroy, John Andrew Crossan, William John Irvine, Alexander Derek Dougan, George Best.

Goals: Medin Zhega (77), William John Irvine (58)

247. 30.03.1966   British Championship
WALES v NORTHERN IRELAND 1-4 (0-2)
Ninian Park, Cardiff
Referee: Not recorded   Attendance: 12,860
WALES: Gareth Sprake, Peter Joseph Rodrigues, Graham Evan Williams, William Terence Hennessey, Harold Michael England, Barrington Gerard Hole, Ronald Raymond Rees, Thomas Royston Vernon, Ronald Wyn Davies, Graham Moore, Gilbert Ivor Reece.   Trainer: David Bowen
NORTHERN IRELAND: Patrick Anthony Jennings, Edward James Magill, Alexander Russell Elder, Martin Harvey, William John Terence Neill, James Joseph Nicholson, Eric Welsh, Samuel Wilson, William John Irvine, Alexander Derek Dougan, James Christopher McLaughlin.
Goals: Ronald Wyn Davies (#) / William John Irvine (#), Samuel Wilson (#), Eric Welsh (#), Martin Harvey (#)

248. 07.05.1966
NORTHERN IRELAND v WEST GERMANY 0-2 (0-1)
Windsor Park, Belfast
Referee: Hugh Phillips (Scotland)   Attendance: 22,000
NORTHERN IRELAND: Patrick Anthony Jennings, Edward James Magill, John Parke, Martin Harvey, Robert John Napier, William John Terence Neill, Eric Welsh, John Andrew Crossan, Samuel Wilson, Alexander Derek Dougan, Vic McKinney.
WEST GERMANY: Günter Bernard, Friedel Lutz, Horst-Dieter Höttges (46 Josef Piontek), Franz Beckenbauer, Willi Schulz, Wolfgang Weber, Jürgen Grabowski, Wolfgang Overath, Uwe Seeler (Cap), Peter Grosser, Alfred Heiss. Trainer: Helmut Schön
Goals: Uwe Seeler (21), Alfred Heiss (57)

249. 22.06.1966
NORTHERN IRELAND v MEXICO 4-1 (0-0)
Windsor Park, Belfast
Referee: John Keith Taylor (England)   Attendance: 12,000
NORTHERN IRELAND: John McClelland, Edward James Magill, Alexander Russell Elder, Martin Harvey, William John Terence Neill, James Joseph Nicholson, Eric Welsh, William Ferguson, William John Irvine (William Cecil Johnston), Alexander Derek Dougan, David Clements (Samuel John Todd).
MEXICO: Ignacio Calderon, Arturo Chaires, Gustavo Pena, Gabriel Nunez, Guillermo Hernandez, Felipe Ruvalcaba, Isodoro Diaz (39 Javier Vargas), Aaron Padilla, Javier Fragoso, Ernesto Cisneros, Magdaleno Mercado.
Sent off : Ignacio Calderon (38)
Goals: William Johnston (#), Alexander Russell Elder (#), James Joseph Nicholson (#), William Ferguson (#) / Gustavo Pena (52)

250. 22.10.1966   3rd European Champs Qualifiers, British Championship
NORTHERN IRELAND v ENGLAND 0-2 (0-1)
Windsor Park, Belfast
Referee: Robert Holley Davidson (Scotland)   Att: 48,600
NORTHERN IRELAND: Patrick Anthony Jennings (46 William Stewart McFaul), John Parke, Alexander Russell Elder, Samuel John Todd, Martin Harvey, William James McCullough, William Ferguson, John Andrew Crossan, William John Irvine, Alexander Derek Dougan.
ENGLAND: Gordon Banks, George Reginald Cohen, Ramon Wilson, Norbert Peter Stiles, John "Jack" Charlton, Robert Frederick Moore (Cap), Alan James Ball, Geoffrey Charles Hurst, Robert Charlton, Roger Hunt, Martin Stanford Peters. Manager: Alfred Ramsey
Sent off: George Best
Goals: Roger Hunt (40), Martin Stanford Peters (59)

251. 16.11.1966   3rd European Champs Qualifiers, British Championship
SCOTLAND v NORTHERN IRELAND 2-1 (2-1)
Hampden Park, Glasgow
Referee: John Keith Taylor (England)   Attendance: 45,281
SCOTLAND: Robert Ferguson, John Greig (Cap), Thomas Gemmell, William John Bremner, Ronald McKinnon, John Clark, William Henderson, Robert White Murdoch, Joseph McBride, Stephen Chalmers, Robert Lennox. Manager: Malcolm MacDonald
NORTHERN IRELAND: Patrick Anthony Jennings, John Parke, Alexander Russell Elder, Martin Harvey, William John Terence Neill, James Joseph Nicholson, Samuel Wilson, John Andrew Crossan, William John Irvine, Alexander Derek Dougan, David Clements.   Manager: Robert Peacock
Goals: Robert White Murdoch (14), Robert Lennox (35) / James Joseph Nicholson (9)

252. 12.04.1967   3rd European Champs Qualifiers, British Championship
NORTHERN IRELAND v WALES 0-0
Windsor Park, Belfast
Referee: Kevin Howley (England)   Attendance: 17,770
NORTHERN IRELAND: Roderick McKenzie, David James Craig, Alexander Russell Elder, Arthur Stewart, William John Terence Neill, James Joseph Nicholson, Eric Welsh, Daniel Trainor, Alexander Derek Dougan, Walter Bruce, David Clements.
WALES: Anthony Horace Millington, Roderick John Thomas, Graham Evan Williams, Alan Leslie Jarvis, Edward Glyn James, Barrington Gerard Hole, Ronald Raymond Rees, William Alan Durban, Ronald Tudor Davies, Thomas Royston Vernon, Keith David Pring.   Trainer: David Bowen

46

253. 21.10.1967   3rd European Champs Qualifiers, British Championship

NORTHERN IRELAND v SCOTLAND 1-0 (0-0)

Windsor Park, Belfast

Referee: James Finney (England)   Attendance: 55,000

NORTHERN IRELAND: Patrick Anthony Jennings, William McKeag, John Parke, Arthur Stewart, William John Terence Neill, David Clements, William Gibson Campbell, John Andrew Crossan, Alexander Derek Dougan, James Joseph Nicholson, George Best.   Manager: William Bingham

SCOTLAND: Ronald Campbell Simpson, Thomas Gemmell, Edward Graham McCreadie, John Greig (Cap), Ronald McKinnon, John Francombe Ure, William Semple Brown Wallace, Robert White Murdoch, James McCalliog, Denis Law, William Morgan.   Manager: Robert Brown

Goal: David Clements (68)

254. 22.11.1967   3rd European Champs Qualifiers, British Championship

ENGLAND v NORTHERN IRELAND 2-0 (1-0)

Wembley, London

Referee: Leo Callaghan (Wales)   Attendance: 85,000

ENGLAND: Gordon Banks, George Reginald Cohen, Ramon Wilson, Alan Patrick Mullery, David Sadler, Robert Frederick Moore (Cap), Peter Thompson, Roger Hunt, Robert Charlton, Geoffrey Charles Hurst, Martin Stanford Peters.   Manager: Alfred Ramsey

NORTHERN IRELAND: Patrick Anthony Jennings, John Parke, Alexander Russell Elder, Arthur Stewart, William John Terence Neill, Martin Harvey, William Gibson Campbell, William John Irvine, Samuel Wilson, James Joseph Nicholson, David Clements.

Goals: Geoffrey Charles Hurst (43), Robert Charlton (62)

255. 28.02.1968   3rd European Champs Qualifiers, British Championship

WALES v NORTHERN IRELAND 2-0 (0-0)

The Racecourse, Wrexham

Referee: Robert Holley Davidson (Scotland)   Att: 17,548

WALES: Anthony Horace Millington, Peter Joseph Rodrigues, Colin Robert Green, William Terence Hennessey, Harold Michael England, Barrington Gerard Hole, Ronald Raymond Rees, Ronald Wyn Davies, Ronald Tudor Davies, William Alan Durban, Graham Evan Williams.   Trainer: David Bowen

NORTHERN IRELAND: Patrick Anthony Jennings, David James Craig, Alexander Russell Elder, Martin Harvey, Samuel John Todd, William McKeag, William John Irvine, Arthur Stewart, Alexander Derek Dougan, James Joseph Nicholson, John Terence Harkin.

Goals: Ronald Raymond Rees (75), Ronald Wyn Davies (84)

256. 10.09.1968

ISRAEL v NORTHERN IRELAND 2-3 (0-3)

Bloomfield, Jaffa, Tel-Aviv

Referee: Dittmar Huber (Switzerland)   Attendance: 20,000

ISRAEL: Haim Levin (Shmuel Melika), Shraga Bar, Zvi Rozen, Yeshaayahu Schwager, Menahem Bello, Giora Spiegel, Shmuel Rosenthal, Mordechai Spiegler, Rahamin Talbi, Yehosua Feigenbaum, Reuoven Young (George Borba).   Trainer: Imanuel Shefer

NORTHERN IRELAND: Patrick Anthony Jennings, Patrick James Rice, Thomas Jackson, Arthur Stewart, William John Terence Neill, Martin Harvey, David Sloan, Alexander McMordie, Alexander Derek Dougan (Raymond Gaston), William John Irvine, William Eric Ross.

Goals: Mordechai Spiegler (51), Rahamin Talbi (63) / William John Irvine (5, 39), Alexander Derek Dougan (20)

257. 23.10.1968   9th World Cup Qualifiers

NORTHERN IRELAND v TURKEY 4-1 (1-1)

Windsor Park, Belfast

Referee: Willem Schalks (Holland)   Attendance: 38,363

NORTHERN IRELAND: Patrick Anthony Jennings, David James Craig (Arthur Stewart), Martin Harvey, James Joseph Nicholson, William John Terence Neill, David Clements, William Gibson Campbell, Alexander McMordie, Alexander Derek Dougan, William John Irvine, George Best.

TURKEY: Nıhat Akbay, Şükrü Birant, Necdet Yıldırım, Ismail Arca, Yılmaz Şen, Ercan Aktuna, Mesut Şen (Abdullah Çevrim), Sanlı Sarıalioğlu, Ogün Altıparmak, Can Bartu, Ender Konca.   Trainer: Adnan Suvari

Goals: George Best (32), Alexander McMordie (48), Alexander Derek Dougan (65), William Gibson Campbell (76) / Ogün Altıparmak (9)

258. 11.12.1968   9th World Cup Qualifiers

TURKEY v NORTHERN IRELAND 0-3 (0-1)

Mithat Paşa, Istanbul

Referee: Zanlin Ben Ganif (Algeria)   Attendance: 19,110

TURKEY: Ali Artuner, Talat Özkarslı, Hüseyin Yazıcı, Ercan Aktuna, Ergün Acuner, Sanlı Sarıalioğlu, Ayhan Elmastaşoğlu, Gürsel Aksel, Ogün Altıparmak, Fevzi Zemzem, Metin Oktay (Faruk Karadoğan).   Trainer: Adnan Suvari

NORTHERN IRELAND: Patrick Anthony Jennings, David James Craig, Martin Harvey, James Joseph Nicholson, William John Terence Neill, Arthur Stewart, Bryan Hamilton, Alexander McMordie, Alexander Derek Dougan, John Terence Harkin, David Clements.

Goals: John Harkin (34, 87), James Joseph Nicholson (53)

259. 03.05.1969   British Championship
NORTHERN IRELAND v ENGLAND 1-3 (0-1)
Windsor Park, Belfast

Referee: Joseph William Mullan (Scotland)   Att: 23,000

NORTHERN IRELAND: Patrick Anthony Jennings, David James Craig, Martin Harvey (Alexander Russell Elder), Samuel John Todd, William John Terence Neill, James Joseph Nicholson, Alexander McMordie, Thomas Jackson, Alexander Derek Dougan, William John Irvine, George Best.

ENGLAND: Gordon Banks, Keith Robert Newton, Robert McNab, Alan Patrick Mullery, Brian Leslie Labone, Robert Frederick Moore (Cap), Alan James Ball, Francis Henry Lee, Robert Charlton, Geoffrey Charles Hurst, Martin Stanford Peters.   Manager: Alfred Ramsey

Goals: Alexander McMordie (64) / Martin Peters (39), Francis Henry Lee (64), Geoffrey Charles Hurst (74 pen)

260. 06.05.1969   British Championship
SCOTLAND v NORTHERN IRELAND 1-1 (0-1)
Hampden Park, Glasgow

Referee: David Smith (England)   Attendance: 7,483

SCOTLAND: James Herriot, Thomas Gemmell, Edward Graham McCreadie, William John Bremner (Cap), John Greig, Patrick Gordon Stanton, William Henderson, Robert White Murdoch, Colin Anderson Stein, Denis Law, Charles Cooke (75 William McClure Johnston).   Manager: Robert Brown

NORTHERN IRELAND: Patrick Anthony Jennings, David James Craig, Alexander Russell Elder, Samuel John Todd, William John Terence Neill, James Joseph Nicholson, George Best, Alexander McMordie, Alexander Derek Dougan, Thomas Jackson, David Clements.   Manager: William Bingham

Goals: Colin Anderson Stein (53) / Alexander McMordie (11)

261. 10.05.1969   British Championship
NORTHERN IRELAND v WALES 0-0
Windsor Park, Belfast

Referee: Not recorded   Attendance: 12,500

NORTHERN IRELAND: Patrick Anthony Jennings, David James Craig, Alexander Russell Elder, Samuel John Todd, William John Terence Neill, James Joseph Nicholson, George Best, Alexander McMordie, Alexander Derek Dougan, Thomas Jackson, David Clements (John Terence Harkin).

WALES: Gareth Sprake, Peter Joseph Rodrigues (Colin Robert Green), Roderick John Thomas, William Alan Durban, David Powell, Alwyn Derek Burton, Ronald Tudor Davies, John Benjamin Toshack, Ronald Wyn Davies, Graham Moore, Barrie Spencer Jones.   Trainer: David Bowen

262. 10.09.1969   9th World Cup Qualifiers
NORTHERN IRELAND v SOVIET UNION 0-0
Windsor Park, Belfast

Referee: Michel Kitabdjian (France)   Attendance: 35,138

NORTHERN IRELAND: Patrick Anthony Jennings, Patrick James Rice, Alexander Russell Elder, Samuel John Todd, William John Terence Neill, James Joseph Nicholson, William Gibson Campbell, Alexander McMordie, Alexander Derek Dougan, David Clements (Thomas Jackson), George Best.

SOVIET UNION: Evgeniy Rudakov, Revaz Dzodzuashvili, Albert Shesternev (Cap), Evgeniy Lovchev, Vladimir Kaplichniy, Valentin Afonin, Vladimir Muntyan, Nikolay Kiselev, Anatoliy Puzach, Galimzyan Khusainov, Vitaliy Khmelnitzkiy (75 Gennadiy Evryuzhikhin).
Trainer: Gavril Kachalin

263. 22.10.1969   British Championship
SOVIET UNION v NORTHERN IRELAND 2-0 (1-0)
Lenin, Moskva

Referee: Rudolf Scheurer (Switzerland)   Att: 102,000

SOVIET UNION: Evgeniy Rudakov, Revaz Dzodzuashvili, Albert Shesternev (Cap), Evgeniy Lovchev, Vladimir Kaplichniy, Viktor Serebryanikov, Vladimir Muntyan, Kakhi Asatiani, Mikhail Gershkovich (68 Anatoliy Puzach), Anatoliy Byshovets, Givi Nodia.   Trainer: Gavril Kachalin

NORTHERN IRELAND: Patrick Anthony Jennings, David James Craig, Martin Harvey, Alan Hunter, William John Terence Neill, James Joseph Nicholson, Daniel Hegan, Thomas Jackson, Alexander Derek Dougan, John Terence Harkin, David Clements.

Goals: Givi Nodia (24), Anatoliy Byshovets (79)

264. 18.04.1970   British Championship
NORTHERN IRELAND v SCOTLAND 0-1 (0-1)
Windsor Park, Belfast

Referee: Eric Jennings (England)   Attendance: 31,000

NORTHERN IRELAND: Patrick Anthony Jennings, David James Craig, David Clements, Samuel John Todd (46 William James O'Kane), William John Terence Neill (Cap), James Joseph Nicholson, William Gibson Campbell (75 Desmond Dickson), Robert John Lutton, Alexander Derek Dougan, Alexander McMordie, George Best.
Manager: William Bingham

SCOTLAND: Robert Brown Clark, David Hay, William Dickson, Francis McLintock (Cap), Ronald McKinnon, Robert Moncur, Thomas McLean, William McInnany Carr, John O'Hare, Alan John Gilzean (70 Colin Anderson Stein), William McClure Johnston.   Manager: Robert Brown

Goal: John O'Hare (58)

265. 21.04.1970   British Championship
ENGLAND v NORTHERN IRELAND 3-1 (1-0)
Wembley, London
Referee: Gaspar Pintado Viu (Spain)   Attendance: 100,000

ENGLAND: Gordon Banks, Keith Robert Newton (82 Colin Bell), Emlyn Walter Hughes, Alan Patrick Mullery, Robert Frederick Moore, Norbert Peter Stiles, Ralph Coates, Brian Kidd, Robert Charlton (Cap), Geoffrey Charles Hurst, Martin Stanford Peters.   Manager: Alfred Ramsey

NORTHERN IRELAND: Patrick Anthony Jennings, David James Craig, David Clements, William James O'Kane, William John Terence Neill (Cap), James Joseph Nicholson, Alexander McMordie, George Best, Alexander Derek Dougan, Anthony O'Doherty (Samuel Nelson), Robert John Lutton (John Cowan).   Manager: William Bingham

Goals: Martin Peters (6), Geoffrey Charles Hurst (57), Robert Charlton (81) / George Best (50)

266. 25.04.1970   British Championship
WALES v NORTHERN IRELAND 1-0 (1-0)
Vetch Field, Swansea
Referee: Not recorded   Attendance: 28,000

WALES: Anthony Horace Millington, Peter Joseph Rodrigues, Roderick John Thomas, William Terence Hennessey, Harold Michael England, David Powell, Richard Lech Krzywicki, William Alan Durban, Ronald Tudor Davies, Graham Moore, Ronald Raymond Rees.   Trainer: David Bowen

NORTHERN IRELAND: William Stewart McFaul, David James Craig, Samuel Nelson, William James O'Kane, William John Terence Neill (Cap), James Joseph Nicholson, William Gibson Campbell (Anthony O'Doherty), George Best, Desmond Dickson, Alexander McMordie, David Clements.   Manager: William Bingham

Goal: Ronald Raymond Rees

267. 11.11.1970   4th European Champs Qualifiers
SPAIN v NORTHERN IRELAND 3-0 (1-0)
Ramón Sánchez Pizjuán, Sevilla
Referee: Gyula Emsberger (Hungary)   Attendance: 26,215

SPAIN: José Ángel Iribar, Joaquin Rifé, Francisco Fernández "Gallego", Juan Carlos Cruz Sol (46 Juan López Hita), Enrique Alvarez Costas, José Luis Violeta, Estéban Arieta, LUIS Aragonés (Cap), Enrique Castro "Quini" (46 Enrique Lora), José Martínez "Pirri", Carlos Rexach.
Trainer: Ladislao Kubala

NORTHERN IRELAND: William Stewart McFaul, David James Craig, Samuel Nelson, Thomas Jackson, William John Terence Neill, William James O'Kane, David Sloan, George Best, Alexander Derek Dougan (Cap) (21 Samuel John Todd), John Terence Harkin, David Clements.
Manager: William Bingham

Goals: Carlos Rexach (39), José Martínez "Pirri" (59), LUIS Aragonés (76)

268. 03.02.1971   4th European Champs Qualifiers
CYPRUS v NORTHERN IRELAND 0-3 (0-0)
GSP, Nicosia
Referee: Francesco Francescon (Italy)   Attendance: 9,119

CYPRUS: Herodotos Koupanos, Kóstas Hristou Kattos (75 Lakis Theodorou), Dimos Kavazis, Kyriakos Koureas, Stefanis Mihaíl, Kallis Konstantínou, Níkos Haralámpous, Pamboulis Papadopoulos, Pavlos Vasileiou, Pashalis Fokkis, Andreas Stylianou.   Trainer: Ray Wood

NORTHERN IRELAND: Patrick Anthony Jennings, David James Craig, Samuel Nelson, Alan Hunter, William John Terence Neill, Samuel John Todd, Bryan Hamilton, Alexander McMordie, Alexander Derek Dougan (Cap), James Joseph Nicholson, George Best.   Manager: William Bingham

Goals: James Nicholson (53), Alexander Derek Dougan (55), George Best (86 pen)

269. 21.04.1971   4th European Champs Qualifiers
NORTHERN IRELAND v CYPRUS 5-0 (2-0)
Windsor Park, Belfast
Referee: Jacques Colling (Luxembourg)   Attendance: 19,153

NORTHERN IRELAND: Patrick Anthony Jennings, David James Craig, David Clements, Martin Harvey, Alan Hunter, Samuel John Todd (86 Peter Watson), Bryan Hamilton, Alexander McMordie, Alexander Derek Dougan (Cap), James Joseph Nicholson, George Best.   Manager: William Bingham

CYPRUS: Herodotos Koupanos, Kokos Mihaíl (54 Lakis Theodorou), Dimos Kavazis, Stefanis Mihaíl (65 Takis Papettas), Kyriakos Koureas, Kallis Konstantínou, Tassos Konstantínou, Pavlos Vasileiou, Pamboulis Papadopoulos, Pashalis Fokkis, Andreas Stylianou.   Trainer: Ray Wood

Goals: Alexander Dougan (20), George Best (44, 47, 56), James Joseph Nicholson (85)

270. 15.05.1971   British Championship
NORTHERN IRELAND v ENGLAND 0-1 (0-0)
Windsor Park, Belfast
Referee: Alistair McKenzie (Scotland)   Attendance: 33,000

NORTHERN IRELAND: Patrick Anthony Jennings, Patrick James Rice, Samuel Nelson, William James O'Kane, Alan Hunter, James Joseph Nicholson, Bryan Hamilton, Alexander McMordie (Thomas Cassidy), Alexander Derek Dougan (Cap), David Clements, George Best.   Manager: William Bingham

ENGLAND: Gordon Banks, Paul Edward Madeley, Terence Cooper, Peter Edwin Storey, Roy Leslie McFarland, Robert Frederick Moore (Cap), Francis Henry Lee, Alan James Ball, Martin Harcourt Chivers, Allan John Clarke, Martin Stanford Peters.   Manager: Alfred Ramsey

Goal: Allan John Clarke (80)

49

271. 18.05.1971   British Championship
SCOTLAND v NORTHERN IRELAND 0-1 (0-1)
Hampden Park, Glasgow

Referee: Clive Thomas (Wales)   Attendance: 31,643

SCOTLAND: Robert Brown Clark, David Hay, James Andrew Brogan, John Greig, Francis McLintock (71 Francis Michael Munro), Robert Moncur (Cap), Peter Patrick Lorimer, Anthony Green, Edwin Gray, Hugh Patrick Curran, John O'Hare (46 Andrew Jarvie).   Manager: Robert Brown

NORTHERN IRELAND: Patrick Anthony Jennings, Patrick James Rice, Samuel Nelson, William James O'Kane, Alan Hunter, James Joseph Nicholson, Bryan Hamilton, Alexander McMordie (67 David James Craig), Alexander Derek Dougan (Cap), David Clements, George Best.
Manager: William Bingham

Goal: John Greig (14 own goal)

272. 22.05.1971   British Championship
NORTHERN IRELAND v WALES 1-0 (1-0)
Windsor Park, Belfast

Referee: Not recorded   Attendance: 20,000

NORTHERN IRELAND: Patrick Anthony Jennings, Patrick James Rice, Samuel Nelson, William James O'Kane, Alan Hunter, James Joseph Nicholson (Martin Harvey), Bryan Hamilton, Alexander McMordie, Alexander Derek Dougan (Cap), David Clements, George Best.
Manager: William Bingham

WALES: Gareth Sprake, Peter Joseph Rodrigues, Roderick John Thomas, Edward Glyn James, John Griffith Roberts, Terence Charles Yorath, Leighton Phillips (Ronald Raymond Rees), William Alan Durban, Ronald Tudor Davies, John Benjamin Toshack, Gilbert Ivor Reece.
Trainer: David Bowen

Goal: Bryan Hamilton (#)

273. 22.09.1971   4th European Champs Qualifiers
**SOVIET UNION
v NORTHERN IRELAND 1-0** (1-0)
Lenin, Moskva

Referee: Ove Dahlberg (Sweden)   Attendance: 75,000

SOVIET UNION: Evgeniy Rudakov, Revaz Dzodzuashvili, Albert Shesternev (Cap), Valeriy Zykov, Murtaz Khurtzilava, Viktor Kolotov, Vladimir Muntyan, Oleg Dolmatov, Vladimir Fedotov, Vitaliy Shevchenko (74 Levon Ishtoyan), Gennadiy Evryuzhikhin.   Trainer: Vladimir Nikolaev

NORTHERN IRELAND: William Stewart McFaul, David James Craig (70 Bryan Hamilton), William John Terence Neill (Cap), Alan Hunter, Samuel Nelson, Daniel Hegan, David Clements, James Joseph Nicholson, William James O'Kane, Alexander Derek Dougan, George Best.
Manager: Terence Neill

Goal: Vladimir Muntyan (43 pen)

274. 13.10.1971   4th European Champs Qualifiers
**NORTHERN IRELAND
v SOVIET UNION 1-1** (1-1)
Windsor Park, Belfast

Referee: Rolf Nyhus (Norway)   Attendance: 16,573

NORTHERN IRELAND: Patrick Anthony Jennings, Patrick James Rice, Samuel Nelson, James Joseph Nicholson, Alan Hunter, William James O'Kane, Alexander McMordie, Bryan Hamilton (65 Martin Hugh Michael O'Neill), William John Terence Neill (Cap), Alexander Derek Dougan (46 Thomas Cassidy), David Clements.   Manager: Terence Neill

SOVIET UNION: Evgeniy Rudakov, Revaz Dzodzuashvili, Albert Shesternev (Cap), Evgeniy Lovchev, Murtaz Khurtzilava, Viktor Kolotov, Nikolay Kiselev, Oleg Dolmatov, Anatoliy Konkov, Anatoliy Byshovets, Vitaliy Shevchenko (60 Levon Ishtoyan).   Trainer: Vladimir Nikolaev

Goals: James Joseph Nicholson (13) / Anatoliy Byshovets (32)

275. 16.02.1972   4th European Champs Qualifiers
NORTHERN IRELAND v SPAIN 1-1 (0-1)
Boothferry Park, Hull

Referee: John Keith Taylor (England)   Attendance: 19,925

NORTHERN IRELAND: Patrick Anthony Jennings, Patrick James Rice, Samuel Nelson, William John Terence Neill, Alan Hunter, David Clements, Bryan Hamilton (46 Martin Hugh Michael O'Neill), Alexander McMordie, Samuel John Morgan, Samuel Baxter McIlroy, George Best.   Manager: Terence Neill

SPAIN: José Ángel Iribar, Juan Carlos Cruz Sol, Francisco Fernández "Gallego" (Cap), Enrique Alvarez Costas, Antonio Alfonso Moreno "Tonono", Gregorio Benito, Francisco Javier Aguilar, Enrique Lora (67 Miguel Ramos "Migueli"), Joaquín Sierra "Quino", Enrique Castro "Quini" (28 Manuel Rios "Manolete"), José Francisco Rojo I.   Trainer: Ladislao Kubala

Goals: Samuel John Morgan (72) / José Francisco Rojo (41)

276. 20.05.1972   British Championship
SCOTLAND v NORTHERN IRELAND 2-0 (0-0)
Hampden Park, Glasgow

Referee: Clive Thomas (Wales)   Attendance: 39,710

SCOTLAND: Robert Brown Clark, John Jack Brownlie, William Donachie, Robert Moncur, William McNeill, James Connolly Johnstone (61 Peter Patrick Lorimer), William John Bremner (Cap), George Graham, Archibald Gemmill, John O'Hare, Denis Law.   Manager: Thomas Docherty

NORTHERN IRELAND: Patrick Anthony Jennings, Patrick James Rice, Samuel Nelson, William John Terence Neill, Alan Hunter, David Clements (83 David James Craig), Daniel Hegan, Alexander McMordie (68 Samuel Baxter McIlroy), Alexander Derek Dougan, William John Irvine, Thomas Jackson.   Manager: Terence Neill

Goals: Denis Law (86), Peter Patrick Lorimer (89)

50

277. 23.05.1972   British Championship
ENGLAND v NORTHERN IRELAND 0-1 (0-1)
Wembley, London

Referee: William John Gow (Wales)   Attendance: 64,000

ENGLAND: Peter Leslie Shilton, Colin Todd, Emlyn Walter Hughes, Peter Edwin Storey, Laurence Valentine Lloyd, Norman Hunter, Michael George Summerbee, Colin Bell (Cap), Malcolm Ian Macdonald (69 Martin Harcourt Chivers), Rodney William Marsh, Anthony William Currie (58 Martin Stanford Peters).   Manager: Alfred Ramsey

NORTHERN IRELAND: Patrick Anthony Jennings, Patrick James Rice, Samuel Nelson, William John Terence Neill (Cap), Alan Hunter, David Clements, Daniel Hegan, Alexander McMordie, Alexander Derek Dougan, William John Irvine, Thomas Jackson.   Manager: Terence Neill

Goal: William John Terence Neill (33)

278. 27.05.1972   British Championship
WALES v NORTHERN IRELAND 0-0
The Racecourse, Wrexham

Referee: John Taylor (England)   Attendance: 15,647

WALES: Gareth Sprake, Malcolm Edward Page, Roderick John Thomas, Harold Michael England, John Griffith Roberts, Terence Charles Yorath (Peter Joseph Rodrigues), William Alan Durban, Ronald Wyn Davies, Gilbert Ivor Reece, Ronald Tudor Davies, Leighton Phillips.   Trainer: David Bowen

NORTHERN IRELAND: Patrick Anthony Jennings, Patrick James Rice, Samuel Nelson, William John Terence Neill (Cap), Alan Hunter, David Clements, Daniel Hegan, Alexander McMordie, Alexander Derek Dougan (Martin Hugh Michael O'Neill), William John Irvine, Thomas Jackson.   Manager: Terence Neill

279. 18.10.1972   10th World Cup Qualifiers
BULGARIA v NORTHERN IRELAND 3-0 (1-0)
Vasil Levski, Sofia

Referee: Gerhard Schulenburg (West Germany)   Att: 40,000

BULGARIA: Iordan Filipov, Ivan Zafirov, Kiril Stankov, Viktor Ionov, Bojil Kolev, Dimitar Penev, Mladen Vasilev, Hristo Bonev (Cap), Georgi Denev, Ivan Stoianov, Bogomil Simov (69 Georgi Tsvetkov).   Trainer: Hristo Mladenov

NORTHERN IRELAND: Patrick Anthony Jennings, Patrick James Rice, Samuel Nelson, Alan Hunter, William John Terence Neill (Cap), David Clements, Bryan Hamilton (62 Samuel John Morgan), Daniel Hegan, Alexander McMordie, Alexander Derek Dougan, George Best.
Manager: Terence Neill

Goals: Hristo Bonev (18 pen, 85 pen), Bojil Kolev (59)

280. 14.02.1973   10th World Cup Qualifiers
CYPRUS v NORTHERN IRELAND 1-0 (0-0)
GSP, Nicosia

Referee: Aurel Bentu (România)   Attendance: 5,328

CYPRUS: Fanos Stylianou, Nicolis Stylianou, Lakis Theodorou, Staúros Stylianou, Kyriakos Koureas, Stefanis Mihaíl, Paníkos Efthymiadis (88 Paníkos Giolitis), Níkos Haralámpous, Pamboulis Papadopoulos, Kokos Antoníou, Andreas Stylianou (85 Mihális Tartaros).
Trainer: Pampos Avraamides

NORTHERN IRELAND: Patrick Anthony Jennings, Patrick James Rice, William John Terence Neill (Cap), Alan Hunter, David James Craig, Daniel Hegan, David Clements, Bryan Hamilton, Desmond Dickson, Alexander Derek Dougan, Samuel Nelson.   Manager: Terence Neill

Goal: Kokos Antoníou (88)

281. 28.03.1973   10th World Cup Qualifiers
NORTHERN IRELAND v PORTUGAL 1-1 (1-0)
Highfield Road, Coventry

Referee: Paul Schiller (Austria)   Attendance: 11,238

NORTHERN IRELAND: Patrick Anthony Jennings, William James O'Kane, Samuel Nelson, William John Terence Neill (Cap), Alan Hunter, David Clements, Bryan Hamilton, Robert Irvine Coyle, Samuel John Morgan, Desmond Dickson, Martin Hugh Michael O'Neill.   Manager: Terence Neill

PORTUGAL: JOSÉ HENRIQUE de Rodrigues Marques, ARTUR Manuel Soares CORREIA, Carlos Alexandre Fortes Alhinho, Fernando António José FREITAS Alexandrino, ADOLFO António da Cruz Calisto, Fernando Pascoal Neves "Pavão" (67 Joaquim António Dinis), Augusto Matine, António SIMÕES da Costa, Tamagnini Manuel Gomes Baptista "Nené", ABEL Fernando Miglieti, EUSÉBIO da Silva Ferreira (Cap).
Trainer: José Augusto

Goals: Martin O'Neill (18) / EUSÉBIO (87 pen)

282. 08.05.1973   10th World Cup Qualifiers
NORTHERN IRELAND v CYPRUS 3-0 (3-0)
Craven Cottage, Fulham, London

Referee: Iorwerth Price Jones (Wales)   Attendance: 6,090

NORTHERN IRELAND: William Stewart McFaul, William James O'Kane, Alan Hunter (46 Robert Irvine Coyle), William John Terence Neill, David James Craig, Bryan Hamilton (46 Robert John Lutton), Thomas Jackson, David Clements, Samuel John Morgan, Martin Hugh Michael O'Neill, Trevor Anderson.   Manager: Terence Neill

CYPRUS: Hristofi Varnavas, Nicolis Stylianou (46 Giannis Mertakkas), Lakis Theodorou, Staúros Stylianou, Kyriakos Koureas, Stefanis Mihaíl, Paníkos Efthymiadis, Kallis Konstantínou, Dimitris Koudas, Pamboulis Papadopoulos, Andreas Stylianou (46 Savvas Rotsidis).
Trainer: Pampos Avraamides

Goals: Samuel John Morgan (4), Trevor Anderson (32, 44)

283. 12.05.1973   British Championship
ENGLAND v NORTHERN IRELAND 2-1 (1-1)

Goodison Park, Liverpool

Referee: Clive Thomas (Wales)   Attendance: 29,865

ENGLAND: Peter Leslie Shilton, Peter Edwin Storey, David John Nish, Colin Bell, Roy Leslie McFarland, Robert Frederick Moore (Cap), Alan James Ball, Michael Roger Channon, Martin Harcourt Chivers, John Peter Richards, Martin Stanford Peters.   Manager: Alfred Ramsey

NORTHERN IRELAND: Patrick Anthony Jennings, Patrick James Rice, David James Craig, William John Terence Neill (Cap), Alan Hunter, David Clements, Bryan Hamilton, Thomas Jackson, Samuel John Morgan, Martin Hugh Michael O'Neill, Trevor Anderson.   Manager: Terence Neill

Goals: Martin Chivers (9, 82) / David Clements (22 pen)

284. 16.05.1973   British Championship
SCOTLAND v NORTHERN IRELAND 1-2 (0-2)

Hampden Park, Glasgow

Referee: Kenneth Burns (England)   Attendance: 39,018

SCOTLAND: Peter McCloy, Daniel Fergus McGrain, William Donachie, James Allan Holton, Derek Joseph Johnstone, Patrick Gordon Stanton (Cap) (50 William John Bremner), George Graham (77 Luigi Macari), David Hay, William Morgan, Kenneth Mathieson Dalglish, Colin Anderson Stein.   Manager: William Esplin Ormond

NORTHERN IRELAND: Patrick Anthony Jennings, Patrick James Rice, David James Craig, William John Terence Neill (Cap), Alan Hunter, David Clements, Bryan Hamilton, Thomas Jackson, Samuel John Morgan, Martin Hugh Michael O'Neill, Trevor Anderson (65 Robert John Lutton).   Manager: Terence Neill

Goals: Kenneth Mathieson Dalglish (89) / Martin Hugh Michael O'Neill (3), Trevor Anderson (17)

285. 19.05.1973   British Championship
NORTHERN IRELAND v WALES 1-0 (1-0)

Goodison Park, Liverpool

Referee: Not recorded   Attendance: 4,946

NORTHERN IRELAND: Patrick Anthony Jennings, Patrick James Rice, David James Craig, William John Terence Neill (Cap), Alan Hunter, David Clements, Bryan Hamilton (Robert John Lutton), Thomas Jackson, Samuel John Morgan, Martin Hugh Michael O'Neill, Trevor Anderson (Robert Irvine Coyle).   Manager: Terence Neill

WALES: Gareth Sprake, Peter Joseph Rodrigues, Roderick John Thomas, Trevor Hockey (William John Emanuel), David Frazer Roberts, John Griffith Roberts, John Francis Mahoney, Malcolm Edward Page, Gilbert Ivor Reece, Ronald Wyn Davies, Leighton James.   Trainer: David Bowen

Goal: Bryan Hamilton (#)

286. 26.09.1973   10th World Cup Qualifiers
NORTHERN IRELAND v BULGARIA 0-0

Hillsborough, Sheffield (England)

Referee: Rolf Nyhus (Norway)   Attendance: 6,206

NORTHERN IRELAND: William Stewart McFaul, Patrick James Rice, David James Craig, William James O'Kane, Alan Hunter, David Clements (Cap), Bryan Hamilton, Thomas Jackson (Robert Irvine Coyle), Samuel John Morgan, Trevor Anderson, Martin Hugh Michael O'Neill (Thomas Cassidy).   Manager: Terence Neill

BULGARIA: Rumiancho Goranov, Ivan Zafirov, Kiril Ivkov, Stefan Aladjov, Bojil Kolev, Dobromir Jechev, Atanas Aleksandrov (55 Krasimir Borisov), Hristo Bonev (Cap), Kiril Milanov, Ivan Stoianov, Georgi Denev.
Trainer: Hristo Mladenov

287. 14.11.1973   10th World Cup Qualifiers
PORTUGAL v NORTHERN IRELAND 1-1 (1-0)

José Alvalade, Lisboa

Referee: Pablo Augusto Sánchez Ibañez (Spain)   Att: 6,713

PORTUGAL: Vítor Manuel Alfonso DAMAS de Oliveira (Cap), Minervino José Lopes Pietra, HUMBERTO Manuel de Jesus COELHO, Carlos Alexandre Fortes Alhinho, ADOLFO António da Cruz Calisto, OCTÁVIO Joaquim Coelho Machado, António José da Conceiçao Oliveira "Toni" (77 ABEL Fernando Miglieti), Samuel Ferreira Fraguito, Tamagnini Manuel Gomes Baptista "Nené", Rui Manuel Trindade Jordão (77 VÍTOR Manuel Ferreira BAPTISTA), Joaquim António Dinis.   Trainer: José Augusto

NORTHERN IRELAND: Patrick Anthony Jennings, Patrick James Rice, David James Craig, Robert John Lutton, William James O'Kane, David Clements (Cap), Thomas Jackson (53 Robert Irvine Coyle), Martin Hugh Michael O'Neill, Samuel John Morgan, Trevor Anderson, George Best.   Manager: Terence Neill

Goals: Jordão (33) / William James O'Kane (68)

288. 11.05.1974   British Championship
SCOTLAND v NORTHERN IRELAND 0-1 (0-1)
Hampden Park, Glasgow

Referee: Iorwerth Price-Jones (Wales)   Attendance: 53,775

SCOTLAND: David Harvey, William Pullar Jardine, William Donachie (46 James Smith), Martin McLean Buchan, James Allan Holton, Thomas Hutchison, William John Bremner (Cap), David Hay, William Morgan, Kenneth Mathieson Dalglish, Denis Law (65 Joseph Jordan).
Manager: William Esplin Ormond

NORTHERN IRELAND: Patrick Anthony Jennings, Patrick James Rice, Samuel Nelson, William James O'Kane, Alan Hunter, David Clements (Cap), Bryan Hamilton (48 Thomas Jackson), Thomas Cassidy, Samuel John Morgan, Samuel Baxter McIlroy, Roland Christopher McGrath.
Manager: Terence Neill

Goal: Thomas Cassidy (40)

289. 15.05.1974   British Championship
ENGLAND v NORTHERN IRELAND 1-0 (0-0)
Wembley, London

Referee: Robert Holley Davidson (Scotlasnd)   Att: 45,500

ENGLAND: Peter Leslie Shilton, David John Nish, Michael Pejic, Emlyn Walter Hughes (Cap), Roy Leslie McFarland (36 Norman Hunter), Colin Todd, Kevin Joseph Keegan, Keith Weller, Michael Roger Channon, Colin Bell, Stanley Bowles (55 Frank Stewart Worthington).   Manager: Joseph Mercer

NORTHERN IRELAND: Patrick Anthony Jennings, Patrick James Rice, Samuel Nelson (Thomas Jackson), William James O'Kane, Alan Hunter, David Clements (Cap), Bryan Hamilton (Martin Hugh Michael O'Neill), Thomas Cassidy, Samuel John Morgan, Samuel Baxter McIlroy, Roland Christopher McGrath.
Manager: Terence Neill

Goal: Keith Weller (67)

290. 18.05.1974   British Championship
WALES v NORTHERN IRELAND 1-0 (1-0)
The Racecourse, Wrexham

Referee: Not recorded   Attendance: 9,311

WALES: Gareth Sprake, Malcolm Edward Page, Roderick John Thomas, John Francis Mahoney, John Griffith Roberts (Cap), Gilbert Ivor Reece, Terence Charles Yorath, David Paul Smallman (Anthony Keith Villars), Leighton Phillips, Leslie Cartwright, Leighton James.   Trainer: David Bowen

NORTHERN IRELAND: Patrick Anthony Jennings, Patrick James Rice, Hugh Oliver Dowd, William James O'Kane, Alan Hunter, David Clements (Cap), Bryan Hamilton (Thomas Jackson), Thomas Cassidy, Samuel Baxter McIlroy, Roland Christopher McGrath, Martin Hugh Michael O'Neill.
Manager: Terence Neill

Goal: David Paul Smallman

291. 04.09.1974   5th European Champs Qualifiers
NORWAY v NORTHERN IRELAND 2-1 (0-1)
Ullevaal, Oslo

Referee: Alfred Delcourt (Belgium)   Attendance: 6,585

NORWAY: Geir Karlsen, Reidar Goa, Torkild Brakstad, Jan Birkelund, Svein Grøndalen, Egil Austbø, Tor Egil Johansen, Svein Kvia, Jan Fuglset, Tom Lund, Harry Hestad.
Trainers: Kjell Schau Andreassen & Nils Arne Eggen

NORTHERN IRELAND: Patrick Anthony Jennings, Patrick James Rice, David James Craig (46 Hugh Oliver Dowd), William James O'Kane, Alan Hunter, David Clements (Cap), Bryan Hamilton, Thomas Cassidy, Thomas Finney, Samuel Baxter McIlroy, Roland Christopher McGrath (67 Thomas Jackson).   Manager: Terence Neill

Goals: Tom Lund (50, 72) / Thomas Finney (3)

292. 30.10.1974   5th European Champs Qualifiers
SWEDEN v NORTHERN IRELAND 0-2 (0-2)
Råsunda, Stockholm

Referee: Theodorus Boosten (Holland)   Attendance: 16,657

SWEDEN: Ronnie Carl Hellström, Roland Andersson, Kent Karlsson, Björn Nordqvist, Björn Andersson, Staffan Tapper, Bo Göran Larsson, Conny Torstensson (46 Jan Mattsson), Ove Kindvall (73 Thomas Nordahl), Ralf Edström, Roland Sandberg.   Trainer: Georg Ericsson

NORTHERN IRELAND: Patrick Anthony Jennings, William James O'Kane, Samuel Nelson (46 Ronald Victor Blair), Hugh Oliver Dowd, Alan Hunter, Christopher James Nicholl, Thomas Jackson, Martin Hugh Michael O'Neill, Samuel John Morgan, Samuel Baxter McIlroy, Bryan Hamilton.

Goals: Christopher Nicholl (7), Martin O'Neill (23)

293. 16.04.1975   5th European Champs Qualifiers
NORTHERN IRELAND v YUGOSLAVIA 1-0 (1-0)
Windsor Park, Belfast

Referee: Robert Wurtz (France)   Attendance: 25,847

NORTHERN IRELAND: Patrick Anthony Jennings, Patrick James Rice, Samuel Nelson, Christopher James Nicholl, Alan Hunter, David Clements, Bryan Hamilton, Martin Hugh Michael O'Neill, Derek William Spence, Samuel Baxter McIlroy, Thomas Jackson.

YUGOSLAVIA: Ognjen Petrović, Luka Peruzović, Džemal Hadžiabdić, Ivan Buljan, Josip Katalinski (Cap), Dražen Mužinić, Slobodan Janković, Momčilo Vukotić (46 Franjo Vladić), Branko Oblak, Jure Jerković (77 Ivica Miljković), Ivan Šurjak.   Trainer: Ante Mladinić

Goal: Bryan Hamilton (22)

294. 17.05.1975   British Championship
NORTHERN IRELAND v ENGLAND   0-0
Windsor Park, Belfast

Referee: Thomas Reynolds (Wales)   Attendance: 36,500

NORTHERN IRELAND: Patrick Anthony Jennings, Patrick James Rice, William James O'Kane, Christopher James Nicholl, Alan Hunter, David Clements, Bryan Hamilton (Thomas Finney), Martin Hugh Michael O'Neill, Derek William Spence, Samuel Baxter McIlroy, Thomas Jackson.

ENGLAND: Raymond Neal Clemence, Steven Whitworth, Emlyn Walter Hughes, Colin Bell, David Victor Watson, Colin Todd, Alan James Ball (Cap), Colin Viljeon, Malcolm Ian Macdonald (70 Michael Roger Channon), Kevin Joseph Keegan, Dennis Tueart.   Manager: Donald Revie

295. 20.05.1975   British Championship
SCOTLAND v NORTHERN IRELAND   3-0 (2-0)
Hampden Park, Glasgow

Referee: Patrick Partridge (England)   Attendance: 64,696

SCOTLAND: Stewart Kennedy, William Pullar Jardine (Cap) (89 Alexander Forsyth), Daniel Fergus McGrain, Francis Michael Munro, Gordon McQueen, Robert Sharp Robinson (76 Alfred James Conn), Bruce David Rioch, Kenneth Mathieson Dalglish, Arthur Duncan, Derek James Parlane, Edward John MacDougall.
Manager: William Esplin Ormond

NORTHERN IRELAND: Patrick Anthony Jennings, Patrick James Rice, William James O'Kane, Christopher James Nicholl, Alan Hunter (83 Ronald Victor Blair), David Clements, Thomas Finney, Martin Hugh Michael O'Neill (87 Trevor Anderson), Derek William Spence, Samuel Baxter McIlroy, Thomas Jackson.

Goals: Edward John MacDougall (15), Kenneth Dalglish (21), Derek James Parlane (80)

296. 24.05.1975   British Championship
NORTHERN IRELAND v WALES   1-0 (1-0)
Windsor Park, Belfast

Referee: Not recorded   Attendance: 17,000

NORTHERN IRELAND: Patrick Anthony Jennings, Peter William Scott, Patrick James Rice, Christopher James Nicholl, Alan Hunter, David Clements, Ronald Victor Blair, Thomas Jackson, Derek William Spence, Samuel Baxter McIlroy, Thomas Finney.

WALES: William David Davies, Roderick John Thomas, Malcolm Edward Page, John Francis Mahoney, David Frazer Roberts, Leighton Phillips, Arfon Trevor Griffiths, Brian Flynn, Gilbert Ivor Reece (David Paul Smallman), Derek Showers, Leighton James.   Trainer: Michael Smith

Goal: Thomas Finney (33)

297. 03.09.1975   5th European Champs Qualifiers
NORTHERN IRELAND v SWEDEN   1-2 (1-1)
Windsor Park, Belfast

Referee: Hans Joachim Weyland (West Germany)
Attendance: 14,622

NORTHERN IRELAND: Patrick Anthony Jennings, Patrick James Rice, Samuel Nelson, David Clements, Alan Hunter, Christopher James Nicholl, Ronald Victor Blair, Bryan Hamilton (Samuel John Morgan), Derek William Spence, Samuel Baxter McIlroy, Thomas Jackson.

SWEDEN: Ronnie Carl Hellström, Roland Andersson, Kent Karlsson, Björn Nordqvist, Jörgen Augustsson, Anders Linderoth, Curt Olsberg (46 Staffan Tapper), Eine Fredriksson, Thomas Sjöberg, Conny Torstensson, Jan Mattsson.
Trainer: Georg Ericsson

Goals: Alan Hunter (32) /
Thomas Sjöberg (45), Conny Torstensson (54)

298. 29.10.1975   5th European Champs Qualifiers
NORTHERN IRELAND v NORWAY   3-0 (2-0)
Windsor Park, Belfast

Referee: Gudjón Finnbogason (Iceland)   Attendance: 8,923

NORTHERN IRELAND: Patrick Anthony Jennings, Patrick James Rice, Samuel Nelson, Christopher James Nicholl, Alan Hunter, Thomas Jackson, Bryan Hamilton, Samuel Baxter McIlroy, Samuel John Morgan (George Terence Cochrane), John Jamison, Thomas Finney.

NORWAY: Geir Karlsen (68 Tom Rüsz Jacobsen), Trond Pedersen, Svein Grøndalen (50 Børge Josefsen), Helge Karlsen, Sigbjørn Slinning, Jan Hansen, Svein Kvia, Helge Skuseth, Gabriel Høyland, Pål Jacobsen, Harry Hestad.
Trainers: Kjell Schau Andreassen & Nils Arne Eggen

Goals: Samuel John Morgan (2), Samuel Baxter McIlroy (5), Bryan Hamilton (53)

299. 19.11.1975   5th European Champs Qualifiers
YUGOSLAVIA v NORTHERN IRELAND   1-0 (1-0)
JNA, Beograd

Referee: Antonio Camacho Jimenez (Spain)   Att: 21,545

YUGOSLAVIA: Ognjen Petrović, Ivan Buljan, Džemal Hadžiabdić, Branko Oblak, Josip Katalinski, Dražen Mužinić, Jure Jerković, Momčilo Vukotić, Ivan Šurjak, Franjo Vladić, Dragan Džajić (Cap).   Trainer: Ante Mladinić

NORTHERN IRELAND: Patrick Anthony Jennings, Patrick James Rice, Peter William Scott, Christopher James Nicholl, Alan Hunter, David Clements, Bryan Hamilton, Samuel Baxter McIlroy, Samuel John Morgan, Thomas Jackson (31 Martin Hugh Michael O'Neill), Thomas Finney.

Goal: Branko Oblak (21)

300. 03.03.1976
ISRAEL v NORTHERN IRELAND 1-1 (1-0)
Bloomfield, Jaffa, Tel-Aviv
Referee: Werner Spiegel (Austria)   Attendance: 9,000
ISRAEL: Yosef Sorinov, Eli Leventhal, Alon Ben-Dor, Avraham Lev, Haim Bar, Meir Nimni, Yaron Oz, Itzhak Shum, Moshe Schweitzer (Uri Malmilian), Gideon Damti, Meir Barad (Viktor Peretz).   Trainer: David Schweitzer
NORTHERN IRELAND: Patrick Anthony Jennings (James Archibald Platt), Peter William Scott, James Michael Nicholl, Alan Hunter, Patrick James Rice, Ronald Victor Blair, Samuel Nelson, Bryan Hamilton, Trevor Anderson (Roland Christopher McGrath), Derek William Spence, Warren Feeney.
Goals: Gideon Damti (36) / Avraham Lev (58 own goal)

301. 08.05.1976   British Championship
SCOTLAND v NORTHERN IRELAND 3-0 (2-0)
Hampden Park, Glasgow
Referee: Thomas Reynolds (Wales)   Attendance: 49,897
SCOTLAND: Alan Roderick Rough, Daniel Fergus McGrain, William Donachie, Thomas Forsyth, Colin MacDonald Jackson, Archibald Gemmill (Cap), Donald Sandison Masson, Bruce David Rioch (56 Richard Asa Hartford), Kenneth Mathieson Dalglish, William Pettigrew (66 Derek Joseph Johnstone), Joseph Jordan.
Manager: William Esplin Ormond
NORTHERN IRELAND: Patrick Anthony Jennings, Peter William Scott, Christopher James Nicholl, Alan Hunter, Patrick James Rice, Bryan Hamilton, Thomas Cassidy, Patrick Gerald Sharp Sharkey (61 David McCreery), Samuel Baxter McIlroy, Samuel John Morgan (85 Derek William Spence), Thomas Finney.   Manager: David Clements
Goals: Archibald Gemmill (23), Donald Masson (47), Kenneth Mathieson Dalglish (52)

302. 11.05.1976   British Championship
ENGLAND v NORTHERN IRELAND 4-0 (2-0)
Wembley, London
Referee: Clive Thomas (Wales)   Attendance: 48,000
ENGLAND: Raymond Neal Clemence, Colin Todd, Michael Dennis Mills, Philip Brian Thompson, Brian Greenhoff, Raymond Kennedy, Kevin Joseph Keegan (65 Joseph Royle), Gerald Charles James Francis (Cap), Stuart James Pearson, Michael Roger Channon, Peter John Taylor (60 Anthony Mark Towers).   Manager: Donald Revie
NORTHERN IRELAND: Patrick Anthony Jennings, Patrick James Rice, Samuel Nelson (Peter William Scott), David Clements, Alan Hunter, Christopher James Nicholl, Bryan Hamilton, Thomas Cassidy, David McCreery, Derek William Spence, Samuel Baxter McIlroy.   Manager: David Clements
Goals: Gerald Francis (35), Michael Channon (36 pen, 77), Stuart James Pearson (63)

303. 14.05.1976   British Championship
WALES v NORTHERN IRELAND 1-0 (1-0)
Vetch Field, Swansea
Referee: Not recorded   Attendance: 9,935
WALES: William David Davies, Leighton Phillips, Malcolm Edward Page, John Francis Mahoney, David Frazer Roberts, Ian Peter Evans, Arfon Trevor Griffiths, Brian Flynn, Terence Charles Yorath (Cap), Alan Thomas Curtis, Leighton James.
Trainer: Michael Smith
NORTHERN IRELAND: Patrick Anthony Jennings, Peter William Scott, Patrick James Rice, Christopher James Nicholl, Alan Hunter, David Clements, Bryan Hamilton, Samuel Baxter McIlroy, Derek William Spence (Samuel John Morgan), Thomas Cassidy (James Michael Nicholl), David McCreery.
Goal: Leighton James

304. 13.10.1976   11th World Cup Qualifiers
HOLLAND v NORTHERN IRELAND 2-2 (0-1)
Feyenoord, Rotterdam
Referee: Angelo Franco Martinez (Spain)   Att: 56,000
HOLLAND: Eddy Treijtel, Willy van de Kerkhof (46 René van de Kerkhof), Adri van Kraay, Wim Rijsbergen, Ruud Krol, Wim Jansen, Johan Neeskens, Arie Haan, Ruud Geels (60 Willy van der Kuylen), Johan Cruijff (Cap), Robert Rensenbrink.
Trainer: Johannes Zwartkruis
NORTHERN IRELAND: Patrick Anthony Jennings, James Michael Nicholl, Thomas Jackson, Patrick James Rice, Alan Hunter, Bryan Hamilton, George Best, Samuel Baxter McIlroy, Roland Christopher McGrath (Derek William Spence), David McCreery, Trevor Anderson.
Goals: Ruud Krol (64), Johan Cruijff (66) / Roland Christopher McGrath (4), Derek William Spence (88)

305. 10.11.1976   11th World Cup Qualifiers
BELGIUM v NORTHERN IRELAND 2-0 (1-0)
Maurice Dufrasne "Sclessin", Liège
Referee: Adolf Prokop (East Germany)   Attendance: 25,081
BELGIUM: Christian Piot (Cap), Eric Gerets, Hugo Broos, Erwin Vandendaele, Michel Renquin, François Vander Elst, Ludo Coeck, Paul Courant, Julien Cools, Roger Van Gool, Raoul Lambert.   Trainer: Guy Thys
NORTHERN IRELAND: Patrick Anthony Jennings, James Michael Nicholl, Patrick James Rice (80 Samuel Nelson), Thomas Jackson, Alan Hunter, Bryan Hamilton, George Best, Samuel Baxter McIlroy, Roland Christopher McGrath, David McCreery, Trevor Anderson.
Goals: Roger Van Gool (28), Raoul Lambert (53)

306. 27.04.1977
**WEST GERMANY
v NORTHERN IRELAND 5-0** (0-0)
Müngersdorfer, Köln

Referee: Károly Palotai (Hungary)   Attendance: 58,000

WEST GERMANY: Josef Maier (46 Bernd Franke), Hans-Hubert Vogts (Cap), Manfred Kaltz, Peter Nogly, Bernhard Dietz, Rainer Bonhof, Heinz Flohe, Rudiger Abramczik, Klaus Fischer, Dieter Müller, Bernd Hölzenbein.
Trainer: Helmut Schön

NORTHERN IRELAND: Patrick Anthony Jennings, Patrick James Rice, Samuel Nelson, Thomas Jackson, Alan Hunter, David McCreery (Thomas Cassidy), Bryan Hamilton, George Best, Gerard Joseph Armstrong (Derek William Spence), Roland Christopher McGrath, Trevor Anderson.

Goals: Rainer Bonhof (55 pen), Klaus Fischer (58), Dieter Müller (65), Klaus Fischer (84), Heinz Flohe (90)

307. 28.05.1977   British Championship
NORTHERN IRELAND v ENGLAND 1-2 (1-1)
Windsor Park, Belfast

Referee: Brian McGinlay   Attendance: 35,000

NORTHERN IRELAND: Patrick Anthony Jennings, James Michael Nicholl, Patrick James Rice, Thomas Jackson, Alan Hunter, Bryan Hamilton, Roland Christopher McGrath, Samuel Baxter McIlroy, Gerard Joseph Armstrong (Martin Hugh Michael O'Neill), David McCreery, Trevor Anderson (Derek William Spence).

ENGLAND: Peter Leslie Shilton, Trevor John Cherry, Michael Dennis Mills, Brian Greenhoff, David Victor Watson, Colin Todd, Raymond Colin Wilkins (65 Brian Ernest Talbot), Michael Roger Channon (Cap), Paul Mariner, Trevor David Brooking, Dennis Tueart.   Manager: Donald Revie

Goals: Roland Christopher McGrath (4) /
Michael Roger Channon (27), Dennis Tueart (86)

308. 01.06.1977   British Championship
SCOTLAND v NORTHERN IRELAND 3-0 (1-0)
Hampden Park, Glasgow

Referee: William John Gow (Wales)   Attendance: 44,699

SCOTLAND: Alan Roderick Rough, Daniel Fergus McGrain, William Donachie, Thomas Forsyth, Gordon McQueen, Donald Sandison Masson, Bruce David Rioch (Cap), Richard Asa Hartford, William McClure Johnston (86 Archibald Gemmill), Kenneth Mathieson Dalglish, Joseph Jordan (69 Luigi Macari).   Manager: Alistair MacLeod

NORTHERN IRELAND: Patrick Anthony Jennings, James Michael Nicholl, Patrick James Rice, Thomas Jackson, Alan Hunter, Bryan Hamilton, Roland Christopher McGrath, Samuel Baxter McIlroy, Martin Hugh Michael O'Neill (56 Derek William Spence), David McCreery, Trevor Anderson.
Manager: Robert Denis Blanchflower

Goals: Kenneth Dalglish (34, 79), Gordon McQueen (61)

309. 03.06.1977   British Championship
NORTHERN IRELAND v WALES 1-1 (0-1)
Windsor Park, Belfast

Referee: Not recorded   Attendance: 15,000

NORTHERN IRELAND: Patrick Anthony Jennings, James Michael Nicholl, Samuel Nelson, Christopher James Nicholl, Alan Hunter, Bryan Hamilton, Roland Christopher McGrath, Samuel Baxter McIlroy, Thomas Jackson, David McCreery (Gerard Joseph Armstrong), Trevor Anderson (Derek William Spence).

WALES: William David Davies, Roderick John Thomas, Joseph Patrick Jones, David Frazer Roberts, Ian Peter Evans, John Francis Mahoney, Peter Anthony Sayer (Alan Thomas Curtis), Brian Flynn, Terence Charles Yorath (Cap), Nicholas Simon Deacy, Leighton James (Michael Reginald Thomas).
Trainer: Michael Smith

Goals: Samuel Nelson (#) / Nicholas Simon Deacy (#)

310. 11.06.1977   11th World Cup Qualifiers
ICELAND v NORTHERN IRELAND 1-0 (1-0)
Laugardalsvöllur, Reykjavík

Referee: Rudolf Glöckner (East Germany)   Att: 10,269

ICELAND: Sigurður Dagsson, Ólafur Sigurvinsson, Janus Guðlaugsson, Marteinn Geirsson, Jóhannes Eðvaldsson (Cap), Gísli Torfason, Guðgeir Leifsson, Ingi Björn Albertsson, Ásgeir Sigurvinsson, Teitur Þórðarson, Guðmundur Þorbjörnsson (65 Atli Eðvaldsson).   Trainer: Anthony Knapp

NORTHERN IRELAND: Patrick Anthony Jennings, Patrick James Rice, Samuel Nelson, James Michael Nicholl, Alan Hunter, Bryan Hamilton, Roland Christopher McGrath, Samuel Baxter McIlroy, Thomas Jackson (Derek William Spence), David McCreery, Trevor Anderson (Gerard Joseph Armstrong).

Goal: Ingi Björn Albertsson (33)

311. 21.09.1977   11th World Cup Qualifiers
NORTHERN IRELAND v ICELAND 2-0 (0-0)
Windsor Park, Belfast

Referee: Henning-Lund Sørensen (Denmark)   Att: 15,000

NORTHERN IRELAND: Patrick Anthony Jennings, Patrick James Rice, James Michael Nicholl, Samuel Nelson, Alan Hunter, David McCreery, Roland Christopher McGrath, George Best, Samuel Baxter McIlroy, Martin Hugh Michael O'Neill, Trevor Anderson.

ICELAND: Sigurður Dagsson, Viðar Halldórsson, Janus Guðlaugsson, Marteinn Geirsson, Jóhannes Eðvaldsson (Cap), Jón Gunnlaugsson, Guðgeir Leifsson, Atli Eðvaldsson, Matthías Hallgrímsson (65 Ólafur Danívalsson), Árni Sveinsson, Ásgeir Elíasson (46 Kristinn Björnsson).
Trainer: Anthony Knapp

Goals: Roland McGrath (62), Samuel Baxter McIlroy (76)

312. 12.10.1977   11th World Cup Qualifiers
NORTHERN IRELAND v HOLLAND 0-1 (0-1)

Windsor Park, Belfast

Referee: Antonio José da Silva Garrido (Portugal)
Attendance: 30,000

NORTHERN IRELAND: Patrick Anthony Jennings, Patrick James Rice, Samuel Nelson, James Michael Nicholl, Alan Hunter, Martin Hugh Michael O'Neill, Samuel Baxter McIlroy, George Best, David McCreery, Roland Christopher McGrath, Trevor Anderson.

HOLLAND: Jan Jongbloed, Wim Suurbier, Wim Rijsbergen (50 Johnny Dusbaba), Ruud Krol (Cap), Hugo Hovenkamp, Wim Jansen, Willy van de Kerkhof, Wim van Hanegem, Johnny Rep, Johan Cruijff (71 Willy van der Kuylen), René van de Kerkhof.   Trainer: Ernst Happel

Goal: Willy van de Kerkhof (74)

313. 16.11.1977   11th World Cup Qualifiers
NORTHERN IRELAND v BELGIUM 3-0 (1-0)

Windsor Park, Belfast

Referee: Georges Konrath (France)   Attendance: 8,000

NORTHERN IRELAND: Patrick Anthony Jennings, Patrick James Rice, Samuel Nelson, James Michael Nicholl, Alan Hunter (54 Christopher James Nicholl), Samuel Baxter McIlroy, Roland Christopher McGrath, David McCreery, Gerard Joseph Armstrong, David Charles Stewart, Trevor Anderson.

BELGIUM: Jean-Marie Pfaff, Eric Gerets, Hugo Broos, Walter Meeuws, Michel Renquin, Julien Cools (Cap), Ludo Coeck, Frank Vercauteren, Raymond Mommens, Willy Wellens, Jan Ceulemans.   Trainer: Guy Thys

Goals: Gerard Joseph Armstrong (42, 74), Roland Christopher McGrath (58)

314. 13.05.1978   British Championship
SCOTLAND v NORTHERN IRELAND 1-1 (1-1)

Hampden Park, Glasgow

Referee: William John Gow (Wales)   Attendance: 64,433

SCOTLAND: Alan Roderick Rough, William Pullar Jardine, Martin McLean Buchan (37 Kenneth Burns), Thomas Forsyth, Gordon McQueen, Donald Sandison Masson, Bruce David Rioch (Cap), Archibald Gemmill, John Neilson Robertson, Joseph Jordan (46 Kenneth Mathieson Dalglish), Derek Joseph Johnstone.   Manager: Alistair MacLeod

NORTHERN IRELAND: James Archibald Platt, Bryan Hamilton, Peter William Scott, Christopher James Nicholl, James Michael Nicholl, Samuel Baxter McIlroy, David McCreery, Martin Hugh Michael O'Neill, Trevor Anderson (63 William Robert Hamilton), Gerard Joseph Armstrong, Roland Christopher McGrath (77 George Terence Cochrane).   Manager: Robert Denis Blanchflower

Goals: Derek Joseph Johnstone (36) / Martin O'Neill (26)

315. 16.05.1978   British Championship
ENGLAND v NORTHERN IRELAND 1-0 (1-0)

Wembley, London

Referee: John Robertson Gordon (Scotland)   Att: 55,000

ENGLAND: Raymond Neal Clemence, Philip George Neal, Michael Dennis Mills, Raymond Colin Wilkins, David Victor Watson, Emlyn Walter Hughes (Cap), Anthony William Currie, Steven James Coppell, Stuart James Pearson, Anthony Stewart Woodcock, Brian Greenhoff.   Manager: Ronald Greenwood

NORTHERN IRELAND: James Archibald Platt, Bryan Hamilton, Peter William Scott, Christopher James Nicholl, James Michael Nicholl, Samuel Baxter McIlroy, David McCreery, Martin Hugh Michael O'Neill, Trevor Anderson, Gerard Joseph Armstrong, Roland Christopher McGrath (George Terence Cochrane).
Manager: Robert Denis Blanchflower

Goal: Philip George Neal (45)

316. 20.05.1978   British Championship
WALES v NORTHERN IRELAND 1-0 (0-0)

The Racecourse, Wrexham

Referee: Not recorded   Attendance: 9,077

WALES: William David Davies, William Byron Stevenson, Joseph Patrick Jones, David Frazer Roberts, Gareth Davies, Terence Charles Yorath (Cap) (Michael Reginald Thomas), John Francis Mahoney, Brian Flynn, Carl Stephen Harris, Phillip John Dwyer, Nicholas Simon Deacy.
Trainer: Michael Smith

NORTHERN IRELAND: James Archibald Platt, Bryan Hamilton, Peter William Scott (Thomas Eugene Connell), Christopher James Nicholl, James Michael Nicholl, Martin Hugh Michael O'Neill, David McCreery, Samuel Baxter McIlroy, Trevor Anderson (George Terence Cochrane), Gerard Joseph Armstrong, Roland Christopher McGrath.

Goal: Nicholas Simon Deacy (# penalty)

317. 20.09.1978   6th European Champs Qualifiers
REPUBLIC OF IRELAND v NORTHERN IRELAND 0-0

Lansdowne Road, Dublin

Referee: Francis Rion (Belgium)   Attendance: 46,000

IRELAND: Michael Kearns, Anthony Patrick Grealish, Mark Thomas Lawrenson, Noel Synnott, James Paul Holmes, William Brady, Gerard Anthony Daly, John Michael Giles (Cap), Paul Gerard McGee, Francis Anthony Stapleton (54 Michael Anthony Walsh), Stephen Derek Heighway (63 Daniel Joseph Givens).   Manager: John Michael Giles

NORTHERN IRELAND: Patrick Anthony Jennings, Patrick James Rice, Samuel Nelson, Christopher James Nicholl, Alan Hunter (Bryan Hamilton), James Michael Nicholl, Martin Hugh Michael O'Neill, David McCreery, Gerard Joseph Armstrong, Samuel Baxter McIlroy, Derek William Spence (George Terence Cochrane).

318. 25.10.1978   6th European Champs Qualifiers
NORTHERN IRELAND v DENMARK 2-1 (0-0)
Windsor Park, Belfast
Referee: Rolf Haugen (Norway)   Attendance: 25,000
NORTHERN IRELAND: Patrick Anthony Jennings, Patrick James Rice, Samuel Nelson, James Michael Nicholl, Alan Hunter, David McCreery, Martin Hugh Michael O'Neill, Samuel Baxter McIlroy, Gerard Joseph Armstrong, Samuel John Morgan (Derek William Spence, Trevor Anderson), George Terence Cochrane.
DENMARK: Ole Kjær, Flemming Nielsen, Per Røntved (Cap), Lars Larsen, John Andersen, Ole Rasmussen, Carsten Nielsen, Ove Flindt Bjerg, Henrik Agerbeck (Jan Sørensen II), Henning Jensen, Jørgen Kristensen.   Trainer: Kurt Nielsen
Goals: Derek William Spence (63), Trevor Anderson (85) / Henning Jensen (51)

319. 29.11.1978   6th European Champs Qualifiers
BULGARIA v NORTHERN IRELAND 0-2 (0-1)
Vasil Levski, Sofia
Referee: Hilmi Ok (Turkey)   Attendance: 25,000
BULGARIA: Rumiancho Goranov, Nikolai Grancharov, Petar Stankov, Roman Karakolev, Georgi Dimitrov, Borislav Sredkov, Rusi Gochev, Georgi Slavkov, Stoicho Mladenov (67 Spas Djevizov), Pavel Panov (Cap), Angel Stankov (46 Chavdar Tsvetkov).   Trainer: Tsvetan Ilchev
NORTHERN IRELAND: Patrick Anthony Jennings, Bryan Hamilton, Samuel Nelson, Christopher James Nicholl, James Michael Nicholl, David McCreery, Martin Hugh Michael O'Neill, Samuel Baxter McIlroy (86 Victor Moreland), Gerard Joseph Armstrong, William Thomas Caskey, George Terence Cochrane (54 Roland Christopher McGrath).
Goals: Gerard Armstrong (17), William Thomas Caskey (83)

320. 07.02.1979   6th European Champs Qualifiers
ENGLAND v NORTHERN IRELAND 4-0 (1-0)
Wembley, London
Referee: Ulf Eriksson (Sweden)   Attendance: 91,244
ENGLAND: Raymond Neal Clemence, Philip George Neal, Michael Dennis Mills, Anthony William Currie, David Victor Watson, Emlyn Walter Hughes (Cap), Kevin Joseph Keegan, Steven James Coppell, Robert Dennis Latchford, Trevor David Brooking, Peter Simon Barnes.   Manager: Ronald Greenwood
NORTHERN IRELAND: Patrick Anthony Jennings (Cap), Patrick James Rice, Samuel Nelson, Christopher James Nicholl, James Michael Nicholl, David McCreery, Martin Hugh Michael O'Neill, Samuel Baxter McIlroy, Gerard Joseph Armstrong, William Thomas Caskey (Derek William Spence), George Terence Cochrane (Roland Christopher McGrath).   Manager: Robert Denis Blanchflower
Goals: Kevin Joseph Keegan (25), Robert Latchford (46, 64), David Victor Watson (50)

321. 02.05.1979   6th European Champs Qualifiers
NORTHERN IRELAND v BULGARIA 2-0 (2-0)
Windsor Park, Belfast
Referee: Anders Mattsson (Finland)   Attendance: 20,000
NORTHERN IRELAND: Patrick Anthony Jennings, Bryan Hamilton, Samuel Nelson, Christopher James Nicholl (75 Victor Moreland), James Michael Nicholl, David McCreery, Martin Hugh Michael O'Neill, Samuel Baxter McIlroy, Gerard Joseph Armstrong, William Thomas Caskey (77 Derek William Spence), George Terence Cochrane.
BULGARIA: Stoian Stoianov, Tsonio Vasilev, Kiril Ivkov (Cap), Georgi Bonev, Liuben Kolev, Aleksandar Rainov, Radoslav Zdravkov (65 Georgi Iliev), Borislav Sredkov, Spas Djevizov, Pavel Panov, Chavdar Tsvetkov.
Trainer: Yanko Dinkov
Goals: Christopher Nicholl (16), Gerard Armstrong (33)

322. 19.05.1979   British Championship
NORTHERN IRELAND v ENGLAND 0-2 (0-2)
Windsor Park, Belfast
Referee: Ian Foote (Scotland)   Attendance: 35,000
NORTHERN IRELAND: Patrick Anthony Jennings, Patrick James Rice, Samuel Nelson, Christopher James Nicholl, James Michael Nicholl, Victor Moreland (57 Roland Christopher McGrath), Bryan Hamilton, Samuel Baxter McIlroy, Gerard Joseph Armstrong, William Thomas Caskey, George Terence Cochrane (68 Derek William Spence).
ENGLAND: Raymond Neal Clemence, Philip George Neal, Michael Dennis Mills (Cap), Philip Brian Thompson, David Victor Watson, Raymond Colin Wilkins, Steven James Coppell, Terence McDermott, Robert Dennis Latchford, Anthony William Currie, Peter Simon Barnes.
Manager: Ronald Greenwood
Goals: David Victor Watson (9), Steven James Coppell (16)

323. 22.05.1979   British Championship
SCOTLAND v NORTHERN IRELAND 1-0 (0-0)
Hampden Park, Glasgow
Referee: Clive Thomas (Wales)   Attendance: 28,524
SCOTLAND: George Wood, George Elder Burley, Francis Tierney Gray, Paul Anthony Hegarty, Gordon McQueen, John Wark (46 David Narey), Graeme James Souness, Richard Asa Hartford, Arthur Graham (89 Francis Peter McGarvey), Kenneth Mathieson Dalglish (Cap), Joseph Jordan.
Manager: John Stein
NORTHERN IRELAND: Patrick Anthony Jennings, Patrick James Rice, Samuel Nelson, James Michael Nicholl, Alan Hunter, Victor Moreland (62 Peter William Scott), Bryan Hamilton, Samuel Baxter McIlroy, Gerard Joseph Armstrong, Thomas Sloan, Derek William Spence (77 William Thomas Caskey).   Manager: Robert Denis Blanchflower
Goal: Arthur Graham (76)

324. 25.05.1979   British Championship
NORTHERN IRELAND v WALES 1-1 (1-0)

Windsor Park, Belfast

Referee: Not recorded   Attendance: 6,500

NORTHERN IRELAND: Patrick Anthony Jennings, Patrick James Rice, Samuel Nelson, Christopher James Nicholl, Alan Hunter, James Michael Nicholl, David McCreery (46 Thomas Sloan), Samuel Baxter McIlroy, Gerard Joseph Armstrong, Derek William Spence, Bryan Hamilton.

WALES: William David Davies, William Byron Stevenson, Joseph Patrick Jones, Leighton Phillips, Phillip John Dwyer, John Francis Mahoney, Terence Charles Yorath (Cap), Brian Flynn, Robert Mark James, John Benjamin Toshack, Alan Thomas Curtis (76 Peter Nicholas).   Trainer: Michael Smith

Goals: Derek William Spence (#) / Robert Mark James (#)

325. 06.06.1979   6th European Champs Qualifiers
DENMARK v NORTHERN IRELAND 4-0 (2-0)

Idrætsparken, København

Referee: Rudolf Frickel (West Germany)   Att: 16,500

DENMARK: Ole Kjær, Ole Højgaard (Peter Poulsen), Sten Ziegler (Cap), Søren Busk, John Andersen, Klaus Nørregaard (Per Røntved), Frank Arnesen, Morten Olsen, Søren Lerby, Allan Rodenkam Simonsen, Preben Elkjær-Larsen.
Trainer: Kurt Nielsen

NORTHERN IRELAND: Patrick Anthony Jennings, Patrick James Rice, Samuel Nelson, James Michael Nicholl, Alan Hunter, David McCreery, Martin Hugh Michael O'Neill (65 Thomas Sloan), Gerard Joseph Armstrong, Samuel Baxter McIlroy (68 William Thomas Caskey), Derek William Spence, Bryan Hamilton.

Goals: Preben Elkjær-Larsen (31, 33, 82), Allan Rodenkam Simonsen (63)

326. 17.10.1979   6th European Champs Qualifiers
NORTHERN IRELAND v ENGLAND 1-5 (0-2)

Windsor Park, Belfast

Referee: Alexis Ponnet (Belgium)   Attendance: 17,755

NORTHERN IRELAND: Patrick Anthony Jennings, Patrick James Rice, Samuel Nelson, James Michael Nicholl, Alan Hunter (46 Peter Rafferty), David McCreery, Thomas Cassidy, Samuel Baxter McIlroy, Gerard Joseph Armstrong, Thomas Finney (68 William Thomas Caskey), Victor Moreland.

ENGLAND: Peter Leslie Shilton, Philip George Neal, Michael Dennis Mills, Philip Brian Thompson, David Victor Watson, Raymond Colin Wilkins, Kevin Joseph Keegan (Cap), Steven James Coppell, Trevor John Francis, Trevor David Brooking (83 Terence McDermott), Anthony Stewart Woodcock.
Manager: Ronald Greenwood

Goals: Victor Moreland (pen) / Trevor John Francis (18, 62), Anthony Woodcock (34, 71), James Nicholl (74 own goal)

327. 21.11.1979   6th European Champs Qualifiers
**NORTHERN IRELAND
v REPUBLIC OF IRELAND 1-0** (0-0)

Windsor Park, Belfast

Referee: André Daina (Switzerland)   Attendance: 15,000

NORTHERN IRELAND: Patrick Anthony Jennings, James Michael Nicholl, Samuel Nelson, Christopher James Nicholl, Alan Hunter, David McCreery, Martin Hugh Michael O'Neill (Thomas Cassidy), Samuel Baxter McIlroy, Gerard Joseph Armstrong, Derek William Spence, Victor Moreland.

IRELAND: Michael Kearns, John Anthony Devine, David Anthony O'Leary, Michael Paul Martin (Cap), Augustine Ashley Grimes, Gerard Anthony Daly (53 Joseph John Wary Waters), Pierce O'Leary, Anthony Patrick Grealish, Francis Anthony Stapleton, Paul Gerard McGee (75 Daniel Joseph Givens), Stephen Derek Heighway.
Manager: John Michael Giles

Goal: Gerard Joseph Armstrong (54)

328. 26.03.1980   12th World Cup Qualifiers
ISRAEL v NORTHERN IRELAND 0-0

National, Ramat-Gan, Tel-Aviv

Referee: Stjepan Glavina (Yugoslavia)   Attendance: 40,000

ISRAEL: Arie Haviv, Gadi Machnes, Haim Bar, Itzhak Shum, Yaacov Cohen, Rifat Turk, Giora Spiegel, Avi Cohen I, Gideon Damti, Viktor Peretz, Moshe Gariani (Oded Machnes).
Trainer: Jack Mansell

NORTHERN IRELAND: Patrick Anthony Jennings, James Michael Nicholl, Samuel Nelson, Christopher James Nicholl, John Patrick O'Neill, Martin Hugh Michael O'Neill, Samuel Baxter McIlroy, Thomas Cassidy, Gerard Joseph Armstrong, Thomas Finney (Derek William Spence), George Terence Cochrane.   Manager: William Bingham

329. 16.05.1980   British Championship
NORTHERN IRELAND v SCOTLAND 1-0 (1-0)

Windsor Park, Belfast

Referee: Clive Thomas (Wales)   Attendance: 18,000

NORTHERN IRELAND: James Archibald Platt, James Michael Nicholl, Malachy Martin Donaghy, Christopher James Nicholl, John Patrick O'Neill, Thomas Cassidy (70 David McCreery), Samuel Baxter McIlroy, William Robert Hamilton (52 John McClelland), Gerard Joseph Armstrong, Thomas Finney, Noel Brotherston.   Manager: William Bingham

SCOTLAND: William Thomson, George Elder Burley, Daniel Fergus McGrain, David Narey, Alexander McLeish, Gordon David Strachan, Graeme James Souness (59 Joseph Jordan), Archibald Gemmill (Cap), Peter Russell Weir (59 David Alexander Provan), Kenneth Mathieson Dalglish, Steven Archibald.   Manager: John Stein

Goal: William Robert Hamilton (36)

330. 20.05.1980 British Championship
ENGLAND v NORTHERN IRELAND 1-1 (0-0)
Wembley, London
Referee: Gwyn Pierce Owen (Wales)   Attendance: 33,676
ENGLAND: Joseph Thomas Corrigan, Trevor John Cherry, Kenneth Graham Sansom, Emlyn Walter Hughes (Cap), David Victor Watson, Raymond Colin Wilkins, Kevin Peter Reeves (70 Paul Mariner), Terence McDermott, David Edward Johnson, Trevor David Brooking, Alan Ernest Devonshire. Manager: Ronald Greenwood
NORTHERN IRELAND: James Archibald Platt, James Michael Nicholl, Malachy Martin Donaghy, Christopher James Nicholl, John Patrick O'Neill, Thomas Cassidy (73 David McCreery), Samuel Baxter McIlroy, William Robert Hamilton (73 George Terence Cochrane), Gerard Joseph Armstrong, Thomas Finney, Noel Brotherston. Manager: William Bingham
Goals: David Johnson (81) / George Terence Cochrane (83)

331. 23.05.1980 British Championship
WALES v NORTHERN IRELAND 0-1 (0-1)
Ninian Park, Cardiff
Referee: Not recorded   Attendance: 12,913
WALES: William David Davies, Peter Nicholas, Joseph Patrick Jones, Terence Charles Yorath (Cap), Leighton Phillips, Paul Terence Price, David Charles Giles, Brian Flynn (Carl Stephen Harris), Ian James Rush, Leighton James, Michael Reginald Thomas.   Trainer: Harold Michael England
NORTHERN IRELAND: James Archibald Platt, James Michael Nicholl, Malachy Martin Donaghy, Christopher James Nicholl, John Patrick O'Neill, Thomas Cassidy (David McCreery), Samuel Baxter McIlroy, William Robert Hamilton (George Terence Cochrane), Gerard Joseph Armstrong, Thomas Finney, Noel Brotherston. Manager: William Bingham
Goal: Noel Brotherston (#)

332. 11.06.1980
AUSTRALIA v NORTHERN IRELAND 1-2 (0-1)
Sydney Cricket Ground, Sydney
Referee: P. Rampley (Australia)   Attendance: 12,486
AUSTRALIA: Greg Woodhouse, Steve Perry, Ivo Prskalo, James Muir, James Tansey (80 Kevin Mullen), Anthony Henderson, John Yzendoorn, Theo Selemides (18 Ken Boden), Mark Jankovics (70 James Rooney), Gary Cole (46 Eddie Krncevic), Peter Sharne.   Trainer: Rudi Gutendorf
NORTHERN IRELAND: James Archibald Platt, James Michael Nicholl, Christopher James Nicholl, John Patrick O'Neill, John McClelland, Thomas Cassidy (84 David McCreery), Noel Brotherston (46 George Terence Cochrane), William Robert Hamilton (84 Derek William Spence), Gerard Joseph Armstrong, Thomas Finney (84 Bryan Hamilton), Martin Hugh Michael O'Neill.   Manager: William Bingham
Goals: Peter Sharne (75) / Christopher James Nicholl (11), Martin Hugh Michael O'Neill (63)

333. 15.06.1980
AUSTRALIA v NORTHERN IRELAND 1-1 (1-0)
Olympic Park, Melbourne
Referee: S. Mellings (Australia)   Attendance: 10,000
AUSTRALIA: Yakka Banovic, John Yzendroon, James Tansey, Anthony Henderson, Ivo Prskalo, James Muir, Peter Sharne (85 Alan Davidson), Gary Cole (73 Ken Boden), Eddie Krncevic, James Rooney (Mark Jankovics), Murray Barnes.   Trainer: Rudi Gutendorf
NORTHERN IRELAND: James Archibald Platt, James Michael Nicholl, Christopher James Nicholl, John Patrick O'Neill, John McClelland, Thomas Cassidy, Noel Brotherston, David McCreery (66 George Terence Cochrane), Gerard Joseph Armstrong, Thomas Finney, Martin Hugh Michael O'Neill.   Manager: William Bingham
Goals: Peter Sharne (18) / Martin Hugh Michael O'Neill (82)

334. 18.06.1980
AUSTRALIA v NORTHERN IRELAND 1-2 (1-0)
Dindmarsh, Adelaide
Referee: Not recorded   Attendance: 10,000
AUSTRALIA: Martin Crook, Steve Perry, James Tansey (Theo Selemidis), Anthony Henderson, Ivan Prskalo (John Nyskohus), Peter Sharne, Eddie Krncevic, James Rooney (Mark Jankovics), Ken Boden, John Yzendroon, James Muir.   Trainer: Rudi Gutendorf
NORTHERN IRELAND: James Archibald Platt, James Michael Nicholl, Christopher James Nicholl, John Patrick O'Neill, John McClelland, Thomas Cassidy (Bryan Hamilton), George Terence Cochrane, William Robert Hamilton (Colin Charles McCurdy), Gerard Joseph Armstrong, Martin Hugh Michael O'Neill, Noel Brotherston.   Manager: William Bingham
Goals: Peter Sharne (#) / Noel Brotherston (67), Colin Charles McCurdy (77)

335. 15.10.1980   12th World Cup Qualifiers
NORTHERN IRELAND v SWEDEN 3-0 (3-0)
Windsor Park, Belfast
Referee: Alexis Ponnet (Belgium)   Attendance: 20,000
NORTHERN IRELAND: James Archibald Platt, James Michael Nicholl, Malachy Martin Donaghy, Thomas Cassidy (76 David McCreery), Christopher James Nicholl, John McClelland, Noel Brotherston, Martin Hugh Michael O'Neill, William Robert Hamilton (76 George Terence Cochrane), Gerard Joseph Armstrong, S. McIlroy.
Manager: William Bingham
SWEDEN: Jan Möller, Hans Borg, Håkan Arvidsson, Bo Börjesson, Tord Holmgren, Lennart Larsson, Sten-Ove Ramberg (46 Ingemar Erlandsson), Peter Nilsson, Thomas Nilsson, Ralf Edström, Billy Ohlsson (68 Thomas Sjöberg).
Trainer: Lars Arnesson
Goals: Noel Brotherston (24), Samuel Baxter McIlroy (28), James Michael Nicholl (37)

336. 19.11.1980   12th World Cup Qualifiers
PORTUGAL v NORTHERN IRELAND 1-0 (0-0)
da Luz, Lisboa
Referee: Georges Konrath (France)   Attendance: 70,000
PORTUGAL: Manuel Galrinho Bento (Cap), GABRIEL Azevedo Mendes, Carlos António Fonseca Simões, João Gonçalves Laranjeira, Minervino José Lopes Pietra, Shéu Han, CARLOS MANUEL Correia dos Santos (46 Tamagnini Manuel Gomes Baptista "Nené"), João António Ferreira Resende Alves (84 Adelino de Jesus Teixeira), José Alberto Costa, Fernando Albino de Sousa Chalana, Rui Manuel Trindade Jordão.
Trainer: Júlio Cernadas Pereira "Juca"
NORTHERN IRELAND: James Archibald Platt, James Michael Nicholl, Malachy Martin Donaghy, Thomas Cassidy (78 David McCreery), Christopher James Nicholl, John Patrick O'Neill, Noel Brotherston, Martin Hugh Michael O'Neill (Cap), William Robert Hamilton (78 George Terence Cochrane), Gerard Joseph Armstrong, Samuel Baxter McIlroy.
Manager: William Bingham
Goal: Rui Manuel Trindade Jordão (60)

337. 25.03.1981   12th World Cup Qualifiers
SCOTLAND v NORTHERN IRELAND 1-1 (0-0)
Hampden Park, Glasgow
Referee: Klaus Scheurell (West Germany)   Att: 78,444
SCOTLAND: Alan Roderick Rough (80 William Thomson), Daniel Fergus McGrain, Francis Tierney Gray, William Fergus Miller, Alexander McLeish, John Wark, Kenneth Burns (77 Richard Asa Hartford), Archibald Gemmill (Cap), John Neilson Robertson, Steven Archibald, Andrew Mullen Gray.
Manager: John Stein

NORTHERN IRELAND: Patrick Anthony Jennings, James Michael Nicholl, Samuel Nelson, John McClelland, Christopher James Nicholl, John Patrick O'Neill, George Terence Cochrane, David McCreery, William Robert Hamilton (78 Derek William Spence), Gerard Joseph Armstrong, Samuel Baxter McIlroy.   Manager: William Bingham
Goals: John Wark (75) / William Robert Hamilton (70)

338. 29.04.1981   12th World Cup Qualifiers
NORTHERN IRELAND v PORTUGAL 1-0 (0-0)
Windsor Park, Belfast
Referee: Svein Inge Thime (Norway)   Attendance: 18,000
NORTHERN IRELAND: Patrick Anthony Jennings, James Michael Nicholl, Samuel Nelson, David McCreery, Christopher James Nicholl, John Patrick O'Neill, George Terence Cochrane, Martin Hugh Michael O'Neill, William Robert Hamilton, Gerard Joseph Armstrong, Samuel Baxter McIlroy.
Manager: William Bingham
PORTUGAL: Manuel Galrinho Bento, GABRIEL Azevedo Mendes, HUMBERTO Manuel de Jesus COELHO (Cap), Carlos António Fonseca Simões, Minervino José Lopes Pietra, Shéu Han, CARLOS MANUEL Correia dos Santos, João António Ferreira Resende Alves, José Alberto Costa, António Luís Alves Ribeiro Oliveira (61 Tamagnini Manuel Gomes Baptista "Nené"), Rui Manuel Trindade Jordão.
Trainer: Júlio Cernadas Pereira "Juca"
Goals: Gerard Joseph Armstrong (71)

339. 19.05.1981   British Championship
SCOTLAND v NORTHERN IRELAND 2-0 (1-0)
Hampden Park, Glasgow
Referee: Patrick Partridge (England)   Attendance: 22,248
SCOTLAND: William Thomson, Daniel Fergus McGrain (Cap), Francis Tierney Gray, William Fergus Miller, Alexander McLeish, Raymond Strean McDonald Stewart, Thomas Burns, Richard Asa Hartford, John Neilson Robertson, Paul Whitehead Sturrock, Steven Archibald.   Manager: John Stein
NORTHERN IRELAND: Patrick Anthony Jennings, James Michael Nicholl, Samuel Nelson (70 Malachy Martin Donaghy), John McClelland, Christopher James Nicholl, John Patrick O'Neill, George Terence Cochrane, Martin Hugh Michael O'Neill, Gerard Joseph Armstrong, Samuel Baxter McIlroy, William Robert Hamilton.
Manager: William Bingham
Goals: Raymond Strean McDonald Stewart (5), Steven Archibald (49)

340. 03.06.1981   12th World Cup Qualifiers
SWEDEN v NORTHERN IRELAND 1-0 (0-0)
Råsunda, Stockholm

Referee: Paolo Bergamo (Italy)   Attendance: 21,431

SWEDEN: Thomas Ravelli, Stig Fredriksson, Glenn Ingvar Hysén, Bo Börjesson, Ingemar Erlandsson, Tony Persson, Hans Borg, Peter Nilsson, Thomas Nilsson (69 Torbjörn Nilsson), Thomas Sjöberg, Jan Svensson (83 Andreas Ravelli). Trainer: Lars Arnesson

NORTHERN IRELAND: Patrick Anthony Jennings, James Michael Nicholl (62 John McClelland), Samuel Nelson, David McCreery, Christopher James Nicholl, John Patrick O'Neill, George Terence Cochrane, Martin Hugh Michael O'Neill, William Robert Hamilton (70 Derek William Spence), Gerard Joseph Armstrong, Samuel Baxter McIlroy.
Manager: William Bingham

Goal: Hans Borg (49)

341. 14.10.1981   12th World Cup Qualifiers
NORTHERN IRELAND v SCOTLAND 0-0
Windsor Park, Belfast

Referee: Valeriy Butenko (Soviet Union)   Att: 22,248

NORTHERN IRELAND: Patrick Anthony Jennings, James Michael Nicholl, Christopher James Nicholl, John Patrick O'Neill, Malachy Martin Donaghy, Martin Hugh Michael O'Neill, Samuel Baxter McIlroy, David McCreery, Gerard Joseph Armstrong, William Robert Hamilton, Noel Brotherston.   Manager: William Bingham

SCOTLAND: Alan Roderick Rough, Raymond Strean McDonald Stewart, Francis Tierney Gray, William Fergus Miller, Alan David Hansen, Gordon David Strachan, Graeme James Souness (76 Andrew Mullen Gray), Richard Asa Hartford (Cap), John Neilson Robertson, Kenneth Mathieson Dalglish, Steven Archibald.   Manager: John Stein

342. 18.11.1981   12th World Cup Qualifiers
NORTHERN IRELAND v ISRAEL 1-0 (1-0)
Windsor Park, Belfast

Referee: Emilio Carlos Guruceta Muro (Spain)   Att: 40,000

NORTHERN IRELAND: Patrick Anthony Jennings, James Michael Nicholl, Christopher James Nicholl, John Patrick O'Neill, Malachy Martin Donaghy, David McCreery, Thomas Cassidy, Samuel Baxter McIlroy, Gerard Joseph Armstrong, William Robert Hamilton, Noel Brotherston.
Manager: William Bingham

ISRAEL: Arie Haviv, Gadi Machnes, Haim Bar, Avi Cohen I, Yaacov Cohen, Uri Malmilian, Yaacov Ekhoiz, Itzhak Shum, Beni Lam (64 Moshe Sinai), Gideon Damti, Beni Tabak.
Trainer: Jack Mansell

Goal: Gerard Joseph Armstrong (27)

343. 23.02.1982   British Championship
ENGLAND v NORTHERN IRELAND 4-0 (1-0)
Wembley, London

Referee: Gwyn Pierce Owen (Wales)   Attendance: 54,900

ENGLAND: Raymond Neal Clemence, Vivian Alexander Anderson, Kenneth Graham Sansom, Raymond Colin Wilkins, David Victor Watson, Stephen Brian Foster, Kevin Joseph Keegan (Cap), Bryan Robson, Trevor John Francis (65 Cyrille Regis), Glenn Hoddle, Anthony William Morley (77 Anthony Stewart Woodcock).   Manager: Ronald Greenwood

NORTHERN IRELAND: Patrick Anthony Jennings, James Michael Nicholl, Samuel Nelson, Malachy Martin Donaghy, Christopher James Nicholl, John Patrick O'Neill, Noel Brotherston (65 George Terence Cochrane), Martin Hugh Michael O'Neill (77 David McCreery), Gerard Joseph Armstrong, Samuel Baxter McIlroy, William Robert Hamilton.
Manager: William Bingham

Goals: Bryan Robson (1), Kevin Joseph Keegan (47), Raymond Colin Wilkins (84), Glenn Hoddle (86)

344. 24.03.1982
FRANCE v NORTHERN IRELAND 4-0 (2-0)
Parc des Princes, Paris

Referee: Roger Verhaeghe (Belgium)   Attendance: 34,000

FRANCE: Jean Castaneda, Manuel Amoros, Christian Lopez (68 Patrick Battiston), Marius Trésor (Cap), Maxime Bossis, Jean-François Larios, Alain Giresse (76 René Girard), Bernard Genghini, Alain Couriol (75 Gérard Soler), Bruno Bellone, Bruno Zénier.   Trainer: Michel Hidalgo

NORTHERN IRELAND: James Archibald Platt, James Michael Nicholl, John Patrick O'Neill, Christopher James Nicholl, Malachy Martin Donaghy, David McCreery (64 William Thomas Caskey), Martin Hugh Michael O'Neill, Samuel Baxter McIlroy (64 Derek William Spence), Noel Brotherston, Gerard Joseph Armstrong, George Terence Cochrane (38 Ian Edwin Stewart).
Manager: William Bingham

Goals: Bruno Zénier (31), Alain Couriol (45), Jean-François Larios (57 pen), Bernard Genghini (80)

345. 28.04.1982   British Championship
NORTHERN IRELAND v SCOTLAND 1-1 (0-1)
Windsor Park, Belfast

Referee: John Hunting (England)   Attendance: 20,000

NORTHERN IRELAND: James Archibald Platt, Malachy Martin Donaghy, Samuel Nelson, John Patrick O'Neill, John McClelland, James Cleary, Noel Brotherston, Martin Hugh Michael O'Neill, Robert McFaul Campbell, Samuel Baxter McIlroy, Patrick Joseph Healy.   Manager: William Bingham

SCOTLAND: George Wood, Daniel Fergus McGrain (Cap), Arthur Richard Albiston, Allan James Evans, Alexander McLeish (75 Alan David Hansen), David Alexander Provan, John Wark, Richard Asa Hartford, John Neilson Robertson (80 Paul Whitehead Sturrock), Kenneth Mathieson Dalglish, Alan Bernard Brazil.   Manager: John Stein

Goals: Samuel Baxter McIlroy (55) / John Wark (32)

346. 27.05.1982   British Championship
WALES v NORTHERN IRELAND 3-0 (1-0)
The Racecourse, Wrexham

Referee: Not recorded   Attendance: 2,315

WALES: Neville Southall, Christopher Marustik, Joseph Patrick Jones, Peter Nicholas, Nigel Charles Ashley Stevenson, William Byron Stevenson, Alan Thomas Curtis (Ian Patrick Walsh), Robert Mark James, Brian Flynn (Cap), Ian James Rush, Leighton James (Michael Reginald Thomas).
Trainer: Harold Michael England

NORTHERN IRELAND: Patrick Anthony Jennings (46 James Archibald Platt), James Michael Nicholl, Malachy Martin Donaghy, John McClelland, Christopher James Nicholl, James Cleary (Robert McFaul Campbell), Noel Brotherston, Patrick Joseph Healy, Gerard Joseph Armstrong, Samuel Baxter McIlroy (Cap), William Robert Hamilton.
Manager: William Bingham

Goals: Alan Thomas Curtis (#), Ian James Rush (#), Peter Nicholas (#)

347. 17.06.1982   12th World Cup, 1st Round
NORTHERN IRELAND v YUGOSLAVIA 0-0
La Romareda, Zaragoza

Referee: Erik Fredriksson (Sweden)   Attendance: 25,000

NORTHERN IRELAND: Patrick Anthony Jennings, James Michael Nicholl, Christopher James Nicholl, John McClelland, Malachy Martin Donaghy, Samuel Baxter McIlroy, Martin Hugh Michael O'Neill (Cap), David McCreery, Gerard Joseph Armstrong, William Robert Hamilton, Norman Whiteside.
Manager: William Bingham

YUGOSLAVIA: Dragan Pantelić, Nikola Jovanović, Miloš Hrstić, Ivan Gudelj, Velimir Zajec, Nenad Stojković, Vladimir Petrović, Edhem Šljivo, Ivan Šurjak (Cap), Safet Sušić, Zlatko Vujović.   Trainer: Miljan Miljanić

348. 21.06.1982   12th World Cup, 1st Round
HONDURAS v NORTHERN IRELAND 1-1 (0-1)
La Romareda, Zaragoza

Referee: Chan Tam Sung (Hong Kong)   Attendance: 15,000

HONDURAS: Julio Arzu, Efrain Gutiérrez, Jaime Villegas, Julio Allan Costly, José Luis Cruz, Ramón Maradiaga (Cap), Gilberto Yearwood, Héctor Zelaya, Prudencio Norales (56 Eduardo Antonio Laing), Portfirio Armando Betancourt, Roberto Figueroa.   Trainer: José la Paz Herrera

NORTHERN IRELAND: Patrick Anthony Jennings, James Michael Nicholl, Christopher James Nicholl, John McClelland, Malachy Martin Donaghy, Martin Hugh Michael O'Neill (Cap) (77 Patrick Joseph Healy), David McCreery, Samuel Baxter McIlroy, Gerard Joseph Armstrong, William Robert Hamilton, Norman Whiteside (86 Noel Brotherston).
Manager: William Bingham

Goals: Eduardo Antonio Laing (60) / Gerard Armstrong (9)

349. 25.06.1982   12th World Cup, 1st Round
SPAIN v NORTHERN IRELAND 0-1 (0-0)
Luis Casanova, Valencia

Referee: Hector Froilan Ortiz Ramirez (Paraguay)
Attendance: 49,562

SPAIN: Luis Miguel Arkonada (Cap), José Antonio Camacho, Miguel Tendillo, José Ramón Alexanco, Rafael Gordillo, Enrique Saura, Miguel Ángel "Perico" Alonso, José Vicente Sánchez, Juan Enrique Gómez "Juanito", Jesús María Satrústegui (46 Enrique Castro González "Quini"), Roberto López Ufarte (77 Ricardo Gallego).
Trainer: José Emilio Santamaría Iglesias

NORTHERN IRELAND: Patrick Anthony Jennings, James Michael Nicholl, Christopher James Nicholl, John McClelland, Malachy Martin Donaghy, David McCreery, Martin Hugh Michael O'Neill (Cap), Samuel Baxter McIlroy (50 Thomas Cassidy), Gerard Joseph Armstrong, William Robert Hamilton, Norman Whiteside (73 Samuel Nelson).
Manager: William Bingham

Sent off: Malachy Martin Donaghy (62)

Goal: Gerard Joseph Armstrong (48)

350. 01.07.1982   12th World Cup, 2nd Round
AUSTRIA v NORTHERN IRELAND 2-2 (0-1)
Vicente Calderon, Madrid

Referee: Adolf Prokop (East Germany)   Attendance: 24,000

AUSTRIA: Friedrich Koncilia, Bernd Krauss, Bruno Pezzey, Erich Obermayer, Anton Pichler, Maximilian Hagmayr (46 Kurt Welzl), Josef Pregesbauer (46 Reinhold Hintermaier), Herbert Prohaska, Ernst Baumeister, Walter Schachner, Gernot Jurtin.   Trainers: Felix Latzke & Georg Schmidt

NORTHERN IRELAND: James Archibald Platt, James Michael Nicholl, Christopher James Nicholl, John McClelland, Samuel Nelson, David McCreery, Martin Hugh Michael O'Neill (Cap), Samuel Baxter McIlroy, Gerard Joseph Armstrong, William Robert Hamilton, Norman Whiteside (66 Noel Brotherston).   Manager: William Bingham

Goals: Bruno Pezzey (50), Reinhold Hintermaier (68) / William Robert Hamilton (27, 75)

351. 04.07.1982   12th World Cup, 2nd Round
FRANCE v NORTHERN IRELAND 4-1 (1-0)
Vicente Calderón, Madrid

Referee: Alojzy Jarguz (Poland)   Attendance: 37,000

FRANCE: Jean-Luc Ettori, Manuel Amoros, Gérard Janvion, Marius Trésor, Maxime Bossis, Jean Amadou Tigana, Alain Giresse, Bernard Genghini, Michel Platini (Cap), Gérard Soler (63 Didier Six), Dominique Rocheteau (83 Alain Couriol). Trainer: Michel Hidalgo

NORTHERN IRELAND: Patrick Anthony Jennings, James Michael Nicholl, Christopher James Nicholl, Malachy Martin Donaghy, John McClelland, David McCreery (86 John Patrick O'Neill), Martin Hugh Michael O'Neill (Cap), Samuel Baxter McIlroy, Gerard Joseph Armstrong, Norman Whiteside, William Robert Hamilton.   Manager: William Bingham

Goals: Alain Giresse (33, 80), Dominique Rocheteau (46, 68) / Gerard Joseph Armstrong (75)

352. 13.10.1982   7th European Champs Qualifiers
AUSTRIA v NORTHERN IRELAND 2-0 (2-0)
Gerhard Hanappi, Wien

Referee: Andrei Butenko (Soviet Union)   Attendance: 9,885

AUSTRIA: Friedrich Koncilia, Bernd Krauss, Bruno Pezzey, Erich Obermayer, Josef Degeorgi, Herbert Prohaska, Heribert Weber, Felix Gasselich, Walter Schachner, Maximilian Hagmayr (69 Peter Pacult), Gernot Jurtin (69 Ernst Baumeister).   Trainer: Erich Hof

NORTHERN IRELAND: James Archibald Platt, James Michael Nicholl, John Patrick O'Neill, John McClelland, Malachy Martin Donaghy Martin Hugh Michael O'Neill, Ian Edwin Stewart (79 Patrick Joseph Healy), David McCreery, Samuel Baxter McIlroy (59 Noel Brotherston), Gerard Joseph Armstrong, William Robert Hamilton.
Manager: William Bingham

Goals: Walter Schachner (3, 41)

353. 17.11.1982   7th European Champs Qualifiers
NORTHERN IRELAND v WEST GERMANY 1-0 (1-0)
Windsor Park, Belfast

Referee: Rolf Nyhus (Norway)   Attendance: 25,000

NORTHERN IRELAND: James Archibald Platt, James Michael Nicholl, Malachy Martin Donaghy, John Patrick O'Neill, John McClelland, Martin Hugh Michael O'Neill, Noel Brotherston, Samuel Baxter McIlroy, Norman Whiteside, William Robert Hamilton, Ian Edwin Stewart.
Manager: William Bingham

WEST GERMANY: Harald Schumacher, Manfred Kaltz, Ulrich Stielike, Gerhard Strack, Bernd Förster, Bernd Schuster (72 Rudolf Völler), Lothar Herbert Matthäus (72 Stephan Engels), Hans-Peter Briegel, Pierre Littbarski, Klaus Allofs, Karl-Heinz Rummenigge (Cap).   Trainer: Josef Derwall

Goal: Ian Edwin Stewart (18)

354. 15.12.1982   7th European Champs Qualifiers
ALBANIA v NORTHERN IRELAND 0-0
Qemal Stafa, Tiranë

Referee: Jozef Nemčovský (Czechoslovakia)   Att: 25,000

ALBANIA: Perlat Musta, Pedro Ruçi, Arian Hametaj, Muhedin Targaj, Arian Bimo (46 Bedri Omuri), Haxhi Ballgjini, Luan Vukatana, Ferid Rragami, Roland Luçi (46 Shkëlqim Muça), Arben Minga, Agustin Kola.
Trainer: Shyqyri Rreli

NORTHERN IRELAND: James Archibald Platt, Malachy Martin Donaghy, James Michael Nicholl, John Patrick O'Neill, John McClelland, Martin Hugh Michael O'Neill, Noel Brotherston, Samuel Baxter McIlroy, Norman Whiteside, William Robert Hamilton, Ian Edwin Stewart.
Manager: William Bingham

355. 30.03.1983   7th European Champs Qualifiers
NORTHERN IRELAND v TURKEY 2-1 (2-0)
Windsor Park, Belfast

Referee: Alain Delmer (France)   Attendance: 20,000

NORTHERN IRELAND: James Archibald Platt, James Michael Nicholl, Malachy Martin Donaghy, John Patrick O'Neill, John McClelland, Martin Hugh Michael O'Neill (Cap), Noel Brotherston, Samuel Baxter McIlroy, Norman Whiteside, Gerard Joseph Armstrong, Ian Edwin Stewart.
Manager: William Bingham

TURKEY: Eser Özaltındere, Erdoğan Arica, Fatih Terim, Yusuf Altıntaş, Hakan Küfükçüoğlu, Eren Talu (83 Arif Kocabıyık), Raşit Çetiner, Hüseyin Çakıroğlu, Metin Tekin, Selçuk Yula, Hasan Şengün.   Trainer: Coşkun Özarı

Goals: Martin O'Neill (5), John McClelland (17) / Hasan Şengün (56)

356. 27.04.1983 7th European Champs Qualifiers
NORTHERN IRELAND v ALBANIA 1-0 (0-0)
Windsor Park, Belfast

Referee: Ib Nielsen (Denmark)   Attendance: 12,000

NORTHERN IRELAND: Patrick Anthony Jennings, James Michael Nicholl, John McClelland, John Patrick O'Neill, Malachy Martin Donaghy, Martin Hugh Michael O'Neill (Cap), Samuel Baxter McIlroy, Noel Brotherston (63 Gerald Mullan), William Robert Hamilton, Gerard Joseph Armstrong, Ian Edwin Stewart.   Manager: William Bingham

ALBANIA: Perlat Musta, Pedro Ruçi, Arian Hametaj, Muhedin Targaj, Kristaq Eksarko (46 Sulejman Mema), Bedri Omuri, Sulejman Demollari, Luan Vukatana, Ilir Lame, Shkëlqim Muça, Arben Minga.   Trainer: Shyqyri Rreli

Goal: Ian Edwin Stewart (54)

357. 24.05.1983 British Championship
SCOTLAND v NORTHERN IRELAND 0-0
Hampden Park, Glasgow

Referee: Keith Hackett (England)   Attendance: 16,238

SCOTLAND: William Thomson, Richard Charles Gough, Alistair John Dawson, David Narey, Paul Anthony Hegarty (Cap), Thomas Burns, Neil Simpson (65 Gordon David Strachan), John Wark, Eamonn John Peter Bannon, Andrew Mullen Gray, Charles Nicholas.   Manager: John Stein

NORTHERN IRELAND: Patrick Anthony Jennings, James Michael Nicholl, Malachy Martin Donaghy, John Patrick O'Neill (46 Christopher James Nicholl), John McClelland, Martin Hugh Michael O'Neill (Cap), Gerald Mullan, Samuel Baxter McIlroy, Gerard Joseph Armstrong, William Robert Hamilton (89 Noel Brotherston), Ian Edwin Stewart.   Manager: William Bingham

358. 28.05.1983 British Championship
NORTHERN IRELAND v ENGLAND 0-0
Windsor Park, Belfast

Referee: Howard William King (Wales)   Attendance: 22,000

NORTHERN IRELAND: Patrick Anthony Jennings, James Michael Nicholl, Malachy Martin Donaghy, John McClelland, Christopher James Nicholl, Martin Hugh Michael O'Neill (Cap), Gerald Mullan (Noel Brotherston), Samuel Baxter McIlroy, Gerard Joseph Armstrong, William Robert Hamilton, Ian Edwin Stewart.   Manager: William Bingham

ENGLAND: Peter Leslie Shilton (Cap), Philip George Neal, Kenneth Graham Sansom, Glenn Hoddle, Terence Ian Butcher, Graham Paul Roberts, Gary Vincent Mabbutt, Luther Loide Blissett (69 John Charles Bryan Barnes), Peter Withe, Gordon Sidney Cowans, Trevor John Francis.   Manager: Robert Robson

359. 31.05.1983 British Championship
NORTHERN IRELAND v WALES 0-1 (0-0)
Windsor Park, Belfast

Referee: Hugh Alexander (Scotland)   Attendance: 8,000

NORTHERN IRELAND: Patrick Anthony Jennings, James Michael Nicholl, Malachy Martin Donaghy, John McClelland, Christopher James Nicholl, Samuel Baxter McIlroy, Noel Brotherston, Gerald Mullan (James Cleary), Gerard Joseph Armstrong, William Robert Hamilton, Ian Edwin Stewart.   Manager: William Bingham

WALES: Neville Southall, Jeffrey Hopkins, Joseph Patrick Jones, Kevin Ratcliffe, Paul Terence Price (72 David Charles Giles), Peter Nicholas (Cap), Brian Flynn, Gordon John Davies, Jeremy Melvyn Charles, Michael Reginald Thomas, Alan Davies.   Trainer: Harold Michael England

Goal: Gordon John Davies (#)

360. 21.09.1983 7th European Champs Qualifiers
NORTHERN IRELAND v AUSTRIA 3-1 (1-0)
Windsor Park, Belfast

Referee: Erik Fredriksson (Sweden)   Attendance: 18,013

NORTHERN IRELAND: Patrick Anthony Jennings), Paul Christopher Ramsey, Christopher James Nicholl, John McClelland, Malachy Martin Donaghy, Martin Hugh Michael O'Neill (Cap), Samuel Baxter McIlroy, Ian Edwin Stewart, William Robert Hamilton, Gerard Joseph Armstrong, Norman Whiteside.   Manager: William Bingham

AUSTRIA: Friedrich Koncilia, Bernd Krauss, Bruno Pezzey, Reinhard Kienast (71 Josef Degeorgi), Leopold Lainer, Heribert Weber, Herbert Prohaska, Felix Gasselich, Martin Gisinger (71 Gerald Willfurth), Walter Schachner, Johann Krankl.   Trainer: Erich Hof

Goals: William Hamilton (28), Norman Whiteside (67), Martin Hugh Michael O'Neill (89) / Felix Gasselich (82)

361. 12.10.1983 7th European Champs Qualifiers
TURKEY v NORTHERN IRELAND 1-0 (1-0)
19 Mayis, Ankara

Referee: Romualdas Yushka (Soviet Union)   Att: 35,000

TURKEY: Adem Ibrahimoğlu, Ismail Demiriz, Fatih Terim, Yusuf Altıntaş, Erdoğan Arica, Halil Ibrahim Eren (41 Riza Çalımbay), Sedat III Özden, Raşit Çetiner, Ilyas Tüfekçi, Hasan Şengün, Selçuk Yula.   Trainer: Coşkun Özarı

NORTHERN IRELAND: Patrick Anthony Jennings, James Michael Nicholl, Malachy Martin Donaghy, Christopher James Nicholl, John McClelland, Martin Hugh Michael O'Neill (Cap), Noel Brotherston (78 James Cleary), Samuel Baxter McIlroy, William Robert Hamilton (64 David McCreery), Norman Whiteside, Ian Edwin Stewart.   Manager: William Bingham

Goal: Selçuk Yula (17)

362. 16.11.1983   7th European Champs Qualifiers
WEST GERMANY v NORTHERN IRELAND 0-1 (0-0)
Volkspark, Hamburg

Referee: Károly Palotai (Hungary)   Attendance: 61,418

WEST GERMANY: Harald Schumacher, Wolfgang Dremmler, Ulrich Stielike (84 Gerhard Strack), Karlheinz Förster, Hans-Peter Briegel, Klaus Augenthaler, Wolfgang Rolff, Lothar Herbert Matthäus, Norbert Meier (68 Pierre Littbarski), Herbert Waas, Karl-Heinz Rummenigge (Cap). Trainer: Josef Derwall

NORTHERN IRELAND: Patrick Anthony Jennings, James Michael Nicholl, Gerard McElhinney, John McClelland, Malachy Martin Donaghy, Paul Christopher Ramsey, Martin Hugh Michael O'Neill (Cap), Gerard Joseph Armstrong, Norman Whiteside, William Robert Hamilton, Ian Edwin Stewart. Manager: William Bingham

Goal: Norman Whiteside (50)

363. 13.12.1983   British Championship
NORTHERN IRELAND v SCOTLAND 2-0 (1-0)
Windsor Park, Belfast

Referee: Neil Midgley (England)   Attendance: 12,000

NORTHERN IRELAND: Patrick Anthony Jennings, James Michael Nicholl, Malachy Martin Donaghy, John McClelland, Gerard McElhinney, Paul Christopher Ramsey, George Terence Cochrane (86 John Patrick O'Neill), Samuel Baxter McIlroy (Cap), William Robert Hamilton, Norman Whiteside, Ian Edwin Stewart. Manager: William Bingham

SCOTLAND: James Leighton, Richard Charles Gough, Douglas Rougvie, Robert Sime Aitken, Alexander McLeish, Gordon David Strachan, Paul Michael Lyons McStay, Graeme James Souness (Cap), Peter Russell Weir, David Dodds, Francis Peter McGarvey (60 Mark Edward McGhee). Manager: John Stein

Goals: Norman Whiteside (17), Samuel Baxter McIlroy (56)

364. 04.04.1984   British Championship
ENGLAND v NORTHERN IRELAND 1-0 (0-0)
Wembley, London

Referee: Ronald Bridges (Wales)   Attendance: 24,000

ENGLAND: Peter Leslie Shilton, Vivian Alexander Anderson, Graham Paul Roberts, Terence Ian Butcher, Alan Philip Kennedy, Samuel Lee, Raymond Colin Wilkins, Bryan Robson (Cap), Graham Rix, Trevor John Francis, Anthony Stewart Woodcock. Manager: Robert Robson

NORTHERN IRELAND: James Archibald Platt, James Michael Nicholl, John McClelland, Gerard McElhinney, Malachy Martin Donaghy, Gerard Joseph Armstrong, Martin Hugh Michael O'Neill (Cap), William Robert Hamilton, Norman Whiteside, Samuel Baxter McIlroy, Ian Edwin Stewart. Manager: William Bingham

Goal: Anthony Stewart Woodcock (49)

365. 22.05.1984   British Championship
WALES v NORTHERN IRELAND 1-1 (0-0)
Vetch Field, Swansea

Referee: Brian Robert McKinley (Scotland)   Att: 7,845

WALES: Neville Southall, David Owen Phillips, Joseph Patrick Jones, Kevin Ratcliffe, Jeffrey Hopkins, Alan Davies, Robert Mark James, Kenneth Francis Jackett, Gordon John Davies (Nigel Mark Vaughan), Ian James Rush, Mark Leslie Hughes. Trainer: Harold Michael England

NORTHERN IRELAND: Patrick Anthony Jennings (38 James Archibald Platt), Malachy Martin Donaghy, Nigel Worthington, John McClelland, Gerard McElhinney, Martin Hugh Michael O'Neill (Cap), Samuel Baxter McIlroy, Gerard Joseph Armstrong, Norman Whiteside, William Robert Hamilton, Ian Edwin Stewart. Manager: William Bingham

Goals: Mark Hughes (51) / Gerard Joseph Armstrong (75)

366. 27.05.1984   13th World Cup Qualifiers
FINLAND v NORTHERN IRELAND 1-0 (0-0)
Porin, Pori

Referee: Karl-Heinz Tritschler (Germany)   Att: 8,000

FINLAND: Olavi Huttunen, Esa Pekonen, Pauno Kymäläinen, Jukka Ikäläinen (48 Jari Europaeus), Erkka Petäjä, Hannu Turunen, Leo Houtsonen, Kari Ukkonen, Jari Rantanen, Pasi Rautiainen, Ari Valvee. Trainer: Martti Kuusela

NORTHERN IRELAND: Patrick Anthony Jennings, James Michael Nicholl, John McClelland, Gerard McElhinney, Malachy Martin Donaghy, Martin Hugh Michael O'Neill (Cap), Samuel Baxter McIlroy (78 Nigel Worthington), Gerard Joseph Armstrong (64 George Terence Cochrane), William Robert Hamilton, Norman Whiteside, Ian Edwin Stewart. Manager: William Bingham

Goal: Ari Valvee (55)

367. 12.09.1984   13th World Cup Qualifiers
NORTHERN IRELAND v ROMANIA 3-2 (1-1)
Windsor Park, Belfast

Referee: Alexis Ponnet (Belgium)   Attendance: 26,000

NORTHERN IRELAND: Patrick Anthony Jennings, James Michael Nicholl, John McClelland, Gerard McElhinney, Malachy Martin Donaghy, Gerard Joseph Armstrong, Martin Hugh Michael O'Neill (Cap), David McCreery, Ian Edwin Stewart, William Robert Hamilton, Norman Whiteside. Manager: William Bingham

ROMANIA: Silviu Lung, Mircea Rednic, Gino Iorgulescu, Costică Ştefănescu (Cap), Nicolae Ungureanu, Aurel Ţicleanu (81 Lică Movilă), Ioan Andone, Michael Klein, Mircea Irimescu (72 Ion Geolgău), Ionel Augustin, Gheorghe Hagi. Trainer: Mircea Lucescu

Goals: Gino Iorgulescu (34 own goal), N. Whiteside (66), Martin Hugh Michael O'Neill (72) / Gheorghe Hagi (36), Ion Geolgău (80)

368. 16.10.1984
NORTHERN IRELAND v ISRAEL 3-0 (3-0)
Windsor Park, Belfast

Referee: Howard William King (Wales)   Attendance: 10,000

NORTHERN IRELAND: George Dunlop, John Patrick O'Neill, John McClelland (Cap), Paul Christopher Ramsey, Nigel Worthington, James Cleary, Stephen Alexander Penney, Lee Doherty, James Martin Quinn, Norman Whiteside (73 Martin McGaughey), Ian Edwin Stewart (73 Noel Brotherston).   Manager: William Bingham

ISRAEL: Boni Ginzburg, Shlomo Shirazi, Nissim Barda, Avi Cohen, David Pizanti, Rifat Turk (Hanan Azulay), Yaacov Ekhoiz, Baruch Maman (Efraim Davidi), Gili Landau, Zahi Armeli, Eli Ohana (Eli Yani).   Trainer: Yosef Mirmovich

Goals: Norman Whiteside (3), James Martin Quinn (35), Lee Doherty (44)

369. 14.11.1984   13th World Cup Qualifiers
NORTHERN IRELAND v FINLAND 2-1 (1-1)
Windsor Park, Belfast

Referee: Alder Dante da Silva dos Santos (Portugal)   Attendance: 22,000

NORTHERN IRELAND: Patrick Anthony Jennings, James Michael Nicholl, John Patrick O'Neill, John McClelland, Malachy Martin Donaghy, Martin Hugh Michael O'Neill (Cap), Samuel Baxter McIlroy, Gerard Joseph Armstrong, James Martin Quinn, Norman Whiteside, Ian Edwin Stewart.   Manager: William Bingham

FINLAND: Olavi Huttunen, Aki Lahtinen, Pauno Kymäläinen, Jari Europaeus, Esa Pekonen, Hannu Turunen, Leo Houtsonen, Kari Ukkonen, Jukka Ikäläinen, Mika Lipponen, Ari Hjelm.   Trainer: Martti Kuusela

Goals: John Patrick O'Neill (42), Gerard Armstrong (50 pen) / Mika Lipponen (22)

370. 27.02.1985   13th World Cup Qualifiers
NORTHERN IRELAND v ENGLAND 0-1 (0-0)
Windsor Park, Belfast

Referee: Volker Roth (West Germany)   Attendance: 28,500

NORTHERN IRELAND: Patrick Anthony Jennings, James Michael Nicholl, John McClelland, John Patrick O'Neill, Malachy Martin Donaghy, Samuel Baxter McIlroy (Cap), Paul Christopher Ramsey, Gerard Joseph Armstrong, Ian Edwin Stewart, James Martin Quinn, Norman Whiteside.   Manager: William Bingham

ENGLAND: Peter Leslie Shilton, Vivian Alexander Anderson, Kenneth Graham Sansom, Alvin Edward Martin, Terence Ian Butcher, Trevor McGregor Steven, Raymond Colin Wilkins (Cap), Gary Andrew Stevens, Anthony Stewart Woodcock (78 Trevor John Francis), Mark Wayne Hateley, John Charles Bryan Barnes.   Manager: Robert Robson

Goal: Mark Wayne Hateley (77)

371. 27.03.1985
SPAIN v NORTHERN IRELAND 0-0
Insular, Palma de Mallorca

Referee: Coşkun Kutay (Turkey)   Attendance: 30,000

SPAIN: Luis Miguel Arkonada (Cap), GERARDO Miranda Concepción, Andoni Goikoetxea, Antonio Maceda, JULIO ALBERTO Moreno Casas, Juan Antonio Señor, ROBERTO Fernández, Ricardo Gallego (46 VÍCTOR Muñoz Manrique), Rafael Gordillo, Francisco Javier Clos (70 Hipólito Rincón), Emilio Butragueño (70 Juan Carlos Pérez Rojo).   Trainer: Miguel Muñoz

NORTHERN IRELAND: Patrick Anthony Jennings, James Michael Nicholl, John McClelland (Cap), John Patrick O'Neill, Malachy Martin Donaghy, Gerard Joseph Armstrong (65 Nigel Worthington), Paul Christopher Ramsey, Norman Whiteside (65 David McCreery), Ian Edwin Stewart, William Robert Hamilton, James Martin Quinn.   Manager: William Bingham

372. 01.05.1985   13th World Cup Qualifiers
NORTHERN IRELAND v TURKEY 2-0 (1-0)
Windsor Park, Belfast

Referee: Bruno Galler (Switzerland)   Attendance: 16,000

NORTHERN IRELAND: Patrick Anthony Jennings, James Michael Nicholl, John McClelland, John Patrick O'Neill, Malachy Martin Donaghy, Samuel Baxter McIlroy (Cap), Paul Christopher Ramsey, Noel Brotherston, Norman Whiteside, James Martin Quinn, Ian Edwin Stewart.   Manager: William Bingham

TURKEY: Erhan Arslan, Ismail Demiriz, Hasan Kemal Özdemir, Abdülkerim Durmaz, Semih Yuvakuran, Ilyas Tüfekçi, Raşit Çetiner, Yusuf Altintaş, Müjdat Yetkiner, Metin Tekin, Hasan Vezir.   Trainer: Kálmán Mészöly

Goals: Norman Whiteside (45, 54)

373. 11.09.1985   13th World Cup Qualifiers
TURKEY v NORTHERN IRELAND 0-0
Atatürk, Izmir

Referee: Michel Vautrot (France)   Attendance: 32,500

TURKEY: Yaşar Duran, Ismail Demiriz, Erdoğan Arica, Raşit Çetiner, Sedat III Özden, Müjdat Yetkiner, Hasan Vezir, Metin Tekin, Şenol Çorlu, Ilyas Tüfekçi (74 Bahattin Güneş), Ali Erdal Keser (31 Tanju Çolak).   Trainer: Coşkun Özarı

NORTHERN IRELAND: Patrick Anthony Jennings, James Michael Nicholl, John McClelland, John Patrick O'Neill, Malachy Martin Donaghy, Paul Christopher Ramsey, James Martin Quinn, Samuel Baxter McIlroy (Cap) (74 David McCreery), Stephen Alexander Penney, Gerard Joseph Armstrong, Nigel Worthington.   Manager: William Bingham

374. 16.10.1985   13th World Cup Qualifiers
ROMANIA v NORTHERN IRELAND 0-1 (0-1)
23 August, București
Referee: Henning Lund Sørensen (Denmark)   Att: 45,000
ROMANIA: Silviu Lung, Nicolae Negrilă (46 Ion Geolgău), Ștefan Iovan, Gino Iorgulescu, Nicolae Ungureanu, Dorin Mateuț, Mircea Rednic, Ladislau Bölöni, Michael Klein, Gheorghe Hagi (Cap), Marcel Coraș (62 Victor Pițurcă). Trainer: Mircea Lucescu
NORTHERN IRELAND: Patrick Anthony Jennings, James Michael Nicholl, Malachy Martin Donaghy, John Patrick O'Neill, Alan McDonald, David McCreery, Stephen Alexander Penney (72 Gerard Joseph Armstrong), Samuel Baxter McIlroy (Cap), James Martin Quinn, Norman Whiteside, Ian Edwin Stewart (46 Nigel Worthington).   Manager: William Bingham
Goal: James Martin Quinn (29)

375. 13.11.1985   13th World Cup Qualifiers
ENGLAND v NORTHERN IRELAND 0-0
Wembley, London
Referee: Erik Fredriksson (Sweden)   Attendance: 70,500
ENGLAND: Peter Leslie Shilton, Gary Michael Stevens, Kenneth Graham Sansom, Glenn Hoddle, Mark Wright, Terence William Fenwick, Paul William Bracewell, Raymond Colin Wilkins (Cap), Kerry Michael Dixon, Gary Winston Lineker, Christopher Roland Waddle.
Manager: Robert Robson
NORTHERN IRELAND: Patrick Anthony Jennings, James Michael Nicholl, Malachy Martin Donaghy, John Patrick O'Neill, Alan McDonald, David McCreery, Stephen Alexander Penney (59 Gerard Joseph Armstrong), Samuel Baxter McIlroy (Cap), James Martin Quinn, Norman Whiteside, Ian Edwin Stewart (72 Nigel Worthington). Manager: William Bingham

376. 26.02.1986
FRANCE v NORTHERN IRELAND 0-0
Parc des Princes, Paris
Referee: Alphonse Constantin (Belgium)   Att: 28,909
FRANCE: Joël Bats, William Ayache (46 Yvon Le Roux), Patrick Battiston, Maxime Bossis, Manuel Amoros, Alain Giresse, Luis Fernandez, Thierry Tusseau (65 Jean-Marc Ferreri), Michel Platini (Cap), Dominique Rocheteau, Jean-Pierre Papin.   Trainer: Henri Michel
NORTHERN IRELAND: Patrick Anthony Jennings, James Michael Nicholl, Malachy Martin Donaghy, John Patrick O'Neill, Alan McDonald, Colin John Clarke, David McCreery (80 John McClelland), Samuel Baxter McIlroy (Cap), Norman Whiteside, Stephen Alexander Penney (70 Mark Caughey), James Martin Quinn (80 Gerard Joseph Armstrong).
Manager: William Bingham

377. 26.03.1986
NORTHERN IRELAND v DENMARK 1-1 (1-0)
Windsor Park, Belfast
Referee: Rodger Gifford (Wales)   Attendance: 20,000
NORTHERN IRELAND: Patrick Anthony Jennings, Malachy Martin Donaghy, Nigel Worthington, John Patrick O'Neill, Alan McDonald, David McCreery (46 Gerard Joseph Armstrong), Stephen Alexander Penney, Samuel Baxter McIlroy (Cap), Colin John Clarke (70 James Martin Quinn), Norman Whiteside, Ian Edwin Stewart (70 Mark Caughey).
Manager: William Bingham
DENMARK: Troels Rasmussen, John Sivebæk, Kent Nielsen, Morten Olsen (Cap) (46 Per Frimann), Jan Bartram, Klaus Berggreen, Allan Rodenkam Simonsen (46 Flemming Christensen), Jan Mølby, John Lauridsen, Michael Laudrup (66 Henrik Andersen), Jesper Olsen.   Trainer: Josef Piontek
Goals: Alan McDonald (39) / Flemming Christensen (79)

378. 23.04.1986
NORTHERN IRELAND v MOROCCO 2-1 (1-0)
Windsor Park, Belfast
Referee: Keith Cooper (Wales)   Attendance: 12,000
NORTHERN IRELAND: Patrick Anthony Jennings (46 James Archibald Platt), Paul Christopher Ramsey, Malachy Martin Donaghy, Bernard Anthony McNally, John Patrick O'Neill, Alan McDonald, Stephen Alexander Penney (76 James Martin Quinn), Samuel Baxter McIlroy (Cap), Colin John Clarke, Norman Whiteside (46 William Robert Hamilton), Ian Edwin Stewart (66 David Anthony Campbell).
Manager: William Bingham
MOROCCO: Abdelfatah Moudami, Labd Khalifa, Fadili, Mustafa Biaz, Nouredine Bouyahiaoui, Abdelmajid Dolmy, Abderrahim (79 Otmani), Abderrazak Khairi, Krimau, Mohamed Timoumi, Azebdine Amanallah.
Trainer: José Madhi Faria
Goals: Colin John Clarke (13), James Martin Quinn (85)

379. 03.06.1986   13th World Cup, 1st Round
ALGERIA v NORTHERN IRELAND 1-1 (0-1)
Trez de Marzo, Guadalajara
Referee: Valeri Butenko (Soviet Union)   Attendance: 22,000
ALGERIA: Larbi El Hadi, Abdullah Liegeon Medjadi, Nourredine Kourichi, Mahmoud Guendouz (Cap), Fawzi Mansouri, Mahmoud Kaci-Said, Hakim Ben Mabrouk, Karim Maroc, Rabah Madjer (33 Rachid Harkouk), Djamal Zidane (71 Lakhdar Belloumi), Salah Assad.
Trainer: Ranah Saadane

NORTHERN IRELAND: Patrick Anthony Jennings, James Michael Nicholl, Malachy Martin Donaghy, John Patrick O'Neill, Alan McDonald, Nigel Worthington, Stephen Alexander Penney (67 Ian Edwin Stewart), Samuel Baxter McIlroy (Cap), David McCreery, William Robert Hamilton, Norman Whiteside (82 Colin John Clarke).
Manager: William Bingham

Goals: Djamal Zidane (59) / Norman Whiteside (6)

380.   07.06.1986   13th World Cup, 1st Round
SPAIN v NORTHERN IRELAND   2-1 (2-0)
Trez de Marzo, Guadalajara

Referee: Horst Brummeier (Austria)   Attendance: 28,000

SPAIN: Andoni Zubizarreta, Pedro Tomás, Andoni Goikoetxea, Ricardo Gallego, José Antonio Camacho (Cap), José Miguel González "Míchel", VÍCTOR Muñoz Manrique, FRANCISCO Javier López, Rafael Gordillo (53 Ramón María Calderé), JULIO SALINAS Fernández (79 Juan Antonio Señor), Emilio Butragueño.   Trainer: Miguel Muñoz

NORTHERN IRELAND: Patrick Anthony Jennings, James Michael Nicholl, Malachy Martin Donaghy, John Patrick O'Neill, Alan McDonald, Nigel Worthington (70 William Robert Hamilton), Stephen Alexander Penney (54 Ian Edwin Stewart), Samuel Baxter McIlroy (Cap), David McCreery, Colin John Clarke, Norman Whiteside.
Manager: William Bingham

Goals: Emilio Butragueño (2), Julio Salinas (18) / Colin John Clarke (48)

381.   12.06.1986   13th World Cup, 1st Round
BRAZIL v NORTHERN IRELAND   3-0 (2-0)
Jalisco, Guadalajara

Referee: Siegfried Kirschen (East Germany)   Att: 51,000

BRAZIL: CARLOS Roberto Gallo, JOSIMAR Higino Pereira, JÚLIO CÉSAR da Silva, Édino Nazareth Filho "Edinho", Cláudio Ibrahim Vaz Leal "Branco", ELZO Aloísio Coelho, Ricardo Rogério de Brito "Alemão", SÓCRATES Brasileiro Sampaio Vieira de Oliveira (68 Arthur Antunes Coimbra "Zico"), Leovegildo Lins Gama Júnior, Luís Antônio Corrêa da Costa "Müller" (26 Wálter Casagrande Júnior), Antônio de Oliveira Filho "Careca".   Trainer: Telê SANTANA da Silva

NORTHERN IRELAND: Patrick Anthony Jennings, James Michael Nicholl, Malachy Martin Donaghy, John Patrick O'Neill, Alan McDonald, David McCreery, Samuel Baxter McIlroy (Cap), Ian Edwin Stewart, Colin John Clarke, Norman Whiteside (67 William Robert Hamilton), David Anthony Campbell (71 Gerard Joseph Armstrong).
Manager: William Bingham

Goals: Antônio de Oliveira Filho "Careca" (15, 88), Josimar (42)

382.   15.10.1986   8th European Champs Qualifiers
ENGLAND v NORTHERN IRELAND   3-0 (1-0)
Wembley, London

Referee: Alphonse Constantin (Belgium)   Att: 35,300

ENGLAND: Peter Leslie Shilton, Vivian Alexander Anderson, Kenneth Graham Sansom, Glenn Hoddle, David Watson, Terence Ian Butcher, Bryan Robson (Cap), Stephen Brian Hodge, Gary Winston Lineker, Peter Andrew Beardsley (84 Anthony Richard Cottee), Christopher Roland Waddle.
Manager: Robert Robson

NORTHERN IRELAND: Philip Anthony Hughes, Gary James Fleming, Alan McDonald, John McClelland (Cap), Nigel Worthington, Malachy Martin Donaghy, Norman Whiteside (84 Samuel Baxter McIlroy), Stephen Alexander Penney (74 James Martin Quinn), Colin John Clarke, David Anthony Campbell, Ian Edwin Stewart.   Manager: William Bingham

Goals: Gary Lineker (33, 80), Christopher Waddle (74)

383.   12.11.1986   8th European Champs Qualifiers
TURKEY v NORTHERN IRELAND   0-0
Atatürk, Izmir

Referee: Ştefan Dan Petrescu (România)   Att: 21,919

TURKEY: Fatih Uraz, Ismail Demiriz, Yusuf Altıntaş, Ismail Tanış, Kadir Akbulut, Savaş Demiral, Uğur Tütüneker, Metin Tekin, Rıdvan Dilmen, Tanju Çolak (46 Orhan Kapucu), Şenol Çorlu.   Trainer: Coşkun Özarı

NORTHERN IRELAND: Philip Anthony Hughes, Malachy Martin Donaghy, Alan McDonald, John McClelland (Cap), Nigel Worthington (75 Bernard Anthony McNally), Stephen Alexander Penney, Daniel Joseph Wilson, David McCreery, James Martin Quinn (71 Lawrence Phillip Sanchez), Colin John Clarke, David Anthony Campbell.
Manager: William Bingham

384.   18.02.1987
ISRAEL v NORTHERN IRELAND   1-1 (0-1)
National, Ramat-Gan, Tel-Aviv

Referee: Tullio Lanese (Italy)   Attendance: 4,081

ISRAEL: Avi Ran, Avi Cohen II, Menashe Shimonov, Avi Cohen I (46 Efraim Davidi), Zion Marili, Uri Malmilian, Nir Klinger, Moshe Sinai (71 Eli Yani), Daniel Brailovsky, Moshe Eisenberg (Eli Driks), Eli Ohana.   Trainer: Miljenko Mihić

NORTHERN IRELAND: Philip Anthony Hughes, Gary James Fleming, Alan McDonald, John McClelland (Cap), Malachy Martin Donaghy, Stephen Alexander Penney (79 Ian Edwin Stewart), Paul Christopher Ramsey, Daniel Joseph Wilson, Kevin James Wilson, Norman Whiteside, Nigel Worthington.   Manager: William Bingham

Goals: Zion Marili (87) / Stephen Alexander Penney (38)

385. 01.04.1987   8th European Champs Qualifiers
NORTHERN IRELAND v ENGLAND   0-2 (0-2)
Windsor Park, Belfast

Referee: Emilio Soriano Aladren (Spain)   Att: 20,578

NORTHERN IRELAND: George Dunlop, Gary James Fleming, Malachy Martin Donaghy, John McClelland (Cap), Alan McDonald, Paul Christopher Ramsey, David Anthony Campbell (59 Daniel Joseph Wilson), David McCreery, Kevin James Wilson, Norman Whiteside, Nigel Worthington. Manager: William Bingham

ENGLAND: Peter Leslie Shilton (46 Christopher Charles Eric Woods), Vivian Alexander Anderson, Kenneth Graham Sansom, Gary Vincent Mabbutt, Mark Wright, Terence Ian Butcher, Bryan Robson (Cap), Stephen Brian Hodge, Peter Andrew Beardsley, Gary Winston Lineker, Christopher Roland Waddle.   Manager: Robert Robson

Goals: Bryan Robson (19), Christopher Roland Waddle (43)

386. 29.04.1987   8th European Champs Qualifiers
NORTHERN IRELAND v YUGOSLAVIA   1-2 (1-0)
Windsor Park, Belfast

Referee: Werner Föckler (West Germany)   Att: 5,482

NORTHERN IRELAND: George Dunlop, Gary James Fleming, Malachy Martin Donaghy, John McClelland (Cap), Alan McDonald, David Anthony Campbell (76 Raymond McCoy), David McCreery (46 Paul Christopher Ramsey), Colin John Clarke, Kevin James Wilson, Norman Whiteside, Nigel Worthington.   Manager: William Bingham

YUGOSLAVIA: Tomislav Ivković, Zoran Vujović, Mirsad Baljić, Srećko Katanec (46 Zoran Vulić), Marko Elsner, Faruk Hadžibegić, Dragan Stojković, Milan Janković, Darko Pančev, Aljoša Asanović (77 Admir Smajić), Zlatko Vujović (Cap).   Trainer: Ivan Osim

Goals: Colin John Clarke (39) /
Dragan Stojković (47), Zlatko Vujović (80)

387. 14.10.1987   8th European Champs Qualifiers
YUGOSLAVIA v NORTHERN IRELAND   3-0 (2-0)
Grbavica, Sarajevo

Referee: Klaus Peschel (East Germany)   Attendance: 14,075

YUGOSLAVIA: Mauro Ravnić, Zoran Vujović, Mirsad Baljić, Srećko Katanec, Faruk Hadžibegić, Ljubomir Radanović, Zlatko Vujović (Cap), Marko Mlinarić (76 Dragoljub Brnović), Fadilj Vokri (76 Dejan Savićević), Mehmed Baždarević, Borislav Cvetković.   Trainer: Ivan Osim

NORTHERN IRELAND: Allen Darrell McKnight, Paul Christopher Ramsey, Nigel Worthington, Malachy Martin Donaghy, Alan McDonald, David McCreery (Cap), David Anthony Campbell (55 Anton Gerard Patrick Rogan), Daniel Joseph Wilson, Colin John Clarke (46 James Martin Quinn), Bernard Anthony McNally, Kevin James Wilson. Manager: William Bingham

Goals: Fadilj Vokri (13, 35), Faruk Hadžibegić (74 pen)

388. 11.11.1987   8th European Champs Qualifiers
NORTHERN IRELAND v TURKEY   1-0 (0-0)
Windsor Park, Belfast

Referee: Peter Mikkelsen (Denmark)   Attendance: 3,931

NORTHERN IRELAND: Allen Darrell McKnight, Gary James Fleming, Nigel Worthington, Malachy Martin Donaghy, Alan McDonald, John McClelland (Cap), Norman Whiteside, Daniel Joseph Wilson (66 Lee Doherty), Colin John Clarke, James Martin Quinn, Kevin James Wilson (56 David Anthony Campbell).   Manager: William Bingham

TURKEY: Okan Gedikali, Ismail Demiriz, Gökhan Keskin, Yusuf Altıntaş, Semih Yuvakuran, Riza Çalımbay, Savaş Demiral, Uğur Tütüneker, Metin Tekin (65 Hamı Mandıralı), Tanju Çolak (79 Ali Gültiken), Ali Erdal Keser. Trainer: Mustafa Denizli

Goal: James Martin Quinn (47)

389. 17.02.1988
GREECE v NORTHERN IRELAND   3-2 (0-1)
Olympiako, Athína

Referee: Zdravko Đokić (Yugoslavia)   Attendance: 12,000

GREECE: Antónis Minou (46 Giánnis Gitsioudis), Efstratios Apostolakis, Konstantinos Kolomitrousis, Stélios Manolas, Pétros Mihos (46 Konstantinos Mavridis), Giórgos Skartados (46 Panagiótis Tsalouhidis), Dimítris Saravakos (Cap), Vasílis Karapialis, Vasílis Dimitriadis (66 Stéfanos Borbokis), Anastásios Mitropoulos, Sávvas Kofidis (46 Nikolaos Nioplias).   Trainer: Miltos Papapostolou

NORTHERN IRELAND: Allen Darrell McKnight, Gary James Fleming, Anton Gerard Patrick Rogan, Malachy Martin Donaghy, John McClelland (Cap), Nigel Worthington, Daniel Joseph Wilson, Bernard Anthony McNally (77 Kevin James Wilson), Colin John Clarke, James Martin Quinn, Michael Andrew Martin O'Neill (66 David Anthony Campbell). Manager: William Bingham

Goals: Stélios Manolas (61, 79), Anastásios Mitropoulos (89) / Colin John Clarke (32, 76)

390. 23.03.1988
NORTHERN IRELAND v POLAND   1-1 (1-1)
Windsor Park, Belfast

Referee: Rodger Gifford (Wales)   Attendance: 4,903

NORTHERN IRELAND: Allen Darrell McKnight, Gary James Fleming, Nigel Worthington, Norman Whiteside (Cap), Alan McDonald, Malachy Martin Donaghy, Daniel Joseph Wilson, Stephen Alexander Penney (70 David Anthony Campbell), Colin John Clarke, James Martin Quinn (78 Kevin James Wilson), Michael Andrew Martin O'Neill (60 Anton Gerard Patrick Rogan).   Manager: William Bingham

POLAND: Józef Wandzik, Dariusz Kubicki, Damian Łukasik, Dariusz Wdowczyk, Ryszard Tarasiewicz (46 Jan Karaś), Ryszard Komornicki (85 Wiesław Cisek), Zbigniew Boniek, Jan Urban, Jacek Ziober (64 Jarosław Araszkiewicz), Dariusz Dziekanowski, Roman Kosecki.   Trainer: Wojciech Łazarek

Goals: Daniel Joseph Wilson (2) / Dariusz Dziekanowski (32)

391. 27.04.1988
NORTHERN IRELAND v FRANCE   0-0
Windsor Park, Belfast

Referee: Keith Cooper (Wales)   Attendance: 6,250

NORTHERN IRELAND: Allen Darrell McKnight, Malachy Martin Donaghy, Nigel Worthington, Norman Whiteside (40 James Martin Quinn), Alan McDonald, John McClelland (Cap), Daniel Joseph Wilson, Stephen Alexander Penney, Colin John Clarke (83 Kevin James Wilson), Michael Andrew Martin O'Neill, Robert Dennison (60 Kingsley Terence Black). Manager: William Bingham

FRANCE: Bruno Martini, Luc Sonor, Sylvain Kastendeuch, Bernard Casoni, Manuel Amoros, Domonique Bijotat, Luis Fernandez (Cap), Philippe Vercruysse (83 Jean-Marc Ferreri), Jean-Philippe Durand, Yannick Stopyra, Patrice Garande (83 Philippe Fargeon).   Trainer: Henri Michel

392. 21.05.1988   14th World Cup Qualifiers
NORTHERN IRELAND v MALTA   3-0 (3-0)
Windsor Park, Belfast

Referee: Carlos Alberto da Silva Valente (Portugal) Attendance: 9,000

NORTHERN IRELAND: Allen Darrell McKnight, Malachy Martin Donaghy, Nigel Worthington, John McClelland (Cap), Alan McDonald, Michael Andrew Martin O'Neill, Daniel Joseph Wilson, Stephen Alexander Penney (81 Bernard Anthony McNally), Colin John Clarke, James Martin Quinn, Robert Dennison (85 Kingsley Terence Black). Manager: William Bingham

MALTA: David Cluett, Edwin Camilleri (46 Charles Micallef II), Alex Azzopardi, Joseph Galea, Joseph Brincat, John Buttigieg (Cap), Carmel Busuttil, Charles Scerri, David Carabott, Martin Scicluna, Michael Degiorgio (59 John Caruana).   Trainer: Horst Heese

Goals: James Quinn (15), Stephen Alexander Penney (23), Colin John Clarke (25)

393. 14.09.1988   14th World Cup Qualifiers
**NORTHERN IRELAND
v REPUBLIC OF IRELAND   0-0**
Windsor Park, Belfast

Referee: Michel Vautrot (France)   Attendance: 19,873

NORTHERN IRELAND: Allen Darrell McKnight, Malachy Martin Donaghy (46 Anton Gerard Patrick Rogan), Alan McDonald, John McClelland (Cap), Nigel Worthington, Stephen Alexander Penney, Daniel Joseph Wilson, Michael Andrew Martin O'Neill, Kingsley Terence Black, James Martin Quinn, Colin John Clarke.   Manager: William Bingham

IRELAND: Gerald Joseph Peyton, Christopher Barry Morris, Michael Joseph McCarthy, Kevin Bernard Moran (Cap), Christopher William Gerard Hughton, Raymond James Houghton, Paul McGrath, Ronald Andrew Whelan, Kevin Mark Sheedy, Anthony Guy Cascarino, John William Aldridge. Manager: John Charlton

394. 19.10.1988   14th World Cup Qualifiers
HUNGARY v NORTHERN IRELAND   1-0 (0-0)
Népstadion, Budapest

Referee: Kurt Röthlisberger (Switzerland)   Att: 18,000

HUNGARY: Péter Disztl, Sándor Sallai, Antal Nagy, Géza Mészöly (46 László Dajka), János Sass, István Kozma, György Bognár, Lajos Détári, Imre Garaba, József Kiprich, Gyula Hajszán (82 István Vincze).   Trainer: György Mezey

NORTHERN IRELAND: Allen Darrell McKnight, Anton Gerard Patrick Rogan, Nigel Worthington, John McClelland (Cap), Alan McDonald, Malachy Martin Donaghy, Robert Dennison, Daniel Joseph Wilson, Colin John Clarke (81 James Martin Quinn), Michael Andrew Martin O'Neill (58 Kevin James Wilson), Kingsley Terence Black.
Manager: William Bingham

Goal: István Vincze (85)

395. 21.12.1988   14th World Cup Qualifiers
SPAIN v NORTHERN IRELAND 4-0 (1-0)
Ramón Sánchez Pizjuán, Sevilla
Referee: Marcel van Langenhove (Belgium)   Att: 70,000
SPAIN: Andoni Zubizarreta, Enrique Sánchez "Quique" Flores, Manuel Jiménez, Genar Andrinúa, Alberto Górriz, José Miguel González "Míchel", ROBERTO Fernández, Rafael Martín Vázquez, Manuel Sánchez "Manolo" (78 JULIO SALINAS Fernández), Emilio Butragueño (Cap), Aítor Beguiristáin (65 Ricardo Jesús Serna).   Trainer: Luis Suárez
NORTHERN IRELAND: Allen Darrell McKnight, Anton Gerard Patrick Rogan, Alan McDonald, John McClelland (Cap), Nigel Worthington, David McCreery (54 James Martin Quinn), Malachy Martin Donaghy (72 Michael Andrew Martin O'Neill), Stephen Alexander Penney, Colin John Clarke, Kevin James Wilson, Kingsley Terence Black.   Manager: William Bingham
Goals: Anton Gerard Patrick Rogan (30 own goal), Emilio Butragueño (55), José Miguel González "Míchel" (60 pen), Alan McDonald (64 own goal)

396. 08.02.1989   14th World Cup Qualifiers
NORTHERN IRELAND v SPAIN 0-2 (0-1)
Windsor Park, Belfast
Referee: Dieter Pauly (West Germany)   Attendance: 15,000
NORTHERN IRELAND: Allen Darrell McKnight, Paul Christopher Ramsey, Anton Gerard Patrick Rogan, Malachy Martin Donaghy, John McClelland (Cap), Daniel Joseph Wilson (68 Colin John Clarke), Robert Dennison (63 Michael Andrew Martin O'Neill), Lawrence Phillip Sanchez, James Martin Quinn, Kevin James Wilson, Kingsley Terence Black.   Manager: William Bingham
SPAIN: Andoni Zubizarreta, Miguel Porlán Noguera "Chendo" (39 EUSEBIO Sacristán), Manuel Jiménez, Genar Andrinúa, Ricardo Jesús Serna, Alberto Górriz, José María Bakero (70 Manuel Sánchez "Manolo"), José Miguel González "Míchel", Emilio Butragueño (Cap), ROBERTO Fernández, Rafael Martín Vázquez.   Trainer: Luis Suárez
Goals: Genar Andrinúa (3), Manuel Sánchez "Manolo" (84)

397. 26.04.1989   14th World Cup Qualifiers
MALTA v NORTHERN IRELAND 0-2 (0-0)
National, Ta'Qali
Referee: Ştefan Dan Petrescu (România)   Att: 15,150
MALTA: David Cluett, John Buttigieg, Edwin Camilleri, Dennis Cauchi (62 Silvio Vella), Joseph Galea, Michael Degiorgio, Carmel Busuttil, Raymond Vella (Cap), David Carabott (78 Jesmond Delia), Charles Scerri, Martin Gregory.   Trainer: Horst Heese

NORTHERN IRELAND: Thomas James Wright, Gary James Fleming, Malachy Martin Donaghy, John McClelland (Cap), Nigel Worthington (86 Anton Gerard Patrick Rogan), David McCreery, Daniel Joseph Wilson, Lawrence Phillip Sanchez (70 Michael Andrew Martin O'Neill), James Martin Quinn, Colin John Clarke, Kevin James Wilson.   Manager: William Bingham
Goals: Colin John Clarke (56), Michael O'Neill (73)

398. 26.05.1989
NORTHERN IRELAND v CHILE 0-1 (0-1)
Windsor Park, Belfast
Referee: George Brian Smith (Scotland)   Attendance: 6,850
NORTHERN IRELAND: Thomas James Wright, Gary James Fleming, Alan McDonald, Malachy Martin Donaghy (Cap), Anton Gerard Patrick Rogan, Daniel Joseph Wilson (75 Robert Dennison), David McCreery (75 Colin O'Neill), Michael Andrew Martin O'Neill, Kevin James Wilson (64 Kingsley Terence Black), James Martin Quinn (64 Liam Coyle), Colin John Clarke.   Manager: William Bingham
CHILE: Roberto Antonio Rojas, Leonel Contreras, Rubén Alberto Espinoza, Hugo Armando González, Fernando Astengo (46 Juvenal Olmos), Oscar Patricio Reyes, Jaime Andrés Vera, Alejandro Manuel Hisis Araya, Jaime Augusto Pizarro, Osvaldo Heriberto Hurtado (85 Luis Pérez), Juan Carlos Letelier Pizarro (46 Juan Covarrubias).   Trainer: Orlando Aravena
Goal: Fernando Astengo (44)

399. 06.09.1989   14th World Cup Qualifiers
NORTHERN IRELAND v HUNGARY 1-2 (0-2)
Windsor Park, Belfast
Referee: Erik Fredriksson (Sweden)   Attendance: 15,000
NORTHERN IRELAND: Thomas James Wright, Gary James Fleming, Nigel Worthington, Anton Gerard Patrick Rogan, Alan McDonald, David McCreery, Daniel Joseph Wilson, James Martin Quinn (64 Michael Andrew Martin O'Neill), Colin John Clarke, Norman Whiteside (Cap), Kingsley Terence Black.   Manager: William Bingham
HUNGARY: Péter Disztl, László Disztl, Sándor Sallai, Ervin Kovács, Zsolt Limperger, József Keller, János Sass, Lajos Détári, György Bognár (84 Zoltán Bognár), Pál Fischer (88 Gyula Hajszán), Kálmán Kovács.   Trainer: Bertalan Bicskei
Goals: Norman Whiteside (89) /
Kálmán Kovács (13), György Bognár (43)

400. 11.10.1989   14th World Cup Qualifiers
**REPUBLIC OF IRELAND
v NORTHERN IRELAND 3-0** (1-0)
Lansdowne Road, Dublin
Referee: Pietro d'Elia (Italy)   Attendance: 45,800

IRELAND: Patrick Bonner, Christopher Barry Morris, Michael Joseph McCarthy (Cap), Kevin Bernard Moran, Stephen Staunton (77 David Anthony O'Leary), Ronald Andrew Whelan, Andrew David Townsend, Raymond James Houghton, John William Aldridge, Anthony Guy Cascarino, Kevin Mark Sheedy.   Manager: John Charlton

NORTHERN IRELAND: George Dunlop, Gary James Fleming, Nigel Worthington, Malachy Martin Donaghy (Cap), Alan McDonald, David McCreery (72 Colin O'Neill), Daniel Joseph Wilson, Michael Andrew Martin O'Neill (80 Kevin James Wilson), Colin John Clarke, Norman Whiteside, Robert Dennison.   Manager: William Bingham

Goals: Ronald Andrew Whelan (43), Anthony Cascarino (47), Raymond James Houghton (57)

401. 27.03.1990
NORTHERN IRELAND v NORWAY 2-3 (1-0)
Windsor Park, Belfast
Referee: Howard William King (Wales)   Attendance: 3,900

NORTHERN IRELAND: Paul Victor Kee, Colin Frederick Hill, Malachy Martin Donaghy, John McClelland (Cap) (78 Iain Dowie), Gerald Paul Taggart, David McCreery (19 Anton Gerard Patrick Rogan), Daniel Joseph Wilson, James Martin Quinn, Colin John Clarke, Kevin James Wilson, Kingsley Terence Black.   Manager: William Bingham

NORWAY: Erik Thorstvedt, Hugo Hansen, Erland Johnsen, Jan Halvor Halvorsen, Gunnar Halle, Karl Petter Løken, Per Egil Ahlsen, Tom Gulbrandsen, Bent Skammelsrud, Jørn Andersen, Jan Åge Fjørtoft (79 Jahn Ivar Jakobsen).   Trainer: Ingvar Stadheim

Goals: James Martin Quinn (44), Kevin James Wilson (86) / Bent Skammelsrud (54), Jørn Andersen (57), Erland Johnsen (90)

402. 18.05.1990   Stanley Rous Cup
NORTHERN IRELAND v URUGUAY 1-0 (1-0)
Windsor Park, Belfast
Referee: Keith Cooper (Wales)   Attendance: 3,500

NORTHERN IRELAND: Thomas James Wright, Colin Frederick Hill (80 John Devine), Nigel Worthington, Gerald Paul Taggart, Alan McDonald (Cap), Anton Gerard Patrick Rogan (84 Stephen Joseph Morrow), Robert Dennison (61 David McCreery), Daniel Joseph Wilson, Kevin James Wilson, Iain Dowie, Kingsley Terence Black.
Manager: William Bingham

URUGUAY: Adolfo Javier Zeoli, Nelson Daniel Gutiérrez, Hugo Eduardo De León, José Oscar Herrera (73 José Luis Pintos Saldanha), José Batlle Perdomo, Alfonso Enrique Domínguez, Antonio Alzamendi (63 Carlos Alberto Aguilera), Santiago Javier Ostolaza, Enzo Francéscoli (Cap), Pablo Javier Bengoechea (60 Rúben Walter Paz), Rúben Sosa.
Trainer: Oscar Washington Tabárez

Goal: Kevin James Wilson (39)

403. 12.09.1990   9th European Champs Qualifiers
NORTHERN IRELAND v YUGOSLAVIA 0-2 (0-1)
Windsor Park, Belfast
Referee: Jacob Uilenberg (Holland)   Attendance: 9,008

NORTHERN IRELAND: Paul Victor Kee, Malachy Martin Donaghy, Nigel Worthington, Gerald Paul Taggart, Alan McDonald, Anton Gerard Patrick Rogan, Robert Dennison (66 Colin John Clarke), Daniel Joseph Wilson, Iain Dowie, Kevin James Wilson, Kingsley Terence Black.
Manager: William Bingham

YUGOSLAVIA: Tomislav Ivković, Zoran Vulić, Predrag Spasić, Davor Jozić, Faruk Hadžibegić (Cap), Ilija Najdoski, Robert Prosinečki, Dejan Savićević, Darko Pančev (88 Željko Petrović), Dragan Stojković (89 Vlada Stošić), Dragiša Binić.
Trainer: Ivan Osim

Goals: Darko Pančev (37), Robert Prosinečki (90)

404. 17.10.1990   9th European Champs Qualifiers
NORTHERN IRELAND v DENMARK 1-1 (0-1)
Windsor Park, Belfast
Referee: Roger Philippi (Luxembourg)   Attendance: 9,079

NORTHERN IRELAND: Paul Victor Kee, Malachy Martin Donaghy, Nigel Worthington, Gerald Paul Taggart, Alan McDonald, Anton Gerard Patrick Rogan, Daniel Joseph Wilson, Colin O'Neill (72 Stephen McBride), Iain Dowie, Colin John Clarke, Kingsley Terence Black.
Manager: William Bingham

DENMARK: Peter Schmeichel, John Sivebæk, Kent Nielsen, Lars Olsen (Cap), Jan Heintze, Jan Bartram, John Larsen, Kim Vilfort, Flemming Povlsen, Michael Laudrup (80 John Helt), Brian Laudrup (70 Lars Elstrup).
Trainer: Richard Møller Nielsen

Goals: Colin John Clarke (58) / Jan Bartram (11 pen)

405. 14.11.1990   9th European Champs Qualifiers
AUSTRIA v NORTHERN IRELAND 0-0
Prater, Wien

Referee: Gérard Biguet (France)   Attendance: 7,062

AUSTRIA: Michael Konsel, Heinz Peischl, Robert Pecl, Andreas Poiger, Peter Schöttel, Gerald Willfurth, Andreas Ogris, Peter Artner, Anton Polster (66 Peter Pacult), Manfred Linzmaier, Alfred Hörtnagl.   Trainer: Alfred Riedl

NORTHERN IRELAND: Paul Victor Kee, Malachy Martin Donaghy, Nigel Worthington, Gerald Paul Taggart, Alan McDonald, Anton Gerard Patrick Rogan, Robert Dennison, Daniel Joseph Wilson, Colin John Clarke (62 Iain Dowie), Kevin James Wilson, Kingsley Terence Black (Stephen Joseph Morrow).   Manager: William Bingham

406. 05.02.1991
NORTHERN IRELAND v POLAND 3-1 (1-1)
Windsor Park, Belfast

Referee: Keith Walter Burge (Wales)   Attendance: 8,000

NORTHERN IRELAND: Paul Victor Kee, Colin Frederick Hill, Stephen Joseph Morrow, Gerald Paul Taggart, Malachy Martin Donaghy, James Magilton, Robert Dennison (89 Stephen McBride), Michael Andrew Martin O'Neill, Colin John Clarke, Kevin James Wilson, Kingsley Terence Black.   Manager: William Bingham

POLAND: Kazimierz Sidorczuk (46 Jarosław Bako), Dariusz Kubicki (Cap), Roman Szewczyk, Piotr Soczyński, Piotr Jegor (46 Kazimierz Moskal), Robert Warzycha, Janusz Nawrocki, Andrzej Lesiak, Adam Zejer, Tomasz Cebula (46 Piotr Czachowski), Ryszard Kraus (46 Tomasz Dziubiński).   Trainer: Andrzej Strejlau

Goals: Gerald Paul Taggart (44), James Magilton (51 pen), Gerald Paul Taggart (82) / Robert Warzycha (17)

407. 27.03.1991   9th European Champs Qualifiers
YUGOSLAVIA v NORTHERN IRELAND 4-1 (1-1)
FK Crvena Zvezda, Beograd

Referee: Yusuf Namoglu (Turkey)   Attendance: 5,086

YUGOSLAVIA: Tomislav Ivković, Zoran Vulić (86 Ilija Najdoski), Robert Jarni, Predrag Spasić, Faruk Hadžibegić (Cap), Davor Jozić, Robert Prosinečki, Dejan Savićević, Darko Pančev, Mehmed Baždarević, Dragiša Binić.   Trainer: Ivan Osim

NORTHERN IRELAND: Paul Victor Kee, Gary James Fleming, Colin Frederick Hill, Malachy Martin Donaghy, Anton Gerard Patrick Rogan, Stephen Joseph Morrow, Robert Dennison (75 James Martin Quinn), James Magilton, Kevin James Wilson (54 Colin John Clarke), Kingsley Terence Black, Iain Dowie.   Manager: William Bingham

Goals: Dragiša Binić (35), Darko Pančev (47, 60, 61) / Colin Frederick Hill (45)

408. 01.05.1991   9th European Champs Qualifiers
NORTHERN IRELAND
v FAROE ISLANDS 1-1 (1-0)
Windsor Park, Belfast

Referee: Michel Piraux (Belgium)   Attendance: 10,000

NORTHERN IRELAND: Paul Victor Kee, Malachy Martin Donaghy, Nigel Worthington, Gerald Paul Taggart, Alan McDonald, James Magilton, Daniel Joseph Wilson (82 Robert Dennison), Colin John Clarke, Iain Dowie (82 Paul Andrew Williams), Kevin James Wilson, Kingsley Terence Black.   Manager: William Bingham

FAROE ISLANDS: Jens Martin Knudsen, Jóannes Jakobsen (Cap), Tummas Eli Hansen, Mikkjal Danielsen, Jan Allan Müller, Allan Mørkøre, Torkil Nielsen, Jan Dam, Ábraham Hansen, Kári Reynheim (75 Ari Thomassen), Kurt Mørkøre (85 Jens Erik Rasmussen).   Trainer: Páll Gudlaugsson

Goals: Colin John Clarke (44) / Kári Reynheim (65)

409. 11.09.1991   9th European Champs Qualifiers
FAROE ISLANDS
v NORTHERN IRELAND 0-5 (0-3)
Idrottsplats, Landskrona (Sweden)

Referee: Simo Ruokonen (Finland)   Attendance: 1,623

FAROE ISLANDS: Jens Martin Knudsen, Jóannes Jakobsen (78 Kurt Mørkøre), Tummas Eli Hansen, Mikkjal Danielsen, Ari Thomassen (57 Jan Allan Müller), Allan Mørkøre, Torkil Nielsen, Jan Dam, Ábraham Hansen, Kári Reynheim, Todi Jónsson.   Trainer: Páll Gudlaugsson

NORTHERN IRELAND: Thomas James Wright, Malachy Martin Donaghy, Stephen Joseph Morrow, Gerald Paul Taggart, Alan McDonald (Cap), James Magilton, Robert Dennison, Kevin James Wilson (68 Stephen McBride), Iain Dowie, Colin John Clarke, Kingsley Terence Black (68 Michael Andrew Martin O'Neill).   Manager: William Bingham

Sent off: Allan Mørkøre (67)

Goals: Kevin Wilson (8), Colin John Clarke (12, 48, 68 pen), Alan McDonald (14)

410. 16.10.1991   9th European Champs Qualifiers
NORTHERN IRELAND v AUSTRIA   2-1 (2-1)
Windsor Park, Belfast

Referee: Leif Sundell (Sweden)   Attendance: 9,000

NORTHERN IRELAND: Thomas James Wright, Colin Frederick Hill, Nigel Worthington, Malachy Martin Donaghy (Cap), Gerald Paul Taggart, James Magilton, Robert Dennison, Iain Dowie, Colin John Clarke (46 Daniel Joseph Wilson), Kevin James Wilson, Kingsley Terence Black.
Manager: William Bingham

AUSTRIA: Wolfgang Knaller, Leopold Lainer, Leopold Rotter, Jürgen Hartmann, Walter Kogler, Manfred Zsak, Andreas Ogris, Peter Artner, Christian Keglevits (62 Andreas Herzog), Peter Stöger (62 Christoph Westerthaler), Herbert Gager.
Trainer: Dietmar Constantini

Goals: Iain Dowie (17), Kingsley Terence Black (41) / Leopold Lainer (45)

411. 13.11.1991   9th European Champs Qualifiers
DENMARK v NORTHERN IRELAND   2-1 (2-0)
Odense Stadion, Odense

Referee: Aleksey Spirin (C.I.S.)   Attendance: 10,881

DENMARK: Peter Schmeichel, Torben Piechnik, Lars Olsen (Cap), Kent Nielsen, John Sivebæk, Kim Vilfort, Johnny Mølby, Kim Christofte, Henrik Larsen, Flemming Povlsen, Lars Elstrup (52 Frank Pingel).   Trainer: Richard Møller Nielsen

NORTHERN IRELAND: Allan William Fettis, Colin Frederick Hill, Nigel Worthington, Malachy Martin Donaghy (Cap), Gerald Paul Taggart, James Magilton, Stephen McBride, Kevin James Wilson, Colin John Clarke (67 Iain Dowie), Michael Eamonn Hughes, Kingsley Terence Black (83 Robert Dennison).   Manager: William Bingham

Goals: Flemming Povlsen (22, 37) / Gerald Paul Taggart (71)

412. 19.02.1992
SCOTLAND v NORTHERN IRELAND   1-0 (1-0)
Hampden Park, Glasgow

Referee: Joseph Bertram Worrall (England)   Att: 13,651

SCOTLAND: Henry George Smith, Stewart McKimmie (46 Gordon Scott Durie), David Robertson, David McPherson, Richard Charles Gough, Gordon David Strachan (Cap), Gary McAllister, Brian John McClair (70 John Angus Paul Collins), Maurice Daniel Robert Malpas, Keith Wright (78 John Grant Robertson), Alistair Murdoch McCoist (46 Kevin William Gallacher).   Manager: Andrew Roxburgh

NORTHERN IRELAND: Thomas James Wright, Malachy Martin Donaghy, Nigel Worthington, Gerald Paul Taggart (84 Stephen Joseph Morrow), Alan McDonald (Cap), James Magilton, Kingsley Terence Black, Kevin James Wilson (81 Michael Andrew Martin O'Neill), Colin John Clarke (46 Iain Dowie), Daniel Joseph Wilson, Michael Eamonn Hughes.
Manager: William Bingham

Goal: Alistair Murdoch McCoist (11)

413. 28.04.1992   15th World Cup Qualifiers
NORTHERN IRELAND v LITHUANIA   2-2 (2-1)
Windsor Park, Belfast

Referee: Rune Pedersen (Norway)   Attendance: 4,000

NORTHERN IRELAND: Allan William Fettis, Malachy Martin Donaghy (46 Gary James Fleming), Nigel Worthington, Gerald Paul Taggart, Alan McDonald (Cap), James Magilton, Kingsley Terence Black, James Martin Quinn, Iain Dowie (80 Anton Gerard Patrick Rogan), Kevin James Wilson, Michael Eamonn Hughes.   Manager: William Bingham

LITHUANIA: Voldemaras Martinkenas, Arunas Mika, Romas Mažeikis, Arvydas Janonis (Cap), Vladimiras Buzmakovas, Arminas Narbekovas, Stasys Danisevičius, Valdas Urbonas, Stasys Baranauskas, Valdas Ivanauskas (89 Robertas Tautkus), Robertas Fridrikas (90 Audrius Žuta).
Trainer: Algimantas Liubinskas

Goals: Kevin James Wilson (13), Gerald Paul Taggart (16) / Arminas Narbekovas (40), Robertas Fridrikas (48)

414. 02.06.1992
GERMANY v NORTHERN IRELAND   1-1 (1-1)
Weser, Bremen

Referee: Alphonse Constantin (Belgium)   Att: 30,000

GERMANY: Bodo Illgner, Manfred Binz, Guido Buchwald, Jürgen Kohler, Stefan Reuter, Matthias Sammer (75 Andreas Thom), Stefan Effenberg, Andreas Brehme, Thomas Häßler (46 Thomas Doll), Rudolf Völler (Cap), Karlheinz Riedle.
Trainer: Hans-Hubert Vogts

NORTHERN IRELAND: Thomas James Wright, Gary James Fleming, Nigel Worthington, Gerald Paul Taggart, Alan McDonald (Cap), Malachy Martin Donaghy, Kingsley Terence Black (79 Stephen Joseph Morrow), James Magilton, Colin John Clarke (87 Michael Andrew Martin O'Neill), Kevin James Wilson, Michael Eamonn Hughes.
Manager: William Bingham

Goals: Manfred Binz (40) / Michael Eamonn Hughes (22)

415. 09.09.1992   15th World Cup Qualifiers
NORTHERN IRELAND v ALBANIA   3-0 (3-0)
Windsor Park, Belfast

Referee: Marnix Sandra (Belgium)   Attendance: 8,000

NORTHERN IRELAND: Thomas James Wright, Gary James Fleming, Nigel Worthington, Gerald Paul Taggart, Alan McDonald, Malachy Martin Donaghy, Kevin James Wilson, James Magilton, Colin John Clarke (78 Michael Andrew Martin O'Neill), Iain Dowie, Michael Eamonn Hughes.
Manager: William Bingham

ALBANIA: Foto Strakosha, Hysen Zmijani, Kastriot Peqini, Artur Lekbello, Rudi Vata, Edmond Abazi, Sokol Kushta, Arben Milori (65 Ferdinand Bilali), Lefter Millo, Ilir Kepa, Altin Rraklli.   Trainer: Bejkush Birçe

Goals: Colin John Clarke (14), Kevin James Wilson (31), James Magilton (44)

416. 14.10.1992   15th World Cup Qualifiers
NORTHERN IRELAND v SPAIN 0-0
Windsor Park, Belfast
Referee: Hellmut Krug (Germany)   Attendance: 32,000
NORTHERN IRELAND: Thomas James Wright, Gary James Fleming, Nigel Worthington, Gerald Paul Taggart, Alan McDonald, Malachy Martin Donaghy, Kingsley Terence Black (61 Stephen Joseph Morrow), Kevin James Wilson, Colin John Clarke, James Martin Quinn, Michael Eamonn Hughes. Manager: William Bingham
SPAIN: Andoni Zubizarreta, Albert Ferrer, Roberto Solozábal, Juan Manuel López, Antonio Muñoz "Toni", José Miguel González "Míchel" (Cap), Guillermo Amor, Fernando Ruiz Hierro, Rafael Martín Vázquez, Manuel Sánchez "Manolo" (62 ALFONSO Pérez), CLAUDIO Barragán Escobar (68 José Guardiola).   Trainer: Javier Clemente
Sent off: Antonio Muñoz "Toni" (83)

417. 18.11.1992   15th World Cup Qualifiers
NORTHERN IRELAND v DENMARK 0-1 (0-0)
Windsor Park, Belfast
Referee: Sándor Puhl (Hungary)   Attendance: 11,000
NORTHERN IRELAND: Allan William Fettis, Gary James Fleming, Nigel Worthington, Gerald Paul Taggart, Alan McDonald, Malachy Martin Donaghy, James Magilton, Kevin James Wilson (53 Kingsley Terence Black), Colin John Clarke (75 Philip Gray), James Martin Quinn, Michael Eamonn Hughes.   Manager: William Bingham
DENMARK: Peter Schmeichel, John Sivebæk (46 Jakob Kjeldbjerg), Marc Rieper, Lars Olsen (Cap), Jan Heintze, Kim Vilfort, John Jensen, Henrik Larsen (74 Bjarne Goldbaek), Flemming Povlsen, Lars Elstrup, Brian Laudrup. Trainer: Richard Møller Nielsen
Goal: Henrik Larsen (51)

418. 17.02.1993   15th World Cup Qualifiers
ALBANIA v NORTHERN IRELAND 1-2 (0-2)
Qemal Stafa, Tiranë
Referee: Veselin Bogdanov (Bulgaria)   Attendance: 12,000
ALBANIA: Xhevahir Kapllani, Hysen Zmijani (46 Ilir Shulku), Rudi Vata, Artur Lekbello (46 Kastriot Peqini), Artan Bano, Salvator Kaçaj, Edmond Abazi, Indrit Fortuzi, Kliton Bozgo, Sulejman Demollari, Altin Rraklli. Trainer: Bejkush Birçe
NORTHERN IRELAND: Thomas James Wright, Gary James Fleming, Stephen Joseph Morrow, Gerald Paul Taggart, Alan McDonald, Malachy Martin Donaghy, James Magilton, Philip Gray, Iain Dowie (74 James Martin Quinn), Michael Andrew Martin O'Neill, Kingsley Terence Black. Manager: William Bingham
Goals: Altin Rraklli (89 /
James Magilton (15), Alan McDonald (41)

419. 31.03.1993   15th World Cup Qualifiers
**REPUBLIC OF IRELAND
v NORTHERN IRELAND 3-0** (3-0)
Lansdowne Road, Dublin
Referee: Kurt Röthlisberger (Switzerland)   Att: 33,000
IRELAND: Patrick Bonner, Joseph Dennis Irwin, Terence Michael Phelan, Kevin Bernard Moran, Paul McGrath, Roy Maurice Keane, Andrew David Townsend (Cap), Raymond James Houghton, Niall John Quinn (84 Edward John Paul McGoldrick), Thomas Coyne (78 Anthony Guy Cascarino), Stephen Staunton.   Manager: John Charlton
NORTHERN IRELAND: Thomas James Wright, Malachy Martin Donaghy, Nigel Worthington, Gerald Paul Taggart, Alan McDonald, Stephen Joseph Morrow, James Magilton (50 James Martin Quinn), Michael Andrew Martin O'Neill (60 Kingsley Terence Black), Iain Dowie, Philip Gray, Michael Eamonn Hughes.   Manager: William Bingham
Goals: Andrew David Townsend (20), Niall John Quinn (22), Stephen Staunton (28)

420. 28.04.1993   15th World Cup Qualifiers
SPAIN v NORTHERN IRELAND 3-1 (3-1)
Benito Villamarin, Sevilla
Referee: Leif Sundell (Sweden)   Attendance: 20,000
SPAIN: Andoni Zubizarreta, Albert Ferrer, Rafael Alkorta, Fernando Giner, Antonio Muñoz "Toni", Fernando Ruiz Hierro, Julen Guerrero, Adolfo Aldana, CLAUDIO Barragán Escobar (58 Kiko), JULIO SALINAS Fernández, Aítor Beguiristáin (Cap) (71 José María Bakero).   Trainer: Javier Clemente
NORTHERN IRELAND: Thomas James Wright, Gary James Fleming, Alan McDonald, Gerald Paul Taggart, Nigel Worthington, Malachy Martin Donaghy, Kevin James Wilson, Michael Eamonn Hughes, Michael Andrew Martin O'Neill (73 Robert Dennison), Kingsley Terence Black (73 Iain Dowie), Philip Gray.   Manager: William Bingham
Goals: Julio Salinas (16, 20), Fernando Ruiz Hierro (40) / Kevin James Wilson (11)

421. 25.05.1993   15th World Cup Qualifiers
LITHUANIA v NORTHERN IRELAND   0-1   (0-1)
Žalgiris, Vilnius

Referee: Esa Antero Palsi (Finland)   Attendance: 6,500

LITHUANIA: Voldemaras Martinkenas, Tomas Žiukas, Virginijus Baltušnikas, Romas Mažeikis, Vladimiras Buzmakovas (67 Deimantas Bička), Viktoras Olšanskis (46 Vaidotas Šlekys), Stasys Baranauskas (Cap), Viaceslavas Sukristovas, Igoris Kirilovas, Robertas Fridrikas, Ričardas Zdančius.   Trainer: Algimantas Liubinskas

NORTHERN IRELAND: Thomas James Wright, Gary James Fleming, Alan McDonald, Gerald Paul Taggart, Nigel Worthington, Malachy Martin Donaghy, James Magilton, Kevin James Wilson, Michael Eamonn Hughes, Michael Andrew Martin O'Neill, Iain Dowie.
Manager: William Bingham

Goal: Iain Dowie (8)

422. 02.06.1993   15th World Cup Qualifiers
LATVIA v NORTHERN IRELAND   1-2   (0-2)
Daugava, Riga

Referee: Piotr Werner (Poland)   Attendance: 2,764

LATVIA: Oļegs Karavajevs, Gatis Erglis, JurijsŠevļakovs, Valerijs Ivanovs, Einars Gnedojs, Jurijs Popkovs, Aleksejs Šarando, Vitālijs Astafjevs, Armands Zeiberliņš (61 Vladimirs Babičevs), Ainars Linards, Jevgenijs Gorjačilovs (46 Aleksandrs Jelisejevs).   Trainer: Janis Gilis

NORTHERN IRELAND: Thomas James Wright, Gary James Fleming, Alan McDonald, Gerald Paul Taggart, Nigel Worthington, Malachy Martin Donaghy, James Magilton, Kevin James Wilson, Michael Eamonn Hughes, Michael Andrew Martin O'Neill (85 James Martin Quinn), Iain Dowie.   Manager: William Bingham

Goals: Ainars Linards (55) /
James Magilton (5), Gerald Paul Taggart (15)

423. 08.09.1993   15th World Cup Qualifiers
NORTHERN IRELAND v LATVIA   2-0   (1-0)
Windsor Park, Belfast

Referee: João Martins Pinto Correia (Portugal)   Att: 6,400

NORTHERN IRELAND: Thomas James Wright, Gary James Fleming, Gerald Paul Taggart, Malachy Martin Donaghy, Nigel Worthington, Kevin James Wilson, James Magilton (59 Keith Rowland), Michael Eamonn Hughes, Philip Gray, James Martin Quinn, Iain Dowie.   Manager: William Bingham

LATVIA: Oļegs Karavajevs, Igors Troickis, Oļegs Aleksejenko, Valerijs Ivanovs, Einars Gnedojs, Jurijs Popkovs, Aleksejs Šarando, JurijsŠevļakovs, Vladimirs Babičevs (46 Aleksandrs Glazovs), Ainars Linards, Aleksandrs Jelisejevs (67 Oļegs Blagonadeždins).   Trainer: Janis Gilis

Goals: James Martin Quinn (35), Philip Gray (80)

424. 13.10.1993   15th World Cup Qualifiers
DENMARK v NORTHERN IRELAND   1-0   (0-0)
Parken, København

Referee: Vadim Zhuk (Belarus)   Attendance: 40,200

DENMARK: Peter Schmeichel, Marc Rieper, Lars Olsen (Cap), Jakob Kjeldbjerg, John Jensen, Kim Vilfort, Brian Steen Nielsen, Michael Laudrup, Brian Laudrup, Frank Pingel (86 Henrik Larsen), Flemming Povlsen.
Trainer: Richard Møller Nielsen

NORTHERN IRELAND: Thomas James Wright, Gary James Fleming, Alan McDonald, Gerald Paul Taggart, Nigel Worthington, Malachy Martin Donaghy, Kevin James Wilson (83 Kingsley Terence Black), James Magilton, Michael Eamonn Hughes, Philip Gray, Iain Dowie (62 James Martin Quinn).   Manager: William Bingham (116)

Goal: Brian Laudrup (83)

425. 17.11.1993   15th World Cup Qualifiers
NORTHERN IRELAND
v REPUBLIC OF IRELAND   1-1   (0-0)
Windsor Park, Belfast

Referee: Ahmet Çakar (Turkey)   Attendance: 10,500

NORTHERN IRELAND: Thomas James Wright, Gary James Fleming, Alan McDonald, Gerald Paul Taggart, Nigel Worthington, Malachy Martin Donaghy, Kevin James Wilson (83 Kingsley Terence Black), James Magilton, Michael Eamonn Hughes, Philip Gray (71 Iain Dowie), James Martin Quinn.   Manager: William Bingham (117)

IRELAND: Patrick Bonner, Joseph Dennis Irwin, Terence Michael Phelan, Alan Nigel Kernaghan, Paul McGrath, Raymond James Houghton (70 Alan Francis McLoughlin), Roy Maurice Keane, Andrew David Townsend (Cap), Edward John Paul McGoldrick, Niall John Quinn, John William Aldridge (80 Anthony Guy Cascarino).
Manager: John Charlton

Goals: James Martin Quinn (73) / Alan McLoughlin (76)

426. 23.03.1994
NORTHERN IRELAND v ROMANIA 2-0 (1-0)
Windsor Park, Belfast
Referee: Keith Walter Burge (Wales)   Attendance: 5,500
NORTHERN IRELAND: Thomas James Wright, Gary James Fleming, Gerald Paul Taggart, Malachy Martin Donaghy, Stephen Joseph Morrow, Kevin James Wilson, James Magilton, Michael Eamonn Hughes (46 Kingsley Terence Black), Stephen Martin Lomas, Philip Gray, James Martin Quinn (76 Iain Dowie).   Manager: Bryan Hamilton
ROMANIA: Florian Prunea (73 Bogdan Stelea), Dan Petrescu, Daniel Claudiu Prodan, Miodrag Belodedici, Dorinel Munteanu, Ioan Ovidiu Sabău (70 Gheorghe Mihali), Gheorghe Popescu (76 Constantin Gâlcă), Ionuț Angelo Lupescu (70 Dinu Viorel Moldovan), Gheorghe Hagi (Cap), Florin Răducioiu (81 Basarab Panduru), Ilie Dumitrescu. Trainer: Anghel Iordănescu
Sent off: Gheorghe Hagi (66)
Goals: Stephen Joseph Morrow (42), Philip Gray (50)

427. 20.04.1994   10th European Champs Qualifiers
**NORTHERN IRELAND
v LIECHTENSTEIN 4-1** (3-0)
Windsor Park, Belfast
Referee: Roelof Luinge (Holland)   Attendance: 7,150
NORTHERN IRELAND: Thomas James Wright, Gary James Fleming, Gerald Paul Taggart, Malachy Martin Donaghy, Nigel Worthington, Kevin James Wilson, James Magilton, Stephen Martin Lomas (80 Michael Andrew Martin O'Neill), Michael Eamonn Hughes, James Martin Quinn, Iain Dowie (77 Philip Gray).   Manager: Bryan Hamilton
LIECHTENSTEIN: Martin Oehri, Heini Stocker (68 Daniel Hasler), Christoph Frick, Wolfgang Ospelt, Roland Moser, Jürg Ritter, Alexander Quaderer, Harry Zech, Mario Frick, Daniel Telser, Christian Matt (64 Thomas Hanselmann). Trainer: Dietrich Weise
Goals: James Martin Quinn (4, 33), Stephen Lomas (25), Iain Dowie (48) / Daniel Hasler (84)

428. 03.06.1994
COLOMBIA v NORTHERN IRELAND 2-0 (2-0)
Foxboro, Boston
Referee: Jack D'Aquila (United States)   Attendance: 21,153
COLOMBIA: Oscar Eduardo Córdoba, Luis Fernando Herrera, Luis Carlos Perea, Andrés Escobar, Wilson Enrique Pérez, Leonel de Jesús Álvarez, Freddy Eusebio Rincón, Gabriel Jaime Gómez, Carlos Alberto Valderrama, José Adolfo Valencia (61 Anthony William De Ávila), Faustino Hernán Asprilla (62 Víctor Hugo Aristizábal).   Trainer: Francisco Maturana
NORTHERN IRELAND: Thomas James Wright, Gary James Fleming, Gerald Paul Taggart, Malachy Martin Donaghy, Nigel Worthington, Kevin James Wilson (59 Stephen Martin Lomas), James Magilton (76 Robert Dennison), Michael Eamonn Hughes, Stephen Joseph Morrow, James Martin Quinn (59 George O'Boyle), Iain Dowie (46 Darren James Patterson).   Manager: Bryan Hamilton
Goals: Wilson Enrique Pérez (29), José Adolfo Valencia (45)

429. 11.06.1994
MEXICO v NORTHERN IRELAND 3-0 (2-0)
Orange Bowl, Miami
Referee: Helder Diaz (United States)   Attendance: 8,418
MEXICO: Jorge Campos, Raúl Gutiérrez, Claudio Suárez, Juan de Dios Ramírez Perales, Jesús Ramón Ramírez, Ignacio Ambríz, Joaquín del Olmo, Luis Antonio Valdéz, Luis García Postigo (33 Benjamín Galindo, 57 Missael Espinoza), Hugo Sánchez (60 Carlos Manuel Hermosillo), Luis Roberto Alves. Trainer: Miguel Mejía Barón
NORTHERN IRELAND: Allan William Fettis (46 Thomas James Wright), Gary James Fleming (83 Stephen Joseph Morrow), Gerald Paul Taggart, Malachy Martin Donaghy, Nigel Worthington, Kevin James Wilson (46 Neil Francis Lennon), James Magilton (46 Darren James Patterson), Michael Eamonn Hughes, Stephen Martin Lomas, George O'Boyle, James Martin Quinn (46 Iain Dowie). Manager: Bryan Hamilton
Goals: Luis García Postigo (18 pen, 30), Carlos Manuel Hermosillo (77)

430. 07.09.1994   10th European Champs Qualifiers
NORTHERN IRELAND v PORTUGAL 1-2 (0-1)
Windsor Park, Belfast
Referee: Rune Pedersen (Norway)   Attendance: 6,000
NORTHERN IRELAND: Allan William Fettis, Gary James Fleming, Nigel Worthington, Stephen Joseph Morrow (81 Gerald Paul Taggart), Alan McDonald, Stephen Martin Lomas, Keith Robert Gillespie (81 George O'Boyle), James Magilton, James Martin Quinn, Philip Gray, Michael Eamonn Hughes. Manager: Bryan Hamilton
PORTUGAL: VÍTOR Manuel Martins BAÍA, JOÃO Manuel Vieira PINTO (Cap), HÉLDER Marino Rodrigues Cristóvão, PAULO Sérgio Braga MADEIRA, João Paulo Maio Santos "Paulinho Santos", PAULO Manuel Carvalho de SOUSA, Vítor Manuel da Costa Araújo "Paneira" (63 António José dos Santos Folha), José Fernando Gomes Tavares, Luis Filipe Madeira Caeiro "Figo", RUI Manuel César COSTA, Ricardo Manuel Silva SÁ PINTO (80 DOMINGOS José Paciência Oliveira). Trainer: António Luís Alves Ribeiro Oliveira
Goals: James Martin Quinn (58 pen) / RUI Manuel César COSTA (8), DOMINGOS José Paciência Oliveira (81)

431. 12.10.1994   10th European Champs Qualifiers
AUSTRIA v NORTHERN IRELAND 1-2 (1-2)
Ernst Happel, Wien

Referee: Antonio Jesús López Nieto (Spain)   Att: 20,000

AUSTRIA: Franz Wohlfahrt, Jürgen Werner-Klausriegler, Wolfgang Feiersinger, Johann Kogler, Peter Schöttel, Adolf Hütter, Peter Stöger, Peter Artner, Christian Prosenik (66 Heimo Pfeifenberger), Anton Polster, Andreas Ogris (46 Ralph Hasenhüttl).   Trainer: Herbert Prohaska

NORTHERN IRELAND: Paul Victor Kee, Gary James Fleming, Nigel Worthington, Gerald Paul Taggart, Alan McDonald, Stephen Martin Lomas, Keith Robert Gillespie (56 Michael Andrew Martin O'Neill), James Magilton, Iain Dowie (74 James Martin Quinn), Philip Gray, Michael Eamonn Hughes.   Manager: Bryan Hamilton

Goals: Anton Polster (24 pen) / Keith Robert Gillespie (3), Philip Gray (36)

432. 16.11.1994   10th European Champs Qualifiers
NORTHERN IRELAND v REPUBLIC OF IRELAND 0-4 (0-3)
Windsor Park, Belfast

Referee: Serge Muhmenthaler (Switzerland)   Att: 10,336

NORTHERN IRELAND: Paul Victor Kee, Gary James Fleming, Nigel Worthington, Gerald Paul Taggart, Stephen Joseph Morrow, Michael Andrew Martin O'Neill (46 Darren James Patterson), Keith Robert Gillespie (62 Kevin James Wilson), James Magilton, Iain Dowie, Philip Gray, Michael Eamonn Hughes.   Manager: Bryan Hamilton

IRELAND: Alan Thomas Kelly, Garry Kelly, Joseph Dennis Irwin, Philip Andrew Babb, Paul McGrath, Stephen Staunton, Roy Maurice Keane (46 Jason Wynn McAteer), Andrew David Townsend (Cap), John Joseph Sheridan, Niall John Quinn, John William Aldridge (80 Thomas Coyne).   Manager: John Charlton

Goals: John William Aldridge (6), Roy Maurice Keane (11), John Joseph Sheridan (38), Andrew David Townsend (54)

433. 29.03.1995   10th European Champs Qualifiers
REPUBLIC OF IRELAND v NORTHERN IRELAND 1-1 (0-0)
Lansdowne Road, Dublin

Referee: Mario van der Ende (Holland)   Attendance: 32,200

IRELAND: Alan Thomas Kelly, Garry Kelly, Joseph Dennis Irwin, Philip Andrew Babb, Paul McGrath, Stephen Staunton, Roy Maurice Keane, Andrew David Townsend (Cap), David Thomas Kelly (74 Jason Wynn McAteer), Niall John Quinn (82 Anthony Guy Cascarino), John Joseph Sheridan.   Manager: John Charlton

NORTHERN IRELAND: Allan William Fettis, Darren James Patterson, Nigel Worthington, Gerald Paul Taggart, Alan McDonald, Stephen Joseph Morrow, Keith Robert Gillespie, James Magilton, Iain Dowie, Colin Frederick Hill, Michael Eamonn Hughes.   Manager: Bryan Hamilton

Goals: Niall John Quinn (47) / Iain Dowie (72)

434. 26.04.1995   10th European Champs Qualifiers
LATVIA v NORTHERN IRELAND 0-1 (0-0)
Daugava, Riga

Referee: Finn Lambeck (Denmark)   Attendance: 1,560

LATVIA: Raimonds Laizāns, Igors Troickis, Vitālijs Astafjevs, Mihails Zemļinskis, Jurijs Ševļakovs, Dzintars Sprogis, Igors N. Stepanovs, Oļegs Blagonadeždins (31 Rihards Butkus, 72 Boriss Moņaks), Vitālijs Teplovs, Vladimirs Babičevs, Aleksandrs Jelisejevs.   Trainer: Janis Gilis

NORTHERN IRELAND: Allan William Fettis, Darren James Patterson, Nigel Worthington, Barry Victor Hunter, Alan McDonald, Colin Frederick Hill, Keith Robert Gillespie (78 George O'Boyle), Kevin James Wilson, Iain Dowie (80 James Martin Quinn), Kevin Horlock, Michael Eamonn Hughes.   Manager: Bryan Hamilton

Goal: Iain Dowie (67 pen)

435. 22.05.1995
CANADA v NORTHERN IRELAND 2-0 (2-0)
Commonwealth, Edmonton

Referee: Brian Hall (United States)   Attendance: 12,112

CANADA: Paul Dolan, Frank Yallop, Iain Fraser, Randolph Fitzgerald Samuel, Mark Watson, Nick Robert Dasovic (75 Marco Rizi), Colin Fyfe Miller, Lyndon Hooper, Geoffrey Aunger (75 Kevin Holness), Paolo Pasquale Peschisolido, Carlo Corazzin.   Trainer: Robert Lenarduzzi

NORTHERN IRELAND: Allan William Fettis, Darren James Patterson, Keith Rowland, Gerald Paul Taggart, Alan McDonald (Cap) (74 Patrick Colm McGibbon), Keith Robert Gillespie (64 Gerard Joseph McMahon), James Magilton, Michael Eamonn Hughes, Kevin Horlock (56 Nigel Worthington), Philip Gray, Iain Dowie (77 George O'Boyle).   Manager: Bryan Hamilton

Goals: Paolo Pasquale Peschisolido (9, 23)

436. 25.05.1995
CHILE v NORTHERN IRELAND 2-1 (0-1)
Commonwealth, Edmonton

Referee: Mike Seifert (Canada)   Attendance: 6,124

CHILE: Marco Antonio Cornéz, Miguel Mauricio Ramírez Pérez, Ronald Hugo Fuentes Núñez, Clarence Acuña Donoso, Gabriel Rafael Mendoza Ibarra, Luis Patricio Mardones Díaz, Luis Eduardo Musrri Saravia (46 Esteban Andrés Valencia Bascuñán), Fabián Guevara Arredondo, Rodrígo Antonio Pérez Albornoz (46 Fabián Raphael Estay), Rodrígo Goldberg (46 Sebastián Rozental Igualt), José Marcelo Salas Melinao. Trainer: Xabier Azkargorta

NORTHERN IRELAND: Allan William Fettis, Patrick Colm McGibbon (85 Darren James Patterson), Alan McDonald (Cap), Gerald Paul Taggart, Nigel Worthington, James Magilton (89 George O'Boyle), Michael Eamonn Hughes, Keith Rowland, Neil Francis Lennon, Gerard Joseph McMahon (82 Keith Robert Gillespie), Iain Dowie (79 Philip Gray). Manager: Bryan Hamilton

Goals: Esteban Andrés Valencia Bascuñán (74), Luis Patricio Mardones Díaz (81) / Iain Dowie (6)

438. 03.09.1995   10th European Champs Qualifiers
PORTUGAL v NORTHERN IRELAND 1-1 (0-0)
das Antas, Porto

Referee: Rémi Harrel (France)   Attendance: 26,780

PORTUGAL: VÍTOR Manuel Martins BAÍA (Cap), Carlos Alberto Oliveira "Secretário", JORGE Paulo COSTA Almeida (74 RUI Gil Soares BARROS), OCEANO Andrade da Cruz, FERNANDO Manuel Silva COUTO, PAULO Manuel Carvalho de SOUSA, Luis Filipe Madeira Caeiro "Figo", João Paulo Maio Santos "Paulinho Santos", DOMINGOS José Paciência Oliveira, RUI Manuel César COSTA (82 PAULO Lourenço Martins ALVES), António José dos Santos Folha. Trainer: António Luís Alves Ribeiro Oliveira

NORTHERN IRELAND: Allan William Fettis, Stephen Joseph Morrow, Nigel Worthington, Colin Frederick Hill, Barry Victor Hunter, Stephen Martin Lomas, Keith Robert Gillespie, James Magilton (79 Keith Rowland), Iain Dowie (76 Philip Gray), Neil Francis Lennon, Michael Eamonn Hughes. Manager: Bryan Hamilton

Goal: Michael Eamonn Hughes (67)

437. 07.06.1995   10th European Champs Qualifiers
NORTHERN IRELAND v LATVIA 1-2 (1-0)
Windsor Park, Belfast

Referee: Juan Ansuategui Roca (Spain)   Attendance: 6,000

NORTHERN IRELAND: Allan William Fettis, Patrick Colm McGibbon (46 Darren James Patterson), Nigel Worthington, Gerald Paul Taggart, Alan McDonald, Stephen Joseph Morrow, Gerard Joseph McMahon, James Magilton, Iain Dowie, Keith Rowland (64 Keith Robert Gillespie), Michael Eamonn Hughes. Manager: Bryan Hamilton

LATVIA: Raimonds Laizāns, Igors Troickis, Vitālijs Astafjevs, Dzintars Sprogis, Artūrs Zakreševskis, Boriss Moņaks, Valerijs Ivanovs, Armands Zeiberliņš, Vits Rimkus (70 Aleksandrs Jelisejevs), Vladimirs Babičevs (82 Vitālijs Teplovs), Imants Bleidelis.   Trainer: Janis Gilis

Goals: Iain Dowie (44) / Armands Zeiberliņš (59), Vitālijs Astafjevs (62)

439. 11.10.1995   10th European Champs Qualifiers
LIECHTENSTEIN
v NORTHERN IRELAND 0-4 (0-1)
Sportpark, Eschen/Mauren

Referee: Luboš Michel (Slovakia)   Attendance: 1,100

LIECHTENSTEIN: Martin Oehri, Patrik Hefti, Christoph Frick (78 Thomas Hanselmann), Roland Hilti (68 Jürgen Ospelt), Daniel Hasler, Peter Klaunzer, Daniel Telser, Heini Stocker (46 Rolf Sele), Franz Schädler, Harry Zech, Ralf Oehri. Trainer: Dietrich Weise

NORTHERN IRELAND: Allan William Fettis (75 Trevor John Wood), Stephen Martin Lomas, Nigel Worthington, Colin Frederick Hill, Barry Victor Hunter, Neil Francis Lennon, Gerard Joseph McMahon (80 Patrick Colm McGibbon), Michael Andrew Martin O'Neill, James Martin Quinn, Philip Gray, Michael Eamonn Hughes (90 Keith Rowland). Manager: Bryan Hamilton

Goals: Michael O'Neill (36), Gerard Joseph McMahon (49), James Martin Quinn (55), Philip Gray (72)

440. 15.11.1995　　10th European Champs Qualifiers
NORTHERN IRELAND v AUSTRIA 5-3 (2-0)
Windsor Park, Belfast
Referee: Leif Sundell (Sweden)　　Attendance: 8,451

NORTHERN IRELAND: Allan William Fettis, Stephen Martin Lomas, Nigel Worthington, Barry Victor Hunter, Colin Frederick Hill, Neil Francis Lennon, Keith Robert Gillespie, Michael Andrew Martin O'Neill, Iain Dowie (81 James Martin Quinn), Philip Gray (78 Alan McDonald), Michael Eamonn Hughes.　Manager: Bryan Hamilton

AUSTRIA: Michael Konsel, Markus Schopp, Walter Kogler, Anton Pfeffer, Wolfgang Feiersinger, Stefan Marasek, Heimo Pfeifenberger, Dietmar Kühbauer (46 Christian Stumpf), Andreas Herzog (46 Arnold Wetl), Peter Stöger, Anton Polster. Trainer: Herbert Prohaska

Goals: Michael O'Neill (27, 78), Iain Dowie (32 pen), Barry Victor Hunter (53), Philip Gray (64) / Markus Schopp (56), Christian Stumpf (70), Arnold Wetl (81)

441. 27.03.1996
NORTHERN IRELAND v NORWAY 0-2 (0-0)
Windsor Park, Belfast
Referee: John Ashman (Wales)　　Attendance: 5,343

NORTHERN IRELAND: Allan William Fettis, Stephen Martin Lomas, Nigel Worthington (56 Keith Rowland), Colin Frederick Hill, Alan McDonald, Keith Robert Gillespie, James Magilton (46 Darren James Patterson), Neil Francis Lennon, Michael Andrew Martin O'Neill (61 Gerard Joseph McMahon), Michael Eamonn Hughes, Iain Dowie. Manager: Bryan Hamilton

NORWAY: Frode Grodås (46 Erik Thorstvedt), Alf Inge Håland, Henning Berg, Ronny Johnsen, Stig Inge Bjørnebye, Øyvind Leonhardsen (24 Jahn Ivar Jakobsen), Kjetil Rekdal, Ståle Solbakken (86 Claus Lundekvam), Petter Rudi, Jan Åge Fjørtoft (75 Egil Østenstad), Ole Gunnar Solskjær. Trainer: Egil Olsen

Sent off: Iain Dowie (86)

Goals: Ole Gunnar Solskjær (51), Egil Østenstad (83)

442. 24.04.1996
NORTHERN IRELAND v SWEDEN 1-2 (0-1)
Windsor Park, Belfast
Referee: Hugh Dallas (Scotland)　　Attendance: 5,666

NORTHERN IRELAND: Aidan John Davison, Darren James Patterson, Colin Frederick Hill, Barry Victor Hunter, Nigel Worthington (77 Stephen James Quinn), Stephen Martin Lomas, Keith Rowland, Michael Andrew Martin O'Neill (65 George O'Boyle), Jonathan David McCarthy, Stephen Joseph Morrow, Gerard Joseph McMahon.
Manager: Bryan Hamilton

SWEDEN: Bengt Andersson, Roland Nilsson, Patrik Jonas Andersson, Joachim Björklund, Gary Sundgren, Jonas Thern, Stefan Schwarz, Klas Ingesson, Peter Wibrån (46 Pär Zetterberg), Kennet Andersson (59 Jörgen Pettersson), Martin Dahlin (80 Henrik Larsson).　Trainer: Tommy Svensson

Goals: Gerard Joseph McMahon (84) / Martin Dahlin (22), Klas Ingesson (58)

443. 29.05.1996
NORTHERN IRELAND v GERMANY 1-1 (0-0)
Windsor Park, Belfast
Referee: William Young (Scotland)　　Attendance: 11,770

NORTHERN IRELAND: Allan William Fettis, Daniel Joseph Griffin, Colin Frederick Hill, Barry Victor Hunter, Nigel Worthington (46 Keith Rowland), Keith Robert Gillespie (66 George O'Boyle), Stephen Martin Lomas, James Magilton, Michael Eamonn Hughes, Gerard Joseph McMahon, Iain Dowie.　Manager: Bryan Hamilton

GERMANY: Oliver Kahn, Thomas Helmer, Jürgen Kohler, Christian Ziege (46 Marco Bode), Mario Basler, Thomas Strunz, Dieter Eilts, Andreas Möller, Mehmet Scholl, Jürgen Klinsmann (Cap) (46 Fredi Bobic), Oliver Bierhoff (46 Stefan Kuntz).　Trainer: Hans-Hubert Vogts

Goals: George O'Boyle (79) / Mehmet Scholl (77)

444. 31.08.1996　　16th World Cup Qualifiers
NORTHERN IRELAND v UKRAINE 0-1 (0-0)
Windsor Park, Belfast
Referee: Alain Sars (France)　　Attendance: 9,358

NORTHERN IRELAND: Allan William Fettis, Daniel Joseph Griffin (52 Michael Andrew Martin O'Neill), Colin Frederick Hill, Stephen Joseph Morrow, Keith Rowland (84 James Magilton), Keith Robert Gillespie, Stephen Martin Lomas, Neil Francis Lennon, Michael Eamonn Hughes, Iain Dowie, Philip Gray.　Manager: Bryan Hamilton

UKRAINE: Oleksandr Shovkovskiy, Oleh Luzhniy (68 Dmytro Parfyonov), Serhiy Bezhenar, Viktor Skrypnyk, Oleksandr Holovko, Ihor Luchkevych (46 Serhiy Rebrov), Yuriy Kalitvintsev (75 Valeriy Kriventsov), Serhiy Popov, Hennadiy Orbu, Yuriy Maxymov, Viktor Leonenko.
Trainer: Jozsef Szabo

Goal: Serhiy Rebrov (80)

445. 05.10.1996   16th World Cup Qualifiers
NORTHERN IRELAND v ARMENIA 1-1 (1-1)
Windsor Park, Belfast

Referee: Krste Danilovski (Macedonia)   Attendance: 12,000

NORTHERN IRELAND: Allan William Fettis, Ian Robert Nolan, Colin Frederick Hill, Barry Victor Hunter, Keith Rowland, Keith Robert Gillespie (80 Michael Andrew Martin O'Neill), Stephen Martin Lomas, Neil Francis Lennon (61 James Magilton), Michael Eamonn Hughes, Iain Dowie, Philip Gray (61 Gerard Joseph McMahon).
Manager: Bryan Hamilton

ARMENIA: Roman Berezovski, Yervand Sukiasyan, Vardan Khachatryan, Sargis Hovsepyan, Harutyun Vardanyan, Sargis Hovhannisyan, Artur Petrosyan (82 Varazdat Avetisyan), Hamlet Mkhitaryan, Aramayis Tonoyan (56 Vardan Minasyan), Eric Assadourian, Karapet Mikaelyan (70 Hakob Ter-Petrosyan).   Trainer: Khoren Oganesyan

Goals: Neil Francis Lennon (30) / Eric Assadourian (8)

446. 09.11.1996   16th World Cup Qualifiers
GERMANY v NORTHERN IRELAND 1-1 (1-1)
Franken, Nürnberg

Referee: Ahmet Çakar (Turkey)   Attendance: 40,718

GERMANY: Andreas Köpke, Stefan Reuter, Jürgen Kohler, Markus Babbel, Michael Tarnat, Thomas Strunz, Dieter Eilts (62 Stephan Paßlack), Thomas Hässler, Andreas Möller, Fredi Bobic (70 Oliver Bierhoff), Jürgen Klinsmann (Cap).
Trainer: Hans-Hubert Vogts

NORTHERN IRELAND: Thomas James Wright, Stephen Joseph Morrow, Gerald Paul Taggart, Ian Robert Nolan, Colin Frederick Hill, Barry Victor Hunter, Stephen Martin Lomas, Neil Francis Lennon (86 Anton Gerard Patrick Rogan), Kevin Horlock, Michael Eamonn Hughes, Iain Dowie (76 Philip Gray).   Manager: Bryan Hamilton

Goals: Andreas Möller (41) / Gerald Paul Taggart (39)

447. 14.12.1996   16th World Cup Qualifiers
NORTHERN IRELAND v ALBANIA 2-0 (2-0)
Windsor Park, Belfast

Referee: Andreas Georgiou (Cyprus)   Attendance: 7,935

NORTHERN IRELAND: Thomas James Wright, Ian Robert Nolan, Gerald Paul Taggart, Colin Frederick Hill, Barry Victor Hunter, Stephen Joseph Morrow (72 Gerard Joseph McMahon), Stephen Martin Lomas, Neil Francis Lennon, Kevin Horlock, Michael Eamonn Hughes, Iain Dowie (90 Stephen James Quinn).   Manager: Bryan Hamilton

ALBANIA: Blendi Nallbani, Saimir Malko, Rudi Vata, Ilir Shulku, Ervin Fakaj, Bledar Kola, Nevil Dede (34 Afrim Tole), Viktor Paço, Altin Haxhi (36 Bajram Fraholli), Altin Rrakllı, Fatmir Vata.   Trainer: Neptun Bajko

Goals: Iain Dowie (13, 22)

448. 22.01.1997
ITALY v NORTHERN IRELAND 2-0 (1-0)
La Favorita, Palermo

Referee: Lutz Michael Fröhlich (Germany)   Att: 30,886

ITALY: Angelo Peruzzi, Ciro Ferrara, Amedeo Carboni, Demetrio Albertini, Paolo Maldini (Cap), Alessandro Costacurta (72 Fabio Cannavaro), Angelo Di Livio (79 Stefano Eranio), Dino Baggio, Pier Luigi Casiraghi (58 Fabrizio Ravanelli) Roberto Di Matteo (58 Diego Fuser), Gianfranco Zola (62 Alessandro Del Piero).   Trainer: Cesare Maldini

NORTHERN IRELAND: Thomas James Wright, Daniel Joseph Griffin, Gerald Paul Taggart, Barry Victor Hunter, Stephen Joseph Morrow, Nigel Worthington, Stephen Martin Lomas, Kevin Horlock, Michael Eamonn Hughes (69 Keith Rowland), Jonathan David McCarthy (83 Robert Dennison), Stephen James Quinn (60 George O'Boyle).
Manager: Bryan Hamilton

Goals: Thomas Wright (9 own goal, 88 own goal)

449. 11.02.1997
NORTHERN IRELAND v BELGIUM 3-0 (1-0)
Windsor Park, Belfast

Referee: John Rowbotham (Scotland)   Attendance: 7,126

NORTHERN IRELAND: Thomas James Wright, Stephen Joseph Morrow, Gerald Paul Taggart, Barry Victor Hunter (46 Daniel Joseph Griffin), Keith Robert Gillespie, Stephen Martin Lomas, Neil Francis Lennon (66 Nigel Worthington), James Magilton, Kevin Horlock (87 Jeffrey Whitley), Gerard Joseph McMahon (46 Philip Patrick Mulryne), Stephen James Quinn (59 George O'Boyle).   Manager: Bryan Hamilton

BELGIUM: Filip De Wilde, Albert De Roover, Dirk Medved, Phillipe Albert, Lorenzo Staelens, Frank Richard Vander Elst, Nico Van Kerckhoven (85 Gunther Schepens), Gert Verheyen (72 Frédéric Pierre), Luc Nilis (46 Emile Lokonda Mpenza), Marc Wilmots (79 Nordin Jbari), Vincenzo Scifo (80 Dominique Lemoine).   Trainer: Georges Leekens

Goals: Stephen James Quinn (14), James Magilton (62 pen), Philip Patrick Mulryne (88)

450. 29.03.1997   16th World Cup Qualifiers
NORTHERN IRELAND v PORTUGAL 0-0
Windsor Park, Belfast

Referee: Graziano Cesari (Italy)   Attendance: 10,500

NORTHERN IRELAND: Thomas James Wright, Stephen Joseph Morrow, Colin Frederick Hill, Gerald Paul Taggart, Ian Robert Nolan, Keith Robert Gillespie, Stephen Martin Lomas, James Magilton, Neil Francis Lennon, Iain Dowie, Stephen James Quinn (69 Gerard Joseph McMahon).
Manager: Bryan Hamilton

PORTUGAL: VÍTOR Manuel Martins BAÍA (Cap), João Paulo Maio Santos "Paulinho Santos", FERNANDO Manuel Silva COUTO, JORGE Paulo COSTA Almeida, DIMAS Manuel Marques Teixeira (63 PEDRO Rui da Mota Vieira MARTINS), SÉRGIO Paulo Marceneiro CONCEIÇÃO, Luis Filipe Madeira Caeiro "Figo", OCEANO Andrade da Cruz (63 Jorge Paulo CADETE Santos Reis), PAULO Manuel Carvalho de SOUSA, RUI Manuel César COSTA, JOÃO Manuel Vieira PINTO. Trainer: Artur Jorge Braga Melo Teixeira

451. 02.04.1997   16th World Cup Qualifiers
UKRAINE v NORTHERN IRELAND 2-1 (1-1)
Olympiyskyi, Kyiv

Referee: Václav Krondl (Czech Republic)   Att: 75,000

UKRAINE: Oleksandr Shovkovskiy, Oleh Luzhniy, Oleksandr Holovko, Serhiy Bezhenar, Viktor Skrypnyk, Yuriy Kalitvintsev (86 Valeriy Kriventsov), Vasyl Kardash, Dmytro Mykhailenko, Vitaliy Kosovskiy (73 Hennadiy Orbu), Serhiy Rebrov, Andriy Shevchenko.   Trainer: Jozsef Szabo

NORTHERN IRELAND: Thomas James Wright, Stephen Joseph Morrow, Colin Frederick Hill, Gerald Paul Taggart, Ian Robert Nolan, Keith Robert Gillespie (79 Gerard Joseph McMahon), Stephen Martin Lomas, Neil Francis Lennon (75 Stephen James Quinn), Michael Eamonn Hughes, Kevin Horlock, Iain Dowie.   Manager: Bryan Hamilton

Goals: Vitaliy Kosovskiy (3), Andriy Shevchenko (71) / Iain Dowie (14 pen)

452. 30.04.1997   16th World Cup Qualifiers
ARMENIA v NORTHERN IRELAND 0-0
Hrazdan, Yerevan

Referee: Karl-Erik Nilsson (Sweden)   Attendance: 10,000

ARMENIA: Roman Berezovski, Yervand Sukiasyan, Vardan Khachatryan, Michel Der Zakarian, Sargis Hovsepyan, Artur Petrosyan (84 Felix Khodzhoyan), Hamlet Mkhitaryan, Arsen Avetisyan (87 Varazdat Avetisyan), Aramais Yepiskoposyan (76 Tigran Yesayan), Eric Assadourian, Karapet Mikaelyan. Trainer: Khoren Oganesyan

NORTHERN IRELAND: Allan William Fettis, Stephen Joseph Morrow, Colin Frederick Hill, Gerald Paul Taggart, Iain Jenkins, Jonathan David McCarthy (71 Philip Patrick Mulryne), Stephen Martin Lomas, Neil Francis Lennon, Kevin Horlock, Iain Dowie, Stephen James Quinn (59 Gerard Joseph McMahon).   Manager: Bryan Hamilton

453. 21.05.1997
THAILAND v NORTHERN IRELAND 0-0
Bangkok

Referee: Pania Hanlumyaung (Thailand)   Att: 10,000

THAILAND: Chaiyong Khumpiam, Tinnakorn, Kritsada Piandit, Surachai Jirisirichote, Promrut, Dusit Chalermsan, Kiimonkolsak, Surachai Jaturapattarapong, Thawatchai Damrong-Ongtrakul (63 Sanor Longsawang), Ongtrakul (72 Pongtorn Thiubthong), Piyapong Pue-On.

NORTHERN IRELAND: Aidan John Davison (46 Roy Carroll), Patrick Colm McGibbon, Daniel Joseph Griffin, Colin Frederick Hill, Iain Jenkins (46 Jeffrey Whitley), Jonathan David McCarthy (46 Gerard Joseph McMahon), Stephen Martin Lomas, Neil Francis Lennon, Kevin Horlock, Philip Patrick Mulryne (46 Stephen James Quinn), Iain Dowie (63 Stephen Robinson).   Manager: Bryan Hamilton

454. 20.08.1997   16th World Cup Qualifiers
NORTHERN IRELAND v GERMANY 1-3 (0-0)
Windsor Park, Belfast

Referee: José Manuel García-Aranda Encinar (Spain)
Attendance: 13,400

NORTHERN IRELAND: Aidan John Davison, Ian Robert Nolan, Colin Frederick Hill, Stephen Joseph Morrow, Gerald Paul Taggart, Keith Robert Gillespie (80 Gerard Joseph McMahon), James Magilton, Neil Francis Lennon (64 Daniel Joseph Griffin), Kevin Horlock, Michael Eamonn Hughes, Stephen James Quinn.   Manager: Bryan Hamilton

GERMANY: Andreas Köpke, Thomas Helmer, Jürgen Kohler, Christian Wörns (64 Thomas Hässler), Jens Nowotny, Jörg Heinrich, Mario Basler (83 Markus Babbel), Andreas Möller, Christian Ziege, Jürgen Klinsmann (Cap), Ulf Kirsten (70 Oliver Bierhoff).   Trainer: Hans-Hubert Vogts

Goals: Michael Eamonn Hughes (60) / Oliver Bierhoff (73, 78, 79)

455. 10.09.1997   16th World Cup Qualifiers
ALBANIA v NORTHERN IRELAND 1-0 (0-0)
Hardturm, Zürich (Switzerland)

Referee: Roger Philippi (Luxembourg)   Attendance: 2,600

ALBANIA: Foto Strakosha, Afrim Tole, Ilir Shulku, Rudi Vata, Arian Xhumba, Altin Haxhi (83 Alpin Gallo), Arjan Peço (66 Mahir Halili), Bledar Kola, Ervin Fakaj, Igli Tare, Alban Bushi (90 Adrian Mema).   Trainer: Astrit Hafizi

NORTHERN IRELAND: Thomas James Wright, Daniel Joseph Griffin, Colin Frederick Hill, Patrick Colm McGibbon (46 Philip Patrick Mulryne), Keith Rowland, Keith Robert Gillespie, Stephen Martin Lomas, Neil Francis Lennon (83 Daniel James Sonner), Kevin Horlock, Iain Dowie, Stephen James Quinn (76 Gerard Joseph McMahon). Manager: Bryan Hamilton

Goal: Altin Haxhi (65)

456. 11.10.1997   16th World Cup Qualifiers
PORTUGAL v NORTHERN IRELAND   1-0 (1-0)
da Luz, Lisboa
Referee: Peter Mikkelsen (Denmark)   Attendance: 31,847
PORTUGAL: SILVINO de Almeida Louro, FERNANDO Manuel Silva COUTO, HÉLDER Marino Rodrigues Cristóvão, João Paulo Maio Santos "Paulinho Santos", DIMAS Manuel Marques Teixeira, OCEANO Andrade da Cruz (Cap), Luis Filipe Madeira Caeiro "Figo", PAULO Manuel Carvalho de SOUSA, SÉRGIO Paulo Marceneiro CONCEIÇÃO (79 Daniel Cruz de Carvalho "Dani"), JOÃO Manuel Vieira PINTO, Pedro Miguel Carreiro Resendes "Pauleta" (63 Jorge Paulo CADETE Santos Reis).   Trainer: Artur Jorge Braga Melo Teixeira

NORTHERN IRELAND: Allan William Fettis, Ian Robert Nolan, Colin Frederick Hill (74 Gerard Joseph McMahon), Stephen Joseph Morrow, Gerald Paul Taggart, James Magilton, Neil Francis Lennon (74 Jonathan David McCarthy), Kevin Horlock, Michael Eamonn Hughes, Stephen Martin Lomas, Iain Dowie.   Manager: Bryan Hamilton

Goal: SÉRGIO Paulo Marceneiro CONCEIÇÃO (17)

457. 25.03.1998
NORTHERN IRELAND v SLOVAKIA   1-0 (0-0)
Windsor Park, Belfast
Referee: Alan Howells (Wales)   Attendance: 7,895

NORTHERN IRELAND: Allan William Fettis, Aaron William Hughes, Colin Frederick Hill, Stephen Joseph Morrow, Iain Jenkins, Keith Robert Gillespie (89 Jonathan David McCarthy), Neil Francis Lennon, Michael Eamonn Hughes, Stephen Martin Lomas, Iain Dowie, Stephen James Quinn (82 George O'Boyle).   Manager: Lawrie McMenemy

SLOVAKIA: Alexander Vencel, Marián Zeman, Milan Timko (81 Tibor Zátek), Dušan Tittel, Marek Špilár, Vladimír Kinder, Ľubomír Moravčík (81 Miroslav Sovič), Samuel Slovák (68 Igor Barbariš) Balíš), Peter Dubovský, Jozef Majoroš, Attila Pinte (46 Szilárd Németh).   Trainer: Jozef Jankech

Goal: Stephen Martin Lomas (51)

458. 22.04.1998
**NORTHERN IRELAND
v SWITZERLAND   1-0** (1-0)
Windsor Park, Belfast
Referee: Hugh Dallas (Scotland)   Attendance: 8,862

NORTHERN IRELAND: Allan William Fettis, Aaron William Hughes, Darren James Patterson, Stephen Joseph Morrow, Iain Jenkins, Keith Robert Gillespie, Neil Francis Lennon, Michael Eamonn Hughes, Stephen Martin Lomas, Iain Dowie, Stephen James Quinn (69 George O'Boyle).
Manager: Lawrie McMenemy

SWITZERLAND: Joël Corminboeuf (46 Pascal Zuberbühler), Stéphane Henchoz, Murat Yakin, Ramon Vega, Raphaël Wicky, Johann Lonfat (72 Adrian Kunz), Johann Vogel (69 Sébastien Jeanneret), Sébastien Fournier, David Sesa, Marco Grassi, Stéphane Chapuisat (63 Patrick Müller).
Trainer: Gilbert Gress

Goal: Darren James Patterson (10)

459. 03.06.1998
SPAIN v NORTHERN IRELAND   4-1 (2-1)
El Sardinero, Santander
Referee: Gilles Veissière (France)   Attendance: 18,120

SPAIN: José Santiago Cañizares, Albert Ferrer, Iván Campo, ABELARDO Fernández (Cap), SERGI Barjuán (46 Agustín Aranzábal), Guillermo Amor, Joseba Etxeberría, Albert Celades, Julen Guerrero (46 Francisco Narváez "Kiko"), RAÚL González (46 ALFONSO Pérez), Juan Antonio Pizzi (46 Fernando Morientes).   Trainer: Javier Clemente Lazaro

NORTHERN IRELAND: Allan William Fettis, Aaron William Hughes, Gerald Paul Taggart, Stephen Joseph Morrow (65 Darren James Patterson), Iain Jenkins, James Magilton (76 Philip Patrick Mulryne), Neil Francis Lennon (90 Jeffrey Whitley), Michael Eamonn Hughes, Jonathan David McCarthy, James Whitley, Iain Dowie.
Manager: Lawrie McMenemy

Goals: Juan Pizzi (29, 37), Fernando Morientes (43, 66) / Gerald Paul Taggart (44)

460. 05.09.1998   11th European Champs Qualifiers
TURKEY v NORTHERN IRELAND   3-0 (1-0)
Ali Sami Yen, Istanbul
Referee: Ryszard Wójcik (Poland)   Attendance: 19,840

TURKEY: Rüştü Reçber, Saffet Akbaş, Mert Korkmaz, Alpay Özalan, Okan Buruk (88 Arif Erdem), Sergen Yalçin, Tayfur Havutçu, Tugay Kerimoğlu (75 Oğuz Çetin), Abdullah Ercan, Oktay Derelioğlu (80 Hamı Mandıralı), Hakan Şükür.
Trainer: Mustafa Denizli

NORTHERN IRELAND: Allan William Fettis, Aaron William Hughes, Kevin Horlock, Philip Patrick Mulryne, Colin Frederick Hill, Stephen Joseph Morrow, Keith Robert Gillespie (73 James Whitley), Neil Francis Lennon, Iain Dowie, Keith Rowland (46 Stephen James Quinn), Michael Eamonn Hughes.   Manager: Lawrie McMenemy

Goals: Oktay Derelioğlu (19, 59), Tayfur Havutçu (50 pen)

461. 10.10.1998   11th European Champs Qualifiers
NORTHERN IRELAND v FINLAND 1-0 (1-0)
Windsor Park, Belfast
Referee: Zoran Arsić (Yugoslavia)   Attendance: 10,200

NORTHERN IRELAND: Allan William Fettis, Aaron William Hughes, Kevin Horlock, Philip Patrick Mulryne, Stephen Joseph Morrow, Darren James Patterson, Keith Robert Gillespie (70 Jonathan David McCarthy), Neil Francis Lennon, Iain Dowie (79 George O'Boyle), Keith Rowland (88 Stephen James Quinn), Michael Eamonn Hughes.
Manager: Lawrie McMenemy

FINLAND: Antti Niemi, Harri Ylönen, Juha Reini, Sami Hyypiä, Tommi Kautonen, Simo Valakari, Jari Ilola, Aki Riihilahti (76 Jari Litmanen), Joonas Kolkka, Mika-Matti Paatelainen (Cap), Jonatan Johansson.
Trainer: Richard Møller-Nielsen

Goal: Keith Rowland (31)

462. 18.11.1998   11th European Champs Qualifiers
NORTHERN IRELAND v MOLDOVA 2-2 (0-1)
Windsor Park, Belfast
Referee: Vladimír Hriňák (Slovakia)   Attendance: 11,137

NORTHERN IRELAND: Allan William Fettis, Daniel Joseph Griffin, Peter Kennedy, Stephen Martin Lomas, Darren James Patterson, Stephen Joseph Morrow, Keith Robert Gillespie (88 Jonathan David McCarthy), Neil Francis Lennon, Iain Dowie, Keith Rowland (77 Philip Gray), Michael Eamonn Hughes.
Manager: Lawrie McMenemy

MOLDOVA: Serghei Dinov, Oleg Fistican, Radu Rebeja, Ion Testimiţanu (85 Vitali Maevici), Alexandru Guzun (71 Ghenadie Puşca), Serghei Stroenco, Alexandru Curtianu, Gheorghe Stratulat (50 Alexandr Suharev), Serghei Epureanu, Vladimir Gaidamaşciuc, Serghei Cleşcenco.
Trainer: Ivan Danilianţ

Sent off: Alexandru Curtianu (66)

Goals: Iain Dowie (49), Neil Francis Lennon (63) / Vladimir Gaidamaşciuc (23), Ion Testimiţanu (58)

463. 27.03.1999   11th European Champs Qualifiers
NORTHERN IRELAND v GERMANY 0-3 (0-2)
Windsor Park, Belfast
Referee: Graziano Cesari (Italy)   Attendance: 14,300

NORTHERN IRELAND: Maik Stefan Taylor, Darren James Patterson, Kevin Horlock, Stephen Martin Lomas, Mark Stuart Williams, Stephen Joseph Morrow, Keith Robert Gillespie (83 Jonathan David McCarthy), Neil Francis Lennon (68 Daniel James Sonner), Iain Dowie, Keith Rowland (68 Peter Kennedy), Michael Eamonn Hughes.
Manager: Lawrie McMenemy

GERMANY: Oliver Kahn, Markus Babbel, Lothar Herbert Matthäus (46 Jens Nowotny), Christian Wörns, Thomas Strunz, Dietmar Hamann, Jens Jeremies, Jörg Heinrich, Olivier Neuville (68 Carsten Jancker), Oliver Bierhoff (Cap), Marco Bode (78 Michael Preetz).   Trainer: Erich Ribbeck

Goals: Marco Bode (11, 43), Dietmar Hamann (62)

464. 31.03.1999   11th European Champs Qualifiers
MOLDOVA v NORTHERN IRELAND 0-0
Republican, Chişinău
Referee: Edo Trivković (Croatia)   Attendance: 9,000

MOLDOVA: Serghei Dinov, Oleg Fistican, Adrian Sosnovschi, Alexandru Guzun, Radu Rebeja, Serghei Stroenco, Alexandru Suharev, Igor Oprea (90 Gheorghe Stratulat), Vladimir Gaidamaşciuc, Serghei Epureanu, Serghei Cleşcenco.
Trainer: Ivan Danilianţ

NORTHERN IRELAND: Maik Stefan Taylor, Darren James Patterson (63 Aaron William Hughes), Kevin Horlock, Stephen Martin Lomas, Mark Stuart Williams, Stephen Joseph Morrow, Keith Robert Gillespie, Neil Francis Lennon, Iain Dowie, Stephen Robinson, Michael Eamonn Hughes.
Manager: Lawrie McMenemy

465. 27.04.1999
NORTHERN IRELAND v CANADA 1-1 (0-0)
Windsor Park, Belfast
Referee: Thomas McCurry (Scotland)   Attendance: 7,663

NORTHERN IRELAND: Maik Stefan Taylor (46 Thomas James Wright), Aaron William Hughes, Kevin Horlock, Barry Victor Hunter, Mark Stuart Williams, Keith Rowland, Philip Patrick Mulryne (82 Daniel James Sonner), Jonathan David McCarthy (59 Rory Hamill), Stephen Martin Lomas, Iain Dowie (74 Glenn Ferguson), Adrian Coote (74 Paul McVeigh).
Manager: Lawrie McMenemy

CANADA: Craig Forrest, Brad Parker, Mark Watson, Jason deVos, Paul Stalteri (66 Garret Kusch), Jeff Clarke, Davide Xausa (59 Marc Bircham), Nick Robert Dasovic, Jason Bent, James Brennan, Paolo Pasquale Peschisolido.
Trainer: Holger Osieck

Goals: Brad Parker (90 own goal) / Marc Bircham (67)

466. 29.05.1999
**REPUBLIC OF IRELAND
v NORTHERN IRELAND 0-1** (0-0)
Lansdowne Road, Dublin
Referee: Ceri Richards (Wales)   Attendance: 12,100
IRELAND: Seamus John Given, Stephen Carr, Kenneth Edward Cunningham (Cap), Philip Andrew Babb, Alan Maybury, Mark Anthony Kinsella (80 Graham Anthony Kavanagh), Lee Kevin Carsley (46 Alan Francis McLoughlin), Damien Anthony Duff (56 Keith Padre Gerard O'Neill), Mark Kennedy, Robert David Keane (56 David James Connolly), Niall John Quinn (72 Anthony Guy Cascarino).   Manager: Michael Joseph McCarthy
NORTHERN IRELAND: Maik Stefan Taylor (46 Roy Carroll), Aaron William Hughes, Darren James Patterson, Barry Victor Hunter, Mark Stuart Williams, Keith Rowland (74 Damien Michael Johnson), Neil Francis Lennon (79 Daniel Joseph Griffin), Jonathan David McCarthy, Iain Dowie (46 Adrian Coote), Stephen James Quinn, Stephen Robinson.   Manager: Lawrie McMenemy
Goal: Daniel Joseph Griffin (85)

467. 18.08.1999
NORTHERN IRELAND v FRANCE 0-1 (0-0)
Windsor Park, Belfast
Referee: William Young (Scotland)   Attendance: 11,804
NORTHERN IRELAND: Maik Stefan Taylor (46 Thomas James Wright), Aaron William Hughes, Mark Stuart Williams, Barry Victor Hunter, Kevin Horlock, Jonathan David McCarthy, Stephen Martin Lomas, Neil Francis Lennon, Peter Kennedy (73 Keith Robert Gillespie), Michael Eamonn Hughes, Iain Dowie (55 Stephen James Quinn).   Manager: Lawrie McMenemy
FRANCE: Fabien Barthez, Lilian Thuram, Laurent Blanc, Marcel Desailly (65 Frank Leboeuf), Bixente Lizarazu (56 Vincent Candela), Patrick Vieira (84 Frédéric Dehu), Alain Boghossian, Robert Pires, Johan Micoud, Sylvain Wiltord (56 Laurent Robert), Lilian Laslandes (77 Tony Vairelles).   Trainer: Roger Lemmere
Goal: Lilian Laslandes (67)

468. 04.09.1999   11th European Champs Qualifiers
NORTHERN IRELAND v TURKEY 0-3 (0-1)
Windsor Park, Belfast
Referee: Alain Sars (France)   Attendance: 270
NORTHERN IRELAND: Maik Stefan Taylor, Aaron William Hughes, Kevin Horlock, Stephen Martin Lomas, Mark Stuart Williams, Barry Victor Hunter, Jonathan David McCarthy (63 Keith Robert Gillespie), Neil Francis Lennon, Iain Dowie (73 Stephen James Quinn), Michael Eamonn Hughes, Peter Kennedy.   Manager: Lawrie McMenemy
TURKEY: Rüştü Reçber, Ali Eren Beşerler, Ogün Temizkanoğlu, Tayfur Havutçu, Alpay Özalan, Arif Erdem (79 Okan Buruk), Abdullah Ercan (75 Hakan Ünsal), Tugay Kerimoğlu, Sergen Yalçin (89 Ümit Karan), Tayfun Korkut, Hakan Şükür.   Trainer: Mustafa Denizli
Goals: Arif Erdem (45, 46, 49)

469. 08.09.1999   11th European Champs Qualifiers
GERMANY v NORTHERN IRELAND 4-0 (4-0)
Westfalen, Dortmund
Referee: Georgios Bikas (Greece)   Attendance: 41,000
GERMANY: Jens Lehmann, Thomas Linke, Lothar Herbert Matthäus, Markus Babbel (30 Thomas Strunz), Jens Jeremies, Jens Nowotny (46 Christian Wörns), Mehmet Scholl, Christian Ziege, Olivier Neuville (67 Bernd Schneider), Oliver Bierhoff (Cap), Marco Bode.   Trainer: Erich Ribbeck
NORTHERN IRELAND: Maik Stefan Taylor, Ian Robert Nolan, Stephen Joseph Morrow, Kevin Horlock, Mark Stuart Williams, Jonathan David McCarthy, Stephen Martin Lomas, Neil Francis Lennon (46 Keith Robert Gillespie), Peter Kennedy, Iain Dowie (46 Stephen James Quinn), Michael Eamonn Hughes.   Manager: Lawrie McMenemy
Goals: Oliver Bierhoff (3), Christian Ziege (16, 33, 45)

470. 09.10.1999   11th European Champs Qualifiers
FINLAND v NORTHERN IRELAND 4-1 (1-0)
Olympiastadion, Helsinki
Referee: Armand Ancion (Belgium)   Attendance: 8,217
FINLAND: Jani Viander, Mika Lehkosuo, Toni Kuivasto, Sami Hyypiä, Hannu Tihinen, Jarkko Wiss (86 Simo Valakari), Joonas Kolkka, Aki Riihilahti (86 Sami Ylä-Jussila), Jari Litmanen (Cap), Mika-Matti Paatelainen, Jonatan Johansson.   Trainer: Richard Møller-Nielsen
NORTHERN IRELAND: Maik Stefan Taylor, Iain Jenkins (78 James Whitley), Stephen Joseph Morrow, Ian Robert Nolan, Mark Stuart Williams, Jonathan David McCarthy, Jeffrey Whitley, Neil Francis Lennon, Peter Kennedy, Michael Eamonn Hughes (74 Damien Michael Johnson), Stephen James Quinn (68 Adrian Coote).
Manager: Lawrie McMenemy
Goals: Jonatan Johansson (9), Sami Hyypiä (63), Joonas Kolkka (73, 83) / Jeffrey Whitley (59)

471. 23.02.2000
LUXEMBOURG v NORTHERN IRELAND 1-3 (1-1)
Josy Barthel, Luxembourg
Referee: Manfred Schuttengruber (Austria)   Att: 1,818
LUXEMBOURG: Alija Besic, Jean Vanek, Roland Schaack, Jeff Strasser, Marc Birsens (6 Christian Alverdi), Jeff Saibene, Sacha Schneider (46 Marcel Christophe), Frank Deville, Luc Holtz (75 Daniel Huss), Manuel Cardoni, Gordon Braun (60 Mikhail Zaritski).   Trainer: Paul Philipp

NORTHERN IRELAND: Roy Carroll (75 Maik Stefan Taylor), Aaron William Hughes, Daniel Joseph Griffin (90 Patrick Colm McGibbon), Ian Robert Nolan, Mark Stuart Williams (65 Colin James Murdock), Keith Robert Gillespie (89 Stephen Robinson), Stephen Martin Lomas, Damien Michael Johnson (78 Michael Eamonn Hughes), James Magilton (75 Daniel James Sonner), Stephen James Quinn (88 Adrian Coote), David Healy.   Manager: Sammy McIlroy

Goals: Manuel Cardoni (41) /
David Healy (21, 48), Stephen James Quinn (87)

472. 28.03.2000
MALTA v NORTHERN IRELAND 0-3 (0-3)
National, Ta'Qali
Referee: Massimo de Santis (Italy)   Attendance: 2,556
MALTA: Ernest Barry (46 Mario Muscat), Brian Said, Silvio Vella (58 Edward Azzopardi), John Buttigieg (46 Noel Turner), Jeffrey Chetcuti, Darren Debono, David Carabott, Carmel Busuttil (62 Nenad Veselji), Adrian Ciantar (46 Adrian Mifsud), Chucks Nwoko (75 George Mallia), Gilbert Agius (46 Ifeani Okonkwo).   Trainer: Josif Ilić

NORTHERN IRELAND: Roy Carroll (85 Maik Stefan Taylor), Daniel Joseph Griffin, Ian Robert Nolan, Mark Stuart Williams, Colin James Murdock (46 Daniel James Sonner), Keith Robert Gillespie (62 Damien Michael Johnson), Stephen Martin Lomas, Neil Francis Lennon, Michael Eamonn Hughes (77 Kevin Horlock), Stephen James Quinn (70 Adrian Coote), David Healy.   Manager: Sammy McIlroy

Goals: Michael Hughes (13 pen), Stephen James Quinn (16), David Healy (41)

473. 26.04.2000
NORTHERN IRELAND v HUNGARY 0-1 (0-0)
Windsor Park, Belfast
Referee: Ceri Richards (Wales)   Attendance: 7,600
NORTHERN IRELAND: Maik Stefan Taylor, Aaron William Hughes, Daniel Joseph Griffin (73 Damien Michael Johnson), Ian Robert Nolan, Gerald Paul Taggart (57 Adrian Coote), Keith Robert Gillespie (76 Colin James Murdock), Daniel James Sonner (85 Stephen Robinson), Neil Francis Lennon, Michael Eamonn Hughes, David Healy, Andrew Kirk (57 Mark Stuart Williams).   Manager: Sammy McIlroy

HUNGARY: Gábor Király, Vilmos Sebők, János Hrutka, János Mátyus, Csaba Fehér, Miklós Lendvai, Pál Dárdai (46 Gábor Halmai), Béla Illés, Zoltán Pető (57 György Korsós), Sándor Preisinger (78 Miklós Herczeg), Ferenc Horváth (89 István Hamar).   Trainer: Bertalan Bicskei

Goal: Ferenc Horváth (61)

474. 16.08.2000
NORTHERN IRELAND v YUGOSLAVIA 1-2 (1-0)
Windsor Park, Belfast
Referee: William Young (Scotland)   Attendance: 6,095
NORTHERN IRELAND: Maik Stefan Taylor, Ian Robert Nolan, Aaron William Hughes, Colin James Murdock (81 Daniel Joseph Griffin), Mark Stuart Williams, Kevin Horlock (73 Keith Robert Gillespie), Jeffrey Whitley, Damien Michael Johnson, James Magilton, David Healy, Philip Patrick Mulryne (68 Stephen James Quinn).   Manager: Sammy McIlroy

YUGOSLAVIA: Željko Cicović, Ivan Dudić, Nenad Sakić, Goran Bunjevčević, Spira Grujić (46 Milan Obradović), Predrag Đorđević, Nenad Grozdić (72 Saša Ilić), Nikola Lazetič, Dejan Stanković, Savo Milošević (60 Mateja Kežman), Predrag Mijatović.   Trainer: Ilija Petković

Goals: David Healy (45) /
Mateja Kežman (63), Predrag Mijatović (78)

475. 02.09.2000   17th World Cup Qualifiers
NORTHERN IRELAND v MALTA 1-0 (0-0)
Windsor Park, Belfast
Referee: Taras Bezubiak (Russia)   Attendance: 8,227
NORTHERN IRELAND: Roy Carroll, Ian Robert Nolan, Aaron William Hughes, Colin James Murdock, Gerald Paul Taggart, Kevin Horlock, Damien Michael Johnson, James Magilton, Stephen Martin Lomas, Stuart Elliott (61 Philip Gray), David Healy.   Manager: Sammy McIlroy

MALTA: Ernest Barry, Brian Said, Jeffrey Chetcuti, Luke Dimech, Daniel Theuma, Darren Debono, David Carabott, Dybrill Sylla (46 Joseph Brincat), Carmel Busuttil, David Camilleri (78 Nenad Veselji), George Mallia (57 Noel Turner).   Trainer: Josif Ilić

Goal: Philip Gray (72)

476. 07.10.2000   17th World Cup Qualifiers
NORTHERN IRELAND v DENMARK 1-1 (1-0)
Windsor Park, Belfast

Referee: Vítor Manuel Melo Pereira (Portugal)   Att: 11,823

NORTHERN IRELAND: Roy Carroll, Aaron William Hughes, Colin James Murdock, Jeffrey Whitley (71 Philip Patrick Mulryne), Gerald Paul Taggart, Kevin Horlock, James Magilton, Stephen Martin Lomas, Neil Francis Lennon, Stuart Elliott (84 Philip Gray), David Healy.
Manager: Sammy McIlroy

DENMARK: Peter Schmeichel (Cap), René Henriksen, Thomas Gravesen, Jan Heintze, Thomas Helveg, Brian Steen Nielsen, Dennis Rommedahl, Jesper Grønkjær (64 Morten Bisgaard), Stig Tøfting, Jon Dahl Tomasson, Ebbe Sand (82 Claus Jensen).   Trainer: Morten Olsen

Goals: David Healy (37) / Dennis Rommedahl (60)

477. 11.10.2000   17th World Cup Qualifiers
ICELAND v NORTHERN IRELAND 1-0 (0-0)
Laugardalsvöllur, Reykjavík

Referee: Markus Merk (Germany)   Attendance: 6,762

ICELAND: Birkir Kristinsson, Auðun Helgason, Eyjólfur Sverrisson (Cap), Arnar Þór Viðarsson, Hermann Hreiðarsson, Heiðar Helguson, Þórður Guðjónsson, Brynjar Björn Gunnarsson, Rúnar Kristinsson (46 Arnar Grétarsson), Eiður Smári Guðjohnsen, Ríkharður Daðason (63 Helgi Sigurðsson).
Trainer: Atli Eðvaldsson

NORTHERN IRELAND: Roy Carroll, Aaron William Hughes, Colin James Murdock, Stephen Martin Lomas, Gerald Paul Taggart (46 Mark Stuart Williams), Kevin Horlock, Damien Michael Johnson, James Magilton, Neil Francis Lennon, Stuart Elliott (82 Philip Gray), David Healy.
Manager: Sammy McIlroy

Goal: Þórður Guðjónsson (88)

478. 28.02.2001   17th World Cup Qualifiers
NORTHERN IRELAND v NORWAY 0-4 (0-3)
Windsor Park, Belfast

Referee: Kenny Clark (Scotland)   Attendance: 7,502

NORTHERN IRELAND: Maik Stefan Taylor, Aaron William Hughes, Gerald Paul Taggart (46 Stuart Elliott), Colin James Murdock, Jonathan David McCarthy (61 Damien Michael Johnson), Jeffrey Whitley (66 Daniel James Sonner), Neil Francis Lennon (46 Mark Stuart Williams), James Magilton, Peter Kennedy (46 Daniel Joseph Griffin), David Healy (69 Philip Gray), Glenn Ferguson (69 Andrew Kirk).
Manager: Sammy McIlroy

NORWAY: Thomas Myhre, André Bergdølmo, Henning Berg (46 Dan Eggen), Claus Lundekvam, Ståle Stensaas, Jo Tessem, Tommy Svindal Larsen, Eirik Bakke (78 Bjarte Lunde Aarsheim), Ole Gunnar Solskjær (78 Trond Andersen), John Carew (62 Frode Johnsen), Thorstein Helstad (78 Morten Berre).   Trainer: Nils Johan Semb

Goals: Thorstein Helstad (20), John Carew (30), Ståle Stensaas (37), Thorstein Helstad (49)

479. 24.03.2001   17th World Cup Qualifiers
**NORTHERN IRELAND
v CZECH REPUBLIC 0-1** (0-1)
Windsor Park, Belfast

Referee: Manuel Enrique Mejuto González (Spain)
Attendance: 10,368

NORTHERN IRELAND: Roy Carroll, Daniel Griffin, Aaron William Hughes, Mark Stuart Williams, Colin James Murdock, James Magilton, Keith Robert Gillespie, Neil Francis Lennon, David Healy (77 Glenn Ferguson), Michael Eamonn Hughes, Stuart Elliott (77 Philip Gray).   Manager: Sammy McIlroy

CZECH REPUBLIC: Pavel Srníček, Tomáš Ujfaluši, Tomáš Votava, Pavel Nedvěd (Cap), Milan Fukal, Roman Týce, Vladimír Šmicer (90 Jiří Němec), Karel Poborský, Jan Koller (72 Vratislav Lokvenc), Tomáš Rosický (80 Jiří Jarošík), Radek Bejbl.   Trainer: Jozef Chovanec

Goal: Pavel Nedvěd (11)

480. 28.03.2001   17th World Cup Qualifiers
BULGARIA v NORTHERN IRELAND 4-3 (2-1)
Balgarska Armia, Sofia

Referee: Vladimír Hriňák (Slovenia)   Attendance: 20,000

BULGARIA: Zdravko Zdravkov, Radostin Kishishev, Predrag Pazhin, Georgi Markov, Krasimir Chomakov, Biser Ivanov, Marian Hristov (68 Svetoslav Petrov), Milen Petkov (59 Stoicho Stoilov), Krasimir Balakov, Martin Petrov, Dimitar Berbatov (82 Georgi Ivanov).   Trainer: Stoicho Mladenov

NORTHERN IRELAND: Roy Carroll, Daniel Griffin, Ian Robert Nolan (90 Jonathan David McCarthy), Mark Stuart Williams, Colin James Murdock, James Magilton, Keith Robert Gillespie (86 Damien Michael Johnson), Neil Francis Lennon (86 Peter Kennedy), David Healy, Michael Eamonn Hughes, Stuart Elliott.   Manager: Sammy McIlroy

Goals: Krasimir Balakov (7), Martin Petrov (17, 78), Krasimir Chomakov (72) / Mark Stuart Williams (15), Stuart Elliott (83), David Healy (90 pen)

481. 2.06.2001   17th World Cup Qualifiers
NORTHERN IRELAND v BULGARIA 0-1 (0-0)
Windsor Park, Belfast

Referee: Massimo Busacca (Switzerland)   Att: 7,663

NORTHERN IRELAND: Maik Stefan Taylor, Ian Robert Nolan (86 Stephen James Quinn), Aaron William Hughes, Daniel Griffin, Colin James Murdock, Damien Michael Johnson, Keith Robert Gillespie, Neil Francis Lennon (78 Philip Patrick Mulryne), David Healy, Michael Eamonn Hughes, Stuart Elliott (78 Glenn Ferguson).   Manager: Sammy McIlroy

BULGARIA: Zdravko Zdravkov, Radostin Kishishev (23 Georgi Peev), Predrag Pazhin, Biser Ivanov, Georgi Markov, Krasimir Chomakov, Marian Hristov (87 Stoicho Stoilov), Milen Petkov, Krasimir Balakov, Georgi Ivanov, Martin Petrov (77 Rosen Kirilov).   Trainer: Stoicho Mladenov

Goal: Georgi Ivanov (52)

482. 06.06.2001   17th World Cup Qualifiers
**CZECH REPUBLIC
v NORTHERN IRELAND 3-1** (1-1)
Na Stínadlech, Teplice

Referee: Leif Sundell (Sweden)   Attendance: 14,050

CZECH REPUBLIC: Pavel Srníček, Tomáš Řepka, Tomáš Votava (46 Radek Bejbl), Pavel Nedvěd (Cap), Tomáš Galásek, Tomáš Rosický, Roman Týce, Karel Poborský (83 Vratislav Lokvenc), Pavel Kuka, Patrik Berger, Jan Koller (64 Milan Baroš).   Trainer: Jozef Chovanec

NORTHERN IRELAND: Maik Stefan Taylor, Ian Robert Nolan, Aaron William Hughes, Mark Stuart Williams, Colin James Murdock, Daniel Griffin, Damien Michael Johnson (77 Glenn Ferguson), Philip Patrick Mulryne (82 Peter Kennedy), David Healy, Michael Eamonn Hughes, Stuart Elliott (66 Stephen James Quinn).   Manager: Sammy McIlroy

Goals: Pavel Kuka (40, 88), Milan Baroš (90) / Philip Patrick Mulryne (45)

483. 01.09.2001   17th World Cup Qualifiers
DENMARK v NORTHERN IRELAND 1-1 (1-0)
Parken, København

Referee: Ryszard Wójcik (Poland)   Attendance: 41,569

DENMARK: Tomas Sørensen (12 Peter Kjær), Stig Tøfting, René Henriksen, Martin Laursen, Jan Heintze (Cap), Thomas Helveg, Peter Nielsen (69 Per Frandsen), Jesper Grønkjær, Jon Dahl Tomasson (79 Marc Nygaard), Dennis Rommedahl, Ebbe Sand.   Trainer: Morten Olsen

NORTHERN IRELAND: Maik Stefan Taylor, Daniel Griffin, Peter Kennedy, Aaron William Hughes, Colin James Murdock, James Magilton, Keith Robert Gillespie, Philip Patrick Mulryne, David Healy, Kevin Horlock, Michael Eamonn Hughes (71 Stuart Elliott).   Manager: Sammy McIlroy

Goals: Dennis Rommedahl (3) / Philip Patrick Mulryne (73)

484. 05.09.2001   17th World Cup Qualifiers
NORTHERN IRELAND v ICELAND 3-0 (0-0)
Windsor Park, Belfast

Referee: Attila Hanacsek (Hungary)   Attendance: 6,625

NORTHERN IRELAND: Maik Stefan Taylor, Daniel Griffin, Peter Kennedy, Aaron William Hughes, George McCartney, James Magilton, Keith Robert Gillespie (89 Paul McVeigh), Philip Patrick Mulryne, David Healy, Kevin Horlock, Michael Eamonn Hughes.   Manager: Sammy McIlroy

ICELAND: Árni Gautur Arason, Auðun Helgason (63 Heiðar Helguson), Arnar Þór Viðarsson, Arnar Grétarsson, Pétur Hafliði Marteinsson, Jóhannes Karl Guðjónsson, Hermann Hreiðarsson, Eyjólfur Sverrisson (Cap), Eiður Smári Guðjohnsen, Helgi Sigurðsson (87 Marel Jóhann Baldvinson), Andri Sigþórsson.   Trainer: Atli Eðvaldsson

Goals: David Healy (49), Michael Eamonn Hughes (58), George McCartney (61)

485. 06.10.2001
MALTA v NORTHERN IRELAND 0-1 (0-0)
National, Ta'Qali

Referee: Manfred Schuttengruber (Austria)   Att: 2,898

MALTA: Mario Muscat, Daniel Theuma (66 George Mallia), Jeffrey Chetcuti, Michael Spiteri, Darren Debono, Brian Said, Gilbert Agius, David Carabott, Michael Mifsud, Chucks Nwoko, Antoine Zahra (82 Hubert Suda).   Trainer: Siegfried Held

NORTHERN IRELAND: Maik Stefan Taylor, Daniel Griffin, Peter Kennedy, George McCartney, Colin James Murdock, James Magilton (Cap), Damien Michael Johnson, Kevin Horlock, David Healy (80 Stephen James Quinn), Michael Eamonn Hughes, Stuart Elliott (80 Grant McCann).   Manager: Sammy McIlroy

Goal: David Healy (58 pen)

486. 13.02.2002
POLAND v NORTHERN IRELAND 4-1 (2-1)
Tsireio, Limassol
Referee: Anastasios Papaioannou (Cyprus)   Att: 221
POLAND: Radosław Majdan (90 Andrzej Bledzewski), Tomasz Wałdoch (Cap), Jacek Bąk, Michał Żewłakow (61 Tomasz Rząsa), Marek Koźmiński, Jacek Krzynówek, Piotr Świerczewski (46 Tomasz Zdebel), Tomasz Iwan (46 Euzebiusz Smolarek), Radosław Kałużny (46 Arkadiusz Bąk), Paweł Kryszałowicz (82 Jacek Zieliński), Emmanuel Olisadebe (46 Marcin Żewłakow).   Trainer: Jerzy Engel
NORTHERN IRELAND: Maik Stefan Taylor, Stephen Martin Lomas, Peter Kennedy (82 Grant McCann), Daniel Griffin (46 Neil Francis Lennon), Aaron William Hughes (Cap), Philip Patrick Mulryne (46 George McCartney), Keith Robert Gillespie, James Magilton (82 Michael Duff), David Healy (60 Stuart Elliott), Damien Michael Johnson (66 Paul McVeigh), Michael Eamonn Hughes.   Manager: Sammy McIlroy
Goals: Paweł Kryszałowicz (6, 67), Radosław Kałużny (11), Marcin Żewłakow (69) / Stephen Martin Lomas (18)

487. 27.03.2002
LIECHTENSTEIN v NORTHERN IRELAND 0-0
Rheinpark, Vaduz
Referee: René Rogalla (Switzerland)   Attendance: 1,080
LIECHTENSTEIN: Peter Jehle (46 Martin Heeb), Martin Telser, Daniel Hasler, Harry Zech, Michael Stocklasa, Frédéric Gigon, Thomas Nigg (72 Franz Burgmeier), Martin Stocklasa, Matthias Beck, Thomas Beck, Ronny Büchel.
Trainer: Ralf Loose
NORTHERN IRELAND: Maik Stefan Taylor (46 Roy Carroll), Stephen Martin Lomas, Mark Stuart Williams, George McCartney, Grant McCann (69 Shaun Holmes), Keith Robert Gillespie, Philip Patrick Mulryne, James Magilton, Damien Michael Johnson, David Healy (83 Stuart Elliott), Warren Feeney (57 Michael Eamonn Hughes).
Manager: Sammy McIlroy

488. 17.04.2002
NORTHERN IRELAND v SPAIN 0-5 (0-1)
Windsor Park, Belfast
Referee: Kenny Clark (Scotland)   Attendance: 20,000
NORTHERN IRELAND: Maik Stefan Taylor (46 Roy Carroll), Ian Robert Nolan, George McCartney, Aaron William Hughes, Mark Stuart Williams, Damien Michael Johnson, Keith Robert Gillespie (77 Patrick McCourt), Kevin Horlock, Stuart Elliott, David Healy, Warren Feeney (64 Lee McEvilly).
Manager: Sammy McIlroy

SPAIN: José Santiago Cañizares (75 Iker Casillas), Carles Puyol, Miguel Ángel Nadal (46 Iván Helguera), Fernando Ruiz Hierro (Cap) (75 SERGIO González), Juan Francisco García "Juanfran", JOAQUÍN Sánchez (46 Gaizka Mendieta), David Albelda (46 Cristóbal Emilio "Curro" Torres), Rubén Baraja, Francisco Javier De Pedro (46 Juan Carlos Valerón), RAÚL González, Fernando Morientes.
Trainer: José Antonio Camacho
Goals: RAÚL González (22, 54), Rubén Baraja (48), Carles Puyol (69), Fernando Morientes (78)

489. 21.08.2002
NORTHERN IRELAND v CYPRUS 0-0
Windsor Park, Belfast
Referee: Simon Jones (Wales)   Attendance: 6,922
NORTHERN IRELAND: Maik Stefan Taylor, Daniel Griffin (46 Michael Duff), Colin James Murdock, Mark Stuart Williams, George McCartney, Peter Kennedy, Keith Robert Gillespie (87 Warren Feeney), Damien Michael Johnson, David Healy, Stephen James Quinn, Kevin Horlock.
Manager: Sammy McIlroy
CYPRUS: Níkos Panayiótou (89 Mihális Simitras), Petros Konnafis, Paníkos Spyrou, Dimitris Daskalakis (46 Mários Nikoláou), Níkos K. Nikoláou (42 Hrýsis Mihaíl), Stélios Okkarídis, Giórgos Theodótou, Leutéris Eleutheríou (70 Mários Hristodoulou), Giánnis Okkás (66 Kóstas Kaïáfas), Marínos Satsiás, Giasemákis Giasemí (61 Mários Agathokleous).   Trainer: Momcilo Vukotić

490. 12.10.2002   12th European Champs Qualifiers
SPAIN v NORTHERN IRELAND 3-0 (1-0)
Carlos Belmonte, Albacete
Referee: Luboš Michel (Slovakia)   Attendance: 16,000
SPAIN: Iker Casillas, Miguel Ángel "Míchel" Salgado, Carles Puyol, Iván Helguera, Raúl Bravo, José María Gutiérrez "Guti" (83 Jesús Capitán "Capi"), Rubén Baraja, JOAQUÍN Sánchez (76 Gaizka Mendieta), Xavier Hernández "Xavi", RAÚL González (Cap) (63 Fernando Morientes), VICENTE Rodríguez.   Trainer: José Ignacio Sáez
NORTHERN IRELAND: Maik Stefan Taylor, Aaron William Hughes, George McCartney, Gerald Paul Taggart (69 Grant McCann), Colin James Murdock, Stephen Martin Lomas, Keith Robert Gillespie, Philip Patrick Mulryne, Damien Michael Johnson, Paul McVeigh (65 David Healy), Kevin Horlock (65 Michael Eamonn Hughes).
Manager: Sammy McIlroy
Goals: Rubén Baraja (19, 89), José María Gutiérrez "Guti" (59)

491. 16.10.2002   12th European Champs Qualifiers
NORTHERN IRELAND v UKRAINE   0-0
Windsor Park, Belfast
Referee: Cosimo Bolognino (Italy)   Attendance: 9,288

NORTHERN IRELAND: Maik Stefan Taylor, Stephen Martin Lomas, Kevin Horlock, George McCartney, Aaron William Hughes, Damien Michael Johnson (83 Colin James Murdock), Keith Robert Gillespie, Philip Patrick Mulryne (90 Grant McCann), David Healy, Paul McVeigh (65 Andrew Kirk), Michael Eamonn Hughes.   Manager: Sammy McIlroy

UKRAINE: Vitaliy Reva, Oleh Luzhniy (Cap), Mykhailo Starostyak, Anatoliy Tymoschuk, Serhiy Kormiltsev (83 Vitaliy Lysytskiy), Andriy Voronin, Hennadiy Zubov, Maxym Kalynychenko (54 Serhiy Rebrov), Andriy Husyn, Andriy Vorobei (75 Oleksandr Melashchenko), Oleksandr Radchenko.
Trainer: Leonid Buryak

492. 12.02.2003
NORTHERN IRELAND v FINLAND   0-1 (0-0)
Windsor Park, Belfast
Referee: Douglas McDonald (Scotland)   Attendance: 6,137

NORTHERN IRELAND: Maik Stefan Taylor (46 Roy Carroll), Aaron William Hughes, Peter Kennedy, Mark Stuart Williams, George McCartney (66 Stephen Craigan), Stephen Martin Lomas, Keith Robert Gillespie, Damien Michael Johnson, David Healy, Stephen James Quinn (59 Andrew Kirk), Paul McVeigh (77 Stuart Elliott).
Manager: Sammy McIlroy

FINLAND: Jussi Jääskeläinen, Toni Kuivasto, Sami Hyypiä (Cap) (70 Markus Heikkinen), Hannu Tihinen, Janne Hietanen, Mika Nurmela, Aki Riihilahti, Simo Valakari, Joonas Kolkka (75 Peter Kopteff), Mika Väyrynen (60 Jonatan Johansson), Mikael Forssell (46 Shefki Kuqi).
Trainer: Antti Muurinen

Goal: Sami Hyypiä (50)

493. 29.03.2003   12th European Champs Qualifiers
ARMENIA v NORTHERN IRELAND   1-0 (0-0)
Republikan, Yerevan
Referee: Roland Beck (Liechtenstein)   Attendance: 10,321

ARMENIA: Roman Berezovski, Yeghishe Melikyan, Karen Dokhoyan, Sargis Hovsepyan, Harutyun Vardanyan, José André Bilibio, Artur Petrosyan (90 Hamlet Mkhitaryan), Aram Voskanyan, Albert Sargisyan (90 Artur Mkrtchyan), Artavazd Karamyan (89 Avgan Mkrtchyan), Arman Karamyan.
Trainer: Mihai Stoichiţă

NORTHERN IRELAND: Maik Stefan Taylor, Aaron William Hughes, Grant McCann, Mark Stuart Williams, Stephen Martin Lomas, Keith Robert Gillespie, Damien Michael Johnson, David Healy, Stephen James Quinn (71 Stuart Elliott), Paul McVeigh, Stephen Craigan.
Manager: Sammy McIlroy

Goal: Artur Petrosyan (86)

494. 02.04.2003   12th European Champs Qualifiers
NORTHERN IRELAND v GREECE   0-2 (0-1)
Windsor Park, Belfast
Referee: Grzegorz Gilewski (Poland)   Attendance: 7,256

NORTHERN IRELAND: Maik Stefan Taylor, Aaron William Hughes, George McCartney, Stephen Craigan, Mark Stuart Williams, Keith Robert Gillespie, Damien Michael Johnson, Grant McCann (68 Andrew Kirk), Stephen Martin Lomas, David Healy (68 Paul McVeigh), Stephen James Quinn.
Manager: Sammy McIlroy

GREECE: Antónis Nikopolidis, Stélios Giannakópoulos, Stélios Venetídis (72 Panagiótis Fyssas), Nikolaos Dabizas, Sotíris Kyrgiakos, Théodoros Zagorakis, Konstantinos Konstantinidis, Giórgos Karagoúnis, Vasílis Tsiártas (76 Pantelís Kafés), Aggelos Haristéas, Thémistoklis Nikolaïdis (42 Zísis Vrízas).   Trainer: Otto Rehhagel

Sent off: Keith Gillespie (69), Stephen James Quinn (38)

Goals: Aggelos Haristéas (3, 56)

495. 03.06.2003   12th European Champs Qualifiers
ITALY v NORTHERN IRELAND   2-0 (1-0)
Nuovo Romagnoli, Campobasso
Referee: Lucillo Cardoso Baptista (Portugal)   Att: 18,270

ITALY: Francesco Toldo, Massimo Oddo, Nicola Legrottaglie (57 Daniele Bonera), Fabio Cannavaro (Cap) (46 Matteo Ferrari), Fabio Grosso (69 Alessandro Birindelli), Simone Perrotta (57 Damiano Tommasi), Massimo Ambrosini, Stefano Fiore, Fabrizio Miccoli (57 Antonio Di Natale), Marco Di Vaio (69 Carlo Nervo), Bernardo Corradi (46 Marco Delvecchio).
Trainer: Giovanni Trapattoni

NORTHERN IRELAND: Maik Stefan Taylor (55 Roy Carroll), Christopher Baird, Aaron William Hughes (Cap), George McCartney, Peter Kennedy (55 Mark Stuart Williams), Daniel Joseph Griffin, Tommy Doherty (86 Stuart Elliott), Damien Michael Johnson (68 Ciaran Toner), David Healy (75 Gary Hamilton), Paul McVeigh (55 Stephen Jones), Andrew Smith.   Manager: Sammy McIlroy (25)

Goals: Bernardo Corradi (31), Marco Delvecchio (67)

496. 11.06.2003   12th European Champs Qualifiers
NORTHERN IRELAND v SPAIN   0-0
Windsor Park, Belfast

Referee: Claus Bo Larsen (Denmark)   Attendance: 11,365

NORTHERN IRELAND: Maik Stefan Taylor, Christopher Baird, Peter Kennedy, Aaron William Hughes, George McCartney, Daniel Joseph Griffin, Tommy Doherty (80 Ciaran Toner), Damien Michael Johnson, David Healy, Andrew Smith (90 Mark Stuart Williams), Stephen Jones (73 Paul McVeigh).   Manager: Sammy McIlroy

SPAIN: Iker Casillas, Carles Puyol, Carlos Marchena, Iván Helguera, Juan Francisco García "Juanfran", Joseba Etxeberría (79 Francisco Javier De Pedro), SERGIO González (66 JOAQUÍN Sánchez), Rubén Baraja, Juan Carlos Valerón, VICENTE Rodríguez (66 Fernando Morientes), RAÚL González (Cap).   Trainer: José Ignacio Sáez

497. 06.09.2003   12th European Champs Qualifiers
UKRAINE v NORTHERN IRELAND   0-0
Centralnyi, Donetsk

Referee: Wolfgang Stark (Germany)   Attendance: 24,000

UKRAINE: Oleksandr Shovkovskiy, Oleh Luzhniy (Cap), Serhiy Fedorov, Anatoliy Tymoschuk, Andriy Nesmachniy, Oleksandr Horshkov, Serhiy Rebrov (72 Oleksandr Melashchenko), Andriy Husyn (16 Oleh Husev), Hennadiy Zubov, Andriy Voronin, Andriy Vorobei.   Trainer: Leonid Buryak

NORTHERN IRELAND: Maik Stefan Taylor, Christopher Baird, Aaron William Hughes, Peter Kennedy, George McCartney, Daniel Joseph Griffin, Keith Robert Gillespie, Damien Michael Johnson, David Healy (62 Andrew Smith), Tommy Doherty (67 Philip Patrick Mulryne), Michael Eamonn Hughes (79 Stephen Jones).   Manager: Sammy McIlroy

498. 10.09.2003   12th European Champs Qualifiers
NORTHERN IRELAND v ARMENIA   0-1 (0-1)
Windsor Park, Belfast

Referee: Anton Stredak (Slovakia)   Attendance: 8,616

NORTHERN IRELAND: Maik Stefan Taylor, Christopher Baird, Aaron Willaim Hughes, Grant McCann, George McCartney, Daniel Joseph Griffin, Keith Robert Gillespie (29 Stephen Jones), Damien Michael Johnson, David Healy (78 Paul McVeigh), Andrew Smith, Tommy Doherty (29 Philip Patrick Mulryne).   Manager: Samuel McIlroy

ARMENIA: Roman Berezovski, Yeghishe Melikyan, José André Bilibio, Sargis Hovsepyan, Marian Zeciu, Romik Khachatryan, Artur Petrosyan (13 Arman Karamyan), Aram Voskanyan, Albert Sargisyan, Artavazd Karamyan (87 Eduard Partsikyan), Andrei Movsesyan (75 Ara Hakobyan).   Trainer: Mihai Stoichiță

Goal: Artavazd Karamyan (27)

499. 11.10.2003   12th European Champs Qualifiers
GREECE v NORTHERN IRELAND   1-0 (0-0)
Apóstolos Nikolaïdis, Athína

Referee: Lucilio Cardoso Cortez Batista (Portugal)   Attendance: 25,000

GREECE: Antónis Nikopolidis, Giórgos Seitaridis, Panagiótis Fyssas, Nikolaos Dabizas (46 Stélios Venetídis), Traïanós Dellas, Aggelos Basinás (90 Théodoros Zagorakis), Paraskevás Antzas, Zísis Vrízas, Aggelos Haristéas (46 Thémistoklis Nikolaïdis), Vasílis Tsiártas, Stélios Giannakópoulos.   Trainer: Otto Rehhagel

NORTHERN IRELAND: Maik Stefan Taylor, Christopher Baird, Peter Kennedy, George McCartney, Aaron William Hughes, Daniel Joseph Griffin (85 Stephen Jones), Keith Robert Gillespie (64 Andrew Smith), Jeffrey Whitley, David Healy, Michael Eamonn Hughes, Stuart Elliott (70 Colin James Murdock).   Manager: Samuel McIlroy

Sent off: George McCartney (69)

Goal: Vasílis Tsiártas (69 pen)

500. 18.02.2004
NORTHERN IRELAND v NORWAY   1-4 (0-3)
Windsor Park, Belfast

Referee: Craig Alexander Thomson (Scotland)   Att: 11,288

NORTHERN IRELAND: Maik Stefan Taylor, Christopher Baird, Aaron William Hughes, George McCartney, Peter Kennedy (77 Stephen Jones), Keith Robert Gillespie (73 Paul McVeigh), Michael Eamonn Hughes, Daniel Joseph Griffin (46 Mark Stuart Williams), Damien Michael Johnson, Andrew Smith, David Healy.   Manager: Lawrie Sanchez

NORWAY: Thomas Myhre (70 Erik Holtan), Hassan El Fakiri, Ronny Johnsen, Brede Poulsen Hangeland, John Arne Riise (70 Erlend Hanstveit), Magne Hoseth, Martin Andresen, Thorstein Helstad (89 Jon Inge Høiland), Steffen Iversen, Morten Gamst Pedersen (81 Alexander Ødegaard), Sigurd Rushfeldt (46 Håvard Flo).   Trainer: Åge Hareide

Goals: David Healy (56) / Morten Gamst Pedersen (17, 36), Steffen Iversen (44), Keith Robert Gillespie (58 own goal)

501. 31.03.2004
ESTONIA v NORTHERN IRELAND   0-1 (0-1)
A Le Coq Arena, Tallinn

Referee: Petteri Kari (Finland)   Attendance: 2,900

ESTONIA: Martin Kaalma, Enar Jääger, Andrei Stepanov, Raio Piiroja (84 Taavi Rähn), Ragnar Klavan, Martin Reim, Maksim Smirnov (86 Ott Reinumäe), Marko Kristal, Indrek Zelinski (67 Ingemar Teever), Meelis Rooba (77 Joel Lindpere), Tarmo Kink (75 Sergei Terehhov).   Trainer: Arno Pijpers

NORTHERN IRELAND: Maik Stefan Taylor, Christopher Baird, Mark Stuart Williams, Stephen Craigan, Anthony Capaldi, Stephen Jones (68 Grant McCann), Daniel James Sonner (78 Michael Duff), Jeffrey Whitley, Philip Patrick Mulryne, David Healy, Andrew Smith.
Manager: Lawrie Sanchez
Goal: David Healy (45)

502. 28.04.2004
**NORTHERN IRELAND
v SERBIA & MONTENEGRO 1-1** (1-1)
Windsor Park Belfast
Referee: Ceri Richards (Wales)   Attendance: 9,690
NORTHERN IRELAND: Maik Stefan Taylor (46 Roy Carroll), Christopher Baird, Mark Stuart Williams, Stephen Craigan, Anthony Capaldi, Keith Robert Gillespie (46 Stephen Jones), Tommy Doherty (78 Michael Eamonn Hughes), Jeffrey Whitley (78 Daniel James Sonner), Philip Patrick Mulryne (46 Paul McVeigh), David Healy (46 Gary Hamilton), Stephen James Quinn (78 Andrew Smith).   Manager: Lawrie Sanchez
SERBIA & MONTENEGRO: Zoran Banović, Milivoje Ćirković (83 Jovan Markoski), Mladen Krstajić, Goran Gavrančić, Dušan Petković, Ivica Dragutinović (46 Milivoje Vitakić), Albert Nađ, Goran Trobok (46 Vladimir Ivić), Zvonimir Vukić, Mateja Kežman, Veljko Paunović (69 Miloš Kolaković).   Trainer: Ilija Petković
Goals: Stephen James Quinn (18) / Veljko Paunović (7)

503. 30.05.2004
BARBADOS v NORTHERN IRELAND 1-1 (1-0)
Waterford National, Bridgetown
Referee: Neil Brizan (Trinidad & Tobago)   Att: 8,000
BARBADOS: Adrian Chase, Rommell Braithwaite, Rudy Grosvenor, John Parris, Dwight James, Randy Burrowes, Norman Forde (46 Gregory Goodridge), Kent Hall, Paul Lovell (John Hawkesworth), Kenroy Skinner (65 Llewellyn Riley), Ryan Lucas (Rommell Burgess).   Trainer: Kenville Layne
NORTHERN IRELAND: Maik Stefan Taylor, Christopher Baird (67 Stephen Jones), Anthony Capaldi (67 Stuart Elliott), Mark Stuart Williams, Keith Robert Gillespie (46 Colin James Murdock), Damien Michael Johnson, Daniel James Sonner (67 Paul McVeigh), Philip Patrick Mulryne (45 Andrew Smith), Stephen James Quinn, David Healy (80 Gary Hamilton), Stephen Craigan.   Manager: Lawrie Sanchez
Sent off: Mark Stuart Williams (30)
Goals: Kenroy Skinner (38) / David Healy (71)

504. 02.06.2004
**ST. KITTS & NEVIS
v NORTHERN IRELAND 0-2** (0-0)
Warner Park, Basseterre
Referee: James Matthew (St. Kitts & Nevis)   Att: 3,500
ST. KITTS & NEVIS: Akil Byron (85 Kayian Benjamin), Dagi Burton (55 Toussaint Riley), Lance Lewis, Thrizen Leader, Keithroy Eddy, Austin Huggins (80 Alexis Saddler), Daryl Gomez, George Isaac, Keithroy Saddler (80 Vernon Sargeant), Ian Lake (59 Jevon Francis), Keith Gumbs.
Trainer: Lenny Lake
NORTHERN IRELAND: Maik Stefan Taylor, Christopher Baird, Anthony Capaldi, Stephen Craigan, Colin James Murdock, Paul McVeigh (63 Philip Patrick Mulryne), Daniel James Sonner (51 Stephen Jones), Jeffrey Whitley (63 Damien Michael Johnson), Stuart Elliott (63 Keith Robert Gillespie), Gary Hamilton (63 David Healy), Andrew Smith.
Manager: Lawrie Sanchez
Goals: David Healy (81), Stephen Jones (84)

505. 06.06.2004
**TRINIDAD & TOBAGO
v NORTHERN IRELAND 0-3** (0-2)
Dwight Yorke, Bacolet
Referee: Barney Callender (Barbados)   Attendance: 7,500
TRINIDAD & TOBAGO: Clayton Ince, Ian Cox, Carlos Edwards, Brent Sancho (46 Keyeno Thomas), Marvin Andrews, Stokely Mason (46 Dwight Yorke), Angus Eve (Cap), Anthony Rougier (76 Darryl Roberts), Kerwyn Jemmott (83 Densil Theobald), Andre Boucaud (68 Hayden Fitzwilliams), Stern John.   Trainer: Bertille St. Clair
NORTHERN IRELAND: Maik Stefan Taylor (82 Alan Mannus), Christopher Baird, Anthony Capaldi, Stephen Craigan (46 Colin James Murdock), Mark Stuart Williams, Stuart Elliott (46 Stephen Jones), Damien Michael Johnson (72 Keith Robert Gillespie), Philip Patrick Mulryne (72 Daniel James Sonner), Jeffrey Whitley, David Healy (65 Paul McVeigh), Stephen James Quinn (61 Andrew Smith).
Manager: Lawrie Sanchez
Goals: David Healy (5, 65), Stuart Elliott (41)

506. 18.08.2004
SWITZERLAND v NORTHERN IRELAND 0-0
Hardturm, Zürich

Referee: Nicolai Vollquartz (Denmark)   Attendance: 4,000

SWITZERLAND: Pascal Zuberbühler, Bernt Haas, Patrick Müller, Murat Yakin (46 Stéphane Henchoz), Christoph Spycher, Benjamin Huggel (46 Ludovic Magnin), Johann Vogel (77 Johann Lonfat), Ricardo Cabanas (82 Alexander Frei), Raphaël Wicky, Hakan Yakin, Johan Vonlanthen (60 André Muff).   Trainer: Jakob Kühn

NORTHERN IRELAND: Roy Carroll, Aaron William Hughes, Stephen Craigan (78 Michael Duff), Mark Stuart Williams (67 Colin James Murdock), Anthony Capaldi, Stuart Elliott (81 Christopher Brunt), Daniel James Sonner, Damien Michael Johnson, Keith Robert Gillespie (51 Paul McVeigh), David Healy (71 Gary Hamilton), Andrew Smith.   Manager: Lawrie Sanchez

507. 04.09.2004   18th World Cup Qualifiers
NORTHERN IRELAND v POLAND 0-3 (0-2)
Windsor Park, Belfast

Referee: Jan W. Wegereef (Holland)   Attendance: 14,000

NORTHERN IRELAND: Maik Stefan Taylor, Aaron William Hughes, Stephen Craigan, Mark Stuart Williams, Anthony Capaldi, Stuart Elliott (62 Paul McVeigh), Michael Eamonn Hughes (53 Stephen Jones), Jeffrey Whitley, Damien Michael Johnson, David Healy, Stephen James Quinn (73 Andrew Smith).   Manager: Lawrie Sanchez

POLAND: Jerzy Dudek, Michał Żewłakow, Jacek Bąk, Arkadiusz Głowacki, Tomasz Rząsa, Jacek Krzynówek (67 Damian Gorawski), Mariusz Lewandowski, Sebastian Mila (76 Arkadiusz Radomski), Marek Zieńczuk, Piotr Włodarczyk, Maciej Żurawski (84 Paweł Kryszałowicz).   Trainer: Paweł Janas

Sent off: Piotr Włodarczyk (79)

Goals: Maciej Żurawski (4), Piotr Włodarczyk (37), Jacek Krzynówek (57)

508. 08.09.2004   18th World Cup Qualifiers
WALES v NORTHERN IRELAND 2-2 (1-2)
Millenium, Cardiff

Referee: Domenico Messina (Italy)   Attendance: 63,500

WALES: Paul Steven Jones, Mark Delaney (25 Robert Earnshaw), James Collins, Daniel Gabbidon, Benjamin David Thatcher (63 Paul Parry), John Morgan Oster, Robert William Savage, Gary Andrew Speed (Cap), Jason Koumas, John Hartson, Craig Douglas Bellamy.   Trainer: Mark Leslie Hughes

NORTHERN IRELAND: Maik Stefan Taylor, Aaron William Hughes, Colin James Murdock, Mark Stuart Williams, Anthony Capaldi (90 George McCartney), Damien Michael Johnson, Jeffrey Whitley, Michael Eamonn Hughes, Mark Clyde, David Healy, Stephen James Quinn (56 Andrew Smith, 87 Paul McVeigh).   Manager: Lawrie Sanchez

Sent off: Robert Savage (9), Michael Eamonn Hughes (9), David Healy (21)

Goals: John Hartson (32), Robert Earnshaw (75) / Jeffrey Whitley (10), David Healy (21)

509. 09.10.2004   18th World Cup Qualifiers
AZERBAIJAN v NORTHERN IRELAND 0-0
Tofik Bakhramov, Baku

Referee: Attila Hanacsek (Hungary)   Attendance: 6,460

AZERBAIJAN: Dzhakhangir Hasanzade, Rafael Amirbekov, Avtandil Gadzhiev, Emin Guliyev, Kamal Guliyev, Mahir Shukurov, Makhmud Kurbanov (58 Anatoli Ponomarev), Ismayil Mammadov (53 Ilgar Kurbanov), Rashad Sadygov (Cap), Samir Aliyev (76 Kurban Kurbanov), Nadir Nabiyev.   Trainer: Carlos Alberto Torres

NORTHERN IRELAND: Maik Stefan Taylor, Mark Clyde, Colin James Murdock, Mark Stuart Williams, Aaron William Hughes, Christopher Baird (9 Keith Robert Gillespie), Damien Michael Johnson, Jeffrey Whitley, Tommy Doherty, Stuart Elliott, Stephen James Quinn (76 Andrew Smith).   Manager: Lawrie Sanchez

510. 13.10.2004   18th World Cup Qualifiers
NORTHERN IRELAND v AUSTRIA 3-3 (1-1)
Windsor Park, Belfast

Referee: Mark Shield (Australia)   Attendance: 20,000

NORTHERN IRELAND: Roy Carroll, Aaron William Hughes (Cap), Mark Stuart Williams, Colin James Murdock (78 Stuart Elliott), Tommy Doherty (86 Stephen Jones), Keith Robert Gillespie, Jeffrey Whitley (89 Paul McVeigh), Damien Michael Johnson, George McCartney, David Healy, Stephen James Quinn.   Manager: Lawrie Sanchez

AUSTRIA: Alexander Manninger, Andreas Ibertsberger, Ferdinand Feldhofer, Martin Hiden, Emanuel Pogatetz, Markus Schopp (Cap) (83 Gernot Sick), Markus Kiesenebner, Dietmar Kühbauer, Roland Kirchler (64 Andreas Ivanschitz), Christian Mayrleb (81 Roland Kollmann), Ivica Vastic.   Trainer: Johann Krankl

Goals: David Healy (35), Colin James Murdock (60), Stuart Elliott (90) / Markus Schopp (14, 72), Christian Mayrleb (61)

511. 09.02.2005
NORTHERN IRELAND v CANADA 0-1 (0-1)
Windsor Park, Belfast
Referee: Joseph Attard (Malta)   Attendance: 11,156
NORTHERN IRELAND: Maik Stefan Taylor (46 Roy Carroll), Christopher Baird, Aaron William Hughes, Colin James Murdock (46 Andrew Kirk), George McCartney, Keith Robert Gillespie (75 Stephen Jones), Jeffrey Whitley, Tommy Doherty (46 Philip Patrick Mulryne) Steven Davis, Anthony Capaldi (79 Stephen Craigan, David Healy (79 Andrew Smith). Manager: Lawrie Sanchez
CANADA: Greg Sutton, Gabriel Gervais, Kevin McKenna (Cap) (46 Michael Klukowski), Marco Reda, Adrian Serioux (88 Jaime Peters), Daniel Imhof, Olivier Occean, Patrice Bernier, James Brennan (87 Iain Hume), Dwayne De Rosario, Joshua Simpson.   Trainer: Frank Yallop
Sent off: Gabriel Gervais (22)
Goal: Olivier Occean (31)

512. 26.03.2005   18th World Cup Qualifiers
ENGLAND v NORTHERN IRELAND 4-0 (0-0)
Old Trafford, Manchester
Referee: Wolfgang Stark (Germany)   Attendance: 65,239
ENGLAND: Paul Robinson, Gary Alexander Neville, John Terry, Rio Gavin Ferdinand, Ashley Cole, David Beckham (71 Kieron Courtney Dyer), Frank James Lampard, Steven Gerrard (71 Owen Hargreaves), Joseph Cole, Wayne Rooney (80 Jermain Defoe), Michael James Owen.
Manager: Sven-Göran Eriksson
NORTHERN IRELAND: Maik Stefan Taylor, Christopher Baird, Aaron William Hughes, Colin James Murdock, Anthony Capaldi, Tommy Doherty (58 Steven Davis), Keith Robert Gillespie, Damien Michael Johnson, Jeffrey Whitley (89 Andrew Kirk), Stuart Elliott, David Healy (89 Stephen Jones). Manager: Lawrie Sanchez
Goals: Joseph Cole (47), Michael James Owen (51), Christopher Baird (54 own goal), Frank James Lampard (62)

513. 30.03.2005   18th World Cup Qualifiers
POLAND v NORTHERN IRELAND 1-0 (0-0)
Wojska Polskiego, Warszawa
Referee: Peter Fröjdtfeld (Sweden)   Attendance: 13,515
POLAND: Jerzy Dudek, Marcin Baszczyński, Jacek Bąk, Tomasz Kłos, Tomasz Rząsa (45 Tomasz Kiełbowicz), Bartosz Karwan (74 Grzegorz Rasiak), Radosław Kałużny (67 Sebastian Mila), Mirosław Szymkowiak, Jacek Krzynówek, Tomasz Frankowski, Maciej Żurawski.   Trainer: Paweł Janas
NORTHERN IRELAND: Maik Stefan Taylor, Christopher Baird, Aaron Hughes, Colin James Murdock, Anthony Capaldi, Mark Stuart Williams (88 Stuart Elliott), Keith Robert Gillespie, Steven Davis, Jeffrey Whitley, Stephen James Quinn (35 Warren Feeney, David Healy(81 Andrew Smith). Manager: Lawrie Sanchez
Goal: Maciej Żurawski (85)

514. 04.06.2005
NORTHERN IRELAND v GERMANY 1-4 (1-1)
Windsor Park, Belfast
Referee: Charles Joseph Richmond (Scotland)   Att: 14,000
NORTHERN IRELAND: Maik Stefan Taylor (77 Michael Ingham), Christopher Baird, Stephen Craigan (77 Christopher Brunt), Mark Clyde, George McCartney, Keith Robert Gillespie (70 Gareth McAuley), Damien Michael Johnson, Steven Davis, Stephen Jones (67 Warren Feeney), Stuart Elliott (67 Andrew Kirk), David Healy (77 Andrew Smith).
Manager: Lawrie Sanchez
GERMANY: Jens Lehmann, Patrick Owomoyela, Per Mertesacker, Robert Huth, Thomas Hitzlsperger, Torsten Frings, Bernd Schneider (46 Sebastian Deisler), Fabian Ernst, Michael Ballack (Cap) (73 Tim Borowski), Gerald Asamoah (46 Bastian Schweinsteiger), Kevin Kuranyi (63 Lukas Podolski).   Trainer: Jürgen Klinsmann
Sent off: Robert Huth (15)
Goals: David Healy (15 pen) / Gerald Asamoah (17), Michael Ballack (62, 66 pen), Lukas Podolski (82)

515. 17.08.2005

MALTA v NORTHERN IRELAND 1-1 (1-1)

National, Ta'Qali

Referee: Mike Riley (England)   Attendance: 1,850

MALTA: Justin Haber, Peter Pullicino (62 Ian Ciantar), Luke Dimech (62 Kenneth Scicluna), Brian Said, Stephen Wellman, Roderick Briffa, Gilbert Agius (74 George Mallia), Orosco Anonam, Ivan Woods, Claude John Mattocks (79 Antoine Zahra I), Andrew Cohen (86 Kevin Sammut).

Trainer: Horst Heese

NORTHERN IRELAND: Maik Stefan Taylor, Stephen Craigan, Aaron Hughes (Cap), Colin James Murdock, Keith Robert Gillespie, Damien Michael Johnson, Jeffrey Whitley (59 Stephen Jones), Steven Davis (89 Philip Patrick Mulryne), Stuart Elliott (59 Christopher Brunt), David Healy, Stephen James Quinn (59 Warren Feeney).   Manager: Lawrie Sanchez

Sent off: Ivan Woods (77), Keith Robert Gillespie (77)

Goals: Ivan Woods (35) / David Healy (9)

516. 03.09.2005   18th World Cup Qualifiers

NORTHERN IRELAND v AZERBAIJAN 2-0 (0-0)

Windsor Park, Belfast

Referee: Dejan Stanišić (Serbia & Montenegro)   Att: 12,000

NORTHERN IRELAND: Maik Stefan Taylor, Christopher Baird, Aaron Hughes (Cap), Anthony Capaldi, Stephen Craigan, Steven Davis, Keith Robert Gillespie, Damien Michael Johnson, David Healy (79 Stephen Jones), Stephen James Quinn (72 Warren Feeney), Stuart Elliott (89 Stephen Robinson).   Manager: Lawrie Sanchez

AZERBAIJAN: Dmitriy Kramarenko, Rafael Amirbekov, Avtandil Gadzhiev, Emin Guliyev, Aslan Kerimov, Makhmud Kurbanov (64 Anatoli Ponomarev), Rashad Sadygov, Yuriy Muzika, Zaur Tagizade (83 Nadir Nabiyer), Emin Imamaliyev, Samir Aliyev (75 Mahir Shukurov).   Trainer: Vagif Sadykov

Goals: Stuart Elliott (60), Warren Feeney (84)

517. 07.09.2005   18th World Cup Qualifiers

NORTHERN IRELAND v ENGLAND 1-0 (0-0)

Windsor Park, Belfast

Referee: Massimo Busacca (Switzerland)   Att: 14,069

NORTHERN IRELAND: Maik Stefan Taylor, Christopher Baird, Anthony Capaldi, Stephen Craigan, Steven Davis, Keith Robert Gillespie, Damien Michael Johnson, David Healy (85 Ivan Sproule), Stephen James Quinn (78 Warren Feeney), Stuart Elliott (90 Michael Duff), Aaron Hughes (Cap).   Manager: Lawrie Sanchez

ENGLAND: Paul Robinson, Luke Young, Ashley Cole, Rio Gavin Ferdinand, James Lee Carragher, Steven Gerrard (76 Jermain Defoe), David Beckham (Cap), Frank James Lampard (81 Owen Hargreaves), Wayne Rooney, Michael James Owen, Shaun Wright-Phillips (54 Joseph Cole).   Manager: Sven-Göran Eriksson

Goal: David Healy (73)

518. 08.10.2005   18th World Cup Qualifiers

NORTHERN IRELAND v WALES 2-3 (0-2)

Windsor Park, Belfast

Referee: Ruud Bossen (Holland)   Attendance: 13,451

NORTHERN IRELAND: Maik Stefan Taylor, Michael Duff (82 Stephen Jones), Anthony Capaldi, Colin James Murdock, Stephen Craigan, Steven Davis, Keith Robert Gillespie, Damien Michael Johnson, David Healy, Stephen James Quinn, Stuart Elliott (65 Christopher Brunt).   Manager: Lawrie Sanchez

WALES: Paul Jones, James Collins (51 Richard Duffy), Mark Delaney, David Partridge, Sam Ricketts (87 Danny Collins), Carl Fletcher, Carl Robinson, Simon Davies, Ryan Giggs (Cap), Robert Earnshaw (77 David Vaughan), John Hartson.   Manager: John Toshack

Goals: Michael Duff (47), Steve Davis (50)

519. 12.10.2005   18th World Cup Qualifiers

AUSTRIA v NORTHERN IRELAND 2-0 (1-0)

Ernst Happel, Wien

Referee: Athanassios Briakos (Greece)   Attendance: 12,500

AUSTRIA: Jürgen Macho, Andreas Dober (46 Andreas Ibertsberger), Martin Stranzl, Paul Scharner, René Aufhauser, Markus Schopp (55 Joachim Standfest), Markus Kiesenebner, Roland Linz, Andreas Ivanschitz, Roman Wallner (77 Ronald Gercaliu), Emanuel Pogatetz.

Trainer: Willibald Ruttensteiner

NORTHERN IRELAND: Maik Stefan Taylor, Christopher Baird, Colin James Murdock, Michael Duff, Stephen Craigan, Steven Davis, Keith Robert Gillespie, Damien Michael Johnson, David Healy (70 Stephen Jones), Stephen James Quinn (57 Warren Feeney), Christopher Brunt (75 Stuart Elliott).   Manager: Lawrie Sanchez

Sent off: Emanuel Pogatetz (74), Damien Johnson (74)

Goals: René Aufhauser (44, 90)

520. 15.11.2005

NORTHERN IRELAND v PORTUGAL 1-1 (0-1)

Windsor Park, Belfast

Referee: Howard Webb (England)   Attendance: 20,000

NORTHERN IRELAND: Maik Stefan Taylor, Christopher Brunt, Colin James Murdock, Stephen Craigan, Anthony Capaldi, Keith Robert Gillespie (87 Ivan Sproule), Stephen Jones (46 Gareth McAuley), Stuart Elliott (46 Grant McCann), Steven Davis, Warren Feeney (87 Dean Shiels), Stephen James Quinn (77 Peter Thompson).   Manager: Lawrie Sanchez

PORTUGAL: Paulo Santos, PAULO Renato Rebocho FERREIRA, RICARDO Alberto Silveira CARVALHO, Fernando José da Silva Freitas Meira, JORGE Miguel de Oliveira RIBEIRO, Armando Gonçalves Teixeira "Petit" (67 JOÃO Artur Rosa ALVES), Francisco José Rodrigues Costa "Costinha", TIAGO Cardoso Mendes (76 Nuno Miguel FRECHAUT Barreto), CRISTIANO RONALDO Santos Aveiro (69 HÉLDER Manuel Marques POSTIGA), Luís BOA MORTE Pereira (62 Marco António Caneira), Pedro Miguel Carreiro Resendes "Pauleta" (46 Nuno Miguel Soares Pereira Ribeiro "Nuno Gomes"). Trainer: Luiz Felipe Scolari

Goals: Warren Feeney (54) / Stephen Craigan (41 own goal)

521. 01.03.2006
NORTHERN IRELAND v ESTONIA 1-0 (1-0)
Windsor Park, Belfast

Referee: Peter Vink (Holland)   Attendance: 13,600

NORTHERN IRELAND: Maik Stefan Taylor (Cap), Gareth McAuley, Michael Duff, Stephen Craigan (46 Brian McLean), Anthony Capaldi, Ivan Sproule (46 Steve Jones), Christopher Baird, Steve Davis (68 Grant McCann), Christopher Brunt (68 Stuart Elliott), David Healy (59 Warren Feeney), James Quinn (59 Peter Thompson).   Manager: Lawrie Sanchez

ESTONIA: Mart Poom (Cap), Enar Jääger, Andrei Stepanov, Raio Piiroja, Urmas Rooba, Ingemar Teever (72 Jürgen Kuresoo), Taavi Rähn (77 Martin Reim), Aleksandr Dmitrijev, Joel Lindpere (54 Andres Oper), Andrei Sidorenkov (82 Jarmo Ahjupera), Tarmo Neemelo.
Trainer: Jelle Goes (Switzerland)

Goal: Ivan Sproule (2)

522. 21.05.2006
URUGUAY v NORTHERN IRELAND 1-0 (1-0)
Giants, New York (United States)

Referee: Arkadiusz Prus (United States)   Attendance: 4,152

URUGUAY: Héctor Farbián Carini, Andrés Scotti, Carlos Adrian Valdez, Diego Roberto Godín, Walter Alberto López, Diego Fernando Pérez, Pablo Gabriel García (Cap), Guillermo Gonzalo Giacomazzi, Fabián Estoyanoff (82 Juan Ignacio Surraco), Washington Sebastián Abreu, Gonzalo Vargas.
Trainer: Oscar Washington Tabárez

NORTHERN IRELAND: Michael Ingham, Michael Duff (83 Sean Webb), Colin James Murdock (83 Gareth McAuley), Stephen Craigan, Anthony Capaldi, Steve Jones (60 Peter Thompson), Steve Davis, Samuel Clingan (82 Mark Hughes), Jeff Hughes (75 Dean Shiels), Ivan Sproule, James Quinn (75 Kyle Lafferty).   Manager: Lawrie Sanchez

Goal: Fabián Estoyanoff (33)

523. 27.05.2006
ROMANIA v NORTHERN IRELAND 2-0 (2-0)
Soldier Field, Chicago

Referee: Mike Kennedy (United States)   Attendance: 15,000

ROMANIA: Dănuţ Coman, Valentin Bădoi, Dorin Goian (56 Adrian Iencsi), Vasile Maftei, Cristian Pulhac (88 Pompiliu Stoica), Bănel Nicoliţă (65 Daniel Opriţa), Tiberiu Bălan (46 Răzvan Cociş), Mirel Rădoi (Cap) (46 Florin Şoavă), Gabriel Boştină, Daniel Niculae (46 Adrian Mutu), Mugurel Buga.
Trainer: Victor Piţurcă

NORTHERN IRELAND: Alan Blayney, Michael Duff, Stephen Craigan (71 Sean Webb), Gareth McAuley (82 Colin James Murdock), Anthony Capaldi (57 Jeff Hughes), Dean Shiels (66 Steve Jones), Samuel Clingan, Steve Davis (Cap), Ivan Sproule (57 Mark Hughes), James Quinn, Peter Thompson (66 Kyle Lafferty).   Manager: Lawrie Sanchez

Goals: Mugurel Buga (7), Daniel Niculae (11)

524. 16.08.2006
FINLAND v NORTHERN IRELAND 1-2 (0-1)
Olympiastadion, Helsinki

Referee: Michael Svendsen (Denmark)   Attendance: 12,500

FINLAND: Jussi Jääskeläinen, Petri Pasanen, Sami Hyypiä (c) (81 Juha Pasoja), Hannu Tihinen, Toni Kallio, Mika Nurmela (74 Jonatan Johansson), Aki Riihilahti (46 Mika Väyrynen), Jari Ilola (46 Jarkko Wiss), Joonas Kolkka (74 Pekka Lagerblom), Alexei Eremenko Jr, Mikael Forssell (57 Shefki Kuqi).   Trainer: Roy Hodgson

NORTHERN IRELAND: Maik Stefan Taylor (46 Roy Carroll), Christopher Baird, Aaron Hughes (65 Michael Duff), Stephen Craigan, Anthony Capaldi, Keith Robert Gillespie (46 Steve Jones), Grant McCann, Samuel Clingan, Stuart Elliott (65 Ivan Sproule), James Quinn (51 Kyle Lafferty), David Healy (Cap) (46 Warren Feeney).   Manager: Lawrie Sanchez

Goals: Mika Väyrynen (74), David Healy (34), Kyle Lafferty (64)

525. 02.09.2006   13th European Champs Qualifiers
NORTHERN IRELAND v ICELAND   0-3 (0-3)
Windsor Park, Belfast

Referee: Tommy Skjerven (Norway)   Attendance: 14,500
NORTHERN IRELAND: Maik Stefan Taylor, Christopher Baird, Aaron Hughes (Cap), Stephen Craigan, Anthony Capaldi (76 Michael Duff), Keith Robert Gillespie, Samuel Clingan, Steve Davis, Stuart Elliott (63 Kyle Lafferty), David Healy, James Quinn (83 Warren Feeney). Manager: Lawrie Sanchez
ICELAND: Árni Gautur Arason, Grétar Rafn Steinsson, Ívar Ingimarsson, Hermann Hreiðarsson, Indriði Sigurðsson, Kári Árnason (33 Helgi Valur Daníelsson), Brynjar Björn Gunnarsson (57 Stefán Gíslason), Jóhannes Karl Guðjónsson, Hannes Þorsteinn Sigurðsson (64 Hjálmar Jónsson), Eiður Smári Guðjohnsen (Cap), Gunnar Heiðar Þorvaldsson.
Trainer: Eyjólfur Sverrisson
Goals: Gunnar Heiðar Þorvaldsson (13), Hermann Hreiðarsson (20), Eiður Smári Guðjohnsen (37).

526. 06.09.2006   13th European Champs Qualifiers
NORTHERN IRELAND v SPAIN   3-2 (1-1)
Windsor Park, Belfast

Referee: Frank de Bleeckere (Belgium)   Attendance: 14,500
NORTHERN IRELAND: Roy Carroll (12 Maik Stefan Taylor), Michael Duff, Stephen Craigan, Aaron Hughes (Cap), Jonathan Evans, Christopher Baird, Keith Robert Gillespie, Samuel Clingan, Steve Davis, Kyle Lafferty (54 James Quinn), David Healy (85 Warren Feeney). Manager: Lawrie Sanchez
SPAIN: Íker Casillas, Sergio Ramos (46 Míchel Salgado), Pablo Ibáñez, Carles Puyol, Antonio López, David Albelda (29 Cesc Fábregas), Xavi Hernández, Xabi Alonso, Fernando Torres (63 Luis García Sanz), Raúl González (Cap), David Villa. Trainer: Luis Aragonés
Goals: David Healy (20, 64, 80)

527. 07.10.2006   13th European Champs Qualifiers
DENMARK v NORTHERN IRELAND   0-0
Parken, København

Referee: Konrad Plautz (Austria)   Attendance: 41,482
DENMARK: Thomas Sørensen (69 Jesper Christiansen), Lars Jacobsen, Michael Gravgaard, Daniel Agger, Niclas Jensen (73 Nicklas Bendtner), Christian Poulsen, Peter Løvenkrands (56 Claus Jensen), Daniel Jensen, Thomas Kahlenberg, Martin Jørgensen, Jon Dahl Tomasson (Cap). Trainer: Morten Olsen
NORTHERN IRELAND: Maik Stefan Taylor, Michael Duff, Stephen Craigan, Aaron Hughes (Cap), Jonathan Evans, Christopher Baird, Samuel Clingan (57 Damien Johnson), Steve Davis, Keith Robert Gillespie, Kyle Lafferty (63 Steve Jones), David Healy (84 Warren Feeney).
Manager: Lawrie Sanchez

528. 11.10.2006   13th European Champs Qualifiers
NORTHERN IRELAND v LATVIA   1-0 (1-0)
Windsor Park, Belfast

Referee: Helmut Fleischer (Germany)   Attendance: 14,500
NORTHERN IRELAND: Maik Stefan Taylor, Christopher Baird, Stephen Craigan, Aaron Hughes (Cap), Jonathan Evans, Keith Robert Gillespie, Steve Davis, Damien Johnson, Samuel Clingan, David Healy (90 Warren Feeney), Kyle Lafferty (88 James Quinn). Manager: Lawrie Sanchez
LATVIA: Aleksandrs Koliņko, Deniss Kačanovs, Māris Smirnovs (46 Kaspars Gorkšs), Igors N. Stepanovs, Dzintars Zirnis, Genādijs Soloņicins (85 Aleksejs Višņakovs), Vitālijs Astafjevs (Cap), Juris Laizāns, Marians Pahars, Ģirts Karlsons, Māris Verpakovskis (78 Gatis Kalniņš).
Trainer: Jurijs Andrejevs
Goal: David Healy (35)

529. 06.02.2007
NORTHERN IRELAND v WALES   0-0
Windsor Park, Belfast

Referee: Charlie Richmond (Scotland)   Attendance: 14,000
NORTHERN IRELAND: Maik Stefan Taylor (46 Michael Ingham), Michael Duff, Stephen Craigan (78 Sean Webb), Aaron Hughes, Anthony Capaldi, Keith Robert Gillespie, Steve Davis, Samuel Clingan (61 Grant McCann), Christopher Brunt, Kyle Lafferty (68 Peter Thompson), Ivan Sproule (68 Dean Shiels). Manager: Lawrie Sanchez
WALES: Danny Coyne, Richard Duffy (46 David Cotterill, 71 Jermaine Easter), Steve Evans, Daniel Collins, Lewin Nyatanga, Simon Davies, Jason Koumas, Carl Phillip Robinson, Paul Parry (83 Andrew Crofts), David Vaughan (46 Samuel Ricketts), Craig Douglas Bellamy. Manager: John Toshack

530. 24.03.2007   13th European Champs Qualifiers
LIECHTENSTEIN
v NORTHERN IRELAND   1-4 (0-0)
Vaduz

Referee: oriekhov (Ukraine)   Attendance: 4,340
LIECHTENSTEIN: Peter Jehle, Oehri (68 Martin Telser), Martin Stocklasa, Christof Ritter, Michael Stocklasa, Martin Buechel, Ronny Buchel (88 Daniel Frick), Franz Burgmeier, Thomas Beck, Mario Frick, Rohrer (84 Stefan Buchel).
NORTHERN IRELAND: Maik Stefan Taylor, Michael Duff, Stephen Craigan, Aaron Hughes, Damien Johnson, Christopher Brunt (68 Gareth McCann), Keith Robert Gillespie, Jonathan Evans, Steve Davis, Kyle Lafferty (56 Warren Feeney), David Healy (84 Stephen Jones).
Manager: Lawrie Sanchez
Goals: Franz Burgmeier (89) / David Healy (52, 74, 83), Grant McCann (90)

531. 28.03.2007 13th European Champs Qualifiers
NORTHERN IRELAND v SWEDEN 2-1 (1-1)
Windsor Park, Belfast

Referee: Eric Braamhaar (Holland)   Attendance: 14,000

NORTHERN IRELAND: Maik Stefan Taylor, Michael Duff, Aaron Hughes, Stephen Craigan, Jonathan Evans, Damien Johnson, Grant McCann, Steven Davis, Christopher Brunt (90 Ivan Sproule), Warren Feeney (79 Kyle Lafferty), David Healy (89 Sean Webb).   Manager: Lawrie Sanchez

SWEDEN: Andreas Isaksson, Erik Edman, Petter Hansson, Mikael Nilsson, Olof Mellberg (69 Daniel Majstorovic), Daniel Andersson, Fredrik Ljungberg, Anders Svensson (46 Kim Källström), Niclas Alexandersson (61 Christian Wilhelmsson), Johan Elmander, Zlatan Ibrahimovic.
Manager: Lars Lagerbäck

Goals: David Healy (31, 58) / Johan Elmander (26)

532. 22.08.2007 13th European Champs Qualifiers
**NORTHERN IRELAND
v LIECHTENSTEIN 3-1** (2-0)
Windsor Park, Belfast

Referee: Radek Matejek (Czech Republic)   Att: 13,000

NORTHERN IRELAND: Maik Stefan Taylor, Michael Duff, George McCartney, Christopher Baird, Stephen Craigan, Samuel Clingan, Keith Robert Gillespie (85 Stephen Jones), Steven Davis, Kyle Lafferty (75 Warren Feeney), David Healy, Christopher Brunt (62 Stuart Elliott).
Manager: Nigel Worthington

LIECHTENSTEIN: Peter Jehle, Michael Stocklasa (38 Yves Oehri), Martin Stocklasa, Daniel Telser, Fabio D'Elia, Michele Polverino, Ronny Buechel, Daniel Frick, Christoph Biedermann (62 Stefan Buechel), Raphael Rohrer (74 Roger Beck), Mario Frick.

Goals: David Healy (5, 35), Kyle Lafferty (56) /
Mario Frick (89)

533. 08.09.2007 13th European Champs Qualifiers
LATVIA v NORTHERN IRELAND 1-0 (0-0)
Skonto, Riga

Referee: Pedro Proenca (Portugal)   Attendance: 7,500

LATVIA: Andris Vanins, Dzintars Zirnis, Kaspars Gorkss, Oskars Klava, Deniss Ivanovs, Imants Bleidelis, Jurijs Laizans, Vitalis Astafjevs, Andrejs Rubins, Maris Verpakovskis (90 Kristaps Blanks), Girts Karlsons (71 Vits Rimkus).

NORTHERN IRELAND: Maik Stefan Taylor, Michael Duff, George McCartney, Christopher Baird, Jonathan Evans, Keith Robert Gillespie, Samuel Clingan, Steven Davis, Stuart Elliott (66 Christopher Brunt), David Healy, Kyle Lafferty (71 Warren Feeney).   Manager: Nigel Worthington

Goal: Christopher Baird (56 own goal)

534. 12.09.2007 13th European Champs Qualifiers
ICELAND v NORTHERN IRELAND 2-1 (1-0)
Laugardalsvöllur, Reykjavík

Referee: Yuri Baskakov (Russia)   Attendance: 2,500

ICELAND: Arni Gautur Arason, Kristjan Orn Sigurdsson, Ragnar Sigurdsson, Ivar Ingimarsson, Hermann Hreidarsson, Kari Arnason (87 Asgeir Asgeirsson), Arnar Vidarsson, Gretar Steinsson, Emil Hallfredsson, Gunnar Thorvaldsson (79 Olafur Skulason), Armann Bjornsson (53 Eidur Gudjohnsen).

NORTHERN IRELAND: Maik Stefan Taylor, Michael Duff, Jonathan Evans, Christopher Baird, George McCartney, Keith Robert Gillespie, Christopher Brunt (83 Stephen Jones), Samuel Clingan, Steven Davis (78 Grant McCann), Warren Feeney, David Healy.   Manager: Nigel Worthington

Goals: Armann Björnsson (6), Keith Gillespie (90 own goal) /
David Healy (72 pen)

535. 17.10.2007 13th European Champs Qualifiers
SWEDEN v NORTHERN IRELAND 1-1 (1-0)
Råsunda, Solna

Referee: Bertrand Layec (France)   Attendance: 33,112

SWEDEN: Andreas Isaksson, Matias Concha, Olof Mellberg, Petter Hansson, Erik Edman, Tobias Linderoth, Anders Svensson, Christian Wilhelmsson (46 Mikael Nilsson), Kim Kallstrom (85 Andreas Johansson), Zlatan Ibrahimovic, Johan Elmander (73 Marcus Allback).

NORTHERN IRELAND: Maik Stefan Taylor, Gareth McAuley, Aaron Hughes, Stephen Craigan, George McCartney (87 Anthony Capaldi), Ivan Sproule, Samuel Clingan, Steven Davis, Christopher Brunt, Kyle Lafferty, David Healy.
Manager: Nigel Worthington

Goals: Olof Mellberg (15) / Kyle Lafferty (72)

536. 17.11.2007 13th European Champs Qualifiers
NORTHERN IRELAND v DENMARK 2-1 (0-0)
Windsor Park, Belfast

Referee: Pieter Vink (Holland)   Attendance: 14,000

NORTHERN IRELAND: Maik Stefan Taylor, Gareth McAuley, Aaron Hughes, Stephen Craigan, Jonathan Evans, Keith Robert Gillespie (74 Ivan Sproule), Samuel Clingan, Steven Davis, Christopher Brunt, Warren Feeney (85 Christopher Baird), David Healy.
Manager: Nigel Worthington

DENMARK: Thomas Sørensen, Brian Priske (72 Rasmus Wurtz), Chris Sørensen, Martin Laursen, Per Kroldrup, Christian Poulsen, Leon Andreasen, Thomas Kahlenberg (46 Dennis Sørensen), Dennis Rommedahl, Martin Jorgensen (79 Simon Poulsen), Nicklas Bendtner.

Goals: Warren Feeney (62), David Healy (80) /
Nicklas Bendtner (51)

537. 21.11.2007   13th European Champs Qualifiers
SPAIN v NORTHERN IRELAND 1-0 (0-0)
Gran Canaria, Las Palmas
Referee: Herbert Fandel (Germany)   Attendance: 31,250
SPAIN: Pepe Reina, Sergio Ramos, Raul Albiol, Pablo Ibanez, Mariano Pernia, Xavi Hernandez (67 David Villa), Cesc Fabregas (46 Joaquin Sánchez), Marcos Senna, David Silva, Andres Iniesta, Daniel Güiza (57 Raul Tamudo).
Trainer: Luis Aragones
NORTHERN IRELAND: Maik Stefan Taylor, Gareth McAuley, Aaron Hughes, Stephen Craigan, Christopher Baird, Ivan Sproule (46 Stephen Robinson), Samuel Clingan, Steven Davis, Christopher Brunt (59 Kyle Lafferty), Warren Feeney (72 Martin Paterson), David Healy.
Manager: Nigel Worthington
Goal: Xavi Hernández (53)

538. 06.02.2008
NORTHERN IRELAND v BULGARIA 0-1 (0-1)
Windsor Park, Belfast
Referee: Douglas McDonald (Scotland)   Attendance: 14,000
NORTHERN IRELAND: Maik Stefan Taylor (83 Alan Mannus), Gareth McAuley, Aaron Hughes, Jonathan Evans (46 Stephen Craigan), George McCartney (46 Christopher Baird), Keith Robert Gillespie (79 Peter Thompson), Samuel Clingan, Damien Johnson (46 Steven Davis), Christopher Brunt, Kyle Lafferty (59 Martin Paterson), David Healy.
Manager: Nigel Worthington
BULGARIA: Georgi Petkov (46 Dimitar Ivankov), Stanislav Angelov, Mihail Venkov (74, Aleksander Tunchev (66 Ivelin Popov), Igor Tomasic, Zhivko Milanov, Martin Petrov, Todor Yanchev (46 Nikolai Dimitrov), Blagoi Georgiev, Dimitar Berbatov (82 Valeri Domovchiyski), Zdravko Lazarov (66 Asen Karaslavov).   Trainer: Plamen Markov
Goal: Jonathan Evans (38 own goal)

539. 26.03.2008
NORTHERN IRELAND v GEORGIA 4-1 (3-0)
Windsor Park, Belfast
Referee: Luc Wilmes (Luxembourg)   Attendance: 13,500
NORTHERN IRELAND: Maik Stefan Taylor (80 Alan Mannus), Christopher Baird, Aaron Hughes, Stephen Craigan (57 Gareth McAuley), Jonathan Evans, Keith Robert Gillespie, Damien Johnson (46 Michael O'Connor), Steven Davis (70 Michael Gault), Stuart Elliott, David Healy (70 Peter Thompson), Kyle Lafferty (46 Warren Feeney).
Manager: Nigel Worthington
GEORGIA: Giorgi Makaridze, Lasha Salukvadze, Kakha Kaladze, Levan Kenia (81 Giorgi Khidesheli), Giorgi Shashiashvili (80 Aleksandre Kobakhidze), Levan Tskitishvili (90 Zaal Eliava), Jaba Kankava, Aleksandre Kvakhadze, David Kvirkvelia, Aleksandre Iashvili.   Trainer: Klaus Toppmöller
Goals: Kyle Lafferty (24, 35), David Healy (32), Peter Thompson (87) / David Healy (54 own goal)

540. 20.08.2008
SCOTLAND v NORTHERN IRELAND 0-0
Hampden Park, Glasgow
Referee: Nicolai Vollquartez (Denmark)   Att: 28,072
SCOTLAND: Craig Gordon (46 Allan McGregor), Graham Alexander, David Weir (72 Christophe Diddier Berra), Stephen McManus (46 Darren Barr), Gary Naysmith, Scott Brown, Darren Fletcher (70 Michael Stewart), Kevin Thomson (46 Barry Robson), James Ronaldo Morrison (62 Kris Commons), James McFadden, Kenny Miller.   Manager: George Burley
NORTHERN IRELAND: Maik Stefan Taylor, Gareth McAuley (76 Michael Duff), Stephen Craigan, Jonathan Evans, Ryan McGivern, Christopher Baird, Martin Paterson (46 Dean Shiels), Steven Davis, Samuel Clingan (59 Michael O'Connor), Christopher Brunt (56 Warren Feeney), David Healy.   Manager: Nigel Worthington

541. 06.09.2008   18th World Cup Qualifiers
SLOVAKIA v NORTHERN IRELAND 2-1 (0-0)
Bratislava
Referee: Nikolai Ivanov (Russia)   Attendance: 5,445
SLOVAKIA: Stefan Senecky, Martin Škrtel, Martin Petras, Peter Pekarik, Miroslav Karhan (Cap) (75 Radoslav Zabavnik), Jan Kozak, Marek Sapara, Robert Vittek (78 Marek Mintal), Martin Jakubko (59 Dusan Svento), Ján Durica, Marek Hamšik.
NORTHERN IRELAND: Maik Stefan Taylor, Aaron Hughes, Stephen Craigan, Jonathan Evans, George McCartney, Christopher Baird (84 Dean Shiels), Keith Robert Gillespie (53 Warren Feeney), Steven Davis, Samuel Clingan, Martin Paterson (66 Christopher Brunt), David Healy.
Manager: Nigel Worthington
Goals: Martin Škrtel (47), Marek Hamšik (70) / Ján Durica (81 own goal)

542. 10.09.2008   18th World Cup Qualifiers
NORTHERN IRELAND v CZECH REPUBLIC 0-0
Windsor Park, Belfast

Referee: Ivan Bebek (Croatia)   Attendance: 14,000

NORTHERN IRELAND: Maik Stefan Taylor, Aaron Hughes, Stephen Craigan, Jonathan Evans, George McCartney, Keith Robert Gillespie (83 Dean Shiels), Christopher Baird, Samuel Clingan (46 Michael O'Connor), Christopher Brunt, Warren Feeney (72 Martin Paterson), David Healy.
Manager: Nigel Worthington

CZECH REPUBLIC: Petr Cech, Zdenek Grygera, Marek Jankulovski, David Rozehnal, Tomas Ujfalusi, Radoslav Kovac, Jaroslav Plasil, Jan Polak, Libor Sionko (67 Zdenek Pospech), Radek Sirl, Milan Baros (78 Miroslav Slepicka).
Trainer: Petr Rada

543. 11.10.2008   18th World Cup Qualifiers
SLOVENIA v NORTHERN IRELAND 2-0 (0-0)
Ljudski, Maribor

Referee: Eduardo Iturralde Gonzalez (Spain)   Att: 12,385

SLOVENIA: Samir Handanovic, Miso Brecko, Marko Suler, Bostjan Cesar, Branko Ilic, Andrej Komac, Mirnes Sisic (80 Valter Birsa), Robert Koren, Andraz Kirm (90 Darijan Matic), Milivoje Novakovic, Zlatko Dedic (68 Zlatan Ljubijankic).
Trainer: Matjaz Kek

NORTHERN IRELAND: Maik Taylor, Gareth McAuley, George McCartney, Jonathan Evans, Chris Baird, Aaron Hughes, Keith Gillespie, Steven Davis, Grant McCann (73 Ryan McGivern), David Healy, Kyle Lafferty.
Manager: Nigel Worthington

Goals: Milivoje Novakovic (84), Zlatan Ljubijankic (85)

544. 15.10.2008   18th World Cup Qualifiers
NORTHERN IRELAND v SAN MARINO 4-0 (2-0)
Windsor Park, Belfast

Referee: Petteri Kari (Finland)   Attendance: 12,957

NORTHERN IRELAND: Maik Taylor, Gareth McAuley (61 Ryan McGivern), George McCartney, Christopher Baird, Michael O'Connor, Keith Gillespie, Steven Davis, David Healy, Kyle Lafferty (82 Warren Feeney), Grant McCann (73 Martin Paterson), Aaron Hughes.   Manager: Nigel Worthington

SAN MARINO: Federico Valentini, Carlo Valentini, Mauro Marani, Nicola Albani, Alessandro Della Valle, Simone Bacchiocchi, Giovanni Bonini (77 Fabio Vitaioli), Michele Marani, Manuel Marani (86 Enrico Cibelli), Andy Selva (46 Matteo Vitaioli), Damiano Vannucci.
Trainer: Gianpaolo Mazza

Goals: David Healy (31), Grant McCann (43), Kyle Lafferty (56), Steven Davis (75)

545. 19.11.2008
NORTHERN IRELAND v HUNGARY 0-2 (0-0)
Windsor Park, Belfast

Referee: Robert Schoergenhofer (Austria)   Att: 6,251

NORTHERN IRELAND: Maik Taylor (46 Jonathan Tuffey), Jonathan Evans, Chris Baird, Ryan McGivern, Michael Duff (55 Niall McGinn), Michael O'Connor (82 Dean Shiels), Sammy Clingan, Chris Brunt (70 Martin Paterson), Keith Gillespie, David Healy (89 Peter Thompson), Kyle Lafferty (46 Warren Feeney).   Manager: Nigel Worthington

HUNGARY: Gabor Babos, Roland Juhasz, Vilmos Vanczak, Peter Halmosi, Laszlo Bodnar, Krisztian Vadocz, Balazs Toth, Szabolcs Huszti, Zoltan Gera, Sandor Torghelle, Gergely Rudolf.   Trainer: Erwin Koeman

Goals: Sandor Torghelle (57), Zoltan Gera (71)

546. 11.02.2009   19th World Cup Qualifier
SAN MARINO v NORTHERN IRELAND 0-3 (0-2)
Olimpico di Serravalle, Serravalle

Referee: Dragomir Stankovic (Serbia)   Attendance: 1,942

SAN MARINO: Federico Valentini, Damiano Vannucci, Carlo Valentini, Davide Simoncini, Alessandro Della Valle, Maicol Berretti, Simone Bacciocchi (73 Fabio Vitaioli), Riccardo Muccioli (66 Matteo Bugli), Michele Marani, Matteo Vitaioli (87 Marco Casadei), Manuel Marani.
Manager: Giampaolo Mazza

NORTHERN IRELAND: Maik Taylor, George McCartney, Stephen Craigan, Aaron Hughes (80 Pat McCourt), Gareth McAuley, Grant McCann, Damien Johnson, Steven Davis, David Healy, Martin Paterson (77 Warren Feeney), Kyle Lafferty (55 Chris Brunt).   Manager: Nigel Worthington

Sent off: Manuel Marani (69)

Goals: G. McAuley (7), Grant McCann (33), Chris Brunt (63)

547. 28.03.2009   19th World Cup Qualifier
NORTHERN IRELAND v POLAND 3-2 (1-1)
Windsor Park, Belfast

Referee: Martin Hansson (Sweden)   Attendance: 13,357

NORTHERN IRELAND: Maik Taylor, Stephen Craigan, Gareth McAuley, Aaron Hughes, Jonny Evans, Grant McCann, Chris Brunt, Damien Johnson, Sammy Clingan, David Healy (90+1 Andy Little), Warren Feeney (84 Chris Baird).
Manager: Nigel Worthington

POLAND: Artur Boruc, Marcin Wasilewski, Michal Zewlakow (65 Bartosz Bosacki), Jakub Wawrzyniak, Tomasz Bandrowski (60 Jakub Blaszczykowski), ROGER Guerreiro, Mariusz Lewandowski, Jacek Krzynówek, Dariusz Dudka, Ireneusz Jelen (71 Marek Saganowski), Robert Lewandowski.
Manager: Leo Beenhakker

Goals: Warren Feeney (10), Jonny Evans (47), Michal Zewlakow (61 og) / Ireneusz Jelen (27), M. Saganowski (90+1)

548.   01.04.2009   19th World Cup Qualifier
NORTHERN IRELAND v SLOVENIA 1-0 (0-0)
Windsor Park, Belfast
Referee: Alon Yefet (Israel)   Attendance: 13,243
NORTHERN IRELAND: Maik Taylor, George McCartney (44 Ryan McGivern), Gareth McAuley (16 Chris Baird), Aaron Hughes, Jonny Evans, Grant McCann, Damien Johnson, Steven Davis, Sammy Clingan, David Healy, Warren Feeney.
Manager: Nigel Worthington
SLOVENIA: Samir Handanovic, Bostjan Cesar, Miso Brecko (85 Ales Mejac), Matej Mavric, Suad Filekovic, Robert Koren, Andrej Komac, Bojan Jokic, Andraz Kirm (77 Andrej Pecnik), Zlatko Dedic (64 Zlatan Ljubijankic), Milivoje Novakovic.
Manager: Matjaz Kek
Goal: Warren Feeney (73)

549.   06.06.2009
ITALY v NORTHERN IRELAND 3-0 (1-0)
Arena Garibaldi, Pisa
Referee: Kevin Blom (Netherlands)   Attendance: 8,000
ITALY: Federico Marchetti, Nicola Legrottaglie, Fabio Grosso (46 Andrea Dossena), Alessandro Gamberini, Davide Santon, Riccardo Montolivo (46 Angelo Palombo), Gennaro Gattuso (46 Matteo Brighi), Gaetano D'Agostino (75 Daniele Galloppa), Giampaolo Pazzini (63 Sergio Pellissier), Giuseppe Mascara (46 Pasquale Foggia), Giuseppe Rossi.
Manager: Marcello Lippi
NORTHERN IRELAND: Jonny Tuffey (63 Alan Mannus), Colin Coates, Chris Casement, Ryan McGivern, Grant McCann, Damien Johnson, Stephen Carson (70 Jamie Lawrie), Michael O'Connor (62 Robert Garrett), Corry John Evans (78 Shane Ferguson), David Healy (46 Niall McGinn), Andy Little (83 Martin Donnelly).   Manager: Nigel Worthington
Goals: Guiseppe Rossi (19), Pasquale Foggia (53), Sergio Pellissier (72)

550.   12.08.2009
NORTHERN IRELAND v ISRAEL 1-1 (1-1)
Windsor Park, Belfast
Referee: Jóhannes Valgeirsson (Iceland)   Att: 10,000
NORTHERN IRELAND: Maik Taylor (46 Jonny Tuffey), George McCartney, Stephen Craigan, Aaron Hughes (46 Gareth McAuley), Chris Baird, Grant McCann, Damien Johnson (46 Niall McGinn), Sammy Clingan (70 Ryan McGivern), Chris Brunt (46 Steven Davis), David Healy (59 Martin Paterson), Kyle Lafferty.
Manager: Nigel Worthington

ISRAEL: Dudu Aouate (46 Nir Davidovitch), Avi Strool (71 Dan Mori), Eyal Meshumar, Avihay Yadin (65 Yoav Ziv), Dedi Ben Dayan, Dekel Keinan (46 Tal Ben Haim), Aviram Baruchyan, Tamir Cohen (46 Biram Kayal), Yossi Benayoun (54 Salim Tuama), Roberto Colautti, Elyaniv Barda.
Manager: Dror Kashtan
Goals: Grant McCann (17) / Elyaniv Barda (26)

551.   05.09.2009   19th World Cup Qualifier
POLAND v NORTHERN IRELAND 1-1 (0-1)
Slaski, Chorzów
Referee: Manuel Enrique Mejuto González (Spain)
Attendance: 38,914
POLAND: Artur Boruc, Pawel Golanski, Michal Zewlakow, Ludovic Obraniak (46 Ebi Smolarek), Rafal Murawski (61 Robert Lewandowski), Mariusz Lewandowski, Jakub Blaszczykowski, Jacek Krzynówek, ROGER Guerreirro, Dariusz Dudka, Pawel Brozek.   Manager: Leo Beenhakker
NORTHERN IRELAND: Maik Taylor, Stephen Craigan, Gareth McAuley, Aaron Hughes, Jonny Evans, Grant McCann, Sammy Clingan, Damien Johnson, Steven Davis, David Healy, Kyle Lafferty (54 Martin Paterson).
Manager: Nigel Worthington
Goals: Mariusz Lewandowski (80) / Kyle Lafferty (38)

552.   09.09.2009   19th World Cup Qualifier
NORTHERN IRELAND v SLOVAKIA 0-2 (0-1)
Windsor Park, Belfast
Referee: Björn Kuipers (Netherlands)   Attendance: 13,019
NORTHERN IRELAND: Maik Taylor, Stephen Craigan, Gareth McAuley, Aaron Hughes, Jonny Evans, Grant McCann (70 Niall McGinn), Damien Johnson, Steven Davis, Sammy Clingan (70 Chris Baird), David Healy, Martin Paterson (76 Chris Brunt).   Manager: Nigel Worthington
SLOVAKIA: Ján Mucha, Martin Skrtel, Peter Pekarík, Ján Durica, Vladimír Weiss (90 Marek Sapara), Zdeno Strba, Kamil Kopúnek, Radoslav Zabavník, Róbert Vittek, Miroslav Stoch (80 Erík Jendrisek), Stanislav Sesták (65 Filip Holosko).
Manager: Vladimir Weiss
Goals: Stanislav Sesták (15), Filip Holosko (66)

553.   14.10.2009   19th World Cup Qualifier
CZECH REPUBLIC v NORTHERN IRELAND 0-0
Synot Tip Aréna, Praha

Referee: Laurent Duhamel (France)   Attendance: 8,002

CZECH REPUBLIC: Petr Cech, Zdenek Pospech, Marek Jankulovski, Tomás Hübschman, Roman Hubník, Tomás Sivok, Tomás Rosicky (72 Jirí Stajner), Jaroslav Plasil, David Jarolím (83 Michal Papadopoulos), Milan Baros, Tomás Necid (58 Adam Hlousek).   Manager: Ivan Hasek

NORTHERN IRELAND: Maik Taylor, Stephen Craigan, Chris Baird, Ryan McGivern, Gareth McAuley, Aaron Hughes, Grant McCann (80 Michael O'Connor), Niall McGinn, Damien Johnson (83 Andy Kirk), Steven Davis, David Healy (69 Warren Feeney).   Manager: Nigel Worthington

554.   14.11.2009
NORTHERN IRELAND v SERBIA 0-1 (0-0)
Windsor Park, Belfast

Referee: Abby Toussaint (Luxembourg)   Attendance: 13,500

NORTHERN IRELAND: Maik Taylor (77 Jonny Tuffey), Stephen Craigan, George McCartney, Chris Baird, Jonny Evans (46 Grant McCann), Aaron Hughes, Steven Davis, Chris Brunt (65 David Healy), Niall McGinn (71 Pat McCourt), Warren Feeney (65 Michael O'Connor), Kyle Lafferty (71 Andy Kirk).   Manager: Nigel Worthington

SERBIA: Bojan Isailovic, Aleksandar Kolarov (67 Jagos Vukovic), Nemanja Vidic (46 Milos Ninkovic), Antonio Rukavina, Aleksandar Lukovic, Radosav Petrovic, Zoran Tosic, Nenad Milijas (46 Milos Krasic), Zdravko Kuzmanovic (52 Gojko Kacar), Danko Lazovic (76 Dejan Lekic), Milan Jovanovic (46 Neven Subotic).   Manager: Radomir Antic

Goal: Danko Lazovic (57)

555.   03.03.2010
ALBANIA v NORTHERN IRELAND 1-0 (1-0)
Qemal Stafa, Tirana

Referee: Elmir Pilav (Bosnia-Herzegovina)   Att: 7,500

ALBANIA: Isli Hidi, Kristi Vangjeli, Andi Lila, Klodian Duro (78 Elis Bakaj), Armend Dallku, Debatik Curri, Ervin Skela (81 Emiljano Vila), Ansi Agolli (64 Jahmir Hyka), Altin Lala (64 Lorik Cana), Ervin Bulku (86 Edmond Kapllani), Erjon Bogdani (46 Hamdi Salihi).   Manager: Josip Kuze

NORTHERN IRELAND: Maik Taylor (72 Jonny Tuffey), George McCartney, Stephen Craigan, Ryan McGivern, Michael O'Connor (46 Corry Evans), Grant McCann, Steven Davis, Niall McGinn (46 Dean Shiels), David Healy (78 Andy Kirk), Andy Little, Kyle Lafferty (64 Rory Patterson).
Manager: Nigel Worthington

Goal: Ervin Skela (26)

556.   26.05.2010
NORTHERN IRELAND v TURKEY 0-2 (0-0)
Veterans Stadium, New Britain (USA)

Referee: Terry Vaughn (USA)   Attendance: 4,000

NORTHERN IRELAND: Alan Blayney, Stephen Craigan, Gareth McAuley, Ryan McGivern (75 Colin Coates), Jamie Mulgrew, Johnny Gorman (66 Michael Bryan), Robert Garrett (80 Jamie Lawrie), Corry Evans, Rory Patterson (60 Rory McArdle), Kevin Braniff (61 Josh Magennis), Andy Little.   Manager: Nigel Worthington

TURKEY: Onur Kivrak, Ibrahim Toraman, Servet Çetin, Sabri Sarioglu, Nuri Sahin (46 Mehmet Topal), Colin Kazim-Richards (61 Semih Sentürk), Selçuk Inan (66 Emre Belözoglu), Hamit Altintop (46 Sercan Yildirim), Ozan Ipek (66 Arda Turan), Caner Erkin (74 Ismail Köybasi), Tuncay Sanli.   Manager: Guus Hiddink

Goals: Sercan Yildirim (48), Semih Sentürk (72)

557.   30.05.2010
CHILE v NORTHERN IRELAND 1-0 (1-0)
Municipal, Chillán

Referee: LÍBER Tabare PRUDENTE González (Uruguay)
Attendance: 12,000

CHILE: MIGUEL Ángel PINTO Jerez, ISMAEL Ignacio FUENTES Castro, PABLO Andrés CONTRERAS Fica, ROBERTO Andrés CERECEDA Guajardo, MAURICIO Anibal ISLA Isla, ARTURO Erasmo VIDAL Pardo (76 CARLOS Esteban ROSS Cotal), Matias Ariel "Mati" FERNÁNDEZ Fernández (89 FELIPE Alejandro GUTIÉRREZ Leiva), MARCO Andrés ESTRADA Quinteros, MARK Dennis GONZÁLEZ Hoffmann (63 FABIÁN Ariel ORELLANA Valenzuela), GONZALO Antonio FIERRO Caniullán, ESTEBAN Efraín PAREDES Quintanilla.
Manager: Marcelo Alberto Bielsa

NORTHERN IRELAND: Alan Blayney (46 Michael McGovern), Stephen Craigan (46 Rory McArdle), Ryan McGivern (55 Colin Coates), Gareth McAuley, Robert Garrett (46 Jamie Lawrie), Michael Bryan (46 Kevin Braniff), Jamie Mulgrew, Johnny Gorman (73 Josh Magennis), Corry Evans, Rory Patterson, Andy Little.   Manager: Nigel Worthington

Goal: ESTEBAN Efraín PAREDES Quintanilla (30)

558. 11.08.2010
MONTENEGRO v NORTHERN IRELAND 2-0 (1-0)
Pod Goricom, Podgorica

Referee: Bosko Jovanetic (Serbia)   Attendance: 5,000

MONTENEGRO: Mladen Bozovic, Elsad Zverotic (83 Faros Beciraj), Luka Pejovic (56 Zarko Tomasevic), Milan Jovanovic (76 Stefan Savic), Savo Pavicevic (52 Drasko Bozovic), Miodrag Dzudovic, Simon Vukcevic, Milorad Pekovic (62 Mitar Novakovic), Vladimir Bozovic, Mirko Vucinic, Radomir Djalovic (78 Andrija Delibasic).   Manager: Zlatko Kranjcar

NORTHERN IRELAND: Maik Taylor, Stephen Craigan, Jonny Evans, Chris Baird (46 Warren Feeney), Ryan McGivern (68 David Healy), Chris Brunt (46 Corry Evans), Sammy Clingan (64 Oliver Norwood), Steven Davis, Kyle Lafferty, Martin Paterson (46 Grant McCann), Andy Little.   Manager: Nigel Worthington

Goals: Radomir Djalovic (43, 58)

559. 03.09.2010   14th European Champs Qualifier
SLOVENIA v NORTHERN IRELAND 0-1 (0-0)
Ljudski vrt, Maribor

Referee: Cristian Balaj (Romania)   Attendance: 12,000

SLOVENIA: Samir Handanovic, Bojan Jokic, Miso Brecko, Bostjan Cesar, Matej Mavric, Robert Koren, Andraz Kirm (75 Josip Ilicic), Aleksander Radosavljevic, Valter Birsa, Zlatan Ljubijankic (88 Tim Matavz), Milivoje Novakovic (74 Zlatko Dedic).   Manager: Matjaz Kek

NORTHERN IRELAND: Maik Taylor, Stephen Craigan, Craig Cathcart, Chris Baird, Gareth McAuley, Aaron Hughes, Steven Davis, Chris Brunt (89 Johnny Gorman), Grant McCann (67 Kyle Lafferty), David Healy (67 Corry Evans), Warren Feeney.   Manager: Nigel Worthington

Goal: Corry Evans (70)

560. 08.10.2010   14th European Champs Qualifier
NORTHERN IRELAND v ITALY 0-0
Windsor Park, Belfast

Referee: Tony Chapron (France)   Attendance: 15,200

NORTHERN IRELAND: Maik Taylor, Gareth McAuley, Aaron Hughes, Jonny Evans, Stephen Craigan, Chris Baird, Grant McCann (80 Corry Evans), Steven Davis, Chris Brunt (71 Niall McGinn), David Healy (66 Kyle Lafferty), Warren Feeney.   Manager: Nigel Worthington

ITALY: Emiliano Viviano, Domenico Criscito, Mattia Cassani, Giorgio Chiellini, Leonardo Bonucci, Simone Pepe (84 Giuseppe Rossi), Stefano Mauri (79 Claudio Marchisio), Andrea Pirlo, Daniele De Rossi, Marco Borriello (74 Giampaolo Pazzini), Antonio Cassano.
Manager: Cesare Prandelli

561. 12.10.2010   14th European Champs Qualifier
FAROE ISLANDS v NORTHERN IRELAND 1-1 (0-0)
Svangaskard, Toftir

Referee: Cyril Zimmermann (Switzerland)   Att: 1,921

FAROE ISLANDS: Jákup Mikkelsen, Jónas Næs, Atli Gregersen, Jóhan Davidsen, Erling Jacobsen, Christian Holst (85 Justinus Hansen), Hjalgrím Elttør, Jóan Edmundsson, Fródi Benjaminsen, Daniel Udsen (68 Jann Ingi Petersen), Símun Samuelsen (78 Arnbjørn Hansen).
Manager: Brian Kerr

NORTHERN IRELAND: Maik Taylor, Gareth McAuley, Aaron Hughes, Jonny Evans, Stephen Craigan, Chris Baird, Niall McGinn (83 Corry Evans), Steven Davis, Chris Brunt, Kyle Lafferty, Warren Feeney (50 David Healy).
Manager: Nigel Worthington

Goals: Christian Holst (60) / Kyle Lafferty (76)

562. 17.11.2010
NORTHERN IRELAND v MOROCCO 1-1 (0-0)
Windsor Park, Belfast

Referee: Tom Harald Hagen (Norway)   Attendance: 15,000

NORTHERN IRELAND: Jonny Tuffey (46 Alan Blayney), Aaron Hughes (46 Rory McArdle), Lee Hodson, Jonny Evans, Ryan McGivern (62 Colin Coates), Johnny Gorman, Adam Barton, Pat McCourt (46 Michael O'Connor), Chris Brunt (47 Josh McQuoid), Niall McGinn (69 Josh Magennis), Rory Patterson.   Manager: Nigel Worthington

MOROCCO: Nadir Lamyaghri, Rachid Soulaimani, Ahmed Kantari, Adil Hermach (89 Karim El Ahmadi), Badr El-Kaddouri, Medhi Benatia (78 Mohammed Berrabeh), Houssine Kharja, Younès Belhanda (75 Chakib Benzoukane), Nacer Chadli, Youssouf Hadji (80 Nabil El Zhar), Marouane Chamakh (71 Youssef El-Arabi).   Manager: Eric Gerets

Goals: Rory Patterson (86 pen) / Marouane Chamakh (55)

563. 09.02.2011   Nations Cup
NORTHERN IRELAND v SCOTLAND 0-3 (0-2)
Aviva Stadium, Dublin

Referee: Tomas Connolly (Republic of Ireland)   Att: 18,742

NORTHERN IRELAND: Jonny Tuffey, Rory McArdle (46 Lee Hodson), Stephen Craigan (66 Adam Thompson), Chris Baird, Gareth McAuley, Pat McCourt, Grant McCann (46 David Healy), Corry Evans, Steven Davis (58 Oliver Norwood), Niall McGinn (72 Liam Boyce), Rory Patterson.
Manager: Nigel Worthington

SCOTLAND: Allan McGregor, Steven Caldwell, Christophe Berra, Phil Bardsley (57 Mark Wilson), Alan Hutton, Kris Commons (72 Craig Conway), Charlie Adam (57 Barry Bannan), Steven Naismith (58 Robert Snodgrass), James Morrison (79 Chris Maguire), James McArthur, Kenny Miller (89 Danny Wilson).   Manager: Craig Levein

Goals: Kenny Miller (19), James McArthur (32), Kris Commons (51)

564.   25.03.2011   14th European Champs Qualifier
SERBIA v NORTHERN IRELAND   2-1 (0-1)
Marakana, Beograd

Referee: Serge Gumienny (Belgium)
Attendance: The match was played behind closed doors

SERBIA: Zeljko Brkic, Neven Subotic, Aleksandar Kolarov, Branislav Ivanovic, Milan Bisevac, Zoran Tosic, Dejan Stankovic, Nenad Milijas (47 Milos Ninkovic), Adem Ljajic (47 Milan Jovanovic), Milos Krasic (86 Radosav Petrovic), Marko Pantelic.   Manager: Vladimir Petrovic

NORTHERN IRELAND: Lee Camp, Gareth McAuley, Aaron Hughes, Jonny Evans (86 Pat McCourt), Craig Cathcart, Chris Baird, Johnny Gorman (78 Warren Feeney), Corry Evans, Sammy Clingan, Chris Brunt, Kyle Lafferty (46 David Healy).   Manager: Nigel Worthington

Goals: Marko Pantelic (65), Zoran Tosic (74) / Gareth McAuley (40)

565.   29.03.2011   14th European Champs Qualifier
NORTHERN IRELAND v SLOVENIA   0-0
Windsor Park, Belfast

Referee: Björn Kuipers (Netherlands)   Attendance: 14,200

NORTHERN IRELAND: Lee Camp, Stephen Craigan, Craig Cathcart, Chris Baird, Gareth McAuley, Jonny Evans, Corry Evans (90+1 Liam Boyce), Sammy Clingan, Chris Brunt, Grant McCann (71 Josh McQuoid), Warren Feeney (82 Pat McCourt).   Manager: Nigel Worthington

SLOVENIA: Samir Handanovic, Bojan Jokic, Miso Brecko, Marko Suler, Matej Mavric, Andraz Kirm, Josip Ilicic (29 Zlatan Ljubijankic), Armin Bacinovic (90 Goran Sukalo), Robert Koren, Valter Birsa, Milivoje Novakovic (84 Zlatko Dedic).   Manager: Matjaz Kek

566.   24.05.2011   Nations Cup
**REPUBLIC OF IRELAND
v NORTHERN IRELAND   5-0** (3-0)
Aviva Stadium, Dublin

Referee: Craig Thomson (Scotland)   Attendance: 12,083

REPUBLIC OF IRELAND: Shay Given (72 David Forde), Keith Treacy, Paul McShane, Stephen Kelly, Séamus Coleman (55 Liam Lawrence), Kevin Foley (70 Stephen Hunt), Stephen Ward, Damien Delaney, Keith Andrews, Robbie Keane (62 Andy Keogh), Simon Cox.   Manager: Giovanni Trapattoni

NORTHERN IRELAND: Alan Blayney, Adam Thompson, Gareth McAuley, Lee Hodson, Craig Cathcart, Josh McQuoid (46 Oliver Norwood), Johnny Gorman (55 Colin Coates), Sammy Clingan, Steven Davis (76 Robert Garrett), Warren Feeney (72 Liam Boyce), Josh Carson (73 Niall McGinn).   Manager: Nigel Worthington

Sent off: Adam Thompson (53)

Goals: Stephen Ward (24), Robbie Keane (37, 54 pen), Craig Cathcart (44 og), Simon Cox (80)

567.   27.05.2011   Nations Cup
WALES v NORTHERN IRELAND   2-0 (1-0)
Aviva Stadium, Dublin

Referee: Alan Kelly (Republic of Ireland)   Attendance: 529

WALES: Wayne Hennessey (75 Lewis Price), Chris Gunter (73 Adam Matthews), Daniel Gabbidon, Danny Collins, Neil Taylor, David Cotterill, Jack Collison (62 Owain Tudur-Jones), David Vaughan, Aaron Ramsey (90 Andy Dorman), Craig Bellamy (62 Robert Earnshaw), Steve Morison (80 Sam Vokes).   Manager: Gary Speed

NORTHERN IRELAND: Jonny Tuffey, Colin Coates, Lee Hodson, Craig Cathcart (63 Stuart Dallas), Gareth McAuley, Johnny Gorman, Robert Garrett (76 Carl Winchester), Oliver Norwood, Niall McGinn (80 Jordan Owens), Warren Feeney (73 Liam Boyce), Josh Carson.   Manager: Nigel Worthington

Goals: Aaron Ramsey (36), Robert Earnshaw (71)

568. 10.08.2011   14th European Champs Qualifier
NORTHERN IRELAND
v FAROE ISLANDS 4-0 (1-0)
Windsor Park, Belfast
Referee: Emir Aleckovic (Bosnia-Herzegovina)   Att: 13,183
NORTHERN IRELAND: Lee Camp, Gareth McAuley (46 Craig Cathcart), Aaron Hughes, Jonny Evans, Chris Baird, Pat McCourt, Grant McCann, Corry Evans (59 Niall McGinn), Steven Davis, Sammy Clingan, David Healy (83 Jamie Ward).
Manager: Nigel Worthington
FAROE ISLANDS: Jákup Mikkelsen, Jónas Næs, Atli Gregersen, Jóhan Davidsen, Súni Olsen (75 Atli Danielsen), Christian Holst (68 Arnbjørn Hansen), Hjalgrím Elttør (75 Christian Mouritsen), Jóan Edmundsson, Fródi Benjaminsen, Daniel Udsen, Rógvi Baldvinsson.   Manager: Brian Kerr
Goals: Aaron Hughes (5), Steven Davis (66), Pat McCourt (71, 88)

569. 02.09.2011   14th European Champs Qualifier
NORTHERN IRELAND v SERBIA 0-1 (0-0)
Windsor Park, Belfast
Referee: Thomas Einwaller (Austria)   Attendance: 13,026
NORTHERN IRELAND: Lee Camp, Gareth McAuley, Aaron Hughes, Jonny Evans, Craig Cathcart, Chris Baird, Grant McCann (71 Warren Feeney), Corry Evans (59 Niall McGinn), Steven Davis, Chris Brunt, David Healy (84 Josh McQuoid).
Manager: Nigel Worthington
SERBIA: Bojan Jorgacevic, Neven Subotic, Slobodan Rajkovic, Aleksandar Kolarov, Branislav Ivanovic, Zoran Tosic (79 Adem Ljajic), Dejan Stankovic, Milos Ninkovic (74 Radosav Petrovic), Zdravko Kuzmanovic (89 Ljubomir Fejsa), Marko Pantelic, Milan Jovanovic.
Manager: Vladimir Petrovic
Goal: Marko Pantelic (67)

570. 06.09.2011   14th European Champs Qualifier
ESTONIA v NORTHERN IRELAND 4-1 (2-1)
A. Le Coq Arena, Tallinn
Referee: Daniel Stålhammar (Sweden)   Attendance: 8,660
ESTONIA: Sergei Pareiko, Raio Piiroja, Dmitriy Kruglov, Enar Jääger, Taavi Rähn, Ragnar Klavan, Martin Vunk, Sander Puri (63 Ats Purje), Konstantin Vassiljev, Tarmo Kink (88 Kaimar Saag), Jarmo Ahjupera (52 Sergei Zenjov).
Manager: Tarmo Rüütli
NORTHERN IRELAND: Lee Camp, Craig Cathcart, Chris Baird, Gareth McAuley, Aaron Hughes, Steven Davis, Sammy Clingan, Chris Brunt, Niall McGinn (65 Josh McQuoid), Grant McCann, David Healy (65 Warren Feeney).
Manager: Nigel Worthington
Goals: M. Vunk (28), Tarmo Kink (32), Sergei Zenjov (59), Kaimar Saag (90+2) / Raio Piiroja (40 og)

571. 07.10.2011   14th European Champs Qualifier
NORTHERN IRELAND v ESTONIA 1-2 (1-0)
Windsor Park, Belfast
Referee: Manuel Gräfe (Germany)   Attendance: 12,768
NORTHERN IRELAND: Lee Camp, Gareth McAuley, Lee Hodson, Craig Cathcart, Chris Baird, Pat McCourt, Grant McCann (83 David Healy), Steven Davis, Sammy Clingan (32 Corry Evans), Chris Brunt, Kyle Lafferty (69 Warren Feeney).
Manager: Nigel Worthington
ESTONIA: Sergei Pareiko, Andrei Stepanov, Raio Piiroja, Dmitriy Kruglov, Enar Jääger, Ragnar Klavan, Martin Vunk, Sander Puri (57 Ats Purje), Aleksandr Dmitrijev, Tarmo Kink (65 Konstantin Vassiljev), Jarmo Ahjupera (46 Sergei Zenjov).
Manager: Tarmo Rüütli
Goals: Steven Davis (22) / Konstantin Vassiljev (77 pen, 84)

572. 11.10.2011   14th European Champs Qualifier
ITALY v NORTHERN IRELAND 3-0 (1-0)
Stadio Adriatico, Pescara
Referee: Antonio Miguel Mateu Lahoz (Spain)   Att: 19,480
ITALY: Gianluigi Buffon (76 Morgan De Sanctis), Mattia Cassani, Federico Balzaretti, Giorgio Chiellini, Andrea Barzagli, Riccardo Montolivo, Andrea Pirlo, Daniele De Rossi, Alberto Aquilani (69 Antonio Nocerino), Sebastian Giovinco, Antonio Cassano (56 Pablo Osvaldo).
Manager: Cesare Prandelli
NORTHERN IRELAND: Maik Taylor, Ryan McGivern, Gareth McAuley, Lee Hodson, Chris Baird, Oliver Norwood (74 Conor McLaughlin), Johnny Gorman (77 Niall McGinn), Corry Evans, Steven Davis, Andy Little, David Healy (65 Warren Feeney).   Manager: Nigel Worthington
Goals: Antonio Cassano (21, 53), Garath McAuley (74 og)

573. 29.02.2012
NORTHERN IRELAND v NORWAY 0-3 (0-1)
Windsor Park, Belfast
Referee: Huw Jones (Wales)   Attendance: 10,500
NORTHERN IRELAND: Lee Camp, Ryan McGivern, Gareth McAuley (57 Lee Hodson), Aaron Hughes (46 Michael Duff), Jonny Evans, Dean Shiels, Shane Ferguson (69 Pat McCourt), Corry Evans (46 Grant McCann), Steven Davis, Sammy Clingan, Martin Paterson (73 David Healy).
Manager: Michael O'Neill
NORWAY: Rune Jarstein, Thomas Rogne, John Arne Risse, Håvard Nordtveit, Tom Høgli (90+2 Espen Ruud), Vadim Demidov (60 Tore Reginiussen), Morten Pedersen, Erik Huseklepp (66 Valon Berisha), Markus Henriksen (78 Ruben Jenssen), Christian Grindheim (60 Tarik Elyounoussi), Mohammed Abdellaoue (46 Daniel Braaten).
Manager: Egil Olsen
Goals: Håvard Nordtveit (44), Tarik Elyounoussi (88), Espen Ruud (90+2)

574. 02.06.2012
NETHERLANDS v NORTHERN IRELAND 6-0 (4-0)

Amsterdam ArenA, Amsterdam

Referee: Robert Schörgenhofer (Austria)   Att: 50,000

NETHERLANDS: Maarten Stekelenburg, Jetro Willems (77 Stijn Schaars), Gregory van der Wiel, John Heitinga, Ron Vlaar, Ibrahim Afellay, Mark van Bommel (57 Rafael van der Vaart), Nigel de Jong, Wesley Sneijder (70 Dirk Kuyt), Robin van Persie (57 Klaas-Jan Huntelaar), Arjen Robben (82 Luciano Narsingh).   Manager: Bert van Marwijk

NORTHERN IRELAND: Lee Camp (46 Roy Carroll), Michael Duff (62 Rory McArdle), Daniel Lafferty (46 Ryan McGivern), James McPake, Lee Hodson, Grant McCann (46 Josh Carson), Shane Ferguson (81 David Healy), Sammy Clingan, Oliver Norwood, Andy Little (56 Niall McGinn), Will Grigg.   Manager: Michael O'Neill

Goals: Robin van Persie (11, 29 pen), Wesley Sneijder (15), Ibrahim Afellay (37, 51), Ron Vlaar (78)

575. 15.08.2012
NORTHERN IRELAND v FINLAND 3-3 (2-2)

Windsor Park, Belfast

Referee: Richard Liesveld (Netherlands)   Attendance: 9,575

NORTHERN IRELAND: Roy Carroll (46 Lee Camp), Craig Cathcart, Ryan McGivern, Gareth McAuley, Lee Hodson (84 Oliver Norwood), Chris Baird, Chris Brunt (46 Jamie Ward), Dean Shiels, Shane Ferguson (84 Josh Carson), Steven Davis, Kyle Lafferty (63 Martin Paterson).
Manager: Michael O'Neill

FINLAND: Niki Mäenpää, Jere Uronen, Joona Toivio, Niklas Moisander, Kari Arkivuo, Alexei Eremenko (69 Përparim Hetemaj), Tim Sparv, Kasper Hämäläinen (69 Toni Kolehmainen), Roman Eremenko, Teemu Pukki (46 Riku Riski), Njazi Kuqi (84 Daniel Sjölund).
Manager: Mixu Paatelainen

Goals: Shane Ferguson (7), Kyle Lafferty (19), Martin Paterson (83 pen) /
Tim Sparv (22), Teemu Pukki (24), Përparim Hetemaj (78)

576. 07.09.2012   20th World Cup Qualifier
RUSSIA v NORTHERN IRELAND 2-0 (1-0)

Stadion Lokomotiv, Moskva

Referee: Antonio Miguel Mateu Lahoz (Spain)   Attendance: 14,300

RUSSIA: Igor Akinfeev, Sergey Ignashevich, Vasiliy Berezutskiy, Aleksandr Anyukov, Roman Shirokov, Dmitriy Kombarov, Viktor Fayzulin (85 Denis Glushakov), Alan Dzagoev (58 Aleksandr Kokorin), Igor Denisov, Vladimir Bystrov, Aleksandr Kerzhakov.   Manager: Fabio Capello

NORTHERN IRELAND: Roy Carroll, Gareth McAuley, Aaron Hughes, Jonny Evans, Craig Cathcart, Jamie Ward (76 Andy Little), Corry Evans (85 Dean Shiels), Steven Davis, Chris Brunt, Chris Baird, Kyle Lafferty.
Manager: Michael O'Neill

Goals: Viktor Fayzulin (30), Roman Shirokov (78 pen)

577. 11.09.2012   20th World Cup Qualifier
NORTHERN IRELAND v LUXEMBOURG 1-1 (1-0)

Windsor Park, Belfast

Referee: Vlado Glodovic (Serbia)   Attendance: 10,674

NORTHERN IRELAND: Roy Carroll, Ryan McGivern, Gareth McAuley, Aaron Hughes, Jonny Evans, Dean Shiels (83 Oliver Norwood), Shane Ferguson (74 Jamie Ward), Steven Davis, Chris Brunt, Chris Baird, Kyle Lafferty.
Manager: Michael O'Neill

LUXEMBOURG: Jonathan Joubert, Ante Bukvic, Tom Schnell, Mathias Jänisch, Guy Blaise, Mario Mutsch, Ben Payal, Lars Gerson (50 Chris Philipps), Gilles Bettmer (90 Eric Hoffmann), Aurélien Joachim (46 Maurice Deville), Daniël Alves Da Mota.   Manager: Luc Holtz

Goals: Dean Shiels (14) / Daniël Alves Da Mota (86)

578. 16.10.2012   20th World Cup Qualifier
PORTUGAL v NORTHERN IRELAND 1-1 (0-1)

Estádio Do Dragão, Porto

Referee: Thorsten Kinhöfer (Germany)   Attendance: 48,711

PORTUGAL: RUI Pedro dos Santos PATRÍCIO, JOÃO Pedro da Silva PEREIRA (74 Éderzito António Macedo Lopes "ÉDER"), Hugo MIGUEL de Almeida Costa LOPES (47 RÚBEN Filipe Marques AMORIM), Képler Laveran Lima Ferreira "PEPE", BRUNO Eduardo Refuge ALVES, MIGUEL Luís Pinto VELOSO, RÚBEN MICAEL Freitas da Ressureição (57 Silvestre Manuel Gonçalves VARELA), JOÃO Filipe Iria Santos MOUTINHO, HÉLDER Manuel Marques POSTIGA, Luís Carlos Almeida da Cunha "NANI", CRISTIANO RONALDO dos Santos Aveiro.
Manager: PAULO Jorge Gomes BENTO

NORTHERN IRELAND: Roy Carroll, Ryan McGivern, Aaron Hughes, Jonny Evans, Craig Cathcart, Oliver Norwood, Niall McGinn, Corry Evans, Steven Davis, Chris Baird, Kyle Lafferty.
Manager: Michael O'Neill

Goals: HÉLDER Manuel Marques POSTIGA (79) /
Niall McGinn (30)

579. 14.11.2012   20th World Cup Qualifier
NORTHERN IRELAND v AZERBAIJAN 1-1 (1-0)
Windsor Park, Belfast
Referee: Viktor Shvetsov (Ukraine)   Attendance: 12.327
NORTHERN IRELAND: Roy Carroll, Daniel Lafferty, Gareth McAuley, Aaron Hughes, Craig Cathcart (81 David Healy), Shane Ferguson, Steven Davis, Chris Baird, Dean Shiels (55 Pat McCourt), Niall McGinn (66 Chris Brunt), Kyle Lafferty. Manager: Michael O'Neill
AZERBAIJAN: Sälahät Agayev, Maksim Medvedev, Vladimir Levin, Rasim Ramaldanov (72 Elhad Näziri), Rahid Ämirguliyev, Ruslan Abisov, Vüqar Nadirov, Javid Hüseynov, Ali Gökdemir (63 Badavi Hüseynov), Rauf Aliyev, Cihan Özkara (78 Vagif Javadov).   Manager: Berti Vogts
Goals: David Healy (90+6) / Rauf Aliyev (5)

580. 06.02.2013
MALTA v NORTHERN IRELAND 0-0
National Stadium, Ta'Qali
Referee: Nikolay Yordanov (Bulgaria)   Attendance: 1,000
MALTA: Andrew Hogg, Alex Muscat, Edward Herrera, Luke Dimech, Andrei Agius (46 Ryan Camilleri), Gareth Sciberras, Paul Fenech, Andrew Cohen, André Schembri (90+2 Shaun Bajada), Michael Mifsud (89 Terence Vella), Clayton Failla. Manager: Pietro Ghedin
NORTHERN IRELAND: Alan Mannus, Gareth McAuley, Daniel Lafferty, Aaron Hughes, Jonny Evans (46 Craig Cathcart), Alex Bruce (72 Pat McCourt), Steven Davis, Chris Brunt, Shane Ferguson (63 Billy McKay), Niall McGinn, Will Grigg (86 Josh Magennis).   Manager: Michael O'Neill

581. 26.03.2013   20th World Cup Qualifier
NORTHERN IRELAND v ISRAEL 0-2 (0-0)
Windsor Park, Belfast
Referee: Hannes Kaasik (Estonia)   Attendance: 7,300
NORTHERN IRELAND: Roy Carroll, Daniel Lafferty, Aaron Hughes, Jonny Evans, Gareth McAuley, Shane Ferguson (73 Josh Magennis), Steven Davis, Sammy Clingan (79 Pat McCourt), Chris Brunt, Niall McGinn, Martin Paterson (83 David Healy).   Manager: Michael O'Neill
ISRAEL: Dudu Aouate, Rami Gershon, Tal Ben Haim, Eitan Tibi, Yuval Shpungin, Bebars Natcho, Maor Melikson (69 Lior Refaelov), Sheran Yeini, Maharan Radi (60 Eran Zahavy), Eden Ben Basat, Itay Shechter (86 Yossi Benayoun). Manager: Eli Guttmann
Goals: Lior Refaelov (77), Eden Ben Basat (84)

582. 14.08.2013   20th World Cup Qualifier
NORTHERN IRELAND v RUSSIA 1-0 (1-0)
Windsor Park, Belfast
Referee: Tom Hagen (Norway)   Attendance: 11,805
NORTHERN IRELAND: Roy Carroll, Daniel Lafferty, Gareth McAuley, Aaron Hughes, Craig Cathcart, Jamie Ward, Oliver Norwood, Niall McGinn (82 Corry Evans), Shane Ferguson, Steven Davis, Martin Paterson (86 Will Grigg). Manager: Michael O'Neill
RUSSIA: Igor Akinfeev, Sergey Ignashevich, Vasiliy Berezutskiy, Aleksandr Anyukov, Roman Shirokov, Dmitriy Kombarov, Viktor Fayzulin, Alan Dzagoev (46 Denis Cheryshev, 52 Aleksandr Samedov), Igor Denisov, Vladimir Bystrov, Aleksandr Kerzhakov (46 Artem Dzyuba). Manager: Fabio Capello
Goal: Martin Paterson (43)

583. 06.09.2013   20th World Cup Qualifier
NORTHERN IRELAND v PORTUGAL 2-4 (1-1)
Windsor Park, Belfast
Referee: Danny Makkelie (Netherlands)   Att: 13,629
NORTHERN IRELAND: Roy Carroll, Gareth McAuley, Lee Hodson, Jonny Evans, Jamie Ward (71 Corry Evans), Oliver Norwood, Niall McGinn (67 Kyle Lafferty), Shane Ferguson (76 Chris Baird), Steven Davis, Chris Brunt, Martin Paterson. Manager: Michael O'Neill
PORTUGAL: RUI Pedro dos Santos PATRÍCIO, JOÃO Pedro da Silva PEREIRA, Adelino André Vieira de Freitas "VIEIRINHA" (65 NÉLSON Miguel Castro OLIVEIRA), Képler Laveran Lima Ferreira "PEPE", BRUNO Eduardo Refuge ALVES, MIGUEL Luís Pinto VELOSO, RAÚL José Trindade MEIRELES (55 Luís Carlos Almeida da Cunha "NANI"), JOÃO Filipe Iria Santos MOUTINHO, FÁBIO Alexandre da Silva COENTRÃO, HÉLDER Manuel Marques POSTIGA, CRISTIANO RONALDO dos Santos Aveiro (90 RÚBEN Filipe Marques AMORIM).   Manager: PAULO Jorge Gomes BENTO
Sent off: HÉLDER Manuel Marques POSTIGA (43), Chris Brunt (61), Kyle Lafferty (80)
Goals: Gareth McAuley (36), Jamie Ward (52) / BRUNO Eduardo Refuge ALVES (21), CRISTIANO RONALDO dos Santos Aveiro (68, 77, 83)

584. 10.09.2013   20th World Cup Qualifier
LUXEMBOURG v NORTHERN IRELAND 3-2 (1-1)
Stade Josy Barthel, Luxembourg

Referee: Robert Malek (Poland)   Attendance: 4,114

LUXEMBOURG: Jonathan Joubert, Chris Philipps, Mathias Jänisch, Mario Mutsch, Laurent Jans, Lars Gerson, Tom Laterza, David Turpel (68 Antonio Luisi), Aurélien Joachim, Stefano Bensi, Daniël Alves Da Mota (89 Ante Bukvic). Manager: Luc Holtz

NORTHERN IRELAND: Roy Carroll, Daniel Lafferty (80 Will Grigg), Gareth McAuley, Lee Hodson, Jonny Evans, Jamie Ward, Oliver Norwood, Niall McGinn (35 Michael O'Connor), Shane Ferguson (60 Billy McKay), Steven Davis, Martin Paterson.   Manager: Michael O'Neill

Goals: Aurélien Joachim (45+2), Stefano Bensi (78), Mathias Jänisch (87) / Martin Paterson (14), Gareth McAuley (82)

585.   11.10.2013   20th World Cup Qualifier
AZERBAIJAN v NORTHERN IRELAND 2-0 (0-0)
Bakcell Arena, Baku

Referee: Andrea De Marco (Italy)   Attendance: 10,100

AZERBAIJAN: Kamran Agayev, Mahir Sükürov, Rasim Ramaldanov, Qara Qarayev, Elnur Allahverdiyev, Rashad Sadygov, Rahid Ämirguliyev, Araz Abdullayev (82 Cihan Özkara), Vüqar Nadirov (46 Javid Hüseynov), Rofat Dadasov (90+3 Badavi Hüseynov), Rauf Aliyev.   Manager: Berti Vogts

NORTHERN IRELAND: Roy Carroll, Gareth McAuley, Lee Hodson (66 Niall McGinn), Jonny Evans, Craig Cathcart, Jamie Ward (84 Will Grigg), Oliver Norwood, Shane Ferguson, Steven Davis, Chris Brunt (74 Billy McKay), Martin Paterson. Manager: Michael O'Neill

Sent off: Jonny Evans (90+4)

Goals: Rofat Dadasov (58), Mahir Sükürov (90+5)

586.   15.10.2013   20th World Cup Qualifier
ISRAEL v NORTHERN IRELAND 1-1 (1-0)
Winter Stadium, Ramat Gan

Referee: Laurent Duhamel (France)   Attendance: 12,785

ISRAEL: Dudu Aouate, Eitan Tibi, Eyal Meshumar, Ofir Davidadze, Tal Ben Haim (46 Dekel Keinan), Sheran Yeini, Lior Refaelov (78 Itay Shechter), Bebars Natcho, Maor Melikson, Eran Zahavy (71 Tal Ben Haim), Eden Ben Basat. Manager: Eli Guttmann

NORTHERN IRELAND: Roy Carroll, Rory McArdle, Daniel Lafferty (78 Shane Ferguson), Lee Hodson, Craig Cathcart, Niall McGinn (65 Jamie Ward), Corry Evans (24 Chris Brunt), Steven Davis, Sammy Clingan, Chris Baird, Martin Paterson.   Manager: Michael O'Neill

Goals: Eden Ben Basat (43) / Steven Davis (72)

Ofir Davidadze is also known as Ofir Davidzada.

587.   15.11.2013
TURKEY v NORTHERN IRELAND 1-0 (1-0)
5 Ocak Stadyumu, Adana

Referee: Bas Nijhuis (Netherlands)   Attendance: 14,000

TURKEY: Tolga Zengin, Semih Kaya, Ersan Gülüm, Gökhan Gönül (72 Tarik Çamdal), Caner Erkin, Arda Turan (89 Ishak Dogan), Bilal Kisa (83 Olcay Sahan), Mehmet Topal, Oguzhan Özyakup (46 Burak Yilmaz), Mevlüt Erdinç (77 Gökhan Töre), Adem Büyük (67 Salih Uçan).   Manager: Fatih Terim

NORTHERN IRELAND: Roy Carroll (46 Alan Mannus), Daniel Lafferty (75 Ryan McGivern), Aaron Hughes, Lee Hodson, Jonny Evans, Oliver Norwood, Steven Davis, Sammy Clingan (75 Billy McKay), Niall McGinn (67 Jonny Steele), Chris Baird, Martin Paterson.   Manager: Michael O'Neill

Goal: Mevlüt Erdinç (45+1)

588.   05.03.2014
CYPRUS v NORTHERN IRELAND 0-0
Neo GSP, Nicosia

Referee: Liran Liany (Israel)   Attendance: 3,000

CYPRUS: Antonis Georgallides, Giorgios Merkis, DOSSA Momad Omar Hassamo JÚNIOR, Marios Antoniades, Mários Nikolaou (58 Kostakis Artymatas), Konstantinos Makridis (64 Costas Charalambidis), Vincent Laban (67 Charalambos Kyriakou), Charis Kyriakou, Nestoras Mytidis (76 Andreas Papathanasiou), Dimitris Christofi (85 Andreas Makris), Efstathios Aloneftis (51 Giorgos Efrem).
Manager: Pambos Christodoulou

NORTHERN IRELAND: Alan Mannus (46 Roy Carroll), Alex Bruce, Ryan McGivern, Gareth McAuley, William Cathcart, Oliver Norwood (74 Pat McCourt), Steven Davis, Chris Brunt, Jamie Ward (63 Billy McKay, 80 Rory McArdle), Niall McGinn (73 Steven Ferguson), Martin Paterson (46 Kyle Lafferty). Manager: Michael O'Neill

Sent off: Gareth McAuley (76)

589.   31.05.2014
URUGUAY v NORTHERN IRELAND   1-0 (0-0)

Estadio Centenario, Montevideo

Referee: LEANDRO Pedro VUADEN (Brazil)   Att: 45,000

URUGUAY: Nestor FERNANDO MUSLERA, DIEGO Alfredo LUGANO Moreno, José MARTÍN CÁCERES Silva (73 ÁLVARO Daniel PEREIRA Barragán), SEBASTIÁN COATES Nion (46 JOSÉ María GIMÉNEZ de Vargas), Victorio Maximiliano "MAXI" PEREIRA Páez, WALTER Alejandro GARGANO Guevara (74 DIEGO Fernando PÉREZ Aguado), CRISTIAN Gabriel RODRÍGUEZ Barrotti, GASTÓN Ezequiel RAMÍREZ Pereyra (65 Marcelo NICOLÁS LODEIRO Benítez), EGIDIO Raúl ARÉVALO Ríos, DIEGO Martín FORLÁN Corazo (46 CHRISTIAN Ricardo STUANI Curbelo), EDINSON Roberto Gómez CAVANI (65 ABEL Mathías HERNÁNDEZ).   Manager: ÓSCAR Washington TABÁREZ Sclavo

NORTHERN IRELAND: Roy Carroll, Luke McCullough, Aaron Hughes, Oliver Norwood (86 Jonny Steele), Corry Evans (87 Conor McLaughlin), Sammy Clingan (74 Paul Paton), Steven Davis, Steven Ferguson (81 Daniel Lafferty), Niall McGinn (61 Josh Magennis), Chris Baird, Billy McKay (81 Ryan McLaughlin).   Manager: Michael O'Neill

Goal: CHRISTIAN Ricardo STUANI Curbelo (61)

590.   05.06.2014
CHILE v NORTHERN IRELAND   2-0 (0-0)

Estadio Elías Figueroa Brander, Valparaíso

Referee: CARLOS Arecio AMARILLA Demarqui (Paraguay)   Attendance: 20,000

CHILE: JHONNY Cristián HERRERA Muñoz, EUGENIO Estenan MENA Reveco, JOSÉ Manuel ROJAS Bahamondes, GARY Alexis MEDEL Soto (77 MAURICIO Ricardo PINILLA Ferrera), MAURICIO Anibal ISLA Isla, FRANCISCO Andrés SILVA Gajardo, JORGE Luis VALDÍVIA Toro (77 ARTURO Erasmo VIDAL Pardo), MARCELO Alfonso DÍAZ Rojas (85 FELIPE Alejandro GUTIÉRREZ Leiva), CARLOS Emilio Tello CARMONA (59 CHARLES Mariano ARÁNGUIZ Sandoval), ESTEBAN Efraín PAREDES Quintanilla (61 EDUARDO Jesús VARGAS Rojas), FABIÁN Ariel ORELLANA Valenzuela (59 ALEXIS Alejandro SÁNCHEZ Sánchez).   Manager: JORGE Luis SAMPAOLI Moya

NORTHERN IRELAND: Roy Carroll, Luke McCullough, Aaron Hughes, Conor McLaughlin, Ryan McLaughlin (71 Niall McGinn), Oliver Norwood (84 Jonathan Steele), Steven Ferguson (78 Daniel Lafferty), Corry Evans (89 Liam Donnelly), Steven Davis, Sammy Clingan, Billy McKay (62 Josh Magennis).   Manager: Michael O'Neill

Goals: EDUARDO Jesús VARGAS Rojas (79), MAURICIO Ricardo PINILLA Ferrera (82)

591.   07.09.2014   15th European Champs Qualifier
HUNGARY v NORTHERN IRELAND   1-2 (0-0)

Groupama Aréna, Budapest

Referee: Deniz Aytekin (Germany)   Attendance: 20,672

HUNGARY: Péter Gulácsi, Vilmos Vanczák, Zoltán Lipták, Roland Juhász, József Varga, Dániel Tözsér, Balász Balogh, Gergely Rudolf (70 István Kovács), Nemanja Nikolic (46 Tamás Priskin), Ádám Gyurcsó (59 Gergö Lovrencsics), Balázs Dzsudzsák.   Manager: Attila Pintér

NORTHERN IRELAND: Roy Carroll, Conor McLaughlin, Gareth McAuley (72 Craig Cathcart), Aaron Hughes, Oliver Norwood (79 Billy McKay), Corry Evans, Steven Davis, Chris Brunt, Jamie Ward (66 Niall McGinn), Chris Baird, Kyle Lafferty.   Manager: Michael O'Neill

Goals: Tamás Priskin (75) /
Niall McGinn (81), Kyle Lafferty (88)

592.   11.10.2014   15th European Champs Qualifier
**NORTHERN IRELAND
v FAROE ISLANDS   2-0** (2-0)

Windsor Park, Belfast

Referee: Alon Yefet (Israel)   Attendance: 10,049

NORTHERN IRELAND: Roy Carroll, Conor McLaughlin, Gareth McAuley (56 Luke McCullough), Aaron Hughes, Shane Ferguson, Steven Davis, Oliver Norwood, Chris Baird, Jamie Ward, Niall McGinn (67 Pat McCourt), Kyle Lafferty (84 Josh Magennis).   Manager: Michael O'Neill

FAROE ISLANDS: Gunnar Nielsen, Viljormur Davidsen, Sonni Nattestad, Jónas Næs, Pól Justinussen (90+1 Kaj Leo í Bartalsstovu), Atli Gregersen, Jóan Edmundsson, Fródi Benjaminsen, Christian Holst (82 Brandur Hendriksson), Hallur Hansson, Páll Klettskard (75 Arnbjørn Hansen).   Manager: Lars Olsen

Goals: Gareth McAuley (6), Kyle Lafferty (20)

Fródi Benjaminsen missed a penalty kick in the 36th minute.

593.   14.10.2014   15th European Champs Qualifier
GREECE v NORTHERN IRELAND   0-2 (0-1)

Stadio Georgios Karaiskáki, Piraeus

Referee: Stéphane Lannoy (France)   Attendance: 18,726

GREECE: Orestis Karnezis, Loukas Vyntra (16 Kostas Stafylidis), Vasilios Torosidis, Sokratis Papastathopoulos, Kostas Manolas, Panagiotis Tachtsidis, Ioannis Maniatis, Georgios Samaras (67 Dimitrios Salpingidis), Kostas Mitroglou, Nikolaos Karelis, Stefanos Athanasiadis (46 Andreas Samaris).   Manager: Claudio Ranieri

NORTHERN IRELAND: Roy Carroll, Conor McLaughlin, Gareth McAuley, Aaron Hughes, Shane Ferguson (78 Ben Reeves), Oliver Norwood, Corry Evans, Steven Davis, Jamie Ward (59 Ryan McGivern), Chris Baird, Kyle Lafferty (72 Josh Magennis).   Manager: Michael O'Neill

Goals: Jamie Ward (9), Kyle Lafferty (51)

594.   14.11.2014   15th European Champs Qualifier
ROMANIA v NORTHERN IRELAND 2-0 (0-0)
Arena Nationala, Bucuresti

Referee: Jonas Eriksson (Sweden)   Attendance: 28,892

ROMANIA: Ciprian Tatarusanu, Razvan Rat, Paul Papp, Dragos Grigore, Vlad Chiriches, Gabriel Torje (80 Ovidiu Hoban), Cristian Tanase (58 Alexandru Maxim), Lucian Sanmartean, Mihai Pintilii, Alexandru Chipciu, Bogdan Stancu (46 Claudiu Keserü).   Manager: Anghel Iordanescu

NORTHERN IRELAND: Roy Carroll, Conor McLaughlin, Ryan McGivern, Gareth McAuley, Aaron Hughes, Oliver Norwood, Corry Evans (78 Billy McKay), Chris Brunt, Niall McGinn (63 Sammy Clingan), Chris Baird, Kyle Lafferty.   Manager: Michael O'Neill

Goals: Paul Papp (74, 79)

595.   25.03.2015
SCOTLAND v NORTHERN IRELAND 1-0 (0-0)
Hampdon Park, Glasgow

Referee: Martin Atkinson (England)   Attendance: 30,000

SCOTLAND: Craig Gordon (46 Allan McGregor), Steven Whittaker (78 Johnny Russell), Gordon Greer, Craig Forsyth, Matt Ritchie, James McArthur (62 James Morrison), Russell Martin (46 Christophe Berra), Shaun Maloney (46 Steven Naismith), Darren Fletcher, Ikechi Anya, Steven Fletcher (63 Jordan Rhodes).   Manager: Gordon Strachan

NORTHERN IRELAND: Michael McGovern, Ben Reeves (70 Ryan McLaughlin), Daniel Lafferty, Aaron Hughes, Jonny Evans (81 Luke McCullough), Oliver Norwood (69 Steven Davis), Stuart Dallas, Paddy McNair, Chris Baird (58 Lee Hodson), Josh Magennis (75 Billy McKay), Will Grigg (58 Pat McCourt).   Manager: Michael O'Neill

Goal: Christophe Berra (85)

596.   29.03.2015   15th European Champs Qualifier
NORTHERN IRELAND v FINLAND 2-1 (2-0)
Windsor Park, Belfast

Referee: Szymon Marciniak (Poland)   Attendance: 10,264

NORTHERN IRELAND: Roy Carroll, Conor McLaughlin, Gareth McAuley, Jonny Evans, Oliver Norwood, Steven Davis (46 Corry Evans), Chris Brunt, Jamie Ward, Niall McGinn (64 Stuart Dallas), Chris Baird, Kyle Lafferty (79 Josh Magennis).   Manager: Michael O'Neill

FINLAND: Lukás Hrádecky, Jere Uronen, Joona Toivio (46 Paulus Arajuuri), Niklas Moisander, Tim Sparv, Sebastian Sorsa, Alexander Ring, Sakari Mattila, Kasper Hämäläinen (43 Joel Pohjanpalo), Roman Eremenko, Teemu Pukki (70 Berat Sadik).   Manager: Mixu Paatelainen

Goals: Kyle Lafferty (33, 38) / Berat Sadik (90+1)

597.   31.05.2015
NORTHERN IRELAND v QATAR 1-1 (0-0)
Alexandra Stadium, Crewe (England)

Referee: Michael Oliver (England)   Attendance: 3,022

NORTHERN IRELAND: Roy Carroll (46 Michael McGovern), Daniel Lafferty, Aaron Hughes (61 Jonny Evans), Craig Cathcart, Conor McLaughlin, Oliver Norwood, Corry Evans, Stuart Dallas (73 Liam Boyce), Niall McGinn (61 Jamie Ward), Paddy McNair (82 Josh Magennis), Will Grigg (73 Pat McCourt).   Manager: Michael O'Neill

QATAR: Amine Lecomte-Addani, Mohammed Kasola, Mohammed Musa, Ahmed Yasser, Dame Traoré (56 Abdelkarim Hassan), Abdelaziz Hatem (56 Karim Boudiaf), Mohammed Muntari (81 Mohammed Jeddo), Ismail Mohammed (56 Hasan Khalid Al Haidos), Ahmed El Sayed, Majdi Siddiq (65 Ali Assadalla), Hamid Ismail.   Manager: José Daniel Carreño

Goals: Stuart Dallas (47) / Karim Boudiaf (70)

598.   13.06.2015   15th European Champs Qualifier
NORTHERN IRELAND v ROMANIA 0-0
Windsor Park, Belfast

Referee: Carlos Velasco Carballo (Spain)   Att: 10,000

NORTHERN IRELAND: Michael McGovern, Conor McLaughlin, Gareth McAuley, Jonny Evans (79 Craig Cathcart), Oliver Norwood, Steven Davis, Stuart Dallas, Chris Brunt, Jamie Ward (79 Corry Evans), Chris Baird, Kyle Lafferty.   Manager: Michael O'Neill

ROMANIA: Ciprian Tatarusanu, László Sepsi, Paul Papp, Dragos Grigore, Vlad Chiriches, Gabriel Torje, Andrei Prepelita, Mihai Pintilii, Alexandru Maxim (90 Gabriel Tamas), Alexandru Chipciu (61 Bogdan Stancu), Claudiu Keserü (72 Florin Andone).   Manager: Anghel Iordanescu

599.   04.09.2015   15th European Champs Qualifier
FAROE ISLANDS
v NORTHERN IRELAND 1-3 (1-1)
Tórsvøllur, Tórshavn
Referee: Felix Zwayer (Germany)   Attendance: 4,513
FAROE ISLANDS: Gunnar Nielsen, Jónas Næs, Sonni Nattestad, Odmar Færø, Christian Holst (76 Pól Justinussen), Brandur Hendriksson (83 Klæmint Olsen), Hallur Hansson, Jóan Edmundsson, Fródi Benjaminsen (87 Rógvi Baldvinsson), Sølvi Vatnhamar, Gilli Rólantsson Sørensen. Manager: Lars Olsen
NORTHERN IRELAND: Michael McGovern, Conor McLaughlin (69 Josh Magennis), Gareth McAuley, Jonny Evans, Oliver Norwood, Steven Davis, Stuart Dallas, Chris Brunt (83 Shane Ferguson), Niall McGinn, Chris Baird, Kyle Lafferty (78 Paddy McNair).   Manager: Michael O'Neill
Sent off: Jóan Edmundsson (65)
Goals: Jóan Edmundsson (36) / Gareth McAuley (12, 71), Kyle Lafferty (75)

600.   07.09.2015   15th European Champs Qualifier
NORTHERN IRELAND v HUNGARY 1-1 (0-0)
Windsor Park, Belfast
Referee: Cüneyt Çakir (Turkey)   Attendance: 10,200
NORTHERN IRELAND: Michael McGovern, Conor McLaughlin, Gareth McAuley, Jonny Evans, Oliver Norwood (75 Josh Magennis), Corry Evans (56 Niall McGinn), Steven Davis, Stuart Dallas (83 Shane Ferguson), Chris Brunt, Chris Baird, Kyle Lafferty.   Manager: Michael O'Neill
HUNGARY: Gábor Király, Tamás Kádár, Richárd Guzmics, Attila Fiola, LEANDRO Marcolini Pedroso de Almeida, Zsolt Kalmár, Ákos Elek (22 Ádám Nagy), Zoltán Gera, Ádám Szalai (68 Tamás Priskin), Krisztián Németh (89 Vilmos Vanczák), Balázs Dzsudzsák.   Manager: Bernd Storck
Sent off: Chris Baird (82)
Goals: Kyle Lafferty (90+3) / Richárd Guzmics (74)

601.   08.10.2015   15th European Champs Qualifier
NORTHERN IRELAND v GREECE 3-1 (1-0)
Windsor Park, Belfast
Referee: Bas Nijhuis (Netherlands)   Attendance: 11,700
NORTHERN IRELAND: Michael McGovern, Craig Cathcart, Gareth McAuley, Corry Evans, Steven Davis, Stuart Dallas, Chris Brunt, Oliver Norwood, Paddy McNair (85 Luke McCullough), Jamie Ward (81 Niall McGinn), Josh Magennis (78 Liam Boyce).   Manager: Michael O'Neill
GREECE: Orestis Karnezis, José Holebas, Sokratis Papastathopoulos, Vasilios Torosidis, Vangelis Moras, Panagiotis Kone (71 Dimitrios Pelkas), Christos Aravidis, Alexandros Tziolis, Andreas Samaris, Nikolaos Karelis (65 Petros Mantalos), Kostas Mitroglou (76 Stefanos Athanasiadis).   Manager: Kostas Tsanas
Goals: Steven Davis (35, 58), Josh Magennis (49) / Christos Aravidis (87)

602.   11.10.2015   15th European Champs Qualifier
FINLAND v NORTHERN IRELAND 1-1 (0-1)
Olympiastadion, Helsinki
Referee: Sergey Karasev (Russia)   Attendance: 14,550
FINLAND: Lukás Hrádecky, Juhani Ojala, Ville Jalasto, Paulus Arajuuri, Jere Uronen, Rasmus Schüller (79 Kasper Hämäläinen), Alexander Ring (44 Robin Lod), Joel Pohjanpalo, Sakari Mattila, Tim Sparv, Berat Sadik (66 Teemu Pukki).   Manager: Markku Kanerva
NORTHERN IRELAND: Michael McGovern, Gareth McAuley, Craig Cathcart, Steven Davis, Stuart Dallas, Chris Brunt, Oliver Norwood, Niall McGinn (71 Shane Ferguson), Chris Baird, Paddy McNair (51 Conor McLaughlin), Kyle Lafferty (79 Josh Magennis).   Manager: Michael O'Neill
Goals: Paulus Arajuuri (87) / Craig Cathcart (31)

603.   13.11.2015
NORTHERN IRELAND v LATVIA 1-0 (0-0)
Windsor Park, Belfast
Referee: Mohammed Al Hoaish (Saudi Arabia)   Att: 11,707
NORTHERN IRELAND: Michael McGovern (46 Roy Carroll), Conor McLaughlin, Gareth McAuley, Jonny Evans, Craig Cathcart, Oliver Norwood (46 Corry Evans), Steven Davis (84 Pat McCourt), Stuart Dallas (69 Shane Ferguson), Chris Baird, James Ward (69 Liam Boyce), Kyle Lafferty (54 Josh Magennis).   Manager: Michael O'Neill
LATVIA: Andris Vanins (74 Pāvels Steinbors), Vitalijs Jagodinskis, Kaspars Gorkss, Vladislavs Gabovs, Antons Kurakins, Artūrs Zjuzins, Olegs Laizāns (78 Jānis Ikaunieks), Aleksejs Visnakovs (69 Artjoms Rudņevs), Igors Tarasovs, Eduards Visnakovs (71 Valērijs Sabala), Deniss Rakels (85 Vladimir Kamess).   Manager: Marian Pahars
Goal: Steven Davis (55)

604. 24.03.2016

WALES v NORTHERN IRELAND 1-1 (0-0)

Cardiff City Stadium, Cardiff

Referee: Steven McLean (Scotland)   Attendance: 21,855

WALES: Wayne Hennessey (46 Danny Ward), Ashley Williams, Adam Matthews, Chris Gunter, James Chester, David Vaughan (71 Joe Allen), Joe Ledley (46 Andrew Crofts), David Cotterill, George Christopher Williams (62 Lloyd Isgrove), Sam Vokes (76 Simon Church), Tom Lawrence (62 Jonathan Williams).   Manager: Chris Coleman

NORTHERN IRELAND: Michael McGovern, Conor McLaughlin (81 Aaron Hughes), Gareth McAuley, Jonny Evans (73 Daniel Lafferty), Craig Cathcart, Oliver Norwood, Steven Davis, Stuart Dallas (90+2 Shane Ferguson), Paddy McNair (73 Paul Paton), Conor Washington (46 Jamie Ward), Kyle Lafferty (81 Billy McKay).   Manager: Michael O'Neill

Goals: Simon Church (89 pen) / Craig Cathcart (60)

605. 28.03.2016

NORTHERN IRELAND v SLOVENIA 1-0 (1-0)

Windsor Park, Belfast

Referee: Kristo Tohver (Estonia)   Attendance: 13,500

NORTHERN IRELAND: Roy Carroll, Michael Smith (71 Conor McLaughlin), Gareth McAuley (46 Aaron Hughes), Jonny Evans, Craig Cathcart, Shane Ferguson (60 Stuart Dallas), Oliver Norwood, Steven Davis, Jamie Ward (60 Kyle Lafferty), Paddy McNair (79 Niall McGinn), Conor Washington (70 Josh Magennis).   Manager: Michael O'Neill

SLOVENIA: Jan Oblak, Nejc Skubic (61 Petar Stojanovic), Miral Samardzic, Bojan Jokic, Bostjan Cesar (80 Aljaz Struna), Jasmin Kurtic (46 Blaz Vrhovec), Rene Krhin, Josip Ilicic (46 Milivoje Novakovic), Valter Birsa, Benjamin Verbic (62 Andraz Kirm), Roman Bezjak (75 Matic Crnic).
Manager: Srecko Katanec

Goal: Conor Washington (41)

Milivoje Novakovic missed a penalty kick (66)

606. 27.05.2016

NORTHERN IRELAND v BELARUS 3-0 (2-0)

Windsor Park, Belfast

Referee: Martin Atkinson (England)   Attendance: 14,229

NORTHERN IRELAND: Roy Carroll (46 Allan Mannus), Conor McLaughlin, Jonny Evans, Craig Cathcart, Corry Evans (74 Niall McGinn), Steven Davis (46 Oliver Norwood), Stuart Dallas (74 Aaron Hughes), Paddy McNair, Chris Baird, Conor Washington (61 Jamie Ward), Kyle Lafferty (61 Will Grigg).
Manager: Michael O'Neill

BELARUS: Andrey Gorbunov, Igor Shitov (78 Sergey Politsevich), Aleksandr Martinovich, Egor Filipenko (38 Mikhail Sivakov), Maksim Volodko, Igor Stasevich (89 Pavel Nekhaychik), Sergey Krivets (60 Aliaksandr Hleb), Nikita Korzun, Sergey Kislyak, Mikhail Gordeychuk, Nikolai Yanush (72 Denis Polyakov).   Manager: Aleksandr Khatskevich

Goals: Kyle Lafferty (6), Conor Washington (44), Will Grigg (88)

607. 04.06.2016

SLOVAKIA v NORTHERN IRELAND 0-0

Stadión Antona Malatinského, Trnava

Referee: Radu Petrescu (Romania)   Attendance: 18,111

SLOVAKIA: Matús Kozácik, Martin Skrtel, Peter Pekarík, Ján Durica, Dusan Svento, Vladimír Weiss, Juraj Kucka (84 Adam Nemec), Patrik Hrosovsky, Marek Hamsík, Michal Duris (65 Ondrej Duda), Róbert Mak (65 Miroslav Stoch).
Manager: Ján Kozák

NORTHERN IRELAND: Michael McGovern, Gareth McAuley, Jonny Evans, Craig Cathcart (30 Aaron Hughes), Shane Ferguson (86 Lee Hodson), Steven Davis, Oliver Norwood (83 Corry Evans), Paddy McNair (90+1 Conor McLaughlin), Chris Baird, Jamie Ward (46 Josh Magennis), Kyle Lafferty (55 Conor Washington).
Manager: Michael O'Neill

608. 12.06.2016   15th European Champs Group C

POLAND v NORTHERN IRELAND 1-0 (0-0)

Allianz Riviera, Nice (France)

Referee: Ovidiu Hategan (Romania)   Attendance: 33.742

POLAND: Wojciech Szczesny, Michal Pazdan, Artur Jedrzejczyk, Kamil Glik, Lukasz Piszczek, Krzysztof Maczynski (78 Tomasz Jodlowiec), Grzegorz Krychowiak, Jakub Blaszczykowski (80 Kamil Grosicki), Bartosz Kapustka (88 Slawomir Peszko), Arkadiusz Milik, Robert Lewandowski.
Manager: Adam Nawalka

NORTHERN IRELAND: Michael McGovern, Conor McLaughlin, Shane Ferguson (66 Conor Washington), Gareth McAuley, Jonny Evans, Craig Cathcart, Chris Baird (76 Jamie Ward), Steven Davis, Oliver Norwood, Paddy McNair (46 Stuart Dallas), Kyle Lafferty.   Manager: Michael O'Neill

Goal: Arkadiusz Milik (51)

609. 16.06.2016   15th European Champs Group C
UKRAINE v NORTHERN IRELAND 0-2 (0-0)
Parc Olympique Lyonnais, Décines-Charpieu (France)
Referee: Pavel Královec (Czech Republic)   Attendance: 51,043
UKRAINE: Andriy Pyatov, Evgen Khacheridi, Vyacheslav Shevchuk, Artem Fedetskiy, Yaroslav Rakitskiy, Taras Stepanenko, Viktor Kovalenko (83 Oleksandr Zinchenko), Sergiy Sydorchuk (76 Denys Garmash), Andriy Yarmolenko, Yevhen Konoplyanka, Evgen Seleznyov (71 Roman Zozulya).   Manager: Mikhail Fomenko
NORTHERN IRELAND: Michael McGovern, Gareth McAuley, Jonny Evans, Aaron Hughes, Craig Cathcart, Steven Davis, Corry Evans (90+3 Paddy McNair), Stuart Dallas, Oliver Norwood, Conor Washington (84 Josh Magennis), Jamie Ward (69 Niall McGinn).   Manager: Michael O'Neill
Goals: Gareth McAuley (49), Niall McGinn (90+6)

610. 21.06.2016   15th European Champs Group C
NORTHERN IRELAND v GERMANY 0-1 (0-1)
Parc des Princes, Paris
Referee: Clément Turpin (France)   Attendance: 44.125
NORTHERN IRELAND: Michael McGovern, Gareth McAuley, Jonny Evans, Aaron Hughes, Craig Cathcart, Steven Davis, Corry Evans (84 Niall McGinn), Stuart Dallas, Oliver Norwood, Conor Washington (59 Kyle Lafferty), Jamie Ward (70 Josh Magennis).   Manager: Michael O'Neill
GERMANY: Manuel Neuer, Jonas Hector, Mats Hummels, Jérôme Boateng (76 Benedikt Höwedes), Sami Khedira (69 Bastian Schweinsteiger), Mesut Özil, Thomas Müller, Toni Kroos, Joshua Kimmich, Mario Götze (55 André Schürrle), Mario Gómez.   Manager: Joachim Löw
Goal: Mario Gómez (30)

611. 25.06.2016   15th Euro Champs Round of 16
WALES v NORTHERN IRELAND 1-0 (0-0)
Parc des Princes, Paris (France)
Referee: Martin Atkinson (England)   Attendance: 44,342
WALES: Wayne Hennessey, Chris Gunter, Neil Taylor, Ben Davies, James Chester, Ashley Williams, Joe Allen, Aaron Ramsey, Joe Ledley (63 Jonathan Williams), Gareth Bale, Sam Vokes (55 Hal Robson-Kanu).   Manager: Chris Coleman
NORTHERN IRELAND: Michael McGovern, Gareth McAuley (84 Josh Magennis), Jonny Evans, Aaron Hughes, Craig Cathcart, Steven Davis, Corry Evans, Stuart Dallas, Oliver Norwood (79 Niall McGinn), Kyle Lafferty, Jamie Ward (69 Conor Washington).   Manager: Michael O'Neill
Goal: Gareth McAuley (75 og)

612. 04.09.2016   21st World Cup Qualifier
CZECH REPUBLIC v NORTHERN IRELAND 0-0
Generali Arena, Praha
Referee: Anasthasios Sidiropoulos (Greece)   Att: 10,731
CZECH REPUBLIC: Tomás Vaclík, Marek Suchy, Michal Kadlec, Pavel Kaderábek, David Pavelka, Filip Novák, Ladislav Krejcí, Vladimír Darida, Milan Skoda (68 Tomás Necid), Jirí Skalák (77 Jan Kopic), Václav Kadlec (83 Matej Vydra).   Manager: Karel Jarolím
NORTHERN IRELAND: Michael McGovern, Conor McLaughlin, Gareth McAuley, Jonny Evans, Oliver Norwood, Shane Ferguson (66 Lee Hodson), Steven Davis, Stuart Dallas, Paddy McNair, Jamie Ward (74 Niall McGinn), Kyle Lafferty (59 Josh Magennis).   Manager: Michael O'Neill

613. 08.10.2016   21st World Cup Qualifier
NORTHERN IRELAND v SAN MARINO 4-0 (1-0)
Windsor Park, Belfast
Referee: István Kovács (Romania)   Attendance: 18,234
NORTHERN IRELAND: Michael McGovern, Conor McLaughlin (77 Paddy McNair), Gareth McAuley, Jonny Evans, Oliver Norwood, Niall McGinn, Shane Ferguson, Steven Davis, Stuart Dallas (65 Conor Washington), Jamie Ward, Josh Magennis (72 Kyle Lafferty).   Manager: Michael O'Neill
SAN MARINO: Aldo Simoncini, Fabio Vitaioli, Davide Simoncini, Alessandro Della Valle, Marco Berardi, Luca Tosi, Mirko Palazzi, Matteo Coppini (71 Enrico Golinucci), Matteo Vitaioli, Mattia Stefanelli (88 Tommaso Zafferani), José Adolfo Hirsch (56 Davide Cesarini).   Manager: Pierangelo Manzaroli
Sent off: Mirko Palazzi (49)
Goals: Steven Davis (26 pen), Kyle Lafferty (79, 90+4), Jamie Ward (85)

614. 11.10.2016   21st World Cup Qualifier
GERMANY v NORTHERN IRELAND 2-0 (2-0)
HDI-Arena, Hannover
Referee: Paolo Tagliavento (Italy)   Attendance: 42,132
GERMANY: Manuel Neuer, Joshua Kimmich, Mats Hummels, Jonas Hector (81 Kevin Volland), Jérôme Boateng (69 Shkodran Mustafi), Mesut Özil (46 Ilkay Gündogan), Toni Kroos, Sami Khedira, Mario Götze, Julian Draxler, Thomas Müller.   Manager: Joachim Löw
NORTHERN IRELAND: Michael McGovern, Gareth McAuley, Aaron Hughes, Lee Hodson, Jonny Evans, Oliver Norwood (73 Paddy McNair), Shane Ferguson, Corry Evans, Steven Davis, Jamie Ward (61 Niall McGinn), Josh Magennis (76 Kyle Lafferty).   Manager: Michael O'Neill
Goals: Julian Draxler (13), Sami Khedira (17)

615. 11.11.2016   21st World Cup Qualifier
NORTHERN IRELAND v AZERBAIJAN 4-0 (2-0)
Windsor Park, Belfast

Referee: Clément Turpin (France)   Attendance: 18,404

NORTHERN IRELAND: Michael McGovern, Jonny Evans, Conor McLaughlin, Gareth McAuley, Shane Ferguson (73 Niall McGinn), Corry Evans (81 Paddy McNair), Steven Davis, Chris Brunt, Oliver Norwood, Josh Magennis, Kyle Lafferty (62 Will Grigg).   Manager: Michael O'Neill

AZERBAIJAN: Kamran Agayev, Maksim Medvedev, Badavi Huseynov, Qara Qarayev, Magomed Mirzabekov, Afran Ismayilov, Arif Dasdemirov, Rahid Amirguliyev, Emin Makhmudov (70 Dimitrij Nazarov), Ruslan Qurbanov (75 Agabala Ramazanov), Ramil Sheydayev (46 Deniz Yilmaz).   Manager: Robert Prosinecki

Goals: Kyle Lafferty (27), Gareth McAuley (40), Conor McLaughlin (66), Chris Brunt (83)

616. 15.11.2016
NORTHERN IRELAND v CROATIA 0-3 (0-2)
Windsor Park, Belfast

Referee: Mark Clattenburg   Attendance: 17,000

NORTHERN IRELAND: Alan Mannus, Gareth McAuley (46 Ryan McGivern), Lee Hodson, Jonny Evans, Matthew Lund (46 Steven Davis), Chris Brunt (46 Conor McLaughlin), Oliver Norwood, Niall McGinn (62 Paul Paton), Paddy McNair, Josh Magennis (56 Kyle Lafferty), Liam Boyce (68 Will Grigg).   Manager: Michael O'Neill

CROATIA: Lovre Kalinic (82 Ivan Vargic), Matej Mitrovic, Marin Leovac, Tin Jedvaj, Domagoj Vida (59 Sime Vrsaljko), Filip Bradaric, Milan Badelj (52 Marcelo Brozovic), Marko Rog (87 Josip Pivaric), Mario Mandzukic (72 Ante Coric), Andrej Kramaric, Duje Cop.   Manager: Ante Cacic

Goals: Mario Mandzukic (9), Duje Cop (35), Andrej Kramaric (68)

617. 26.03.2017   21st World Cup Qualifier
NORTHERN IRELAND v NORWAY 2-0 (2-0)
Windsor Park, Belfast

Referee: Hüseyin Göçek (Turkey)   Attendance: 18,161

NORTHERN IRELAND: Michael McGovern, Conor McLaughlin, Gareth McAuley, Jonny Evans, Craig Cathcart, Oliver Norwood, Steven Davis, Stuart Dallas (87 Matthew Lund), Chris Brunt, Conor Washington (84 Kyle Lafferty), Jamie Ward (79 Niall McGinn).   Manager: Michael O'Neill

NORWAY: Rune Jarstein, Gustav Valsvik, Jørgen Skjelvik, Håvard Nordtveit, Even Hovland, Omar Elabdellaoui, Tarik Elyounoussi (53 Mats Møller Dæhli), Stefan Johansen (74 Sander Berge), Alexander Søderlund (63 Adama Diomandé), Joshua King, Mohamed Elyounoussi.   Manager: Lars Lagerbäck

Goals: Jamie Ward (2), Conor Washington (32)

618. 02.06.2017
NORTHERN IRELAND v NEW ZEALAND 1-0 (1-0)
Windsor Park, Belfast

Referee: Laurent Kopriwa (Luxembourg)   Att: 16,185

NORTHERN IRELAND: Michael McGovern (84 Roy Carroll), Conor McLaughlin, Aaron Hughes, Tom Flanagan, Jonny Evans, Oliver Norwood, Matthew Lund (46 Steven Davis), Stuart Dallas (74 Paul Paton), Chris Brunt (46 Shane Ferguson), Josh Magennis (83 Shay McCartan), Liam Boyce (46 Kyle Lafferty).   Manager: Michael O'Neill

NEW ZEALAND: Stefan Marinovic, Tommy Smith, Andrew Durante, Thomas Doyle (72 Deklan Wynne), Kip Colvey (63 Kosta Barbarouses), Michael Boxall, Ryan Thomas (79 Shane Smeltz), Marco Rojas (63 Monty Patterson), Clayton Lewis (46 Bill Tuiloma), Chris Wood, Michael McGlinchey.   Manager: Anthony Hudson

Goal: Liam Boyce (6)

619. 10.06.2017   21st World Cup Qualifier
AZERBAIJAN v NORTHERN IRELAND 0-1 (0-0)
Tofiq Bakhramov adina Respublika stadionu, Baku

Referee: Javier Estrada Fernández (Spain)   Att: 27,978

AZERBAIJAN: Kamran Agayev, Rashad Sadygov, Pavlo Pashaev, Maksim Medvedev, Badavi Huseynov, Qara Qarayev, Afran Ismayilov (84 Rahid Amirguliyev), RICHARD Almeida de Oliveira, Dimitrij Nazarov (77 Namig Alasgarov), Javid Huseynov, Ramil Sheydayev (90 Araz Abdullayev).   Manager: Robert Prosinecki

NORTHERN IRELAND: Michael McGovern, Conor McLaughlin, Gareth McAuley (25 Niall McGinn, 86 Lee Hodson), Aaron Hughes, Jonny Evans, Oliver Norwood, Steven Davis, Stuart Dallas, Chris Brunt, Josh Magennis, Liam Boyce (77 Kyle Lafferty).   Manager: Michael O'Neill

Goal: Stuart Dallas (90+2)

620. 01.09.2017   21st World Cup Qualifier
SAN MARINO v NORTHERN IRELAND 0-3 (0-0)
Stadio Olimpico, Serravalle

Referee: Enea Jorgji (Albania)   Attendance: 2,544

SAN MARINO: Aldo Simoncini, Andrea Grandoni, Juri Biordi (67 Fabio Vitaioli), Marco Bernardi, Davide Simoncini (76 Alex Gasperoni), Michele Cervellini, Giovanni Bonini, Michael Battistini, Mirko Palazzi, Filippo Berardi (81 Alessandro Golinucci), Danilo Rinaldi.   Manager: Pierangelo Manzaroli

NORTHERN IRELAND: Michael McGovern, Aaron Hughes, Jonny Evans, Conor McLaughlin, Steven Davis, Stuart Dallas (78 Niall McGinn), Chris Brunt, Oliver Norwood, Josh Magennis, Kyle Lafferty (61 Shane Ferguson), Conor Washington (78 Corry Evans).   Manager: Michael O'Neill

Goals: Josh Magennis (71, 75), Steven Davis (78 pen)

621.   04.09.2017   21st World Cup Qualifier
NORTHERN IRELAND
v CZECH REPUBLIC 2-0 (2-0)
Windsor Park, Belfast

Referee: Daniele Orsato (Italy)   Attendance: 18,167

NORTHERN IRELAND: Michael McGovern, Conor McLaughlin, Aaron Hughes, Jonny Evans, Chris Brunt, Oliver Norwood, Corry Evans, Steven Davis, Stuart Dallas (74 Kyle Lafferty), Conor Washington (58 Lee Hodson), Josh Magennis (84 Shane Ferguson).   Manager: Michael O'Neill

CZECH REPUBLIC: Tomás Vaclík, Jan Boril, Marek Suchy, Tomás Kalas, Theodor Gebre Selassie, Filip Novák (66 Borek Dockal), Jakub Jankto (55 Josef Husbauer), Vladimír Darida, Tomás Soucek, Ladislav Krejcí (55 Jan Kliment), Michal Krmencík.   Manager: Karel Jarolím

Goals: Jonny Evans (28), Chris Brunt (41)

622.   05.10.2017   21st World Cup Qualifier
NORTHERN IRELAND v GERMANY 1-3 (0-2)
Windsor Park, Belfast

Referee: Danny Makkelie (Netherlands)   Att: 18,104

NORTHERN IRELAND: Michael McGovern, Conor McLaughlin, Gareth McAuley, Lee Hodson (46 Stuart Dallas), Jonny Evans, Oliver Norwood, Corry Evans (80 George Saville), Steven Davis, Chris Brunt, Josh Magennis, Kyle Lafferty (69 Conor Washington).   Manager: Michael O'Neill

GERMANY: Marc-André ter Stegen, Sebastian Rudy, Marvin Plattenhardt, Joshua Kimmich, Mats Hummels, Jérôme Boateng, Toni Kroos, Leon Goretzka (66 Emre Can), Julian Draxler (72 Leroy Sané), Sandro Wagner, Thomas Müller (83 Lars Stindl).   Manager: Joachim Löw

Goals: Josh Magennis (90+3) / Sebastian Rudy (2), Sandro Wagner (21), Joshua Kimmich (86)

623.   08.10.2017   21st World Cup Qualifier
NORWAY v NORTHERN IRELAND 1-0 (0-0)
Ullevaal Stadion, Oslo

Referee: Sergey Boyko (Ukraine)   Attendance: 10,244

NORWAY: Ørjan Nyland, Tore Reginiussen, Håvard Nordtveit, Birger Meling, Jonas Svensson, Markus Henriksen (83 Ole Selnæs), Sander Berge, Stefan Johansen (88 Martin Linnes), Mohamed Elyounoussi (71 Tarik Elyounoussi), Alexander Sørloth, Alexander Søderlund.
Manager: Lars Lagerbäck

NORTHERN IRELAND: Michael McGovern, Conor McLaughlin, Gareth McAuley, Jonny Evans, Oliver Norwood (46 George Saville), Corry Evans (79 Shane Ferguson), Steven Davis, Stuart Dallas, Chris Brunt, Conor Washington (69 Kyle Lafferty), Josh Magennis.   Manager: Michael O'Neill

Goal: Chris Brunt (71 og)

624. 09.11.2017 21st World Cup Qualifier Play-off
NORTHERN IRELAND
           v SWITZERLAND 0-1 (0-0)
Windsor Park, Belfast

Referee: Ovidiu Hategan (Romania)   Attendance: 18,269

NORTHERN IRELAND: Michael McGovern, Conor McLaughlin, Gareth McAuley, Jonny Evans, Oliver Norwood, Corry Evans (65 George Saville), Steven Davis, Stuart Dallas (52 Jamie Ward), Chris Brunt, Josh Magennis, Kyle Lafferty (78 Conor Washington).   Manager: Michael O'Neill

SWITZERLAND: Yann Sommer, Fabian Schär, Ricardo Rodríguez, Stephan Lichtsteiner, Manuel Akanji, Steven Zuber (87 Admir Mehmedi), Denis Zakaria, Granit Xhaka, Xherdan Shaqiri, Blerim Dzemaili (83 Fabian Frei), Haris Seferovic (77 Breel Embolo).   Manager: Vladimir Petkovic

Goal: Ricardo Rodríguez (58 pen)

625. 12.11.2017 21st World Cup Qualifier Play-off
SWITZERLAND v NORTHERN IRELAND 0-0
St. Jakob-Park, Basel

Referee: Felix Brych (Germany)   Attendance: 36,210

SWITZERLAND: Yann Sommer, Fabian Schär, Ricardo Rodríguez, Stephan Lichtsteiner, Manuel Akanji, Steven Zuber, Denis Zakaria, Granit Xhaka, Xherdan Shaqiri (80 Remo Freuler), Blerim Dzemaili (61 Admir Mehmedi), Haris Seferovic (86 Breel Embolo).   Manager: Vladimir Petkovic

NORTHERN IRELAND: Michael McGovern, George Saville, Gareth McAuley, Aaron Hughes, Jonny Evans, Oliver Norwood (75 Josh Magennis), Steven Davis, Stuart Dallas, Chris Brunt, Conor Washington (82 Paddy McNair), Jamie Ward (74 Jordan Jones).   Manager: Michael O'Neill

626.   24.03.2018
NORTHERN IRELAND v SOUTH KOREA 2-1 (1-1)
Windsor Park, Belfast

Referee: Bobby Madden (Scotland)   Attendance: 18,103

NORTHERN IRELAND: Trevor Carson, Jonny Evans (68 Craig Cathcart), Gareth McAuley, Aaron Hughes (19 Conor McLaughlin), Jamal Lewis, Corry Evans (62 Liam Boyce), George Saville, Oliver Norwood (71 Paddy McNair), Jamie Ward (62 Conor Washington), Josh Magennis, Jordan Jones (82 Paul Smyth).   Manager: Michael O'Neill

SOUTH KOREA: Kim Seung-Gyu, Park Joo-Ho (68 Lee Chang-Min), Kim Jin-Su (35 Kim Min-Woo), Lee Yong, Jang Hyun-Soo, Kim Min-Jae, Ki Sung-Yeung (67 Jung Woo-Young), Lee Jae-Sung (II), Kim Shin-Wook, Son Heung-Min (75 Yeom Ki-Hun), Kwon Chang-Hoon (62 Hwang Hee-Chan).   Manager: Shin Tae-Yong

Goals: Kim Min-Jae (20 og), Paul Smyth (86) / Kwon Chang-Hoon (7)

627. 29.05.2018
PANAMA v NORTHERN IRELAND 0-0
Estadio Rommel Fernández Gutiérrez, Panama City

Referee: HENRY Alberto BEJARANO Matarrita (Costa Rica)
Attendance: 26,000

PANAMA: JOSÉ De Jesús CALDERÓN Frías, ADOLFO Abdiel MACHADO, FELIPE Abdiel BALOY Ramírez (75 ROMÁN Aureliano TORRES Morcillo), LUIS Carlos OVALLE Victoria, FIDEL ESCOBAR Mendieta, GABRIEL Enrique GÓMEZ Girón (46 VALENTIN Enrique PIMENTEL Armuelles), ANÍBAL Cesis GODOY (46 RICARDO Guardia ÁVILA), ARMANDO Enrique COOPER Whitaker (46 MIGUEL Elias CAMARGO Cañizalez), EDGAR Yoel BÁRCENAS Herrera, JOSÉ Luis RODRÍGUEZ Francis (59 ISMAEL DÍAZ De León), LUIS Carlos TEJADA Hansell (46 BLAS Antonio Miguel PÉREZ Ortega).   Manager: HERNÁN Darío GÓMEZ Jaramillo

NORTHERN IRELAND: Trevor Carson (46 Bailey Peacock-Farrell), Aaron Hughes, Gareth McAuley, Jonny Evans, Craig Cathcart, Corry Evans (71 Jordan Thompson), Shane Ferguson (72 Ryan McLaughlin), Stuart Dallas (59 Lee Hodson), Paddy McNair, Josh Magennis (88 Shayne Lavery), Liam Boyce (72 Paul Smyth).   Manager: Michael O'Neill

628. 03.06.2018
COSTA RICA v NORTHERN IRELAND 3-0 (1-0)
Estadio Nacional de Costa Rica, San José

Referee: Fernando Guerrero Ramírez (Mexico)
Attendance: 35,100

COSTA RICA: KEYLOR Antonio NAVAS Gamboa (35' LEONEL Gerardo MOREIRA Ledezma), BRYAN Josué OVIEDO Jiménez, ÓSCAR Esau DUARTE Gaitán (46 FRANCISCO Javier CALVO Quesada), CRISTIAN Esteban GAMBOA Luna (64 IAN Rey SMITH Quiros), GIANCARLO GONZÁLEZ Castro (73 KENDALL Jamaal WASTON Manley), JOHNNY ACOSTA Zamora, CELSO BORGES Mora (64 YELTSIN Ignacio TEJEDA Valverde), DAVID Alberto GUZMÁN Pérez, JOHAN Alberto VENEGAS Ulloa (70 RONALD Alberto MATARRITA Ulate), JOEL Nathaniel CAMPBELL Samuels, DANIEL COLINDRES Solera.
Manager: ÓSCAR Antonio RAMÍREZ Hernández

NORTHERN IRELAND: Trevor Carson (73 Conor Hazard), Aaron Hughes, Gareth McAuley, Jonny Evans, Stuart Dallas, Lee Hodson (60 Conor McLaughlin), Craig Cathcart (73 Luke McCullough), Paddy McNair, Liam Boyce (39 Shay McCartan), Josh Magennis (60 Ryan McLaughlin), Corry Evans (85 Jordan Thompson).   Manager: Michael O'Neill

Goals: JOHAN Alberto VENEGAS Ulloa (30), JOEL Nathaniel CAMPBELL Samuels (46), FRANCISCO Javier CALVO Quesada (66)

629. 08.09.2018   UEFA Nations League – Group B3
**NORTHERN IRELAND
        v BOSNIA & HERZEGOVINA 1-2** (0-1)
Windsor Park, Belfast

Referee: Pavel Královec (Czech Republic)   Att: 16,942

NORTHERN IRELAND: Bailey Peacock-Farrell, Jonny Evans, Craig Cathcart, Conor McLaughlin (70 Liam Boyce), Steve Davis, Niall McGinn (76 Jamie Ward), Oliver Norwood, Stuart Dallas, George Saville, Jamal Lewis, Kyle Lafferty (69 Will Grigg).   Manager: Michael O'Neill

BOSNIA & HERZEGOVINA: Ibrahim Sehic, Toni Sunjic, Ervin Zukanovic, Eldar Civic (76 Goran Zakaric), Miralem Pjanic (83 Riad Bajic), Gojko Cimirot, Edin Visca, Muhamed Besic, Haris Duljevic, Elvis Saric (67 Rade Krunic), Edin Dzeko.   Manager: Robert Prosinecki

Goals: Will Grigg (90+3) /
Haris Duljevic (36), Elvis Saric (64)

630. 11.09.2018
NORTHERN IRELAND v ISRAEL 3-0 (2-0)
Windsor Park, Belfast

Referee: Bas Nijhuis (Netherlands)   Attendance: 12,913

NORTHERN IRELAND: Trevor Carson (46 Michael McGovern), Jonny Evans, Craig Cathcart, Paddy McNair, Steve Davis, Corry Evans (46 Oliver Norwood), Stuart Dallas (77 Shane Ferguson), George Saville (71 Michael Smith), Jordan Jones (65 Gavin Whyte), Jamal Lewis, Will Grigg (65 Conor Washington).   Manager: Michael O'Neill

ISRAEL: Guy Haimov, Taleb Twatiha (40 Samuel Scheimann), Eytan Tibi, Eli Dasa (65 Ben Bitton), Ayad Habashi (46 Nisso Kapiloto), Bibras Natkho, Shiran Yeini, Dor Micha (59 Alon Turgeman), Dor Peretz, Tomer Hemed (59 Dia Seba), Moanes Dabour (75 Dan Leon Glazer).
Manager: Andreas Herzog

Goals: Steve Davis (13), Stuart Dallas (41), Gavin Whyte (67)

631. 12.10.2018   UEFA Nations League – Group B3
AUSTRIA v NORTHERN IRELAND 1-0 (0-0)
Ernst Happel Stadion, Vienna

Referee: Georgi Kabakov (Bulgaria)   Attendance: 22,300

AUSTRIA: Heinz Lindner, Andreas Ulmer, Sebastian Prödl, Stefan Lainer, Martin Hinteregger, Stefan Ilsanker, Marcel Sabitzer (75 Alessandro Schöpf), Peter Zulj, Marko Arnautovic, Guido Burgstaller (83 Florian Kainz), Valentino Lazaro (90+1 Aleksandar Dragovic).   Manager: Franco Foda

NORTHERN IRELAND: Bailey Peacock-Farrell, Jonny Evans, Craig Cathcart, Steve Davis, Shane Ferguson (56 Corry Evans), Oliver Norwood, Stuart Dallas, Paddy McNair, George Saville (77 Kyle Vassell), Jamal Lewis, Josh Magennis (79 Will Grigg).   Manager: Michael O'Neill

Goal: Marko Arnautovic (71)

632. 15.10.2018   UEFA Nations League – Group B3
BOSNIA & HERZEGOVINA
          v NORTHERN IRELAND 2-0 (1-0)
Stadion Grbavica, Sarajevo

Referee: Mattias Gestranius (Finland)   Attendance: 11,050

BOSNIA & HERZEGOVINA: Ibrahim Sehic, Toni Sunjic, Ervin Zukanovic, Ognjen Vranjes, Eldar Civic, Miralem Pjanic, Edin Visca (88 Deni Milosevic), Haris Duljevic (75 Goran Zakaric), Elvis Saric, Edin Dzeko, Muhamed Besic (90 Gojko Cimirot).   Manager: Robert Prosinecki

NORTHERN IRELAND: Bailey Peacock-Farrell, Jonny Evans, Craig Cathcart, Steve Davis, Corry Evans, Oliver Norwood (58 Gavin Whyte), Stuart Dallas, Paddy McNair (71 Kyle Vassell), Jamal Lewis, George Saville, Liam Boyce (80 Josh Magennis).   Manager: Michael O'Neill

Goals: Edin Dzeko (27, 73)

633. 15.11.2018
REPUBLIC OF IRELAND
          v NORTHERN IRELAND 0-0
Aviva Stadium, Dublin

Referee: Slavko Vincic (Slovenia)   Attendance: 31,241

REPUBLIC OF IRELAND: Darren Randolph, Séamus Coleman, Shane Duffy, John Egan, Darragh Lenihan (84 Cyrus Christie), Glenn Whelan (36 Conor Hourihane), James McClean (66 Enda Stevens), Bobbie Brady, Jeff Hendrick, Callum O'Dowda (46 Ronas Curtis), Callum Robinson (66 Seán Maguire, 80 Scott Hogan).   Manager: Martin O'Neill

NORTHERN IRELAND: Bailey Peacock-Farrell, Jonny Evans, Craig Cathcart, Michael Smith (74 Jamie Ward), Steve Davis, Corry Evans (65 Paddy McNair), George Saville, Stuart Dallas, Jamal Lewis, Liam Boyce (71 Kyle Lafferty), Gavin Whyte (61 Jordan Jones).   Manager: Michael O'Neill

634. 18.11.2018   UEFA Nations League – Group B3
NORTHERN IRELAND v AUSTRIA 1-2 (0-0)
Windsor Park, Belfast

Referee: Jonathan Lardot (Belgium)   Attendance: 17,895

NORTHERN IRELAND: Trevor Carson, Gareth McAuley, Jonny Evans, Michael Smith, Steve Davis, Niall McGinn (74 Gavin Whyte), Corry Evans (88 Paddy McNair), George Saville, Jordan Jones, Stuart Dallas, Liam Boyce (74 Kyle Lafferty).   Manager: Michael O'Neill

AUSTRIA: Heinz Lindner, Andreas Ulmer, Alexandar Dragovic, David Alaba, Stefan Lainer, Martin Hinteregger, Julian Baumgartlinger, Stefan Ilsanker (46 Peter Zulj), Michael Gregoritsch (71 Marko Arnautovic), Valentino Lazaro, Xaver Schlager.   Manager: Franco Foda

Goals: Corry Evans (57) /
Xaver Schlager (49), Valentino Lazaro (90+3)

635. 21.03.2019   16th European Champs Qualifiers
NORTHERN IRELAND v ESTONIA 2-0 (0-0)
Windsor Park, Belfast

Referee: Ivan Bebek (Croatia)   Attendance: 18,176

NORTHERN IRELAND: Bailey Peacock-Farrell, Jonny Evans, Craig Cathcart, Steve Davis, Niall McGinn (85 Conor McLaughlin), Stuart Dallas, Paddy McNair, George Saville, Jordan Jones (81 Shane Ferguson), Jamal Lewis, Kyle Lafferty (76 Josh Magennis).   Manager: Michael O'Neill

ESTONIA: Sergei Lepmets, Gert Kams, Joonas Tamm, Nikita Baranov, Karol Mets, Artur Pikk, Madis Vihmann, Artjom Dmitrijev (85 Rauno Sappinen), Mattias Käit, Henri Anier (76 Sergei Zenjov), Henrik Ojamaa (68 Konstantin Vassiljev).   Manager: Martin Reim

Goals: Niall McGinn (56), Steve Davis (75 pen)

636. 24.03.2019   16th European Champs Qualifiers
NORTHERN IRELAND v BELARUS 2-1 (1-1)
Windsor Park, Belfast

Referee: Pawel Raczkowski (Poland)   Attendance: 18,188

NORTHERN IRELAND: Bailey Peacock-Farrell, Jonny Evans, Craig Cathcart, Steve Davis, Niall McGinn (68 Josh Magennis), Stuart Dallas, Paddy McNair, George Saville, Jordan Jones (85 Shane Ferguson), Jamal Lewis, Kyle Lafferty (79 Liam Boyce).   Manager: Michael O'Neill

BELARUS: Andrey Klimovich, Mikhail Sivakov, Igor Shitov (73 Denis Polyakov), Aleksandr Martinovich, Maksim Volodko, Aliaksandr Hleb (66 Anton Putilo), Igor Stasevich, Stanislav Dragun, Ivan Maevski, Pavel Savitskiy (85 Pavel Nekhaychik), Denis Laptev.   Manager: Igor Kriushenko

Goals: Jonny Evans (30), Josh Magennis (87) /
Igor Stasevich (33)

637. 08.06.2019   16th European Champs Qualifiers
ESTONIA v NORTHERN IRELAND 1-2 (1-0)
A. Le Coq Arena, Tallinn

Referee: FÁBIO José Costa VERÍSSIMO (Portugal)
Attendance: 8,378

ESTONIA: Sergei Lepmets, Taijo Teniste (85 Gert Kams), Karol Mets, Artur Pikk, Madis Vihmann, Artjom Dmitrijev, Konstantin Vassiljev, Vlasiy Sinyavskiy, Mattias Käit (85 Joonas Tamm), Sergei Zenjov, Rauno Sappinen (61 Erik Sorga).   Manager: Martin Reim

NORTHERN IRELAND: Bailey Peacock-Farrell, Jonny Evans, Craig Cathcart, Michael Smith (64 Jordan Jones), Steve Davis, Stuart Dallas, Paddy McNair, Jamal Lewis, George Saville (69 Josh Magennis), Liam Boyce (46 Conor Washington), Gavin Whyte.   Manager: Michael O'Neill

Goals: Konstantin Vassiljev (25) /
Conor Washington (77), Josh Magennis (80)

638.　11.06.2019　16th European Champs Qualifiers
BELARUS v NORTHERN IRELAND 0-1 (0-0)

Borisov Arena, Borisov

Referee: Harald Lechner (Austria)　Attendance: 5,250

BELARUS: Alyaksandr Hutor, Denis Polyakov, Igor Shitov (72 Aleh Veratsila), Aleksandr Martinovich, Nikita Naumov, Pavel Nekhaychik, Igor Stasevich, Ivan Maevski, Nikita Korzun (46 Sergey Kislyak), Yuri Kovalev, Yevgeniy Shikavka (58 Denis Laptev).　Manager: Igor Kriushenko

NORTHERN IRELAND: Bailey Peacock-Farrell, Jonny Evans, Craig Cathcart, Michael Smith, Steve Davis, Corry Evans (69 George Saville), Paddy McNair, Jordan Jones, Jamal Lewis, Josh Magennis (56 Stuart Dallas), Conor Washington (72 Kyle Lafferty).　Manager: Michael O'Neill

Goal: Paddy McNair (86)

639.　05.09.2019
NORTHERN IRELAND v LUXEMBOURG 1-0 (1-0)

Windsor Park, Belfast

Referee: Bryn Markham-Jones (Wales)　Attendance: 14,108

NORTHERN IRELAND: Bailey Peacock-Farrell (67 Michael McGovern), Tom Flanagan, Conor McLaughlin, Shane Ferguson (67 Liam Donnelly), George Saville (60 Alfie Mccalmont), Jordan Thompson (88 Steve Davis), Cairon Brown, Kyle Lafferty (59 Shane Lavery), Josh Magennis, Gavin Whyte (88 Ethan Galbraith).　Manager: Michael O'Neill

LUXEMBOURG: Anthony Moris (46 Ralph Schon), Lars Gerson, Kevin Malget (46 Tim Hall), Laurent Jans, Dirk Carlson, Olivier Thill (85 Florian Bohnert), Danel Sinani (74 Daniel Alves da Mota), Vincent Thill, Maurice Deville (60 David Turpel), Gerson Rodrigues, Leandro Barreiro (73 Chris Philipps).　Manager: Luc Holtz

Goal: Kevin Malget (37 og)

640.　09.09.2019　16th European Champs Qualifiers
NORTHERN IRELAND v GERMANY 0-2 (0-0)

Windsor Park, Belfast

Referee: Daniele Orsato (Italy)　Attendance: 18,236

NORTHERN IRELAND: Bailey Peacock-Farrell, Jonny Evans, Craig Cathcart, Jamal Lewis, Steve Davis, Corry Evans, Stuart Dallas, Paddy McNair, George Saville (70 Josh Magennis), Niall McGinn (59 Gavin Whyte), Conor Washington (83 Shane Lavery).　Manager: Michael O'Neill

GERMANY: Manuel Neuer, Marcel Halstenberg, Niklas Süle, Matthias Ginter (40 Jonathan Tah), Joshua Kimmich, Lukas Klostermann, Toni Kroos, Serge Gnabry, Marco Reus (85 Emre Can), Julian Brandt, Timo Werner (68 Kai Havertz).　Manager: Joachim Löw

Goals: Marcel Halstenberg (48), Serge Gnabry (90+3)

641.　10.10.2019　16th European Champs Qualifiers
NETHERLANDS v NORTHERN IRELAND 3-1 (0-0)

De Kuip, Rotterdam

Referee: Benoît Bastien (France)　Attendance: 41,348

NETHERLANDS: Jasper Cilessen, Daley Blind, Virgil van Dijk, Denzel Dumfries (78 Luuk de Jong), Matthijs de Ligt, Georginio Wijnaldum, Marten de Roon (66 Donny van de Beek), Frenkie de Jong, Ryan Babel (66 Donyell Malen), Memphis Depay, Steven Bergwijn.　Manager: Ronald Koeman

NORTHERN IRELAND: Bailey Peacock-Farrell, Jonny Evans, Craig Cathcart, Michael Smith, Steve Davis, Corry Evans (87 Tom Flanagan), Shane Ferguson, Stuart Dallas, Paddy McNair, George Saville (83 Jordan Thompson), Kyle Lafferty (67 Josh Magennis).　Manager: Michael O'Neill

Goals: Memphis Depay (80, 90+4), Luuk de Jong (90+1) / Josh Magennis (75)

642.　14.10.2019
CZECH REPUBLIC v NORTHERN IRELAND 2-3 (0-3)

Generali Arena, Prague

Referee: Ivan Kruzliak (Slovakia)　Attendance: 9,139

CZECH REPUBLIC: Jirí Pavlenka, Jan Kopic, Ondrej Kúdela, Radim Rezník, Stefan Simic (46 Ondrej Celustka), Josef Husbauer (66 Patrik Schick), Ladislav Krejcí (75 Lukás Masopust), Jaromír Zmrhal (46 Jan Boríl), Lukás Kalvach (46 Vladimír Darida), Alex Král, Michael Krmencík (46 Zdenel Ondrásek).　Manager: Jaroslav Silhavy

NORTHERN IRELAND: Michael McGovern, Jonny Evans, Craig Cathcart, Tom Flanagan, Conor McLaughlin, Steve Davis (65 Corry Evans), Stuart Dallas, Paddy McNair, Jordan Thompson (65 George Saville), Liam Boyce (71 Josh Magennis), Gavin Whyte (87 Niall McGinn).　Manager: Michael O'Neill

Goals: Vladimír Darida (67), Alex Král (68) / Paddy McNair (9, 40), Jonny Evans (23)

643. 16.11.2019   16th European Champs Qualifiers
NORTHERN IRELAND v NETHERLANDS 0-0
Windsor Park, Belfast

Referee: Szymon Marciniak (Poland)   Attendance: 18,404

NORTHERN IRELAND: Bailey Peacock-Farrell, Jonny Evans, Craig Cathcart, Jamal Lewis (81 Jordan Thompson), Steve Davis, Corry Evans (70 Niall McGinn), Stuart Dallas, Paddy McNair, George Saville (58 Michael Smith), Josh Magennis, Gavin Whyte.   Manager: Michael O'Neill

NETHERLANDS: Jasper Cillessen, Daley Blind, Joël Veltman, Virgil van Dijk, Matthijs de Ligt, Marten de Roon (36 Davy Pröpper), Donny van de Beek, Frenkie de Jong, Steven Berghuis (65 Luuk de Jong), Quincy Promes, Ryan Babel (90 Nathan Aké).   Manager: Ronald Koeman

644. 19.11.2019   16th European Champs Qualifiers
GERMANY v NORTHERN IRELAND 6-1 (2-1)
Commerzbank Arena, Frankfurt am Main

Referee: Carlos del Cerro Grande (ESP)   Attendance: 42,855

GERMANY: Marc-André ter Stegen, Joshua Kimmich, Jonathan Tah, Lukas Klostermann (65 Niklas Stark), Toni Kroos, Ilkay Gündogan, Jonas Hector, Emre Can, Leon Goretzka (73 Suat Serdar), Serge Gnabry (80 Nadiem Amiri), Julian Brandt.   Manager: Joachim Löw

NORTHERN IRELAND: Bailey Peacock-Farrell, Craig Cathcart, Michael Smith, Tom Flanagan, Steve Davis, Corry Evans (65 Conor McLaughlin), Shane Ferguson, Paddy McNair (77 Liam Boyce), Jordan Thompson, George Saville, Josh Magennis (83 Shane Lavery).   Manager: Michael O'Neill

Goals: Serge Gnabry (19, 47, 60), Leon Goretzka (43, 73), Julian Brandt (90+1) / Michael Smith (7)

645. 04.09.2020   UEFA Nations League – Group B1
ROMANIA v NORTHERN IRELAND 1-1 (1-0)
Arena Nationala, Bucharest

Referee: François Letexier (France)   Attendance: 0

ROMANIA: Ciprian Tatarusanu, Vlad Chiriches, Alin Tosca, Nicolae Stanciu, Nicusor Bancu, Sergiu Hanca (86 Ionut Nedelcearu), Alexandru Maxim, Alexandru Cicâldau (73 Dan Nistor), Ianis Hagi (55 Alexandru Cretu), Denis Alibec, George Puscas.   Manager: Mirel Radoi

NORTHERN IRELAND: Bailey Peacock-Farrell, Craig Cathcart, Stuart Dallas, Jamal Lewis, Daniel Ballard (90+1 Michael Smith), Steven Davis, Paddy McNair, Corry Evans (76 Kyle Lafferty), George Saville, Josh Magennis, Conor Washington (65 Gavin Whyte).   Manager: Ian Baraclough

Goals: George Puscas (25) / Gavin Whyte (86)

Sent off: Josh Magennis (39)

646. 07.09.2020   UEFA Nations League – Group B1
NORTHERN IRELAND v NORWAY 1-5 (1-3)
National Football Stadium at Windsor Park, Belfast

Referee: Bartosz Frankowski (Poland)   Attendance: 0

NORTHERN IRELAND: Bailey Peacock-Farrell, Craig Cathcart, Michael Smith, Shane Ferguson, Stuart Dallas, Daniel Ballard (46 Liam Boyce), Steven Davis, Paddy McNair, George Saville (71 Corry Evans), Jordan Thompson, Conor Washington (77 Shayne Lavery).   Manager: Ian Baraclough

NORWAY: Rune Jarstein, Even Hovland, Omar Elabdellaoui (80 Jonas Svensson), Haitam Aleesami (77 Birger Meling), Kristoffer Ajer, Stefan Johansen (71 Joshua King), Markus Henriksen, Mohamed Elyounoussi, Mathias Normann, Alexander Sørloth, Erling Braut Håland.
Manager: Lars Lagerbäck

Goals: Paddy McNair (6) / Mohamed Elyounoussi (2), Erling Braut Håland (7, 58), Alexander Sørloth (19, 47)

647. 08.10.2020   16th European Champs Qualifiers – Play-off
BOSNIA AND HERZEGOVINA v NORTHERN IRELAND 1-1 (1-0, 1-1) (AET)
Stadion Grbavica, Sarajevo

Referee: Antonio Miguel Mateu Lahoz (Spain)
Attendance: 1,800

BOSNIA AND HERZEGOVINA: Ibrahim Sehic, Sead Kolasinac (118 Haris Hajradinovic), Sinisa Sanicanin, Anel Ahmedhodzic, Branimir Cipetic, Miralem Pjanic, Edin Visca, Gojko Cimirot (106 Stjepan Loncar), Amir Hadziahmetovic (83 Amer Gojak), Edin Dzeko, Rade Krunic (88 Dino Hotic).   Manager: Dusan Bajevic

NORTHERN IRELAND: Bailey Peacock-Farrell, George Saville, Jonny Evans, Craig Cathcart, Stuart Dallas, Jamal Lewis, Steven Davis, Niall McGinn (82 Jordan Jones, 120+1 Conor Washington), Paddy McNair (90+3 Jordan Thompson, 120+1 Liam Boyce), Corry Evans (73 Gavin Whyte), Josh Magennis (90+3 Kyle Lafferty).   Manager: Ian Baraclough

Goals: Rade Krunic (14) / Niall McGinn (53)

Penalties: 1-0 Miralem Pjanic, 1-1 Stuart Dallas, Haris Hajradinovic (missed), 1-2 Kyle Lafferty, Edin Visca (missed), George Saville (missed), 2-2 Dino Hotic, 2-3 Conor Washington, 3-3 Edin Dzeko, 3-4 Liam Boyce

648. 11.10.2020 UEFA Nations League – Group B1
NORTHERN IRELAND v AUSTRIA 0-1 (0-1)
National Football Stadium at Windsor Park, Belfast
Referee: Petr Ardeleánu (Czech Republic)   Attendance: 0

NORTHERN IRELAND: Michael McGovern, Jonny Evans, Craig Cathcart, Conor McLaughlin, Stuart Dallas (73 Jordan Thompson), Jamal Lewis, Steven Davis (73 Corry Evans), Paddy McNair (83 Josh Magennis), Kyle Lafferty (61 Conor Washington), Jordan Jones, Gavin Whyte (83 Liam Boyce).   Manager: Ian Baraclough

AUSTRIA: Pavao Pervan, Aleksandar Dragovic, David Alaba, Stefan Lainer, Martin Hinteregger, Reinhold Ranfti (73 Christopher Trimmel), Julian Baumgartlinger, Stefan Ilsanker, Xaver Schlager, Christoph Baumgartner, Michael Gregoritsch (80 Adrian Grbic).   Manager: Franco Foda

Goal: Michael Gregoritsch (42)

649. 14.10.2020 UEFA Nations League – Group B1
NORWAY v NORTHERN IRELAND 1-0 (0-0)
Ullevaal Stadion, Oslo
Referee: Kristo Tohver (Estonia)   Attendance: 200

NORWAY: André Hansen, Stefan Strandberg, Omar Elabdellaoui, Birger Meling, Kristoffer Ajer, Mohamed Elyounoussi, Mathias Normann (65 Fredrik Midtsjø), Martin Ødegaard (78 Martin Linnes), Sander Berge, Joshua King (65 Alexander Sørloth), Erling Braut Håland (87 Markus Henriksen).   Manager: Lars Lagerbäck

NORTHERN IRELAND: Trevor Carson, Jonny Evans (46 Conor McLaughlin), Michael Smith (60 Stuart Dallas), Shane Ferguson, Tom Flanagan, Daniel Ballard, Corry Evans, George Saville (61 Paddy McNair), Jordan Thompson (85 Steven Davis), Josh Magennis, Conor Washington (75 Gavin Whyte).   Manager: Ian Baraclough

Goal: Stuart Dallas (68 og)

650. 12.11.2020 16th European Champs Qualifiers – Play-off Final
NORTHERN IRELAND
v SLOVAKIA (1-2) (0-1, 1-1) (AET)
National Football Stadium at Windsor Park, Belfast
Referee: Dr. Felix Brych (Germany)   Attendance: 1,060

NORTHERN IRELAND: Bailey Peacock-Farrell, Craig Cathcart (99 Tom Flanagan), Paddy McNair (104 Shane Ferguson), Stuart Dallas, Jonny Evans, Steven Davis, Niall McGinn (77 Kyle Lafferty), George Saville (65 Jordan Thompson), Jamal Lewis, Conor Washington (66 Gavin Whyte), Josh Magennis (77 Liam Boyce).   Manager: Ian Baraclough

SLOVAKIA: Marek Rodák, Tomás Hubocan, Peter Pekarík, Lubomír Satka, Milan Skriniar, Marek Hamsík (107 Ján Gregus), Juraj Kucka, Róbert Mak (65 Michal Duris), Albert Rusnák (118 Norbert Gyömbér), Stanislav Lobotka (65 Patrik Hrosovský), Ondrej Duda (85 Samuel Mráz).   Manager: Stefan Tarkovic

Goals: Milan Skriniar (88 og) / Juraj Kucka (17), Michal Duris (110)

651. 15.11.2020 UEFA Nations League – Group B1
AUSTRIA v NORTHERN IRELAND 2-1 (0-0)
Ernst Happel Stadion, Vienna
Referee: Murizio Mariani (Italy)   Attendance: 0

AUSTRIA: Pavao Pervan, Andreas Ulmer (78 Adrian Grbic), Aleksandar Dragovic (46 Reinhold Ranfti), David Alaba, Stefan Lainer, Martin Hinteregger, Julian Baumgartlinger (78 Louis Schaub), Stefan Ilsanker, Marcel Sabitzer, Xaver Schlager, Michael Gregoritsch (63 Marko Arnautovic).   Manager: Franco Foda

NORTHERN IRELAND: Michael McGovern, Michael Smith, Tom Flanagan, Shane Ferguson (36 Jamal Lewis), Conor McLaughlin, Stuart Dallas, Daniel Ballard (83 Craig Cathcart), Paddy McNair, Alister McCann (83 Steven Davis), Liam Boyce (62 Gavin Whyte), Conor Washington (62 Josh Magennis).   Manager: Ian Baraclough

Goals: Louis Schaub (81), Adrian Grbic (87) / Josh Magennis (75)

652. 18.11.2020 UEFA Nations League – Group B1
NORTHERN IRELAND v ROMANIA 1-1 (0-0)
National Football Stadium at Windsor Park, Belfast
Referee: Sandro Schärer (Switzerland)   Attendance: 0

NORTHERN IRELAND: Bailey Peacock-Farrell, Jonny Evans, Craig Cathcart, Michael Smith (79 Ethan Galbraith), Stuart Dallas, Daniel Ballard, Matthew Kennedy (66 Jamal Lewis), Paddy McNair, Alister McCann, Liam Boyce (66 Conor Washington), Josh Magennis (79 Conor McLaughlin).   Manager: Ian Baraclough

ROMANIA: Ciprian Tatarusanu, Camora, Valentin Cretu (64 Vasile Mogos), Alin Tosca (74 Eric Bicfalvi), Ionut Nedelcearu, Iulian Cristea, Dan Nistor, Razvan Marin, Denis Alibec (87 Alexandru Baluta), Dennis Man (64 Alexandru Maxim), Florin Tanase (87 Cristian Ganea).   Manager: Mirel Radoi

Goals: Liam Boyce (56) / Eric Bicfalvi (81)